BCE = 10

TWENTIETH CENTURY PUBLICATIONS IN SCOTTISH GAELIC

TWENTIETH CENTURY PUBLICATIONS IN SCOTTISH GAELIC

DONALD JOHN MACLEOD

SCOTTISH ACADEMIC PRESS
EDINBURGH
1980

Published by
Scottish Academic Press Ltd
33 Montgomery Street, Edinburgh EH7 5JX

First published 1980
SBN 0 7073 0284 6

Introduction and Notes
© 1980 D. J. Macleod

Thug an Comunn Leabhraichean Gàidhlig
cuideachadh do'n fhoillsichear gus an leabhar
seo a chur an clò

Printed in Great Britain by
Clark Constable Ltd, Edinburgh

PREFACE

I would like to thank all those who helped in the preparation of this bibliography: the staff of all the libraries consulted who were unfailingly courteous and helpful; those who gave access to or reported for me on private collections, e.g. John Lorne Campbell, Professor G. N. M. Collins, Sister Margaret MacDonnel, Professor Calum I. N. MacLeod, Hugh MacPhee and Thomas M. Murchison; John Murray, Editorial Officer of the Gaelic Books Council, who kept me up to date with recent publications; and all those, too numerous to mention, who replied to my queries about particular books and authors. Finally, I would like to thank Professor Derick Thomson, of the Celtic Department, Glasgow University, who suggested this project as part of a Ph.D. programme and who encouraged and advised me throughout.

REFERENCES AND ABBREVIATIONS

Bibliographies

AU — Aberdeen University Library. *Scottish-Gaelic Holdings*. Aberdeen, 1966.

Beaton — D. Beaton. *Bibliography of Gaelic Books, Pamphlets and Magazine Articles for the Counties of Caithness and Sutherland*. Wick, 1923.

Black — G. F. Black. *A List of Works relating to Scotland*. New York, 1916. ["Gaelic Language and Culture," pp 912–930.]

BM — British Museum. *General Catalogue of Printed Books*. London, 1960–.

BUCOP — *British Union Catalogue of Periodicals*. London, 1955–.

Celtic Congress: Exhibition of Celtic Literature to be held in the Jeffrey Room, the Mitchell Library, Glasgow, 12th to 29th August 1953.

Clare — Sister Regina Clare. "Scottish Gaelic books, pamphlets and articles published in Canada and written by Canadians." In *Canadian Library Association Occasional paper No. 53*. Ottawa, 1967.

Dunn — Charles W. Dunn. "Check-list of Scottish Gaelic Writings in North America." In *Irisleabhar Ceilteach*, I.1. Toronto, 1952.

GBC — Gaelic Books Council. *Leabhraichean Gàidhlig*. Glasgow, 1971–.

P. D. Hancock. *A bibliography of works relating to Scotland, 1916–1950, Part 2*. Edinburgh, 1960.

MacLaren — [Bibliographical notes in the margin of a copy of *Typographia Scoto-Gadelica*, chiefly in the hand of James MacLaren of the publishing firm, Alexander MacLaren & Sons.]

National Book League. *Scotland: a select bibliography*. Cambridge, n.d.

National Book League. *The Highlands and Islands of Scotland*. London, 1967; Edinburgh, 1971.

Scottish Council for Research in Education. *List of Gaelic Text-Books*. N.p., n.d.

T S-G — Donald Maclean. *Typographia Scoto-Gadelica*. Edinburgh, 1915.

INTRODUCTION

For the purposes of this bibliography, a publication is regarded as "Gaelic" if it contains approximately 2–3 pages in that language. Sheet music, place-name studies and commercial ephemera are not included nor are offprints from periodicals which are described elsewhere in the bibliography. Newspapers and periodicals containing Gaelic irregularly or in insufficient amounts to warrant separate entries are listed under the heading *Periodicals*. The bibliography covers the period 1900-73.

Since this bibliography is, in effect, a continuation of Donald Maclean's *Typographia Scoto-Gadelica* [Edinburgh, 1915], the rules of description adopted in that work have been followed here as far as was considered practicable. All departures from this standard are in line with the Anglo-American Cataloging Code.

Each entry comprises: (*a*) a heading, giving author's name, title of the work and place and date of publication; (*b*) a full transcript of the title page(s); (*c*) collation and a locations note; (*d*) footnotes.

The following rules apply, within each of these sections.

(*a*) Author's name is always given in English in the heading, since this is the practice in most reference works and because of the lack of uniformity in the spelling of Gaelic surnames. Author's real name is preferred to pseudonyms; in the case of women who have published books under both their maiden and married surnames, the name by which the author is best known is preferred. Authors of the same name are distinguished by designation – place, well-known sobriquet, etc. – as well as by dates. Decisions on the placing of the main entry in difficult cases are made in accordance with the Anglo-American Code: essentially, such entries are placed under the name of "the person or body judged to be principally responsible for the intellectual or artistic content of the work as a whole". (This means, for instance, that a collection of folksongs all recorded from one singer is entered under that name rather than the editor's and that the publications derived from J. F. Campbell's manuscript collection of folklore are entered under his name.) Where several authors are named on the title page, the work is entered under the first named. There is comprehensive cross-referencing.

A short version of the title, in the language of the title page, is used in the headings; where there are English and Gaelic title pages, the Gaelic title is preferred on all occasions except in the case of translations from English or another language.

(*b*) Where a work contains two or more title pages, these are presented as separate paragraphs in the order in which they occur in the work; essential bibliographical information derived from some other part of the work (e.g. verso of title page, colophon) is presented as a separate paragraph after the title page. In the case of serial publications, the title page of the first issue is transcribed in full; all subsequent changes are presented as variations on it. A similar practice has been adopted with reprints of monographs.

(*c*) Pagination and size are in accordance with the Anglo-American Code rather than with *Typographia Scoto-Gadelica*. Sizes are to nearest ten millimetres. Locations of copies of the work are noted after the collation.

(*d*) Footnotes contain all relevant information not contained in the body of the entry.

Books and editions of books referred to in publishers' advertisements and other sources but which have not been traced in libraries, public or private, or any of the bibliographies detailed above are included in this bibliography.

vii

Libraries

AU	Aberdeen University Library
AU:CL	Aberdeen University Celtic Class Library
BM	The British Museum, London
CoS	The Church of Scotland, New College Library, Edinburgh
EPL	Edinburgh Public Library
EU	Edinburgh University Library
EU:CL	Edinburgh University Celtic Class Library
FC	The Free Church College Library, Edinburgh
GU	Glasgow University Library
GU:CL	Glasgow University Celtic Class Library
Harvard	Harvard University Library
Mit.	The Mitchell Library, Glasgow
PC	Private collections
SS	The School of Scottish Studies, Edinburgh
Xavier	St Francis Xavier University Library, Antigonish, N.S., Canada

TWENTIETH CENTURY
PUBLICATIONS IN
SCOTTISH GAELIC

A.M. See Morrison, Angus.

A.M.E. See Henderson, Angus.

Aberdeen University Celtic Society. See Crann.

Aberdeen University Library. [*Scottish-Gaelic Holdings.*] Aberdeen, 1966.
    Aberdeen University Library. Scottish-Gaelic Holdings. Classified List. 1966.
    [2], ii, 109 p. 270 mm. AU, GU.
        Introduction by D. J. MacLeod, the compiler.

Achd Eaglais na h-Alba. See Church of Scotland.

Active Gael. See Gaelic Society of Glasgow. Transactions, Volume IV.

Aifrionn Ann an Gaidhlig. See Catholic Church. *Liturgy and ritual.* [Mass.]

Aird, Dr. Gustavus, 1813–98. [*Analysis of the Shorter Catechism.*] Edinburgh, n.d.
    Cogadh mór na h-Eòrpa. Daorsa agus Saorsa. Aird. [Illus.] Printed by Oliver and
    Boyd, Edinburgh, for The Church of Scotland, The United Free Church of Scotland,
    and The Free Church of Scotland.
    xi, 112 p. 140 mm. NLS.
        A translation of Aird's unpublished "An Analysis of the Westminster Assembly's
        Shorter Catechism". One of a series of religious books published for the use of
        Gaelic-speaking soldiers in the First World War.

Airgiod an Righ. Glasgow, 1942.
    Airgiod an Rìgh. [Illus.; Quotation.] An Comunn Gaidhealach, 131 Sràid Iar Regent,
    Glaschu, C.2. 1942.
    187 p. 140 mm. Mit., NLS.
        Mainly articles reprinted from *An Gaidheal*, the official magazine of An Comunn
        Gaidhealach. Published for distribution to soldiers during the Second World War.
        With "Seirbhis a' Chrùin" and leaflets formed *Am Feachd Gaidhealach* (1944).

Airgiod an Righ. See also *Feachd Gaidhealach.*

Aiseirigh, An. See Dow, William. [*The Resurrection.*]

Aithghearradh Teagasg Chriosta. See Catholic Church. *Catechism.* [Christian Doctrine.]

Aithris is Oideas. London, 1964.
    Aithris is Oideas. (Traditional Gaelic Rhymes and Games.) University of London
    Press Ltd, Warwick Square, London EC4. 1964.
    Publications of the Scottish Council for Research in Education XLIX. Aithris is Oideas.
    (Traditional Gaelic Rhymes and Games.)
    110 p. 230 mm. GU.
        Compiled by the Committee on Bilingualism of the S.C.R.E. (convener, John A.
        Smith). Preface signed by Smith. Printed Rbt. Cunningham & Sons, Alva.

Alasdair agus Mairi Air Chuairt. Glasgow, 1971.
Alasdair agus Màiri air chuairt. Le còmhlan de luchd-teagaisg ás na Hearadh. Dealbhan le Cailean Spencer. Gairm. Glaschu. 1971.
Air fhoillseachadh an co-bhoinn ri Coimitidh nan Leabhraichean-sgoile.
40 p; illus. 210 mm.
    Co-authors: Dolina Ferguson, Ann MacDonald, Effie MacDonald, Alison Mac-Laren, B. A. MacLean, Elizabeth MacLeod, Mary MacLeod, Mary Robertson.

Alba [Miscellany]. See MacLean, Malcolm (joint ed.).

Alba. [Newspaper]. Perth, 1908; Greenock, 1908–9.
Alba. "Alba airson nan Albannach! Saorsa aig an taigh. Aoigheachd do na h-uile neach." Aireamh 1. Peairt, Di-Sathuirne, 8 de'n Ghearran, 1908. A' phrìs sgillinn.
. . . Aireamh 23 Grianaig, Di-Sathuirne, 11 de'n Iuchar, 1908. A' phrìs sgillinn.
    This and subsequent numbers bear the imprint, ". . . air a chur am mach, as leith na feadhainn d'am buin e, le Alasdair Mac Neacail, 7 Sràid Cathcart, Grianaig".
. . . Aireamh 53] 6 de'n Dara-mios, 1909. [Last No.]
    [Frequency] Weekly.
    [Collation] 6 p per issue to No. 18, 4 p thereafter. 530/590 mm.
    [Editors] Alexander M. Nicolson and Angus Henderson.
    [Locations] Mit., NLS.
    [Printers] Milne, Tannahill & Methven, Perth, to No. 22; Orr, Pollock & Co., Greenock, thereafter.
    [Note] Owned by Roderick Erskine of Mar; managed by Alexander M. Nicolson. A weekly newspaper. Its pledged editorial aims were: "(1) Prìomh chòireacha na h-Alba a chosnadh air ais . . .; (2) Am Fearann fhaighinn air ais . . .; (3) An t-Ath-bheothachadh Gàidhealach a sheasamh."

Albannaich. See Comunn nan Albannach.

Almanac. See Am Feillire.

Alston, Charles H. [*Gaelic Names of British Mammals.*] Edinburgh, 1913.
A list of the Gaelic names of British mammals. By Charles H. Alston.
[145]–153 p. 220 mm. Mit.
    Offprint from *The Scottish Naturalist*, No. 19, July 1913.

Am Measg nam Bodach. Glasgow, 1938.
Am Measg nam Bodach. Co-chruinneachadh de sgeulachdan is beul-aithris a chaidh a chraobhsgaoileadh air an fhritheud eadar Samhuinn, 1936, agus An Gearran, 1937. An Comunn Gaidhealach, 131 Sràid Iar Regent, Glaschu, C.2. 1938.
148 p. 190 mm. GU:CL, NLS.
    Preface by Hugh MacPhee, for the B.B.C.

Amhrain Anna Sheumais. See MacKenzie, Anne. [*Amhrain Anna Sheumais.*]

Andersen, Hans Christian, 1805–75. [*The Snow Queen.*] Glasgow, n.d.
Leabhraichean a' Chomuinn. Banrigh an t-Sneachda. Bho Hans Andersen. Air a chur an Gàidhlig le Dòmhnall Grannd. [Illus.] Dealbhan le Luce Lagarde. Clo-bhuailte le Bias am Paris mar a dh'iarr An Comunn Gaidhealach.
24 p; col. illus. 190 mm.
    One of a series of school readers translated from French.

—— [*Thumbelina.*] Glasgow, n.d.
Leabhraichean a' Chomuinn. Ludag Bheag. Bho Hans Andersen. Air a chur an Gàidhlig le Dòmhnall Grannd. [Illus.] Dealbhan le Francoise J. Bertier. Clo-bhuailte le Bias am Paris mar a dh'iarr An Comunn Gaidhealach.
24 p; col. illus. 190 mm.
    1967.

Anderson, Hugh, d. 1909. [*Measan Milis as an Lios.*] Glasgow, 1925.
Measan Milis as an Lios. Orain le Caiptean Eoghan Anderson, nach maireann. [Illus.]
Glascho: Gilleasbaig Mac-na-Ceardadh, 47 Sràid Waterloo. 1925.
31 p, plate. 190 mm. Mit., PC, SSS.
Contains music, in solfa notation.

Anderson, Jonathan Ranken, 1803–59. [*The Marriage Feast.*] Glasgow [1902].
"A' Chuirm Bhainnse." Leis an Urramach Eòin MacRaing Mac Ghille-Anndrais nach
maireann. Translation of John Knox Tracts (No. 15), *The Marriage Feast.* John
MacNeilage, 85 Great Western Road, Glasgow.
12 p.
Not seen. Described in *MacLaren.* Not in T S-G.

—— [*The Marriage Feast.*] Glasgow, 1944.
John Knox Tracts, No. 15. 3d. Duilleagan Leughaidh Iain a' Chnuic. A' Chuirm
Bhainnse. Leis an Urramach Eòin MacRaing Mac Ghille-Anndrais nach maireann.
Air a thionndadh gu Gàidhlig. [Quotation.] The Marriage Feast. Sermon by the late
Rev. Jonathan Ranken Anderson. Translated into Gaelic. An dara clobhualadh.
Glascho: Alasdair Maclabhruinn 's a Mhic, 268 Sràid Earraghaidheal, C.2. 1944.
16 p. 190 mm. PC.

Andersson, Otto, 1879–?. [*Gaelic Folk Music from the Isle of Lewis.*] Abo, 1952.
On Gaelic Folk Music from the Isle of Lewis. A collection of tunes with comparative
notes on waulking customs and waulking songs. By Otto Andersson.
68 p. 230 mm. Mit.
In "Budlaven, organ for brages sektion for folklivsforskning och institutet for Nordisk
etnologi vid abo Akademi", 1952. Contains verses of Gaelic songs, and music in staff
notation.

Ap Siencyn, Ioan (joint ed.). See Irisleabhar Ceilteach.

[*Arabian Nights*], Division I. Inverness, 1906.
Sgeulachdan Arabianach. Tales from the Arabian Nights. Translated into Gaelic from
the English expurgated edition. Division I. Second edition. Price one shilling.
Inverness: *Northern Chronicle* Office. Edinburgh: Norman MacLeod, The Mound.
1906.
[4], 120 p. 190 mm. AU, GU:CL.

[*Arabian Nights*], Division III. Inverness, 1900.
Sgeulachdan Arabianach. Tales from the Arabian Nights. Translated into Gaelic from
the English expurgated edition. Division III. Price one shilling. Inverness: *Northern
Chronicle* Office. Edinburgh: Norman MacLeod, 25 George IV Bridge. 1900.
[4], 126 p. 190 mm. AU, BM, GU:CL.
Division II appeared in 1899. Reprinted from the *Northern Chronicle* newspaper.
Translated by Rev. John Macrury. First published ed. 1717 (in French, edited by
Antoine Galland); standard Vulgate edition 1835.

Arascain is Mhairr, Ruaraidh. See Erskine, The Hon. Ruaraidh, of Mar.

Ath-Ghearradh an Teagasg Chriosd. See Catholic Church. *Liturgy and Ritual.* [Christian
Doctrine.]

Baha'i. See National Spiritual Assembly of the Baha'is of the British Isles. *Sgriobtuirean
Creidimh na Baha-i.*

Bah'u'llah. See National Spiritual Assembly of the Baha'is of the British Isles. *Sgriobtuirean Creideamh na Baha'i.*

Ban-Altrumachd Aig an Tigh. Glasgow, 1939.
Ban-Altrumachd aig an Tigh. Air a dheasachadh le Comhairle Clann an Fhraoich airson Comunn na h-Oigridh. Glaschu: An Comunn Gaidhealach, 131 Sràid West Regent. 1939.
59 p; illus. 220 mm. GU:CL, NLS.
Written, in English, by Dr. Atholl Robertson and translated and edited by the "Clann an Fhraoich" committee. Clann an Fhraoich was an all-Gaelic circle within An Comunn Gaidhealach.

Bannerman, John M., 1901–69. [*Gaol agus Dùthchas.*] See Ceithir Comhraidhean.

Baptie, Charles R. [*Orain Ghaidhlig.*] Paisley, n.d.
Part 1. Orain Ghàidhlig. Gaelic songs with pianoforte accompaniments by Charles R. Baptie. J. and R. Parlane, Paisley. John Menzies and Co., Edinburgh and Glasgow. Houlston and Sons, London. One shilling net.
27 p. 310 mm. AU, Mit.
Reviewed in Transactions of the Gaelic Society of Inverness, 1902; first advertisement seen, 1905. Music in both notations. No more parts appear to have been published.

Bard, Am. Edinburgh, 1901–2.
Am Bàrd. Ar Tìr agus ar Teanga. Leabhar 1. – Aireamh 1. A' Bhuidh Mhios, 1901. Prìs, sgillinn. (Edition de luxe, sia sgillinnean.)
. . . Leabhar II. An t-Iuchar, 1902. Aireamh III. [Last seen.]
[Frequency] Monthly. Vol. I: 5 numbers seen (Jul.–Nov. 1901); Vol. II: 3 numbers (May–Jul. 1902).
[Collation] Vol. I: 80 p (total); Vol. II: 102 p. 310 mm.
[Locations] BM.
[Note] A literary monthly, in Gaelic and English. Contents include the operetta, "Iseabail" by Malcolm MacInnes. Published by Norman MacLeod, Edinburgh, for Roderick Erskine of Mar.

Bard Thighearna Cholla. See MacLean, John. [*Bard Thighearna Cholla.*]

Bardachd na Feinne. N.p., n.d.
Bàrdachd na Féinne.
48 p. 190 mm. PC.
Reprinted from the newspaper *MacTalla.*

Bartlett, Samuel [*Braid air a Bhraid*] Glasgow [*c.* 1935].
Braid air a Bhraid. Leis an Lighiche Somhairle Bartlett. Eadar-theangaichte gu Gàidhlig le Anna Nic Iain. Price, 1/– net. From the Secretary, An Comunn Gaidhealach, Castlebay, Isle of Barra. Copyright, 1935.
Published for An Comunn Gaidhealach, Castlebay Branch, by Alex. MacLaren & Sons, 268 Argyle Street, Glasgow, C.2. Printed in Scotland.
16 p. 190 mm. EPL, Mit.
The English original was apparently not published.

Bartok, Bela, 1881–1945. [*Studia Memoriae Belae Bartok Sacra.*] London, 1959.
Studia Memoriae Belae Bartók Sacra. Editio tertia. Boosey and Hawkes, Limited: London, New York, Sydney, Toronto, Cape Town, Paris, Bonn. 1959.
535 p, 3 tables in folder. 250 mm. AU, GU, Mit.
"Gaelic Folksongs from South Uist" by Margaret Fay Shaw, pp. 419–34. Also offprints of this article from the earlier Hungarian eds: below.

—— [*Studia Memoriae Belae Bartok Sacra.*] See also Shaw, Margaret Fay. Gaelic Folksongs from South Uist. [Offprints.]

Baxter, Richard, 1615–91. [*Saints' Everlasting Rest.*] Edinburgh, 1908.
    The Saints' Everlasting Rest. A treatise on the blessed state of the saints in their enjoy-
    ment of God in Heaven. Rev. Richard Baxter. Translated by the Rev. John Forbes,
    minister of Sleat. Edinburgh, John Grant, 1908.
    Fois Shiorruidh nan Naomh. Solus air staid bheannaichte nan naomh a' mealtainn Dhé
    air Neamh. Le Mr. Richard Bacster. Eadartheangaichte le Iain Foirbeis, ministear
    Shléit. Edinburgh: John Grant. 1908.
    xiv, 375 p. 180 mm. AU.
    1st ed. 1862, of which this is a reprint. English original first published 1650.

—— [*The Saints' Everlasting Rest.*] Stornoway, 1970.
    . . . Translated by the Rev. John Forbes, Minister of Sleat. Edinburgh: John Grant.
    1908. Stornoway Religious Bookshop. Reprinted 1970.
    . . . Eadar-theangaichte le Iain Foirbeis, Ministear Shléit. Edinburgh: John Grant.
    1908. Stornoway Religious Bookshop. Reprinted 1970.
    xiv, 375 p. 220 mm.

Bayne, Ronald, *c.* 1755–1821 (joint author). See Dioghluim o Theagasg nan Aithrichean.

Beagan Gaidhlig. Glasgow, n.d.
    Beagan Gàidhlig. A Scottish Television Publication. Scottish Television Limited.
    [Hope Street, Glasgow.]
    87 p. 250 mm.
    Support material for a series of 24 Gaelic lessons broadcast by Scottish Television
    between Sept. 18th 1971 and Dec. 7th 1971 (repeated, Jan. 20th to June 1st 1972.)
    Comprises: 8 4unbound pages of notes and vocabulary; 3 p, "A Selection of Gaelic
    songs"; miscellaneous leaflets on aspects of Gaelic culture; 1 EP record, with trans-
    cript. The course was devised by George Reid, assisted by David Dunn, Brian
    Mahoney and Donald MacLennan (Gaelic Adviser).

Bean Torra Dhamh. See Macpherson, Mary.

Beaton, D., 1872–19 ? . *Bibliography.* Wick, 1923.
    Bibliography of Gaelic Books, Pamphlets, and Magazine Articles, for the Counties of
    Caithness and Sutherland, with biographical notes. Compiled by Rev. D. Beaton,
    author of "Ecclesiastical History of Caithness", etc. Wick: Peter Reid & Co., Ltd.,
    John O' Groat Journal Office, 1923.
    75 p. 220 mm. NLS.

Beaton, D. (ed.). See Cameron, Neil. [*Collected Works.*]

[Bell, John H.] See Gathan Greine.

Bell, John J., 1871–1934. [*Thread o' Scarlet.*] Glasgow, n.d.
    An Snàithnean Sgàrlaid. Dealbh-chluich an aon sealladh. Gaelic translation of the
    one-act play, Thread o' Scarlet, by J. J. Bell. Air eadar-theangachadh le Iain Mac-
    Fhionghuin. An Comunn Gaidhealach, 131 West Regent Street, Glasgow.
    15 p. 220 mm.
        c. 1950. Printed Caledonian Press, Glasgow. English original first published 1923.

Bellahouston Academy. See School Magazines.

Bernera (Harris) Church of Scotland. Year Book. See A' Charraig.

Bhean Nighe, A'. Glasgow, n.d.
    The Ceilidh Books. Leabhraichean nan Ceilidh. Aireamh 38. A' Bhean Nighe,
    Luideag-an-Uillt. [Illus.] A' phrìs sè sgillinnean. 6d. Alasdair MacLabhruinn agus a
    Mhic, 360–2 Sràid Earraghaidheal, Glascho.
    [195]–222, [334]–366 p. 220 mm. PC.
        From *Guth na Bliadhna.* LIX. 2, 3. 1912.

Bhratach, Am. Glasgow, n.d.
Am Bhratach. Leabhar-meudachaidh do chummanacht na h-Alba. Uimhir 1. An t-Samhuinn.
. . . Uimhir 2. An Gearran.
. . . Uimhir 3. [Last seen.]
[Collation] 4 p each. 380 × 260 mm.
[Locations] NLS.
[Note] *c.* 1940. Approx. one-third Gaelic. Published by J. H. Miller; printed by Unity Press, 65 Burnside Street, Glasgow, C.4.

Bible. The Old Testament, the New Testament and the Psalms, when bound together, are treated as separate monographs if they have separate title pages and pagination.

Bible.
Leabhraichean an t-Seann Tiomnaidh agus an Tiomnaidh Nuaidh; air an tarruing o na ceud channainibh chum Gaidhlig Albannaich. Comunn-Bhìobull Dùthchail na h-Alba; Na h-ard-aitreabhan: 5 Cearnan Naoimh Aindreais, Duneideann; 224 Iar-Shràid Dheòrsa, Glaschu. 1911. Gaelic 24mo Bible.
992 p. 150 mm. NLS, PC.
Ibid. Reprinted 1914, 1921, 1927, 1934, 1951.
. . . 1939. Gaelic Bourgeois 8vo Bible.
789, 264 p. 230 mm.
Printed Geo. C. MacKay, Edinburgh.
Ibid. Reprinted 1950.
1st ed. of the Gaelic New Testament was in 1767; 1st ed. of the Gaelic Old Testament 1801.

Bible. *Reference Bible.*
Leabhraichean an t-Seann Tiomnaidh agus an Tiomnaidh Nuaidh. Air an tarruing o na ceud chanainibh chum Gaelig Albannaich. Revised Edition. The National Bible Society of Scotland: Head Offices: 5 St. Andrew Square, Edinburgh, and 224 West George Street, Glasgow. Gaelic 8vo Ref. Bible. 1953.
1155 p. 200 × 150 mm. NBS, PC.
The first edition was in 1880, of which this is a reprint. It is a revision by Dr Thomas MacLauchlan and Dr Archibald Clerk of the edition of 1826. Contains informative notes, references, variant readings; the 1953 edition does not have the maps of the earlier edition. The Old Testament and Psalms have separate title pages but the pagination is continuous throughout. Printed by Neill & Co., Edinburgh.

Bible. N.T. *Gaelic and English.*
Tiomnadh Nuadh ar Tighearna agus ar Slànuighir Iosa Criosd air a tharruing o'n Ghréigis chum Gàidhlig Albannaich. Comunn Bhìobull Dùthchail na h-Alba. Na h-Ard-aitreabhan, Duneideann agus Glaschu.
The New Testament of our Lord and Saviour Jesus Christ translated out of the original Greek and with the former translations diligently compared and revised by His Majesty's special command appointed to be read in Churches. Printed by authority. The National Bible Society of Scotland: 5 St. Andrew Square, Edinburgh; 224 West George Street, Glasgow. Brevier Octavo.
717 p. 190 mm. NBS.
c. 1938. The Gaelic and English texts are in parallel columns.
Ibid. Reprinted 1965.

Bible. N.T. *National Bible Society.*
Tiomnadh Nuadh ar Tighearna agus ar Slànuighir Iosa Criosd eadar-theangaichte o'n Ghreugais chum Gaelic Albannaich. Comunn-Bhìobull Dùthchail na h-Alba; Na h-Ard-aitreabhan: 5 Ceàrnan Naoimh Aindreais, Dun-éideann, agus 224 Iar-Shràid Dheòrsa, Glaschu. 1900. Gaelic 24mo Testament.
[4], 498 p. 150 mm. GU:CL.

Ibid. Reprinted 1909, 1925, 1979.
Tiomnadh Nuadh ar Tighearna agus ar Slànuighir Iosa Criosd eadar-theangaichte o'n
Ghreugais chum Gaelic Albannaich agus air a chur a mach le h-ùghdarras Ard-
Sheanaidh Eaglais na h-Alba. . . . 1901. Gaelic 8vo New Testament.
[4], 498 p. 230 mm.
    Printed Neill & Co., Edinburgh.
Ibid. Reprinted 1906, 1922, 1952.
. . . The National Bible Society of Scotland. Head Offices: 5 St. Andrew Square, Edinburgh and 224 West George Street, Glasgow. 1907. Gaelic 32mo.
315 p. 119 mm. NBS.
. . . 1909.
264 p. 230 mm. NBS.
. . . 1910.
316 p. 116 mm. NBS.
Tiomnadh Nuadh ar Tighearna agus ar Slànuighir Iosa Criosd, air a tharruing o'n
Ghréigis chum Gàidhlig Albannaich. Comunn-Bhìobull Dùthchail na h-Alba; Na
h-Ard-aitreabhan: 5 Ceàrnan Naoimh Aindreais, Dun-éideann; 224 Iar-Shràid Dheòrsa,
Glaschu.
[2], 220 p. 180 mm.
    Bound with 1908 Old Testament.
. . . 1915.
[4], 448 p. 180 mm. NBS.
. . . 1916. Gaelic 32mo.
451 p. 116 mm. NBS.
    Printed by Turnbull & Spears, Edinburgh.
Ibid. Reprinted 1918, 1922, 1938, n.d.

Bible. N.T. *S.P.C.K.*
Leabhraichean Tiomnaidh Nuaidh ar Tighearn agus ar Slànuighir Iosa Criosd, air an
eadar-theangachadh o'n Ghreugais chum Gàidhlig Albannaich. Air iarrtas agus air
costus na cuideachd urramaich a ta chum eòlas Criosdaidh a sgaoileadh air feadh
Gaidhealtachd agus eileana na h-Alba. Dunèideann. 1902.
    Revised edition. The revision was carried out by a special committee of the Free
    Church and the Church of Scotland, the most active members being Dr. John
    MacLean, Neil Dewar and Rev. Robert Blair.
. . . na h-Alba. An Comunn-Bhìobull Dùthchail na h-Alba; Na h-Ard-aitreabhan: 5
Ceàrnan Naoimh Aindreais, Dun-éideann; 224 Iar-Shràid Dheòrsa, Glaschu.
247 p. 150 mm. NBS.
    Bound with 1904 Old Testament.

Bible. O.T. *National Bible Society.*
Leabhraichean an t-Seann Tiomnaidh, air an tarruing o'n cheud chànain chum Gaelic
Albannaich. An Comunn-Bhìobull Dùthchail na h-Alba; Ard-aitreabh: 5 Ceàrnan
Naoimh Aindreais, Dun-Eidin; agus 224 Iar-Shràid Dheòrsa, Glaschu. 1905. Gaelic
12mo Bible.
[4], 681 p. 180 mm. NBS.
Ibid. Reprinted 1908.
    Printed Morrison & Gibb, Edinburgh.
Leabhraichean an t-Seann Tiomnaidh, air an tarruing o'n cheud chànain chum Gaelic
Albannaich; agus air an cur a mach le h-ùghdarras Ard-Sheanaidh Eaglais na h-Alba.
1904. Gaelic 24mo Bible.
[4], 748 p. 150 mm. NBS.
. . . The National Bible Society of Scotland; Head Offices: 5 St. Andrew Square, Edinburgh; and 224 West George Street, Glasgow. 1902. Gaelic Bourgeois 8vo Bible.
789 p. 230 mm. AU, EU:CL, NBS.
Ibid. Reprinted 1909.

Bible. O.T. *S.P.C.K.*
Leabhraichean an t-Seann Tiomnaidh, air an eadartheangachadh o'n Eabhra chum Gàidhlig Albannaich. Air iarrtas agus air costus na Cuideachd Urramach a ta chum Eòlas Criosdaidh a sgaoileadh air feadh Gaidhealtachd agus eileana na h-Alba. Dun-eideann. 1902.
[2], iv, 904 p. 290 mm. GU, Mit., NLS.
   Revised edition. Printed Morrison & Gibb, Edinburgh.
   See note under New Testament.

Bible. Psalmody. See:
Church of Scotland. *Liturgy and Ritual.* [Sailm Dhaibhidh.]
Free Church of Scotland. *Liturgy and Ritual.* [Fuinn nan Salm Ghaidhlig.]
Hately, T. L. *Seann Fhuinn nan Salm.*
Whitehead, F. W. *The Six Long Gaelic Psalm Tunes.*

Bible. Psalms. *Gaelic and English.*
Sailm Dhaibhidh maille ri laoidhibh air an tarruing o na scriptuiribh naomha chum bhi air an seinn ann an aoradh Dhe. Comunn-Bhìobull Dùthchail na h-Alba. Na h-ard-aitreabhan Duneideann agus Glaschu. Gaelic English. The Psalms of David in metre according to the version approved by The Church of Scotland and appointed to be used in worship. The National Bible Society of Scotland. 5 St. Andrew Square, Edinburgh; 224 West George Street, Glasgow. Brevier Octavo.
240, [13] p. 190 mm. PC.
   Bound with undated ed. of the parallel English and Gaelic N.T. Printed by Turn-bull & Spears, Edinburgh.
   Ibid. Bound with 1965 ed. of N.T., parallel English and Gaelic version.

Bible. Psalms. *National Bible Society.*
Sailm Dhaibhidh ann an Dàn Gaidhealach. Dun-Eidin: clò-bhuailt air son An Comunn Bhìobull Dùthchail na h-Alba.
97 p. 230 mm. NBS.
   Bound with 1901 N.T.
   Ibid. Bound with 1902 Bible, 1906 N.T., 1909 O.T.
Sailm Dhaibhidh maille ri Laoidhibh air an tarruing o na Scriptuiribh Naomha, chum bhi air an seinn ann an aoradh Dhé. Comunn-Bhìobull Dùthchail na h-Alba; Na h-Ard-aitreabhan: 5 Ceàrnan Naoimh Aindreais, Duneideann; 224 Iar-Shràid Dheòrsa, Glaschu.
   Bound with 1916 N.T.
   Ibid. Bound with 1918 N.T.
   Ibid. Bound with 1921, 1927, 1951 eds. of the Bible and the 1925 N.T.
86 p. 150 mm. NBS.
   Ibid. Bound with 1922, 1939, 1952 eds. of N.T. and the 1950 Bible. Also separate eds. of 1930, 1950.
97 p. 230 mm. NBS.
   Ibid. Bound with 1938 N.T.
93 p. 113 mm. NBS.
Sailm Dhaibhidh maille ri Laoidhibh air an tarruing o na Scriptuiribh Naomha, chum bhi air an seinn ann an aoradh Dhé. Air an leasachadh, agus air an cur a mach le h-ùgdarras Ard-Sheanaidh Eaglais na h-Alba. An Comunn-Bhìobull Dùthchail na h-Alba; Ard-aitreabh: 5 Ceàrnan Naoimh Aindreais, Dun-Eidin, agus 224 Iar-Shràid Dheòrsa, Glaschu.
86 p. 150 mm.
   Bound with 1900 N.T.
   Ibid. Bound with 1905 O.T. and 1909 N.T.
   Ibid. Bound with 1905 Bible, 1908 O.T. and undated N.T.
92 p. 180 mm. NBS.
   Ibid. Bound with 1907, 1910 N.T.

95 p. 119 mm. NBS
Ibid. Bound with 1911, 1914, 1934 Bible.
86 p. 150 mm. NLS.
    First National Bible Society edition was in 1880 (revised by Rev. Archibald Clerk
and Rev. Thomas MacLauchlan).

Bible. Psalms. *Ross (Thomas) Version.*
Sailm Dhaibhidh ann an Dan Gaidhealach: do reir na h-Eabhra, agus an eadar-
theangachaidh a's fearr an Laidin, an Gaidhlic, 's an Gall bheurla. Do thionnsgnadh in
Seanadh Earra Ghaidheal sa' bhliadhna 1659, agus do chriochnaicheadh san 1694,
r'an reic ann an eaglaisibh 's ann an teaghlaichibh Gaidhealach. Air an glanadh a nis
o mhearachdaibh lionmhor a' chlodh-bhualaidh, agus air an atharrachadh, le ro bheag
caochladh air na briathraibh, do reir gné sgriobhaidh an t-Seann Tiomnaidh agus an
Tiomnaidh Nuaidh. Le Tomas Ros, LL.D., Ministear an t-Soisgeil ann an Lochbhraoin.
The National Bible Society of Scotland: Head Offices: 5 St. Andrew Square, Edinburgh,
and 224 West George Street, Glasgow.
iv, 396 p. 150 mm. NBS.
    Has 1824 Preface, but is clearly a much later reprint; bound with 1900 ed. of the
Shorter Catechism. Printed by Ballantyne, Hanson & Co., Edinburgh. 1st ed.
1807; based on Synod of Argyll version (1st ed. 1659).

Bible. Psalms. *Smith (Dr John) Version.*
Sailm Dhaibhidh, maille ri Laoidhean o'n Scrioptur Naomha, chum bhi air an seinn
ann an aoradh Dhia. Air an leasachadh, agus air an cuir a mach reir seoladh, iarrtuis,
agus ughdarrais Seanaidh Earra-ghaeil. Le I. Smith, D.D. The National Bible Society
of Scotland: Head Offices: 5 St. Andrew Square, Edinburgh, and 224 West George
Street, Glasgow. 1904. Gaelic Psalms.
396 p. 150 mm. EU:CL, NBS.
    Printed Darien Press.
Ibid. Reprinted 1908, 1921, 1939.
    1st ed. 1787.

Bible. Psalms. *Synod of Argyll Version.*
The Gaelic Psalms 1694, being a reprint of the edition issued by the Synod of Argyll in
that year with an historical introduction by Duncan C. Mactavish. Lochgilphead:
James M. S. Annan. 1934.
xxiv, [6], 282 p. 190 mm. EU:CL, GU:CL, NLS.
    1st ed. of the Synod of Argyll version was in 1659.

Bible. *Summary of Editions.*
New Testament: 1900, 1901, 1902 (Revised), 1904, 1906, 1907, 1908, 1909, 1910,
1915, 1916, 1918, 1922 [*c.* 1938], 1952, 1965, n.d.
Old and New Testaments: 1911, 1914, 1921, 1924, 1927, 1934, 1939, 1950, 1951,
1952, 1965.
Old Testament: 1902, 1902 (Revised), 1904, 1905, 1909.
Psalmody: [1906].
Psalms: 1900, 1901, 1904, 1905[2], 1906, 1907, 1908[2], 1909, 1910, 1911, 1914,
1916, 1918, 1921, 1922[2], 1925, 1927, 1934[2], 1938, 1939[2], 1950, 1951, 1952,
1965, n.d.
Reference Bible: 1953.
    For information on the translation of the Bible into Gaelic, see Rev. Donald Mac-
Kinnon's *The Gaelic Bible and Psalter* (Dingwall, 1930).

Bideau, Georges. [*The Dog with Bootees.*] Glasgow, n.d.
Leabhraichean A' Chomuinn. Peasan, Cuilean nan Cluaran. Le Georges Bideau. A'
Ghaidhlig le Domhnall Grannd. [Illus.] Dealbhan le Luce Lagarde. Clo-bhuailte le
Bias am Paris mar a dh'iarr An Comunn Gaidhealach.
243 p; col. illus. 190 mm.

—— [*Robin Redbreast and His Friends.*] Glasgow, n.d.
Leabhraichean A' Chomuinn. Broidreagan agus a Chuideachd. Le Georges Bideau.
A' Ghaidhlig le Domhnall Grannd. [Illus.] Dealbhan le Grinson. Clo-bhuailte le
Bias am Paris mar a dh'iarr An Comunn Gaidhealach.
243 p; col. illus. 190 mm.
    1969. An elementary school reader, translated from the French. Uniform with the
earlier translations by Grant of tales by Grimm and Andersen. See "Leabhraichean
a' Chomuinn" for list of titles.

Bishop of Argyll and the Isles. See Catholic Church, Argyll and the Isles (Diocese).

Blair, Duncan B., 1815–93. [*Coinneach Odhar.*] Sydney, C.B., 1900.
Coinneach Odhar, am Fiosaiche. Leis an Urr. D. B. Blair, D.D., nach maireann.
Sydney, C. B.: "Mac-Talla" Office, 1900.
[4], 29 p. 160 mm. AU, Mit.

Blar na Saorsa. Glasgow, n.d.
The Ceilidh Books. Leabhraichean nan Ceilidh. Aireamh 32. Blàr na Saorsa. Allt-a'-
Bhàn-Chnuic. [Illus.] Alasdair Mac Labhruinn agus a Mhic, 360-2 Sràid Earraghaidheal, Glascho.
[131]–162 p. 220 mm. NLS.
    Reprinted from *Guth na Bliadhna*, XI, 2, Summer, 1914.

Blar Traigh Ghruinneaird. See Campbell, John F. [*Blar Traigh Ghruinneaird.*]

Board of Agriculture and Fisheries. [*Cloimh Chaorach.*] London, 1910.
Leaflet No. 61 (Gaelic). Bòrd Tuathanachais 's Iasgaich. Clòimh Chaorach. (Sheep-
Scab) . . . 4, Whitehall Place, London, S.W. Chaidh so a sgriobhadh anns a bhliadhna
1899. An dara-sgriobhadh 1910.
7 p. 220 mm. PC.

Bolg Solair, Am. Glasgow, fore. 1907.
Am Bolg Solair. The Pedlar's Pack. With contents collected from many sources and
published in aid of the funds of Féill a' Chomuinn Ghaidhealaich. Published by Archibald Sinclair, Celtic Press, 47 Waterloo Street, Glasgow.
100 p; 12 plates. 210 mm. AU, Mit., NLS.
    "Editor's Note" signed by Elma Story and dated October, 1907.

Bonn-Steidh agus Riaghailtean. See Comunn Gaidhealach. *Bonn-Steidh agus Riaghailtean.*

Bord Tuathanachais 's Iasgaich. See Board of Agriculture and Fisheries.

Borgström, Carl Hj., 1909–. [*The Dialect of Barra.*] Oslo, 1935.
The Dialect of Barra in the Outer Hebrides. By Carl Hj. Borgström.
Norsk Tidsskrift for Sprogvidenskap. Bind VIII. 1935. Saertrykk [offprint].
[2], [71]–242 p. 250 mm. BM, Mit.
    The complete Volume VIII was published in 1937.

—— [*The Dialects of Skye and Ross-shire.*] Oslo, 1941.
Norsk Tidsskrift for Sprogvidenskap. . . Utgitt av Carl J. S. Marstrander. Suppl.
Bind. II. Oslo 1941. H. Aschehoug & Co. (W. Nygaard).
A Linguistic Survey of the Gaelic Dialects of Scotland. Volume II. Carl Hj. Borg-
ström. The Dialects of Skye and Ross-shire. Oslo, 1941. H. Aschehoug & Co. (W.
Nygaard).
168 p [paperback]; map. 250 mm. AU, BM.

—— [*The Dialects of Skye and Ross-shire.*] Oslo, 1941.
. . . Suppl. Bind II. Norwegian Universities Press.
. . . The Dialects of Skye and Ross-shire. Norwegian Universities Press.
Oslo, 1941.
168 p; map. 250 mm. GU:CL.
Hardback; otherwise identical to the above.

—— [*The Dialects of the Outer Hebrides.*] Oslo, 1940.
Norsk Tidsskrift for Sprogvidenskap. . . . Utgitt av Carl J. S. Marstrander. Suppl.
Bind I. Oslo, 1940. H. Aschehoug & Co. (W. Nygaard).
A Linguistic Survey of the Gaelic Dialects of Scotland. Volume I. Carl Hj. Borgström.
The Dialects of the Outer Hebrides. Oslo, 1940. H. Aschehoug & Co. (W. Nygaard).
280 p; map. 260 mm. AU, BM.
    Paperback.

—— [*The Dialects of the Outer Hebrides.*] Oslo, 1940.
. . . Suppl. Bind I. Norwegian Universities Press.
. . . The Dialects of the Outer Hebrides. Norwegian Universities Press.
. . . Oslo, 1940.
280 p; map. 260 mm. GU:CL.
Hardback; otherwise identical to the above.

Bottomley, Gordon, 1874–1948. [*Deirdire.*] Inverness, 1944.
Deirdire. Dealbh-chluich an ceithir earrannan an Gàidhlig is am Beurla. Am briathran
na sgeulachd agus an dàin a fhuair Alasdair MacGhille-Mhìcheil am Barraidh. Le
Gordon Bottomley. Le earrannan leasachaidh air an cur am Beurla le Caitriona F. agus
Daibhidh Urchadan. Inbhir Nis: aig oifis *The Northern Chronicle*, 1944. Còirichean
gu h-iomlan air an dìon.
Deirdire. Drama in four acts in Gaelic and English. Adapted from Alexander Carmichael's Barra story and lay by Gordon Bottomley with the additional passages translated into Gaelic by Catherine F. and David Urquhart. Inverness: at *The Northern
Chronicle Office*, 1944. All rights reserved.
[8], 159 p. 190 mm. AU, BM, GU, Mit.
    English and Gaelic texts on facing pages. Bottomley dramatised an English trans-
lation of the Deirdre story, his play being translated back into Gaelic.

Boulton, Harold E., 1859–1935. [*Our National Songs.*] Volume II. London, *c.* 1924.
Our National Songs. Collected and arranged by Sir Harold Boulton, Bart., C.V.O.
and Arthur Somervell. Volume II. Copyright MCMXXIV by J. B. Cramer & Co.
Ltd. for all countries. Price 4/– net. J. B. Cramer & Co. Ltd.: 139 New Bond Street,
London, W.1. New York: Chappell-Harms (inc.), 185 Madison Avenue. Printed in
England.
[4], 77 p. 310 mm. NLS.
    Contains 3 Gaelic songs, with translations by Neil Shaw.

—— [*Our National Songs.*] Volume III. London, *c.* 1925.
Our National Songs. Collected and arranged by Sir Harold Boulton, Bart., C.V.O.,
and Arthur Somervell. Volume III. Copyright MCMXXV by J. B. Cramer & Co.
Ltd. for all countries. Price 4/– net. J. B. Cramer & Co. Ltd.: 139 New Bond Street,
London, W.1. New York: Edward Schuberth & Co.
[1], 75, [3] p. 310 mm. NLS.
    Contains 2 Gaelic songs, with English translation. Volume I of this series contained
no Gaelic.

—— [*Songs of the North.*] Fiftieth Anniversary Volume. London, [Pref. 1935].
Fiftieth anniversary volume. Songs of the North, gathered together from the Highlands
and Lowlands of Scotland. Edited by Harold Boulton. Music composed and arranged
by Malcolm Louson, Evelyn Sharpe, Robert Macleod, Granville Bantock, Arthur

Somervell, J. Michael Diack. Illustration by J. H. Lorimer, A.R.W.S., Corr. Mem. Institute of France. Price 15/–. London: J. B. Cramer & Co. Ltd., 139 New Bond Street, W.1.; Simpkin, Marshall, Hamilton, Kent & Co. Ltd. New York: Edward Schuberth & Co.

[12], 230 p; plate. 320 mm. Mit.
> Chiefly English and Scots songs; also some original Gaelic songs and translations into Gaelic of Scots and English songs by Neil Shaw and Rev. Alex. MacKinnon. All the songs in this collection were also published separately by J. B. Cramer, London.

—— [*Songs of the North.*] Volume III. London, n.d.
Vol. III. Songs of the North, gathered together from the Highlands and Lowlands of Scotland. Edited by Harold Boulton. Music arranged by Robert Macleod. The Gaelic text edited by Neil Shaw. Illustrated by J. H. Lorimer, A.R.W.S., Corr. Mem. Institute of France. Price 21/– net. London: J. B. Cramer & Co. Ltd., 139 New Bond Street, W.1.; Simpkin, Marshall, Hamilton, Kent & Co. Ltd. New York: Edward Schuberth & Co. (Printed in England.)

[11], 157 p. 320 mm. NLS.
> Contains 14 Gaelic songs out of a total of 53. Of the former, four are original, nine are Gaelic translations of English lyrics by Boulton, and one a translation of a song by Mrs M. Louson; the translations are by Duncan Johnston (1), Rev. Alex. Mac-Kinnon (2), John MacMillan (2), and Neil Shaw (5). Music in staff notation with piano accompaniment. All Gaelic texts have versified English translations on the facing page.

—— [*Unrecorded Miracle of St. Columba.*] London, c. 1930.
An Unrecorded Miracle of St. Columba. By Harold Boulton. With a Gaelic translation by Archibald McDonald and a drawing by Avild Rosenkrantz. London: Philip Allan & Co. Ltd., Quality House, Great Russell Street, W.C.1.
Miorbhuil Neo-sgrìobhte le Calum Cille. Le H. Boulton. Eadar-theangaichte le Gilleasbuig MacDhòmhnuill.

[2], 41 p; plate. 220 mm. AU, BM.
> Bears the imprint, "All rights reserved 1930". Printed The Camelot Press Limited, London and Southampton.

Brandane, John, 1869–1947. [*The Change-House.*] Glasgow, 1950.
Dealbh-chluichean an Gàidhlig. An Tigh-Osda. Dealbh-chluich an aon sealladh. Gaelic translation of the one-act play, The Change-House, by John Brandane. Air eadar-theangachadh le Dòmhnall Mac Dhòmhnaill (Eirisgeidh). An Comunn Gaid-healach, 131 West Regent Street, Glasgow. 1950.

28 p. 190 mm.
> John Brandane was the pen-name of Dr. John MacIntyre.
> English original first published 1921.
> Printed by Alex. Learmonth, Stirling.

—— [*The Glen is Mine.*] Glasgow, 1935.
'S Leam Fhìn an Gleann. Cluich aighearach ann an trì earrannan le John Brandane. Air eadar theangachadh gu Gàidhlig le T. S. Mac-a-Phearsain, Ceannloch. A' cheud duais, Mòd, 1932. An Comunn Gaidhealach, 212 Iar Shràid Sheòrais, Glaschu, C.2. 1935.

123 p. 190 mm. EPL, GU:CL.
> Printed Alex. Learmonth, Stirling. English original first published 1925.

—— [*Rory Aforesaid.*] Glasgow, 1937.
Ruairidh Roimh-Ainmichte. Cluich-àbhachd ann an aon earrainn le John Brandane. Air eadar-theangachadh gu Gàidhlig le Aonghas Mac Mhaoilein. Glascho: Alasdair MacLabhruinn agus a Mhic, 268 Sràid Earra Ghaidheal, C.2. 1937.

29 p. 190 mm. EPL, GU:CL, Mit.
> English original first published 1928.

British Broadcasting Corporation. See Am Measg nam Bodach.

British Broadcasting Corporation. See Learning Gaelic.

Brosnachadh do na Gaidheil. See Comunn nan Albannach. Brosnachadh do na Gaidheil.

Bruce, George, 1909–. [*The Scottish Literary Revival.*] London, 1968.
The Scottish Literary Revival. An anthology of twentieth-century poetry. Edited by
George Bruce. Collier-MacMillan Limited, London. The Macmillan Company, New
York. First printing 1968.
xi, 130 p. 220 mm.
    Contains Gaelic poems by Sorley Maclean and Derick Thomson. Printed Morrison
    & Gibb Ltd., Edinburgh and London.

—— [*Scottish Poetry, Number One.*] Edinburgh, n.d.
Number One. Scottish Poetry. Edited by George Bruce, Maurice Lindsay and Edwin
Morgan for the University Press, Edinburgh.
x, 96 p. 190 mm.
    c. 1965. Contains Gaelic poems by Derick Thomson.

—— [*Scottish Poetry, Number Three.*] Edinburgh, *c.* 1968.
Number Three. Scottish Poetry. Edited by George Bruce, Maurice Lindsay and
Edwin Morgan for the University Press, Edinburgh.
125 p. 190 mm.
    Copyright imprint, " © Edinburgh University Press, 1968". American distributors:
    Aldine Publishing Co., Chicago. Printed T. & A. Constable, Edinburgh. Gaelic
    poems by Sorley Maclean and Derick Thomson. Number Two contained no Gaelic.
Bruce, George J., b.1869. [*Do Luchd-taghaidh Shiorramachd Inbhir-nis.*] Inverness,
n.d.
Do Luchd-taghaidh Shiorramachd Inbhir-nis.
[Signed] Deòrsa Seumas Brus (George James Bruce), Author-Journalist, 161A Strand,
Lunnain.
4 p. 350 mm. NLS.
    An election leaflet of 1918. Contains one and a half pages of Gaelic. Printed
    Highland News Printing and Publishing Works, Inverness.

Buchanan, Dugald, 1716–68. [*Beatha agus Iompachadh.*] Glasgow, 1928.
Beatha agus Iompachadh Dhùghaill Bochannain a dh'eug ann an Ranach sa' bliadhna
1768 (air a sgrìobhadh leis fhéin). Glascho: Alasdair Mac Labhruinn 's a Mhic, 360–
364 Sràid Earraghaidheal, C.2. 1928.
185 p. 170 mm. AU.
    1st ed. 1844, of which this is a reprint.

—— [*Beatha agus Iompachadh Maille r' a Laoidhean.*] Edinburgh, 1908.
The Life and Conversion of Dugald Buchanan who died at Rannach in 1768 (written
by himself) to which is annexed his spiritual hymns. [Quotations.]
Edinburgh: John Grant, 31 George IV Bridge. 1908.
Beatha agus Iompachadh Dhùg. Bochannain a dh'eug ann an Ranach sa' bhliadhna
1768 (air a sgrìobhadh leis fhéin) maille r'a laoidhean spioradail. [Quotations.]
Edinburgh: John Grant, 31 George IV Bridge. 1908.
vi, 185 p; 87 p. 170 mm. PC.
    The hymns have separate fly-title page ("Laoidhean Spioradail le Dùghall Bochan-
    nan") and pagination. This is a reprint of the 1st ed. of 1844. The editor was John
    MacKenzie. An English translation of Buchanan's poems and "Confessions" by
    Lachlan MacBean ("Buchanan the Sacred Bard of the Scottish Highlands") was
    published in 1919.

—— [*Spiritual Songs.*] Edinburgh, 1913.
The Spiritual Songs of Dugald Buchanan. Edited with introduction, notes and vocabulary by Rev. Donald Maclean, author of "The Highlands before the Reformation", "Duthil: Past and Present", "The Literature of the Scottish Gael", etc. New edition. Edinburgh: John Grant, 31 George IV Bridge. 1913.
xii, 114 p. 210 mm. AU, BM, EU:CL, Mit.
    Printed Oliver & Boyd, Edinburgh.

—— [*Dain Spioradail.*] Glasgow, 1946.
Dàin Spioradail le Dùghall Bochanan. The Spiritual Songs of Dugald Buchanan. Glasgow: Alex. MacLaren & Sons, 268 Argyle Street, C.2.
First published 1767. Second edition 1773. Reprinted perhaps forty times. MacLaren's new edition 1946.
[2], 59 p. 190 mm. PC.

Budge, Donald (ed.). See Douglas, Katherine. [*Pein-ora.*]

—— (ed.). See Douglas, Katherine. [*Sar-orain.*]

Bunyan, John, 1628–88. [*Grace Abounding.*] Edinburgh, 1902.
Grace Abounding to the Chief of Sinners. By John Bunyan. [Quotation.] Edinburgh: John Grant, 31 George IV Bridge. 1902.
Gràs am Pailteas do Cheann-feadhna nam Peacach. Le Iain Buinian. [Quotation.] Edinburgh: John Grant, 31 George IV Bridge. 1902.
223 p. 160 mm. AU, Mit.
Printed by Oliver & Boyd, Edinburgh. Contains editorial note signed: "J.M'K. [i.e. John MacKenzie], Edinburgh, 14th June 1847". 1st ed. 1847; English original first published 1666.

—— [*The Holy War.*] Edinburgh, n.d.
Cogadh mòr na h-Eòrpa. An Cogadh Naomh. Part One. [Illus.] Printed by Oliver and Boyd, Edinburgh, for The Church of Scotland, The United Free Church of Scotland, and The Free Church of Scotland.
iv, 63 p. 140 mm. NLS.
. . . Part Two. [Otherwise title page as above.]
xii, [64]–135 p. 140 mm. NLS.
    Issued during World War One.

—— [*The Holy War.*] Edinburgh, n.d.
Cogadh na Saorsa. An Cogadh Naomh. A Cheud Earrann. [Illus.] Printed by Oliver and Boyd, Edinburgh, for The Church of Scotland, The Free Church of Scotland.
iv, 63 p. 140 mm. NLS.
. . . Earrann II. [Otherwise title page as above.]
vii, [64]–135 p. 140 mm. NLS.
    A reprint of the "Cogadh Mor na h-Eòrpa" ed. [see above]; distributed to soldiers in World War Two. Gaelic translation first published 1840; English original first published 1682.

—— [*Pilgrim's Progress.*] Edinburgh, 1912.
The Pilgrim's Progress from this world to the world to come under the similitude of a dream, in three parts, by John Bunyan. [Quotation.] Edinburgh: John Grant, 31 George IV Bridge. 1912.
Cuairt an Eilthirich, no Turas a' Chriosdaidh o'n t-saoghal so chum an t-saoghail a ta ri teachd fo shamhla bruadair, ann an tri earrannan, le Iain Buinian. [Quotation.] Edinburgh: John Grant, 31 George IV Bridge. 1912.
vi, 413 p. 180 mm. AU, GU.
    Translated by John MacKenzie. 1st ed. 1812; the above is a reprint of the 1845 ed.; English original first published 1678–84.

—— [*Pilgrim's Progress.*] London, 1929.
Turus a' Chriosduidh o'n t-saoghal so chum an t-saoghail ri teachd air a chur an riochd aisling le Iain Buinian. [Quotation.] Air a chur an Gaidhlig Albannaich le Calum MacGhillinnein, D.D., an Dun-eideann. (Pilgrim's Progress in Scottish Gaelic.) Comunn nan Trachdannan Diadhaidh an Lunnuinn. 1929.
221 p; 16 plates. 180 mm. AU, PC.
　　Printed The Darien Press, Edinburgh.

—— [*Pilgrim's Progress.*] London, 1953.
. . . 1953.
221 p; 16 plates. 180 mm. PC.
　　Foreword by T. M. Murchison. Printed Lowe and Brydone, London.

—— [*The World to Come.*] Edinburgh, 1903.
The World to Come; or, Visions of Heaven and Hell. By John Bunyan. [Quotations.] Edinburgh: John Grant, 31 George IV Bridge. 1903.
An Saoghal a ta ri teachd; no Seallaidhean Néimh agus Ifrinn. Le Iain Buinian. [Quotations.] Edinburgh: John Grant, 31 George IV Bridge. 1903.
[4], 172 p. 140 mm. AU, Mit.
　　1st ed. 1844, of which this is a reprint. Translated by John Mackenzie.

Burns, Norman (tr.). See Murray, W. [*Adventure at the Castle.*]

Burns, Robert, 1759–96. [*Songs and Poems.*] Glasgow, n.d.
Dain, is luinneagan, Robert Burns, eadartheangaichte do'n Ghaidhlig Albannach.
Songs and poems of Robert Burns. Translated into Scottish Gaelic by Charles Mac-Phater, Glasgow. Glasgow: Alex. M'Laren & Son, 360–362 Argyle Street. Dumfries: R. G. Mann, Courier and Herald Offices.
iv, [i], viii, 355 p; 15 plates. 200 mm. AU, GU, Mit., NLS.
　　Advertised in *An Deo-Greine*, May 1909, as "now in press"; advertised for sale by MacLaren's in *An Deo-Greine*, Nov. 1911. Illus. comprise photos and line drawings.

Cabairneach, An. Portree, 1944, 1945, 1950, 1962.
Comunn na h-Oigridh. Feachd Phortrigh'. An Cabairneach. A' phrìs – Tasdan (co-dhiubh). "An Eachdraidh Thuathach," Inhbir Nis. [Masthead.] An Cabairneach. An t-Og Mhios, 1944.
25 p; illus. 250 mm. NLS, PC.
　　Editor Finlay J. MacDonald.
Comunn na h-Oigridh. Feachd Phortrigh'. An Cabairneach. A' phrìs – Tasdan. "An Eachdraidh Thuathach", Inbhirnis.
[Masthead.] An Cabairneach. An t-Og Mhios, 1945. II. Bean-Deasachaidh – Ceit Nic Dhòmhnuill.
25 p; illus. 250 mm. NLS, PC.
Comunn na h-Oigridh. Feachd Phortrigh'. An Cabairneach. A' phrìs – Tasdan (co-dhiùbh, co-dhiùbh). "An Eachdraidh Thuathach", Inbhir Nis.
[Masthead.] An Cabairneach. An Ceitean, 1950. Fir-Deasachaidh – Murchadh A. Mac-an-Tuairneir, Niall Moireasdan. Comhairle Dheasachaidh – Calum Caimbeul, Alasdair M. MacDhòmhnuill, Niall MacDhòmhnuill, Dòmhnull Mac'Ill'Eathain, Róda NicDhòmhnuill, Mórag Mhoireasdan.
27 p; illus. 250 mm. NLS.
Comunn na h-Oigridh. Feachd Phortrigh'. An Cabairneach. A' phrìs – leth-chrun (co-dhiùbh, co-dhiùbh).
[Masthead.) An Cabairneach. An Céitean, 1962. IV. Fir-Deasachaidh: Iain Mac-Dhùghaill, Dòmhnull Mac 'Ill Fhinnein, Dòmhnull Iain MacLeòid.
23 p; illus. 250 mm. PC.
　　Prepared by the Portree High School branch of Comunn na h-Oigridh. Edited under the supervision of John Steele, then Gaelic master at Portree High School.

Cainnt agus Facail Iomchuidh air son Coinnimh. Glasgow, 1954.
An Comunn Gaidhealach. Clann an Fhraoich. Cainnt agus facail iomchuidh air son coinnimh. Niall Mac Ille Sheathanaich, F.S.A. (Scot.), Ceann-suidhe a' Chomuinn Ghaidhealaich. Dòmhnall MacPhàil, J.P., Fear-gairme na Comhairle. Domhnull Grannd, M.A., B.A., Ed.B. I. M. Moffat-Pender, M.A. 1954.
8 p. 210 mm. PC.

Caimbel, Paruig. See Campbell, Peter.

Caimbeul, Cairstiona. See Campbell, Christina.

Caimbeul, Calum. See Campbell, Calum.

Caimbeul, Catriona. See Campbell, Catherine.

Caimbeul, Iain. See Campbell, John, of Sydney, N.S.

Caimbeul, Iain F. See Campbell, John F.

Caimbeul, Iain Latharna. See Campbell, John L.

Caimbeul, Seonaidh. See Campbell, John, of South Uist, 1859–1945.

Calder, George, 1859–1941. [*Gaelic Grammar.*] Glasgow, [Intro. 1923].
A Gaelic Grammar, containing the parts of speech and the general principles of phonology and etymology, with a chapter on proper and place names. By George Calder, B.D., D.Litt., Lecturer in Celtic, University of Glasgow. Glasgow: Alex. MacLaren & Sons, 360–362 Argyle Street.
xiv, [1], 352 p. 200 mm. AU, BM, GU:CL, Mit.

—— [*Gaelic Grammar.*] Glasgow, 1972.
. . . By George Calder, B.D., D.Litt., Lecturer in Celtic, University of Glasgow. Gairm Publications, Glasgow. 1972.
xiv, [1], 352 p. 140 mm.

—— (ed.). See MacDougall, James. [*Folk Tales and Fairy Lore.*]

—— (ed.). See MacIntyre, Duncan. [*Orain Ghaidhealach.*]

—— (ed.). See Ross, William. [*Orain Ghaidhealach.*]

Calvin, John, 1509–64. [*Catechismus Ecclesiae Genevensis.*]   Edinburgh, 1962.
Adtiomchiol an Chreidimh. The Gaelic Version of John Calvin's Catechismus Ecclesiae Genevensis. A facsimile reprint, including the prefixed poems and the Shorter Catechism of 1659, with Notes and Glossary, and an Introduction. Edited by R. L. Thomson, Lecturer in the Department of English Language and Medieval Literature, University of Leeds. Published by Oliver & Boyd for the Scottish Gaelic Texts Society. Edinburgh. 1962.
Scottish Gaelic Texts; Volume Seven.
xlviii, 264 p. 230 × 160 mm. GU.
    Text, pp. xliii–xlviii, 1–112; Notes, 118–149; Glossary, 151–213; Appendix, 215–250; List of Members, 259–264. 1st ed. 1659. Original first published 1545.

Cameron, Alexander, 1848–1933. [*Orain, Sgriobhaidhean agus Litrichean.*] Edinburgh, 1926.
Am Bard. Orain, Sgrìobhaidhean agus Litrichean Bàrd Thùrnaig (Alasdair Camshron). Air an deasachadh agus air an cur a mach le Iain MacAlasdair Moffat-Pender. Roimh-ràdh le Uilleam I. MacBhatair, M.A., LL.D., Ard-Ollamh na Gaidhlig an Oil-thigh Dhun-Eideann. Dun-Eideann. U. M. Urchardainn agus a Mhac. 1026.
232 p; 7 plates. 230 mm. AU, BM, EU, GU.
    Printed A. Sinclair, Glasgow.

Cameron, Hector, 1893–1940. [*Na Baird Thirisdeach*.] Glasgow, 1932.
Na Baird Thirisdeach. Saothair ar co-luchd-dùthcha aig an tigh 's bho'n tigh. Agus air a dheasachadh leis an Urr. Eachann Camshron. 1932. Air a chur a mach leis A' Chomunn Thirisdeach.
The Tiree Bards. Being the original compositions of natives of Tiree at home and abroad. Edited by the Rev. Hector Cameron. 1932. Published by The Tiree Association.
xxlv, 438 p. 130 mm. AU, BM, EU, Mit.
Printed Eneas Mackay, Stirling.

Cameron, John, of Sutherland. [*Gaelic Names of Plants*.] Glasgow, 1900.
The Gaelic Names of Plants (Scottish, Irish, and Manx), collected and arranged in scientific order, with notes on their etymology, uses, plant superstititions, etc., among the Celts, with copious Gaelic, English, and scientific indices, by John Cameron, Sunderland. [Quotation.] New and revised edition. Glasgow: John Mackay, *Celtic Monthly* Office, 1 Blythswood Drive. 1900.
xv, 160 p; plate. 230 mm. AU, GU, Mit.
   1st ed. 1883. Originally published as articles in the *Scottish Naturalist*, 1879–.

Cameron, John, of Ullapool. See Marshall, Alexander. [*God's Way of Salvation*.]

Cameron, Mrs. [Margaret]. [*M'annsachd*.] Edinburgh, 1916.
M'annsachd agus Rannan Eile le Mrs. Camaran a bha uair-éiginn am Monar. Edinburgh: John Grant, 31 George IV Bridge. 1916.
37 p. 180 mm. FC.
Printed Oliver & Boyd, Edinburgh.

Cameron, Neil, 1854–1932. [*Collected Works*.] Inverness, 1932.
Memoir, Biographical Sketches, Letters, Lectures and Sermons (English and Gaelic) of the Rev. Neil Cameron, Glasgow. Edited by the Rev. D. Beaton, Oban. Inverness: printed by the Northern Counties Newspaper and Printing and Publishing Company, Limited. 1932.
vii, 304 p; plate. 190 mm. PC.
   [271]–304 p of Gaelic.

Cameron Lees, James. See Lees, J. Cameron.

Campbell, Mrs. A. See MacKinnon, Mary A.

Campbell, Angus, *Am Bocsair*, 1908–49. [*Orain Ghaidhlig*.] Glasgow, 1943.
Orain Ghàidhlig le Aonghas Caimbeal, Nis, Leódhas. Gaelic Songs by Angus Campbell, Ness, Lewis. Glasgow: printed by John Thomlison, Ltd., Stanley Works. 1943.
32 p. 190 mm. BM, PC.

Campbell, Angus, *Am Puilean*, 1903–. [*Moll is Cruithneachd*.] Glasgow, 1972.
Moll is Cruithneachd. Le Aonghas Caimbeul (Am Puilean), Mac Alasdair Mhurchaidh òig á Suaineabost, Nis, Leódhas. Gairm. Glaschu. 1972.
Clo-bhualaidhean Gairm, Leabhar 31.
[8], 96 p. 220 mm.
Printed A. Learmonth, Stirling.

—— [*Suathadh ri Iomadh Rubha*.] Glasgow, 1973.
Suathadh ri Iomadh Rubha. Eachdraidh a bheatha le Aonghas Caimbeul (Am Puilean). Deasaichte le Iain Moireach. Gairm. Glaschu. 1973.
Clò-bhualaidhean Gairm, Leabhar 34.
[10], 370 p; 9 plates.
Cover design by Duncan MacAskill. First prizewinner in Gaelic Books Council biography competition, 1970.

Campbell, Calum. [*Laoidhean.*] Stornoway, n.d.
Laoidhean le Calum Caimbeul, a Bhradhagair. (Air an sgrìobhadh leis an Urr. Murchadh Caimbeul.) Printed at the *Gazette* Office, Stornoway.
8 p. 220 mm. FC.
Recent.

Campbell, Catherine, 1931–. [*Laoidhean Ghaidhlig.*] Stornoway, n.d.
Laoidhean Ghàidhlig le Catriona Caimbel. Prìs 3/–.
Published by A. McLeod, Marybank, Stornoway, and printed by Stornoway Gazette Limited, 10 Francis Street, Stornoway.
36 p; 3 plates; illus. 220 mm. PC.
A few tunes in staff, and solfa. Preface by A.M.L. (Angus MacLeod?). Recent.

Campbell, Christina, 1906–. [*Measg Sguaban Bhoais.*] Glasgow, 1971.
Measg Sguaban Bhoais. Laoidhean le: Cairstiona Chaimbeul; Anna Chaimbeul, Belag Chaimbeul, Catriona Chaimbeul. Clo-beag, Glaschu, 1971.
40 p. 210 mm.
Foreword by Donald Smith. Ten poems by Christina Campbell; one each by Ann, Bella and Catherine Campbell.

Campbell, Dugald J. [*A' Phiob-Mhor.*] N.p., n.d.
An ceòl a bu bhinne a chuala Sassunnach riabh, a phiob-mhor.
4 p. 180 mm. PC.
Around the turn of the century.

Campbell, G. Murray. [*Edward VII, King of Scots.*] N.p., 1910.
Edward VII, King of Scots. 7-5-1910. By G. Murray Campbell. English translation by Norman Grieve.
19 p. 150 mm. EU.
English and Gaelic on facing pages. 1 verse per page only.

Campbell, Hilda M. [*Orain na Clàrsaich.*] London, *c.* 1933.
Orain na Clàrsaich (Songs of the Harp). Arranged by Hilda M. Campbell (Airds). English words by Harold Boulton. With Forewords by Hilda Mary Campbell and Harold Boulton. Copyright. Price 3/6. Paterson's Publications Ltd.; London: 36–40 Wigmore Street, W.1.; Edinburgh: 27 George Street. New York: Carl Fischer, Inc., 62 Cooper Square. Canada: Anglo-Canadian Music Co., 144 Victoria Street, Toronto. New Zealand: C. Begg & Co., Ltd., Manners Street, Wellington.
24 p. 310 mm. Mit., NLS.
Songs individually copyrighted 1933; Mitchell Library copy acquired 1933. 8 Gaelic songs with English translations; music in both notations, with harp accompaniments. Cover design by Anna MacBride.

Campbell, James (ed.). See MacKenzie, Lachlan. [*Lectures, Sermons and Writings.*]

Campbell, John, of Glasgow (comp.). See MacColl, Duncan. [*Laoidhean Soisgeulach.*]

Campbell, John, of South Uist, 1859–1945. [*Orain Ghaidhlig.*] Dunfermline, 1936.
Orain Ghàidhlig le Seonaidh Caimbeul (Seonaidh mac Dhòmhnaill 'ic Iain Bhàin). Air an toirt sios le Iain Mac Aonghuis. Air an deasachadh le Iain Latharna Caimbeul (fear-deasachaidh "Duain Ghàidhealach mu Bhliadhna Thearlaich"). Chaidh an leabhar so chlò-bhualadh ann an Alba le I. B. Mac Aoidh agus a Chuideachd, ann an Dun Phàrlain, Fiobha, gu feum an Ughdair, anns a' bhliadhna 1936.
xvii, 130 p; plate. 190 mm. BM, NLS.

—— [*Orain Ghàidhlig.*] Dunfermline, 1937.
Ibid.
A' Chiad Chlò-Bhualadh 1936. An Darna Clò-bhualadh Am Màrt, 1937.
xvii, 130 p; plate. 190 mm. GU, Mit., PC.
Reprint. Printed privately by J. L. Campbell.

Campbell, John, of Sydney, N.S. [*Marbhrann agus Laoidhean Spioradail.*] Sydney, N.S., 1947.
Marbhrann agus Laoidhean Spioradail eadartheangaichte o'n Bheurla le Iain Caimbeul.
Sydney, N.S. 1947.
16 p. 160 mm. PC, Xavier.

—— [*Marbhrann.*] N.p., n.d.
"Marbhrann le Iain Caimbeul Sidini – Air son a bh'ean a caochail 'sa bhliana 1939."
3 p.
> Not seen. Described in *Clare* and *Dunn*.

Campbell, John F., 1822–85. [*Blar Traigh Ghruinneaird.*] Edinburgh, 1950.
Ian Og Ìle. MS. VII, Ian Deòir. Earrann I. Blàr Tràigh Ghruinneaird. John Grant,
Booksellers Ltd., 31 George IV Bridge, Edinburgh. 1950.
[6], 22 p. 220 mm. PC.
> Contains also the stories, "Na Domhnullaich agus na Leathanaich", and "Raonall
> Arrunnach 's Seumas MacDhomhnaill". Tales collected for John F. Campbell by
> John Dewar.

—— [*The Celtic Dragon Myth.*] Edinburgh, 1911.
The Celtic Dragon Myth by J. F. Campbell, with the Geste of Fraoch and the Dragon.
Translated with introduction by George Henderson, Ph.D. (Vienna), B.Litt. (Oxon.),
M.A. (Edin.), Lecturer in Celtic Languages and Literature, University of Glasgow.
Illustrations in colour by Rachel Ainslie Grant Duff. Edinburgh: John Grant, 31
George IV Bridge. 1911.
li, 172 p; 5 plates. 250 mm. AU, GU, Mit.
> Contains also "Na Tri Rathaidean Móra" and "An t-Iasgair". Printed Oliver and
> Boyd, Edinburgh.

—— [*Clann an Righ fo Gheasaibh.*] Glasgow, n.d.
The Ceilidh Books. Leabhraichean nan Céilidh. Aireamh 21. Clann an Rìgh fo
Gheasaibh. Seann sgeul le I. F. Campbell, "Iain Og Ile". [Illus.] A' phrìs, trì sgilli-
nnean, 3d. Alasdair Mac Labhruinn agus a Mhic, 360–2 Sràid Earraghaidheal,
Glascho.
[65]–84 p. 210 mm. PC.
> Reprinted from *An Sgeulaiche*, III.2, Summer, 1911.

—— [*Fear a' Bhratain Uaine.*] Glasgow, 1930.
The Ceilidh Books. Leabhraichean nan Céilidh. Aireamh 23. Fear a' Bhratain Uaine.
Seann sgeul le I. F. Caimbeul, "Iain Og Ile". [Illus.] A' phrìs, trì sgillinnean. 3d.
Alasdair Mac Labhruinn agus a Mhic, 360–2 Sraid Earraghaidheal. 1930.
[502]–520 p. 210 mm. PC.
> Reprinted from *Guth na Bliadhna*, IX.4, Autumn, 1912.

—— [*Gille a' Bhuidseir.*] London, 1912.
Ancient Legends of the Scottish Gael. Gille a' Bhuidseir. The Wizard's Gillie and
other tales. Edited and translated by John G. McKay. From the magnificent Manuscript Collections of the late J. F. Campbell of Islay, compiler of the famous "Popular
Tales of the West Highlands". Saint Catherine Press, Oswaldestre House, 34 Norfolk
Street, Strand, W.C.
141 p; 6 plates. 200 mm. AU, GU.
> Date from 2nd ed.

—— [*Gille a' Bhuidseir.*] Glasgow, 1946.
. . . Glasgow: Alex. MacLaren & Sons, 268 Argyle Street, C.2.
First edition 1912. Second Edition 1946.
127 p. 180 mm.

—— [*Gille nan Cochall Chraiceann.*] Stirling, 1955.
Gille nan Cochall Chraiceann, and other tales. K. C. Craig, M.A., B.Litt. Eneas MacKay, Stirling.
Sgialachdan Gàilig a chruinnich Iain Og Ile, air an taghadh le K. C. Craig, M.A., B.Litt.
54 p. 190 mm. NLS, SS.
  First published 1955.

—— [*Leabhar na Feinne.*] Shannon, 1972.
Leabhar na Feinne. Heroic Gaelic Ballads collected in Scotland chiefly from 1512 to 1871. With an introduction by Derick S. Thomson. Arranged by J. F. Campbell. Irish University Press. Shannon, Ireland. 1972.
Scottish Reprints. Leabhar na Feinne.
[1872 t.p.] Leabhar na Feinne. Vol. 1. Gaelic Texts. Heroic Gaelic Ballads collected in Scotland chiefly from 1512 to 1871. Copied from old manuscripts preserved at Edinburgh and elsewhere, and from rare books; and orally collected since 1859; with lists of collections, and of their contents; and with a short account of the documents quoted. Arranged by J. F. Campbell, Niddry Lodge, Kensington, London, W. October 1872. London: printed for the author by Spottiswoode & Co., New Street Square, E.C. 1872. Price £1.
ix, [1], xxxvi, 224 p. 350 mm.
  A photolithographic facsimile. 1st ed. 1872. Only one volume appeared.

—— [*Leigheas Cas O Cein.*] Stirling, 1950.
Leigheas Cas O Céin. Sgialachd air a gabhail am Paislig an 1870 le Lachlainn Mac Nèill, griasaiche a Ile, agus air a cur sìos air son Iain Oig Ile le Eachann Mac 'Ill 'Eathainn, maighstir sgoileadh Ileach (MSS. Iain Oig Ile Vol. 17). Air a deasachadh le K. C. Craig. Published for K. C. Craig by Eneas MacKay, Stirling. 1950.
[4], 84 p. 200 mm. EU, GU.
  Printed Jamieson & Munro, Stirling.

—— [*Mogan Dearg Mac Iachair.*] Glasgow, n.d.
The Ceilidh Books. Leabhraichean nan Céilidh. Aireamh 20. Mogan Dearg Mac Iachair. Seann sgeul le I. F. Caimbeul, "Iain Og Ile". [Illus.] A' phris, trì sgillinnean, 3d. Alasdair Mac Labhruinn agus a Mhic, 360–2 Sràid Earraghaidheal, Glascho.
[48]–70 p. 220 mm. PC.
  Reprinted from *Guth na Bliadhna*, LX.1, Winter, 1913.

—— [*More West Highland Tales.*] Volume One. Edinburgh, 1940.
More West Highland Tales. Transcribed and translated from the original Gaelic by John G. McKay. Edited by: Professor W. J. Watson, M.A., LL.D., D.Litt.Celt., Hon.F.E.I.S.; The Reverend Professor Donald Maclean, D.D.; Professor H. J. Rose, M.A., F.B.A., F.S.A.S. Volume One. Published for The Scottish Anthropological and Folklore Society by Oliver and Boyd, Edinburgh and London. 1940.
xxxix, 540 p. 240 mm. AU, EU:CL, GU.
  From the J. F. Campbell of Islay MSS. Gaelic and English on facing pages. Secretaries to the Publishing Committee: D. C. Crichton and T. J. M. Mackay.

—— [*More West Highland Tales.*] Volume Two. Edinburgh, 1960.
More West Highland Tales. Transcribed and translated from the original Gaelic MSS. by John G. McKay, translator of The Wizard's Gillie. Editors: Gaelic – Professor Angus Matheson, M.A.; Translation – J. MacInnes, M.A.; Folklore – Professor H. J. Rose, M.A., LL.D., F.B.A.; Notes – Professor K. Jackson, Litt.D., D.Litt.Celt., F.B.A. Volume Two. Published for The Scottish Anthropological and Folklore Society by Oliver and Boyd, Edinburgh and London. 1960.
From the MS. Collections of the late John Francis Campbell of Islay, Iain Og Ile, collector and translator of Popular Tales of the West Highlands.
xvi, 383 p. 240 mm. AU, FU, GU.

Secretaries to the Publishing Committee, David C. Crichton and Thomas J. M. Mackay.

—— [*Na Se Bonnaich Bheaga.*] London, 1912.
Na Se Bonnaich Bheaga, and other Easy Gaelic Fairy Tales. From the unpublished MS. Collections of the late J. F. Campbell of Islay, Iain Og Ile. Arranged by J. G. McKay. Price 3d. Special terms for large quantities. To be had from Miss A. MacLennan, 82 St. John's Hill, Clapham Junction, London, S.W.
12p. 250 mm. AU, PC.
Date from imprint in 2nd ed.

—— [*Na Se Bonnaich Bheaga.*] Glasgow, 1946.
. . . English translation by J. G. McKay. For every story English translations have been prepared, upon which the utmost care has been bestowed, and these translations will be found facing the Gaelic originals, on opposite pages. Glasgow: Alex. MacLaren and Sons, 268 Argyle Street.
First Edition 1912. Second Edition 1946.
[2], 26 p. 220 mm. PC.

Campbell, John L., 1906–. [*Duain Ghaidhealach mu Bhliadhna Thearlaich.*] Edinburgh, 1933.
Duain Ghàidhealach mu Bhliadhna Theàrlaich a dheasaich agus dh'eadar-theangaich Iain Latharna Caimbeul, a chuir Focloir agus Sanasan r'a chéile. Iain Grannd, 31 Drochaid a' Cheathraimh Rìgh Deòrsa, Dùn-Eideann. 1933.
Highland Songs of the Forty-Five. Edited and translated with Glossary and Notes. By John Lorne Campbell. John Grant, 31 George IV Bridge, Edinburgh. 1933.
xxxvi, 327 p; map. 240 mm. AU, BM, EU, GU, Mit.
English translation on facing pages. Some tunes, in staff notation. Printed by Oliver and Boyd, Edinburgh.

—— [*Fr. Allan McDonald of Eriskay.*] Edinburgh, 1954.
Fr. Allan McDonald of Eriskay, 1859–1905, priest, poet, and folklorist. By John L. Campbell. Based upon a broadcast talk recorded at Antigonish, Nova Scotia, in May 1953, and printed to mark the fiftieth anniversary of the consecration of Eriskay Church, built by Fr. Allan. The profits on the sale of this pamphlet are to be devoted towards the upkeep of Eriskay Church. The copyright is the property of the author.
31 p; 4 plates. 220 mm. BM.
Mainly in English with Gaelic quotations.

—— [*Gaelic Folksongs from the Isle of Barra.*] London, n.d.
Gaelic Folksongs from the Isle of Barra. Recorded by J. L. Campbell, President of the Folklore Institute of Scotland. Edited by J. L. Campbell with the collaboration of Annie Johnston and John MacLean, M.A. Published by The Linguaphone Institute for The Folklore Institute of Scotland.
55, [1]; illus. 210 mm. AU, BM, NLS, PC.
    1950. 5 12-inch records were issued with the booklet. Photograph of "Ruairi Iain Bhàin" is on p 4. English translation on facing pages. "Printed for International Catalogues Ltd., 207–209 Regent Street, London, W.1. by W. & J. Mackay & Co. Ltd., Chatham."

—— [*Sia Sgialachdan.*] Edinburgh, 1939.
Sia sgialachdan a chruinnich 's a dheasaich Iain Latharna Caimbeul ann am Barraidh 's an Uidhist a Deas. Six Gaelic stories from Barra and South Uist collected and edited by John Lorne Campbell. With Introduction, English Summary and Glossary. Privately printed by T. and A. Constable, Limited, Edinburgh. 1939.
50 p. [Gaelic tales, pp 19–50.] 220 mm. BM, CoS, Mit.

—— (ed.). See Campbell, John, of Uist. [*Orain Ghaidhlig.*]

—— (ed.). See Hardy, Thomas. [*The Three Strangers.*]

—— (joint ed.). See Lhuyd, Edward. [*Edward Lhuyd in the Scottish Highlands.*]

—— (ed.). See MacCormick, Donald. [*Hebridean Folksongs.*]

—— (ed.). See MacDonald, Fr. Allan. [*Bardachd Mhgr Ailein.*]

—— (ed.). See MacDonald, Fr. Allan. [*Gaelic Words and Expressions from South Uist.*]

—— (comp.). See MacDonald, Duncan, of South Uist. [*Fear na H-Eabaid.*]

—— (ed.). See MacLellan, Angus. [*Saoghal an Treobhaiche.*]

—— (ed.). See Macpherson, John, "The Coddy". [*Tales of Barra.*]

—— (ed.). See Van Dyke, Henry. [*The Other Wise Man.*]

Campbell, Malcolm. See Campbell, Calum.

Campbell, Margaret Shaw. See Shaw, Margaret F.

Campbell, Mrs. Mary A. See MacKinnon, Mary A.

Campbell, Murdoch (ed.). See Campbell, Calum. [*Laoidhean.*]

Campbell, Peter. [*Bardachd Ghaidhlig.*] Inverness, n.d.
Bardachd Ghaidhlig le Paruig Caimbel.
35 p. 190 mm. PC.
  Printed by Duncan Grant, 47 High Street, Inverness.

Caraid nan Gaidheal. See MacLeod, Dr. Norman, Minister of St. Columba's Church, Glasgow, 1783–1862.

Carey, Henry. See "God Save the King".

Carmichael, Alexander, 1832–1912. [*Carmina Gadelica.*] Volume I. Edinburgh, 1900.
Carmina Gadelica. Hymns and incantations, with illustrative notes on words, rites, and customs, dying and obsolete: orally collected in the Highlands and Islands of Scotland and translated into English by Alexander Carmichael. Volume I. Edinburgh: printed for the author by T. and A. Constable, printers to her Majesty, and sold by Norman Macleod, 25 George IV Bridge. 1900.
xxxii, 339 p; plate. 260 mm. AU, BM, GU, Mit.

—— [*Carmina Gadelica.*] Volume I. Edinburgh, 1928.
. . . Volume I. Oliver and Boyd; Edinburgh: Tweeddale Court; London: 33 Paternoster Row, E.C.4. 1928.
xxxvi, 335 p; plate. 240 mm. GU, Mit., SS.
  Special 2nd ed. preface signed by "E.C.W." (i.e. Ella Carmichael Watson, daughter of Alexander Carmichael, wife of W. J. Watson). English translation on facing pages.

—— [*Carmina Gadelica.*] Volume I. Edinburgh, 1972.
. . . Volume I. Scottish Academic Press. Edinburgh & London. 1972.
xxxvi, 335 p; plate. 240 mm.

—— [*Carmina Gadelica.*] Volume II. Edinburgh, 1900.
Carmina Gadelica. Hymns and incantations, with illustrative notes on words, rites, and customs, dying and obsolete: orally collected in the Highlands and Islands of Scotland and translated into English, by Alexander Carmichael. Volume II. Edinburgh: printed for the author by T. and A. Constable, printers to her Majesty, and sold by Norman Macleod, 25 George IV Bridge. 1900.
[2], xi, 350 p. 260 mm. AU, BM, GU, Mit.

—— [*Carmina Gadelica*.]   Volume II.   Edinburgh, 1928.
. . . Volume II.   Oliver and Boyd; Edinburgh: Tweeddale Court; London: 33 Paternoster Row, E.C.4.   1928.
xv, 381 p; [1] ["Soiridh."]   240 mm.   GU, Mit.

—— [*Carmina Gadelica*.]   Volume II.   Edinburgh, 1972.
. . . Volume II.   Scottish Academic Press.   Edinburgh & London.   1972.
xv, 381 p. [1]   240 mm.
   English translation on facing pages.

—— [*Carmina Gadelica*.]   Volume III.   Edinburgh, 1940.
Carmina Gadelica.   Hymns and incantations, with illustrative notes on words, rites, and
customs, dying and obsolete: orally collected in the Highlands and Islands of Scotland
by Alexander Carmichael.   Volume III.   [Illus.]   Oliver & Boyd; Edinburgh: Tweeddale Court; London: 98 Great Russell Street, W.C.   1940.
xxiv, 395 p; 1 plate.   240 mm.   AU, BM, EU, GU, Mit., NLS.
   Edited by James Carmichael Watson, who contributes a Preface.

—— [*Carmina Gadelica*.]   Volume IV.   Edinburgh, 1941.
Carmina Gadelica.   Hymns and incantations, with illustrative notes on words, rites,
and customs, dying and obsolete: orally collected in the Highlands and Islands of
Scotland by Alexander Carmichael.   Volume IV.   [Illus.]   Oliver and Boyd; Edinburgh:
Tweeddale Court; London: 98 Great Russell Street, W.C.   1941.
xlv, [2], 367 p.   240 mm.   AU, BM, EU, GU, Mit., NLS.
   Edited by James Carmichael Watson; published after his death; contains an apprecia-
tion of him.

—— [*Carmina Gadelica*.]   Volume V.   Edinburgh, 1954.
Carmina Gadelica.   Hymns and incantations, with illustrative notes on words, rites,
and customs, dying and obsolete: orally collected in the Highlands and Islands of
Scotland by Alexander Carmichael.   Volume V.   Edited by Angus Matheson,
McCallum-Fleming Lecturer in Celtic, University of Glasgow.   [Illus.]   Oliver and
Boyd; Edinburgh: Tweeddale Court; London: 39A Welbeck Street, W.1.   1954.
xxiv, 402 p; plate.   240 mm.   AU, BM, EU, GU, Mit., NLS.
   Printed T. and A. Constable, Edinburgh.

—— [*Carmina Gadelica*.]   Volume VI.   Edinburgh, 1971.
Carmina Gadelica.   Hymns and incantations, with illustrative notes on words, rites and
customs, dying and obsolete: orally collected in the Highlands and Islands of Scotland
by Alexander Carmichael.   Volume VI: Indexes.   Edited by Angus Matheson, Professor
of Celtic Languages and Literature in the University of Glasgow.   Scottish Academic
Press.   Edinburgh and London.   1971.
[7], 271 p.   240 mm.
   Published after Matheson's death; was prepared for the press by William Matheson.
   Each volume carries the subtitle, "Ortha nan Gaidheal", on the spine.

—— [*Deirdire*.]   Edinburgh, 1905.
Deirdire and the Lay of the Children of Uisne.   Orally collected in the Island of Barra,
and literally translated by Alexander Carmichael.   Edinburgh: Norman MacLeod.
London: David Nutt.   Dublin: Gill & Son.   1905.
[20], 146 p; 200 mm.   BM, GU.
   Printed T. & A. Constable, Edinburgh.

—— [*Deirdire*.]   Edinburgh, 1914.
Paisley: Alexander Gardner.   London (Kensington): Kenneth Mackenzie.   Dublin:
Hodges, Figgis & Co.   1914.   Second Edition.
[20], 155 p.   200 mm.   GU.
   Printed T. & A. Constable, Edinburgh.

—— [*Deirdire.*] Inverness, *c.* 1972.
Club Leabhar. Limited. Inverness.
Deirdire agus Laoidh Chlann Uisne. Sgrìobhta bho bheulachas ann am Barraidh agus
eadar-theangaichte le Alasdair MacGillemhìcheil. Club Leabhar Limited. Inbhirnis.
This edition *c.* 1972. Club Leabhar Limited.
[5], 146 p. 190 mm.
English translation on facing pages in all eds. Printed Eccleslitho, Inverness.

—— (comp.). See Bottomley, Gordon. [*Deirdire.*]

Carmichael, Ella C., *d.* 1928 (ed.). See *Celtic Monthly.*

Carmody, Francis J., 1907–. [*The Interrogative System in Modern Scottish Gaelic.*]
   Berkely, 1945.
The Interrogative System in Modern Scottish Gaelic. By Francis J. Carmody. University of California Publications in Linguistics Volume 1, No. 6, pp 215–26. University
of California Press, Berkely and Los Angeles. 1945.
[215]–226 p. 260 mm. PC.

Carney, James, 1914–. [*Celtic Studies.*] London, 1968.
Celtic Studies. Essays in memory of Angus Matheson, 1912–62. Edited by James
Carney and David Greene. London: Routledge and Kegan Paul.
First published 1968.
x, 182 p; plate. 230 mm.

—— [*Celtic Studies.*] London, 1969.
Ibid.
First published 1968. Reprinted 1969.
x, 182 p; plate. 230 mm. GU.
Scottish Gaelic contents include: poem by Sorley MacLean; "Notes on Gaelic gram-
mar" by Carl Hj. Borgström; "The Gaelic of Carloway, Isle of Lewis" by Donald G.
Howells; "The breaking of original long ē in Scottish Gaelic" by Kenneth Jackson;
"Unpublished verse by Silis Ni Mhic Raghnaill ne Ceapaich" by Kenneth Mac-
Donald; "The Harlaw Brosnachadh" by Derick S. Thomson.

Carswell, John, *c.* 1520–72 (tr.). See Church of Scotland. *Liturgy and Ritual.* [Book of
Common Order.]

Cassie, R. L. [*Comparative Gaelic-Scots Vocabulary.*] Stirling, 1930.
A Comparative Gaelic-Scots Vocabulary. By R. L. Cassie, author of "Byth Ballads",
"Doric Ditties", "Heid or Hert", "The Gangrel Muse", etc. Eneas Mackay, Stirling.
First published 1930.
95 p; plate. 200 mm. AU, GU, Mit.

Catechisms. See:
   Calvin, John. [*Catechismus Ecclesiae Genevensis.*]
   Catholic Church. *Catechism.* [Christian Doctrine.]
   Catholic Church. *Catechism.* [First Communion Catechism.]
   Guthrie, William. [*The Christian's Great Gain.*]
   The Shorter Catechism.

Catholic Church. *Catechism.* [Christian Doctrine.] Oban, 1902.
Aithghearradh Teagasg Chriosta. Le aonta nan Easbuig Ro-Urramach, Easbuig Abair
Eadhain agus Easbuig Earraghaidheal 's nan Eilean. An siathamh clò-bhualadh.
MCMII.
46 p. 130 mm. EU:CL, PC.
The first Gaelic translation of the "Christian Doctrine" was published in 1781
(486 p); the first of the abridged versions was in 1815. The above was printed by
Hugh MacDonald, Oban.

Catholic Church. *Catechism*. [Christian Doctrine.] New Glasgow, N.S., 1920.
Ath-ghearradh an Teagsag Chriosd. Air a cheartachadh 's air ath leasachadh le òrdugh Easbuig Caithliceach na' Sgìreachd. [Illus.] New Glasgow, N.S.: New Glasgow Printery. 1920.
24 p. 140 mm. GU:CL.

Catholic Church. *Catechism*. [Christian Doctrine.] Glasgow, 1940.
Aithghearradh Teagasg Chriosta is Leabhar Urnaigh. Air an tionndadh bho Bheurla gu Gaidhlig le aonta Easbuig Earraghaidheal 's nan Eileanan. Clò-bhuailte le P. Donegan & Co., 145 Trongate, Glasgow, C.1. 1940.
100 p. 140 mm. NLS.

Catholic Church. *Catechism*. [First Communion Catechism.] Dublin, 1950.
Leabhar Cheist na Cloinne Bige. With simplified text and explanations for the pupil and a manual with detailed study guides for the teacher. Prepared by Ellamay Horan, Ph.D., Editor of *The Journal of Religious Instruction*, and the co-author of the Kingdom of God Series. Containing the complete text of the official first communion catechism. The Scottish Hierarchy has approved Leabhar Cheist na Cloinne Bige for the Infant Department and Primary Three of Catholic Schools. Donald A. Campbell, Archbishop of Glasgow, October 10, 1950.
Distributed by The Catholic Truth Society, 18 Renfrew Street, Glasgow, C.2. Air an tionndadh bho Bheurla gu Gaidhlig le aonta Stephen McGill, Easbuig Earraghaidheal 's nan Eileinean. Published by Iona Press, Dublin and Glasgow. Entire contents copyrighted 1950 throughout the United Kingdom by Iona Press by arrangement with William H. Saddler, Inc., New York, and under licence from the Confraternity of Christian Doctrine, Washington. Printed in Dublin by Dakota Limited.
viii, 39 p, [1]; col. illus. 190 mm. PC.

Catholic Church. *Liturgy and ritual*. [Iul a' Chriostaidh.] Antigonish, 1901.
Iul a' Chriostaidh; no Comh-chruinneachadh de ùrnaighean air son a h-uile ama agus staide de bheatha a' Chrìostaidh. An seachdamh clòbhualadh, ath-leasaichte. Antigonish: The Casket Printing and Publishing Company. 1901.
383 p. 150 mm. Xavier.
1st ed. pre-1844.

—— [*Iul a' Chriosdaidh*.] Stirling, 1963.
An ochdamh clobhualadh, ath-leasaichte. Stirling: A. Learmonth & Son, Printers, 9 King Street. 1963.
viii, 463 p. 140 mm. PC.

Catholic Church. *Liturgy and ritual*. [Lòchran an Anma.] Edinburgh, 1906.
Lòchran an Anma. Leabhar-Urnaigh Caitliceach. Sands agus a' Chuideachd, 21 Sraid Anobhair, Dùneideann.
viii, 162 p. 130 × 90 mm. Mit., NLS, PC.
   Imprimatur and Nihil obstat are dated 1906. Printed Oliver and Boyd.

Catholic Church. *Liturgy and ritual*. [Mass.] N.p., n.d.
An Aifrionn ann an Gàidhlig.
16 p. 119 mm. PC.
   Recent.

Catholic Church. *Argyll and the Isles* (*Diocese*). [Pastoral Letter.] Oban, 1942.
[Illus.: Crest of the Bishop of Argyll and the Isles.]
A Pastoral Letter to the Clergy and Laity of the Diocese of Argyll and the Isles. To be read at the Last Mass on the First Sunday in Lent, 1942. Oban Times Ltd., Oban.
10 p. 210 mm. PC.

Catriona Thangaidh. See MacKay, Catherine.

Cattanach, Donald, 1813–91. [*Bardachd*.] Edinburgh, n.d.
Bàrdachd Dhomhnaill Chatanaich, Cinn-Ghiuthsaich.
15 p. 170 mm. PC.
  Reprinted from *The Free Church Record*. Edited by Rev. Donald MacKinnon.
  Printed Turnbull & Spears, Edinburgh.

—— [*Eachdraidh air Bail'-an-Righ*.] Edinburgh, n.d.
Eachdraidh air Bail'-an-Rìgh a bha fo riaghladh nan ceàrd a bhi air a ghlanadh. Le
Dòmhnull Catanach a bh'air an t-Sliabh am Bàideanach (1813–91).
16 p. 170 mm. NLS.
  Date uncertain.

Ceanaideach, An Dr. [*Iain*]. See Kennedy, Dr. John.

Ceathramh Leabhar, air son nan Sgoilean Gae'lach. See Church of Scotland Genera
  Assembly. [*An Ceathramh Leabhar*.]

Ceilidh Books. See Leabhraichean nan Ceilidh.

Ceilidh nan Gaidheal: Leabhar na h-ard-Fheise. Glasgow, 1947.
Leabhar na h-Ard-Fheise. Ceilidh nan Gaidheal, Glaschu, 1896–1946. A' phris 2/6.
Air a chur am mach fo ùghdarras na Comhairle, le Alasdair MacLabhruinn agus a Mhic,
268, Sraid Earra-Ghaidheal, Glaschu. 1947. Printed in Scotland. Air a chlòbhualadh
an Albainn.
51 p; illus. 190 mm. PC.
  Ceilidh nan Gaidheal was a Gaelic cultural association in Glasgow. Foreword by
  Hector MacDougal, President of Ceilidh nan Gaidheal. Contains history, reminis-
  cences and poems about the association and a play, "Se rud a their a màthair, a bhios
  deanta", by Archibald MacCulloch.

Ceilidh Song-Book. See Ceol nam Beann.

Ceist nan Ceist. See Henderson, Angus. [*Spealgadh nan Glasan*.]

Ceithir Comhraidhean. Glasgow, 1931.
Ceithir Còmhraidhean. Ceist nan Ceist, le Donnchadh MacIain, Ile. An Ealdhain Ur,
le Coinneach MacDhòmhnaill, Cunndain. Gaol agus Dùthchas, le Iain R. MacGille na
Brataich. Coinneach Beag agus Dòmhnull Bàn, le Donnchadh MacDhòmhnuill,
Leòdhas. A' phrìs, sè sgillinn. An Comunn Gaidhealach, 212 Sràid West George
Glascho. 1931.
39 p. 190 mm. Mit.

Ceithir Orain Ghaidhlig Eadar-Theangaichte Bho'n Bheurla. See MacLeod, Roderick, of
  Inverness. [*Ceithir Orain Ghaidhlig*.]

Celtia. Dublin, 1901–08.
Celtia. A Pan-Celtic Monthly Magazine.
Vol. I. No. 1, January 1901.
... Vol. VIII, May 1908, No. V. [Last seen.]
  [Frequency] Monthly. (See "Locations" note.)
  [Collation] *c*. 15 p per no. 280 mm.
  [Locations] AU, Mit.; both libraries contain only 9 numbers of Vol. III, 6 of Vol.
  IV, 1 of Vol. V, 8 of Vol. VII and 5 of Vol. VIII; neither library contains Vol. VI,
  no record of Vol. VI in BUCOP.
  [Editor] S-R. John, Wimbledon, England.
  [Note] A Pan-Celtic magazine of popular scholarship; contains fragment of a com-
  parative Celtic dictionary. Published in Dublin.

Celtic Annual. See Dundee Highland Society. [*Year Book/Celtic Annual*.]

Celtic Congress, 1953: *Exhibition of Celtic Literature*. Glasgow, 1953.
Glasgow Corporation Public Libraries. Celtic Congress 1953. Exhibition of Celtic
Literature to be held in the Jeffrey Room, the Mitchell Library, Glasgow, 12th to 29th
August, 1953.
28 p. 210 mm. PC.

Celtic Forum. Toronto, 1934–5.
Toronto Centennial Number. 25c. Celtic Forum. A Journal of Celtic Opinion.
Vol. I, No. 1. St. Andrew's Day, November 30, 1934.
St. Patrick's Number. Vol. I, No. 2. March 1935. Published at 71 Welland Avenue,
Toronto.
Summer Number. Vol. I, No. 3. June 1935.
Science Number. 50c. Vol. I, No. 4. October 1935. [Last seen.]
    [Collation] 32 p per no. 280 mm.
    [Location] NLS.
    [Editor] W. J. Edmonston Scott.

Celtic Monthly. Glasgow, 1893–1917.
[The Celtic Monthly: A Magazine for Highlanders. Edited by John Mackay, Kingston,
Glasgow. Vol. I. Glasgow: Archibald Sinclair, Celtic Press, 10 Bothwell Street, John
Menzies & Co., and William Love. Edinburgh: Norman Macleod and John Grant.
Inverness: William Mackay and John Noble. Oban: Thomas Boyd and Hugh Mac-
Donald. 1893.]
The Celtic Monthly: A Magazine for Highlanders. Edited by John Mackay, 9 Blyths-
wood Drive, Glasgow. Vol. VIII. Glasgow: Archibald Sinclair, 47 Waterloo Street,
John Menzies & Co., William Love, and W. & R. Holmes. Edinburgh: Norman
Macleod and John Grant. Inverness: William Mackay and John Noble. Oban:
Thomas Boyd and Hugh MacDonald. 1900.
. . . Edited by John Mackay, 1 Blythswood Drive, Glasgow. Vol. XI. John Mackay,
Celtic Monthly Office, 1 Blythswood Drive, Glasgow. 1903.
. . . Edited by John Mackay, 10 Bute Mansions, Glasgow. Vol. XIII. John Mackay,
Celtic Monthly Office, 10 Bute Mansions, Glasgow. 1905.
. . . Vol. XIX. A. M. Mackay, 10 Bute Mansions, Hillhead, Glasgow. 1911.
. . . Vol. XXV . . . [Last vol.] 1917.
    [Collation] 20 p per no. *c.* 1–2 plates. 260 mm.
    [Locations] BM, Mit., NLS.
    [Contents] An illustrated monthly; contained Gaelic articles regularly, including a
    serialisation of "Dun-Aluinn", the first Gaelic novel (1913–14).

Celtic Review. Edinburgh, 1904–16.
The Celtic Review. Published quarterly. Consulting Editor: Professor MacKinnon.
Acting Editor: Miss E. C. Carmichael. Volume I. July 1904 to April 1905. Edin-
burgh: Norman MacLeod, 25 George IV Bridge. London: David Nutt, 57–59 Long
Acre, W.C. Dublin: Hodges, Figgis & Co., Ltd., 104 Grafton Street.
The Celtic Review. Published quarterly. Editor: Mrs. W. J. Watson (Miss E. C.
Carmichael). Volume X. December 1914 to June 1916. [Last Vol.]
    [Collation] *c.* 96 p per quarterly issue; plates occasionally. 260 mm.
    [Locations] BM, GU (Vols. I-VII), Mit.
    [Note] Scholarly periodical. Printed T. & A. Constable, Edinburgh. "Mrs. W. J.
    Watson (Miss E. C. Carmichael)" replaces "Miss E. C. Carmichael" from Vol. VII,
    1911–12; David Nutt address changes Vol. VIII, 1912–13.

Celtic Voice. London, 1961.
Celtic Voice. [Illus.: crest with motto, "Guth Cheilteach".] Number One. Summer,
1961. Quarterly. Price One Shilling. Published by Graham Bros., 5 The Street,
Didmarton, Badminton, Glos. All correspondence to: A. Graham, Flat 3, 9 Clydesdale
Road, London W.11. [No more seen.]

[Collation] 12 p; illus. 350 × 120 mm.
[Note] Contains 2 p of Gaelic, "Am Feall-Ghlacadh", Gaelic translation of part of Stevenson's *Kidnapped*.

Central Gaelic Committee, E.I.S. See Thomson, Donald. [*Gaelic Poems for Interpretation.*]

Ceo na Moineadh. See MacLennan, Malcolm. [*Ceo na Moineadh.*]

Ceol nan Beann. Glasgow, n.d.
Ceòl nam Beann. [Illus.] Dionnasg Gàidhlig na h-Alba. The Ceilidh Song Sheet. 42 of the best songs in Gaelic.
[4] p. 360 × 270 mm. PC.
Folded sheet, containing the 44 pages of the volume described below. Also a version entitled, "Gaelic Community Song Sheet".

Ceol nan Beann. Glasgow, n.d.
Ceòl nam Beann. [Illus.: Gaelic League Crest.] The Ceilidh Song-book. 42 of the best songs in Gaelic. Price 6d.
[44] p. 130 mm. GU:CL.
Printed by the North-West Printing Co., Glasgow, for the Gaelic League of Scotland.

Ceol nan Beann. Glasgow, n.d.
Ceòl nam Beann. [Illus.: Gaelic League Crest.] The Ceilidh Song-book. 60 of the best songs in Gaelic. Revised edition. Price 1/-.
62 p. 130 mm.
Printed Learmonth, Stirling.

Ceol nan Beann. Glasgow, 1969.
[Cover.] Ceòl nam Beann. Dionnasg Gàidhlig na h-Alba.
The Ceilidh Song-book. 60 of the best songs in Gaelic. Revised edition. Price 1/6.
Printed by A. Learmonth & Son, 9 King Street, Stirling. 1969.
62 p, [1] plate. 130 mm.

Ceud-Fhuasgladh do na Daoine Leointe. Glasgow, 1939.
Ceud-Fhuasgladh do na Daoine Leointe. Air a dheasachadh le Comhairle Clann an Fhraoich airson Comunn na h-Oigridh. Glaschu: An Comunn Gaidhealach, 131 Sràid West Regent. 1939.
62 p; illus. 220 mm. GU:CL, NLS, PC.
Foreword in English by Dr. Atholl Robertson, Oban, of whose English manuscript this is a translation. Clann an Fhraoich was a section of An Comunn Gaidhealach.

Ceum, An. Glasgow, 1946–9.
An Ceum. The official organ of Dionnasg Gaidhlig na h-Alba (The Gaelic League of Scotland). Uimhir 1. Leabhar 1. An Damhair, 1946. Pris gach mios 2 sgillinn.
... Leabhar 2. Uimhir 9. An t-Og-mhios, 1949. [Last seen.]
[Frequency] Monthly, Vol. I, 1-7; no more seen of Vol. 1, but Vol. 2 begins in Sept. 1947, suggesting that 12 monthly numbers of Vol. 1 were issued. Approx. quarterly, Vol. 2.
[Collation] 8 p per no. 220 × 180 mm.
[Locations] NLS (incomplete set).
[Note] In Gaelic and English. Replaced "Crois Tara" (1938–9) as magazine of the Gaelic League of Scotland.

Ceum, An. See also Crois Tara.

Chapbook. Glasgow, 1946.
Chapbook. [Illus.] Number Two. Sixpence. [1st March, 1946.]
... Number Eight. ... [14th January 1947.]
[Frequency] 12 numbers issued, between Jan. 1946 and July 1947.
[Collation] *c.* 18 p each. 250 mm.

[Location] BM.

[Note] Edited by Alex Donaldson. Numbers 2–8 contained "An Duilleag Ghàidhlig" edited by Alexander Nicolson. Published by Scroop Books Ltd. (later known as A. & J. Donaldson, Glasgow).

Charraig, A'. Bernera, 1971.

A' Charraig. Leabhar Bliadhnail Eaglais Bhearnaraigh. Aireamh 1, 1971. A' phrìs 5/– (25p).

Thug "An t-Eileanach", Beàrnaraigh na Hearadh, an leabhar seo am follais ann an 1971.

48 p; illus.

Foreword by Roderick MacLeod, editor. Printed by Sankey, Nelson, Lancs.

Choisir-Chiuil, A'. [In parts.] Paisley, n.d.

Part I. A' Choisir-chiùil. The St. Columba Collection of Gaelic Songs arranged for Part-singing. J. and R. Parlane, Paisley. J. Menzies and Co., Edinburgh and Glasgow. Houlston and Sons, London. Price Sixpence – Staff or Sol-fa.

16 p. 250 mm. NLS.

1892.

Part II . . .

[17]–32 p. 250 mm. NLS.

Part III . . .

[33]–48 p. 250 mm. NLS.

Part IV . . .

[49]–64 p. 250 mm. NLS.

Part V . . .

[65]–80 p. 250 mm. NLS.

Addition to imprint: "Norman MacLeod, 3 Geo. IV Bridge, Edinburgh".

Part VI . . .

[81]–96 p. 250 mm. NLS.

Four parts were planned originally. Part IV was published in 1900. According to *MacLaren*, Part V was published in 1913 and Part VI shortly thereafter. Part VI not issued separately.

Choisir-chiuil, A'. Paisley, n.d.

A' Choisir-chiùil. The St. Columba Collection of Gaelic Songs. Arranged for Part-singing. J. and R. Parlane, Paisley. J. Menzies and Co., Edinburgh and Glasgow. Houlston and Sons, London.

[4], 64 p. 250 mm. Mit.

The first bound volume, pre-1900. Parts I–IV.

—— Paisley, n.d.

A' Choisir-chiùil. The St. Columba Collection of Gaelic Songs, arranged for Part-singing. J. and R. Parlane, Paisley. John Menzies and Co., Edinburgh and Glasgow. Madgwick Houlston and Co., Ltd., London. Norman MacLeod, 25 Geo. IV Bridge, Edinburgh.

[43], 80 p. 250 mm. AU, Mit.

Containing Parts I–V. *MacLaren* states that Part V was issued by Parlane in 1913.

—— Paisley, n.d.

Ibid.

[43], 96 p. 250 mm.

Parts I–VI.

—— London, n.d.

A' Choisir-chiùil. The St. Columba Collection of Gaelic Songs, arranged for Part-singing. London: Bayley & Ferguson, 2 Great Marlborough Street, W.; Glasgow: 54 Queen Street.

[4], 100 p. 250 mm. Mit.

Parts I–VI and 4 other songs. A' Choisir-Chiùil was edited and most of the music arranged by Archibald Ferguson, conductor of the St. Columba Church Gaelic Choir.

Choral Music for Children's Competitions. See An Comunn Gaidhealach. [*National Mod.*] Choral Music for Children's Competitions.

Christian Doctrine. See Roman Catholic Church. *Liturgy and ritual.* [Christian Doctrine.]

Chruit Oir, A'. Edinburgh, [Intro. 1919].
Cogadh mór na h-Eòrpa. A' Chruit Oir. [Illus.] Printed by Oliver and Boyd, Edinburgh, for The Church of Scotland, The United Free Church of Scotland, and The Free Church of Scotland.
xii, 148 p. 140 mm. NLS.
This was the 19th and last in the series of religious booklets issued by the Joint Committee of the three Churches for soldiers in the First World War. Contains religious verse.

Church of Scotland. [*Church of Scotland Act*, 1921.] Edinburgh, 1921.
Achd Eaglais na h-Alba, 1921.
8 p. 170 mm. PC.

Church of Scotland. [*Life and Work.*] See *Life and Work: Na Duilleagan Gaidhlig.*

Church of Scotland. *Liturgy and ritual.* [Book of Common Order.] Edinburgh, 1970.
Foirm na n-urrnuidheadh. John Carswell's Gaelic translation of the Book of Common Order. Edited by R. L. Thomson, Senior Lecturer in English and Superior of Celtic Studies, University of Leeds; in part from materials collected by the late Angus Matheson, Professor of Celtic, University of Glasgow. Published by Oliver & Boyd for the Scottish Gaelic Texts Society. Edinburgh. 1970.
Scottish Gaelic Texts. Volume Eleven.
xc, 243 p. 230 mm.
Text, pp 1–113; Notes, pp 115–72; Appendices, pp 173–86; Glossary, pp 187–243.

Church of Scotland. *Liturgy and Ritual.* [A Cuir air leth Ceisdeir.] N.p., n.d.
Cumadh agus ordugh na seirbhis airson a bhi a cuir air leth ceisdeir.
8 p. 170 × 120 mm. PC.

Church of Scotland. *Liturgy and Ritual.* [Laoidheadair Gaidhlig.] Glasgow, 1902.
Laoidheadair Gàidhlig. Comh-chruinneachadh do Laoidhean Spioradail, a réir an Laoidheadair Beurla a chuireadh a mach le ùghdarras Eaglais na h-Alba. Glasgow: Archibald Sinclair, Printer, Celtic Press, 47 Waterloo Street.
170 p. 170 mm. TS-G.
"1902 Proof Copy": *TS-G*. Not seen. The first draft (46 p) was in 1899.

—— [*Laoidheadair Gaidhlig.*] Glasgow, 1904.
Ibid.
1904 Proof Copy.
96 p. 170 mm. [No music.] FC, Mit., NLS.

—— [*An Laoidheadair Gaidhlig.*] Glasgow, 1905.
An Laoidheadair Gàidhlig. [Illus.] Glasgow: Archibald Sinclair, Printer, "Celtic Press", 47 Waterloo Street.
Proof Copy 1905.
133 p. 170 mm. Mit.
"An Laoidheadair Gàidhlig" (translations), pp 3–83 (87 hymns); "Laoidhean Spioradail" (translations), pp 84–99 (17 hymns); "Laoidhean agus Dàin Spioradail" (original), pp 100–33 (27 hymns). No music.

—— [*Laoidhean Gaidhlig.*] Glasgow, 1907.
Laoidhean Gàidhlig. [Illus.] Air an cur a mach le ùghdarras Eaglais na h'Alba.
Glaschu: Gilleasbuig Mac-na-Ceàrdadh, 47 Sràid Waterloo. 1907.
xii, 130 p. 190 mm. CoS, NLS.
    Preface signed, "Norman MacLeod, Cl: Eccl: Scot". Contains 131 hymns; no music.

—— [*An Laoidheadair.*] Glasgow, 1935.
An Laoidheadair. [Illus.] Air a chur a mach le ùghdarras Eaglais na h-Alba. Church
of Scotland Committee on Publications: 121 George Street, Edinburgh; 232 St. Vincent Street, Glasgow. 1935.
Air a chur a mach le còmhnadh nan comunnan so: Highlands and Islands, Public Worship
and Aids to Devotion, Publications.
xiv, [13], 175 p. 190 mm. Mit., NLS.
    Edited by Malcolm MacLennan and Malcolm MacLeod. In three sections:
Earrann I (pp 1–126), "Laoidhean Gàidhlig"; Earrann II (pp 127–58), "Laoidhean
air an tionndadh gu Gàidhlig o'n Bheurla, cuid dhiubh le fuinn ùra is cuid eile le
seann fhuinn a tha air an deanamh freagarrach dhaibh"; Earrann III (pp 159–75),
"Laoidhean a tha air an tionndadh gu Gàidhlig o'n Bheurla anns a' cheart mheadar
agus leis na ceart fhuinn a gheibhear orra anns an Laoidheadair Bheurla." Music in
both notations. Based on *The Church Hymnary*, with some original Gaelic hymns.

Church of Scotland. *Liturgy and Ritual.* [Sailm Dhaibhidh.] London, 1906.
Sailm Dhaibhidh agus Laoidhean air an tarruing o na Sgriobtuiribh Naomha: maille ri
fonnaibh iomchuidh. Air an cur a mach le h-ùghdarras Ard-Sheanadh Eaglais na h-Alba.
London: T. Nelson & Sons, Paternoster Row; Edinburgh and New York. 1906.
[16], 239 p, [218] p. 170 mm. PC.
    1st ed. Split pages; 239 p of metrical Psalms, 218 p of tunes. Bound with "St.
Columba Church Hymnary". 1906.

Church of Scotland (sponsors). See Bible.

Church of Scotland (joint sponsors). See Cogadh Mor na h-Eorpa. [For cross-references
    to individual titles in this series.]

Church of Scotland (joint sponsors). See Cogadh na Saorsa. [For cross-references to
    individual titles in this series.]

Church of Scotland. See The Shorter Catechism.

Church of Scotland. See Westminster Confession of Faith.

Church of Scotland, Bernera (Harris) Parish. See A' Charraig.

Church of Scotland, General Assembly. [*An Ceathramh Leabhar.*] Edinburgh, 1901.
An Ceathramh Leabhar air son nan Sgoilean Gae'lach a ta air an cumail suas le Comunn
Ard-Sheanaidh Eaglais na h-Alba. An dara clòdh-bhualadh. Duneidin: air a chlòdh-
bhualadh le Uilleam Blackwood agus a Mhic. 1901.
144 p. 150 mm. Mit.

Church of Scotland. [*An Ceathramh Leabhar.*] Edinburgh, 1907.
. . . 1907.
144 p. 150 mm. PC.
    1st ed. 1826, of which these are reprints.

Church of Scotland, Home Mission Committee. [*Tracts.*] Edinburgh, n.d.
. . . Issued by The Church of Scotland Home Mission Committee. Air a chur a mach le
"Home Board" Eaglais na h-Alba.
4 p each. 190 mm. PC.
    Gaelic tracts issued twice yearly for several years; edited by Thomas M. Murchison.
All undated.

Ciobair, An. Glasgow, 1970.
>An Cìobair. Le còmhlan a thainig cruinn aig Cruinneachadh an Luchd-teagaisg Ghàidhlig an Inbhirnis, 1968. Dealbhan le Cailean Spencer. Gairm. Glaschu. 1970.
>An Cìobair. Sreath na Sgoile (air fhoillseachadh an co-bhoinn ri Coimitidh nan Leabhraichean-sgoile), Leabhar 7. Clo-bhualaidhean Gairm, Leabhar 20.
>[12] p; illus. 210 mm.

Clachan. See Highland Village Association.

Clann an Fhraoich. See:
>Ban-Altrumachd aig an Tigh.
>Cainnt agus facail iomchuidh air son Coinnimh.
>Ceud-Fhuasgladh do na Daoine Leointe.
>Cleasan Gaidhealach.

Clann an Fhraoich. See also Comunn na h-Oigridh.

Clann na h-Alba. [*Brosnachadh.*] London, n.d.
>Clann na h-Alba Pamphlets, No. 1. Brosnachadh.
>2 p. 220 mm. NLS.
>½ p in Gaelic. Printed by the Malvina Press, London, W.

Clanranald, Book of. [*The MacDonald History.*] N.p., n.d.
>The Book of Clanranald. The MacDonald History.
>44 p. 220 mm. PC.
>A reprint of the text published in Alexander Cameron's *Reliquiae Celticae*, Vol. II, 1894, without English translation. Not an off-print: the text has not been changed, but the type has been reset and the pagination changed. The condition of the copies seen suggests they were issued about the turn of the century.

Clanranald, Book of. See Lloyd, Joseph. *Alasdair Mac Colla.*

Clar-Eagair Obair nam Feachd. See Comunn na h-Oigridh.

Clark, Mrs. M. See Macpherson, Mary.

Clarsach na h-Alba. See Harp of Caledonia.

Clarsair Dall. See Morison, Roderick.

Cleasan Gaidhealach. Glasgow, 1936.
>Cleasan Gaidhealach airson Comunn na h-Oigridh. Le Comhairle Clann an Fhraoich. An Comunn Gaidhealach, 131 Sràid West Regent, Glaschu. 1936.
>24 p. 220 mm. PC.
>Originally appeared in "An Gaidheal", May–Dec. 1935. Mostly from R. C. MacLagan's "The Games and Diversions of Argyllshire" (London, 1901) and a manuscript collection by Katherine Whyte Grant. Printed Learmonth, Stirling.

Clerk, Archibald, 1813–87. [*The Old, Old Story.*] N.p., n.d.
>The Old, Old Story. An Seann, Seann Sgeul, ann an da earrainn. Air eadartheangachadh gu Gàidhlig le G. Cleireach, LL.D., ministeir Chill mhaillidh. Am treas clò-bhualadh.
>16 p. 160 mm. PC.
>1st ed. 1883, of which this is a reprint. *MacLaren* gives May 1915 as the publication date. Gaelic and English on facing pages.

Clerk, Archibald (ed.). See MacLeod, Dr. Norman, Minister of St. Columba's Church, Glasgow. [*Caraid nan Gaidheal.*]

Cloimh Chaorach. See Board of Agriculture and Fisheries. [*Cloimh Chaorach.*]

Co-Chomunn an Spioraid Naoimh Airson Aonadh Criosdachd an t-Saoghail. See Holy Spirit Association.

Cocaire, An. Glasgow, 1969.
An Còcaire. Le còmhlan de luchd-teagaisg a thainig cruinn aig Cruinneachadh an Luchd-teagaisg an Inbhirnis, 1968. Dealbhan le Cailean Spencer. Gairm. Glaschu. 1969.
An Còcaire. Sreath na Sgoile (air fhoillseachadh an co-bhoinn ri Coimitidh nan Leabhraichean-sgoile), Leabhar 5. Clo-bhualaidhean Gairm, Leabhar 17.
[12] p; illus. 210 mm.

Cocker, W. D. [*The Miller's Wooing.*] Glasgow, n.d.
Dealbh-chluichean an Gaidhlig. [Illus.] Dealbhchluich an aon sealladh. Gaelic translation of the one-act play, The Miller's Wooing, by W. D. Cocker. Air eadar-theangachadh le Iain Walker. An Comunn Gaidhealach, 65 Sràid West Regent, Glaschu.
20 p. 210 mm.
c. 1950. Printed A. Sinclair, Glasgow.
"The Miller's Wooing" (1942) is an English version by the author of his Scots "The Wooin' O't" (1925).

Coddy, The. See MacPherson, John, "The Coddy".

Cogadh mor na h-Eorpa. [A series of religious booklets issued between 1916 and 1919 by a joint committee of the Church of Scotland, the Free Church of Scotland and the United Free Church of Scotland for distribution to soldiers in World War One. Edited by Rev. Malcolm MacLennan and Rev. Donald MacLean.] See:
Aird, Dr. Gustavus. [*Analysis of The Shorter Catechism.*]
Bunyan, John. [*The Holy War.*]
Cameron Lees, James. [*Life and Conduct.*]
Chruit Oir, A'.
Faire agus Urnuigh.
Kennedy, Dr. John. [*Searmon agus Oraid.*]
Hodge, Archibald A. [*Atonement.*]
McCheyne, R. M. [*Guth mo Ghraidh.*]
MacKenzie, Lachlan. [*Ros o Sharon.*]
MacLaurin, John. [*The Cross of Christ.*]
Marshall, Walter. [*Sanctification.*]
Martin, Donald J. [*Teagasg nam Miorbhuilean.*]
Martin, Hugh. [*The Shadow of Calvary.*]
Mil nan Dan.
Owen, John. [*The Glory of Christ.*]
Owen, John. [*The Holy Spirit.*]
Spurgeon, C. H. [*Deagh Mhisneachd do na Diobarraich.*]
Teasgasg nan Aithrichean.

Cogadh Naomh. See Bunyan, John. [*The Holy War.*]

Cogadh na Saorsa. [A series of religious booklets issued by the Church of Scotland and the Free Church of Scotland for distribution to soldiers in World War Two. Six are reprints of "Cogadh mhor na h-Eorpa" booklets]. See:
Bunyan, John. [*The Holy War.*]
Eilean mo Ghaoil.
Faire agus Urnuigh.
Martin, Donald J. [*Teagasg nam Miorbhuilean.*]
Martin, Hugh. [*The Shadow of Calvary.*]
Mil nan Dan.
Sguaban o Achaidhean nan Aithrichean.
Solus Lathail.
Teasgasg nan Aithrichean.

Coisir a' Mhoid, 1–5. Coisir a' Mhoid [First Issue]. Paisley, n.d.

Coisir a' Mhòid. The Mòd Collection of Gaelic Part Songs. 1896–1910. Published for An Comunn Gaidhealadh by J. and R. Parlane, Paisley. John Menzies and Co., Ltd., Edinburgh and Glasgow. T. D. MacDonald, Secretary of An Comunn Gaidhealach, 108 Hope Street, Glasgow. A. M'Laren and Son, 360 and 362 Argyle Street, Glasgow.

[4], 56 p. 250 × 160 mm. Mit., NLS, SS.

Staff and sol-fa versions.

Coisir a' Mhòid I. The Mod Collection of Gaelic Part Songs. 1896–1912 (First Book). An Comunn Gaidhealach; Secy.: Neil Shaw. Printed and published for An Comunn Gaidhealach by Alex. MacLaren & Sons, Argyle Street, Glasgow.

[2], 62 p. 250 mm. AU, Mit., NLS, SS.

This is the sol-fa version. The staff edition had Shaw and MacLaren's addresses on the title page, and contained 6 unnumbered pages.

Coisir a' Mhòid II. The Mod Collection of Gaelic part songs (Second Book). 1913–1925. Clar-amais. . . . Printed and published for An Comunn Gaidhealach by Alex. Maclaren & Sons, Gaelic Printers and Booksellers, 360–362 Argyle Street, Glasgow, C.2.

[2], 66 p. 250 mm. AU, SS.

Both notations.

. . . Published by MacLaren's Gaelic Songs, 29 Waterloo Street, Glasgow.

[2], 66 p. 250 mm.

1972. Staff only.

Coisir a' Mhòid 3. The Mod Collection of Gaelic part songs. Third Book, 1925–31. Clàr-amais. . . . Printed and published for An Comunn Gaidhealach by Alex. MacLaren & Sons, Printers and Booksellers, 268 Argyle Street, Glasgow, C.2. 1935.

63 p. 250 mm. Mit.

1973. Both notations.

Coisir a' Mhòid 4. The Mod Collection of Gaelic part songs. Fourth Book, 1932–7. Clàr-amais. . . . Printed and published for An Comunn Gaidhealach by Alex. Mac-Laren & Sons, Printers and Booksellers, 268 Argyle Street, Glasgow, C.2. 1940.

71 p. 250 mm. Mit.

Staff and sol-fa versions.

. . . Published by Gairm Publications, 29 Waterloo Street, Glasgow.

71 p. 250 mm.

Dec. 1973. Staff and sol-fa.

Coisir a' Mhòid 5. The Mod Collection of Gaelic part songs. Fifth Book, 1938–47. Clàr-amais. . . . Printed and published for An Comunn Gaidhealach by Alex. Mac-Laren & Sons, Printers and Booksellers, 268 Argyle Street, Glasgow, C.2. 1953.

[2], 60 p. 250 mm. PC.

Staff and sol-fa versions.

. . . Published by Gairm Publications, 29 Waterloo Street, Glasgow.

[2], 60 p. 250 mm.

1973. Sol-fa version only.

Coisirean Oigridh. See An Comunn Gaidhealach. [*National Mod*.] Choral Music for Children's Competitions.

Coisir na Cloinne. Glasgow, n.d.

Coisir na Cloinne. Forty Gaelic songs with sol-fa. Special musical arrangements by well-known composers for Rural and Juvenile Gaelic Choirs. Published for An Comunn Gaidhealach by Alex. MacLaren & Sons, Argyle Street, Glasgow.

24 p. 210 mm. PC.

1925.

[*Coisir na Cloinne*.] Glasgow, 1949.

. . . Published for An Comunn Gaidhealach by Alex. MacLaren & Sons, 19 Wellington Street, Glasgow.
24 p. 210 mm. PC.
At end of text: "Reprinted 1949". The title page alteration has been pasted over the previous entry.

Collinson, Francis. [*The Traditional and National Music of Scotland.*] London, 1966.
The Traditional and National Music of Scotland. By Francis Collinson. Routledge and Kegan Paul. London.
First published, 1966.
xvii, 294 p. 250 mm. Mit.
Gaelic songs, texts and discussion, pp 32–118.

Comhairle Clann an Fhraoich. See:
Ban-Altrumachd aig an Tigh.
Ceud-Fhuasgladh do na Daoine Leointe.
Cleasan Gaidhealach Airson na Cloinne.

Comhlan, a thainig cruinn aig Cruinneachadh an Luchd teagaisg Ghaidhlig a nInbhirnis, 1968. See:
Ciobair, An.
Cocaire, An.
Fear Na Butha.
Fear Nam Fiaclan.
Fear-Smalaidh.
Fraochan is Peasan.
Iasgair, An t-.
Post, Am.

Comhlan de luchd-teagaisg as na Hearadh. See Alasdair agus Mairi air Chuairt.

Committee on Bilingualism. The Scottish Council for Research into Education. See *Aithris is Oideas.*

Comunn-Bhiobull Duthchail na h-Alba. See National Bible Society of Scotland.

Comhraidhean Gaidhlig. Glasgow, n.d.
Còmhraidhean Gaidhlig. Gaelic Dialogues. Book I. 1. Am Maighstir-Sgoile agus Calum Posta. 2. Fionnlagh Piobaire, agus Para Mor, an oidhche mu'n d'fhag iad Glascho. 3. Eadar Cuairtear nan Gleann agus Eachann Tiristeach. 4. Tormod Mac Uisdein is Seonaid, bantrach an t-Saoir. Glascho: Alasdair MacLabhruinn is a Mhic, 360–362 Sràid Earraghaidheal, C.2.
32 p. 190 mm. AU, GU:CL, NLS.
The first three by Dr. Norman MacLeod, the fourth by Hector MacDougall. First advertised 1925.

Comunn Gaidhealach. *Bonn-Steidh agus Riaghailtean.* Glasgow, 1938.
An Comunn Gaidhealach. [Illus.] Bonn-stéidh agus Riaghailtean. Constitution and Rules. Frith-laghannan. Bye-laws. An t-Sultuin, 1938.
39 p. 190 mm. Mit., PC.
Gaelic and English on facing pages. Printed Archibald Sinclair, Glasgow.

Comunn Gaidhealach. *Coisir a' Mhoid.* See *Coisir a' Mhoid.*

Comunn Gaidhealach. *Coisir na Cloinne.* See *Coisir na Cloinne.*

Comunn Gaidhealach. *An Deo-Greine.* See *An Deo-Greine.*

Comunn Gaidhealach. *An Earail.* Glasgow, n.d.
[Illus.] Earail do Bhuill a' Chomuinn.
7 p. 180 mm. PC.

Comunn Gaidhealach. *Facal do na Gaidheil.* Glasgow, n.d.
An Comunn Gaidhealach. Facal do na Gaidheil. A word to the Gaidheal from An Comunn Gaidhealach.
2 p. 270 mm. NLS.
Gaelic and English.

Comunn Gaidhealach. [*Féill a' Chomuinn Ghaidhealaich.*] *Buth nan Ealdhain.* Glasgow, n.d.
Feill a' Chomuinn Ghaidhealaich, Buth nan Eadlain. Leabhar Bhuth nan Eadlain ('The Industry Stall Book'), being information relating to Home Industries, collected from the districts represented at the Stall. "An rud a tha feumail tha e priseil." ("What is useful is valuable.")
73 p; illus. 108 mm. Mit.
1 song in Gaelic.

Comunn Gaidhealach. Féill a' Chomuinn Ghaidhealaich.
Books published in aid of An Comunn Gaidhealach's "Feill" of 1907. See also:
Bolg Solair.
Feill Cookery Book.
Parker, Winifred. [*Na Daoine Sidhe.*]
Sop as Gach Seid.

Comunn Gaidhealach. *Gaelic Orthography.* Glasgow, 1954.
[Illus.] Gaelic Orthography. Recommended Forms. An Comunn Gaidhealach, 65 West Regent Street, Glasgow, C.2. 1954.
[4]. 260 × 190 mm. PC.

Comunn Gaidhealach. An Gaidheal. See *An Gaidheal.*

Comunn Gaidhealach. Gailig. See *An Gaidheal.*

Comunn Gaidhealach. [*National Mod.*] Baird a' Chomuinn. See MacKinnon, Lachlan. [*Baird a' Chomuinn.*]

Comunn Gaidhealach. [*National Mod.*] Choral Music for Children's Competitions. Coisirean Oigridh. Glasgow, 1923.
An Comunn Gaidhealach. Inverness Mod. 1923. Choral Music for Children's Competitions. Printed and published for An Comunn Gaidhealach by Alex. Mac-Laren & Sons, Gaelic Printers and Booksellers, 360–362 Argyle Street, Glasgow.
Music for Children's Competitions. Mod of 1924. Choral Songs.
Ibid. 1926, 1929–31, 1934–5; minus "Choral Songs", 1936–40.
An Comunn Gaidhealach. Mod, 1947. Earrann na h-Oigridh.
Ibid. 1947–52.
An Comunn Gaidhealach. Jubilee Mod, 1953. Coisirean Oigridh.
Ibid. 1953–73.
[Collation] 4 p, 1923–40; 4–8 p, 1947–52; 8 p, 1953–63; 12 p, 1964–9; 20 p, 1970–3.
320 × 190 mm.

Comunn Gaidhealach. [*National Mod.*] Choral Test Songs. Glasgow, 1915 1924, 1930.
Test Song for Mod of 1915. Tog Orm mo Phìob. (Hand me my Pipes.) Lament for Sir Roderick M'Leod of Dunvegan. Air composed by his piper, Para Mór M'Crimmon, A.D. 1626. A Gaelic melody arranged for mixed voices (unaccompanied). English text by Rev. M. N. Munro, M.A. Arranged by Julian H. W. Nesbitt. Price 2d net, postage extra. Printed by J. and R. Parlane, Paisley.
[8] p. 250 mm. PC.
An Comunn Gaidhealach. Twenty-Eighth Mod to be held at Perth, 1924. Cumha Mhic Criomainn. Choral Test Song. For conditions of competition see Syllabus 1924

Mod, from the Secretary of An Comunn Gaidhealach, 114 West Campbell Street, Glasgow. Price 6d. Printed and published for An Comunn Gaidhealach by Alex. Maclaren & Sons, Gaelic Printers and Booksellers, 360–362 Argyle Street, Glasgow.
7 p. 240 mm. PC.
Cruachan Beann.
  Music arranged by T. S. Drummond, advertised in 1930; referred to as "Mod Choral Test Song". Not seen.

Comunn Gaidhealach. [*National Mod.*] Co-Fharpaisean 8, 9, 11, 12. Glasgow, 1948
An Comunn Gaidhealach. 1948. Co-fharpaisean 8, 9, Urram do'n Ollamh Blackie: Am Bru-Dearg ag gabhail fasgaidh bho'n doininn; Badan roid, bho thaobh an tobair. Co-fharpais 11: Sìle. Co-fharpais 12: Eilean na h-Oige.
8 p. 190 mm.

Comunn Gaidhealach. [*National Mod.*] Coisir a' Mhoid. See *Coisir a' Mhoid.*

Comunn Gaidhealach. [*National Mod.*] Coisir na Cloinne. See *Coisir na Cloinne.*

Comunn Gaidhealach. [*National Mod.*] Earrann na h-Ealdhain. Glasgow, 1912–14.
Earrann na h-Ealdhain agus na Lamh-Oibre. Riaghailtean nan Comh-fharpuis agus a' Mhargaidh Bhliadhnail, 1912.
7 p. 230 mm. PC.
  1912–14 only seen.

Comunn Gaidhealach. [*National Mod.*] Earrann na h-Oigridh. Glasgow, 1928–.
An Comunn Gaidhealach. Mod Inbhir-nis, 1928. Earrann na h-Oigridh.
Ibid. 1930, 1932, 1934, 1936–9, 1946–8, 1952–.
[Collation] 7–8 p. 190 mm.
[Note] Passages of prose and verse for recitation. Some have subtitle, "Beul Aithris".

Comunn Gaidhealach. [*National Mod.*] Orain a' Mhoid. Glasgow, 1924–40.
Orain a' Mhòid. 1924. Gaelic Songs for Solo Singing; Poem and Prose for Recitation. Leabhar I. Book One. Glascho: Alasdair MacLabhruinn 's a Mhic, 360–362 Sràid Earra-Ghaidheal.
Ibid (date omitted after Vol. II). Vols. I–XVII, 1924–40. Vols. I–X issued as bound volume.
[Collation] 16 p each vol. 210 mm.

Comunn Gaidhealach. [*National Mod.*] Orain-aon-Neach. Glasgow, 1948–.
An Comunn Gaidhealach. Orain-aon-Neach. Mod, 1948. An Comunn Gaidhealach, 131 Sràid West Regent, Glaschu, C.2.
... Mod, 1949. Leabhar 2. ...
Ibid. 1950–2; with locations of Mod, 1953–.
[Collation] 8–30 p. 250 mm.
[Note] Address of An Comunn Gaidhealach changes to "65 Sràid West Regent, Glaschu, C.2." from Vol. 4, 1951.

Comunn Gaidhealach. [*National Mod.*] Orain na h-Oigridh/Orain na Cloinne. Glasgow, 1947–.
Orain na h-Oigridh. Mod, 1947. ...
An Comunn Gaidhealach. Orain aon neach, rosg is bàrdachd (Earrann na h-Oigridh). Mòd, 1949. (Copyright reserved.) An Comunn Gaidhealach, 131 Sràid West Regent, Glaschu, C.2.
Ibid. 1950–2.
An Comunn Gaidhealach. Orain na Cloinne. Mod an Iubili, 1953, anns an Oban. Copyright reserved. An Comunn Gaidhealach, 65 Sràid West Regent, Glaschu, C.2.
Ibid. 1953–.

[Collation] 6–16 p. 210 mm.

[Note] Address of An Comunn Gaidhealach changes to "65 Sràid West Regent, Glaschu, C.2." 1951. Addresses of other An Comunn Gaidhealach offices added later.

Comunn Gaidhealach. [*National Mod.*] Senior Choral Competition, Puirt-a-Beul. Glasgow, 1952.

An Comunn Gaidhealach. Forty-Ninth Mod. Rothesay 1952. Senior Choral Competition, Puirt-a-Beul. . . . Price 3/–. Published by An Comunn Gaidhealach. Printed in Great Britain by Mozart Allan, 84 Carlton Place, Glasgow, C.5. Copyright 1952. Staff.

7 p. 250 mm. PC.

Comunn Gaidhealach. [*National Mod.*] Songs for Choral Competitions. Glasgow, 1938–.

An Comunn Gaidhealach. Forty-Second Mod. Glasgow, 1938. Songs for Choral Competitions. Price 1/– each. Printed and published for An Comunn Gaidhealach by Alex. MacLaren & Sons, Gaelic Printers and Booksellers, 268 Argyle Street, Glasgow, C.2. Printed in Scotland.

Ibid. 1939, 1947, 1949–54, 1956, 1958–66.

[Collation] 12–30 p; average 20 p. 240 mm.

[Note] Printer imprint varies. Printed by MacLaren, Glasgow, 1938–49; W. A. Doogan, Glasgow, 1950–1; Mozart Allan, Glasgow, 1952–66.

Comunn Gaidhealach. [*National Mod.*] Songs for Rural Choirs' Competitions. Glasgow, 1951–.

An Comunn Gaidhealach. Forty-Eighth Mod. Edinburgh 1951. Songs for Rural Choirs' Competitions. . . . Price 3/6 net. Published by An Comunn Gaidhealach. Printed in Great Britain. Copyright 1951. Staff.

Ibid. 1952–3, 1957.

An Comunn Gaidhealach. Fifty-Ninth Mod. Oban 1962. Rural Choirs. Co-fharpais 58. Oran do Reisimeid Earra-Ghaidheal. Price 3/6. Published by An Comunn Gaidhealach, 65 West Regent Street, Glasgow, C.2. Printed in Great Britain by Mozart Allan, 84 Carlton Place, Glasgow, C.5. Copyright 1962. Staff and sol-fa.

[Collation] 12 p, 11 p, 4 p, 4 p, 8 p respectively. 240 mm.

Comunn Gaidhealach. [*National Mod.*] Song for Choral Competition. (Individual songs) Glasgow, 1947, 1949.

Song for Choral Competition. Muile nam Fuar-Bheann Mor. An t-òran agus fonn le Iain Mac Dhòmhnuill (Liosach). For conditions of competition see Syllabus from the Secretary of An Comunn Gaidhealach, 131 West Regent Street, Glasgow, C.2. Price 6d. Printed and published for An Comunn Gaidhealach by Alex. MacLaren & Sons, Gaelic Printers and Booksellers, 268 Argyle Street, Glasgow, C.2. Copyright 1947.

[4] p. 270 mm. PC.

An Comunn Gaidhealach. Song for Choral Competition. Tuireadh Iain Ruaidh. For conditions of competition see Syllabus from the Secretary of An Comunn Gaidhealach, 131 West Regent Street, Glasgow, C.2. Price 9d.

7 p. 250 mm. PC.

Copyright 1949.

Comunn Gaidhealach. [*National Mod.*] Syllabus and Prize List. Glasgow, 1910–57.

An Comunn Gaidhealach. Syllabus and Prize-List of the Nineteenth Mod, to be held in the Music Hall, Edinburgh, on 5th, 6th and 7th October 1910. An Comunn Gaidhealach. Clàr-Innsidh agus Duaisean an Naoidheamh-Mòid-Dheug, a tha ri chumail ann an Talla-a'-Chiùil, an Dun-éideann, air a' chóigeamh, an t-seathamh, agus an t-seachdamh là de Mhios October 1910.

Gaelic and English. Earlier eds. mostly in English.

Ibid. 1910–40, 1946–56.

An Comunn Gaidhealach. Patron H.M. The Queen. Syllabus, Prize List and Rules of The National Mod. Price 1/3. N.B.—"Particulars of all prescribed pieces are published annually in a supplement." An Comunn Gaidhealach. Clàr-iomairt, duaisean agus riaghailtean A' Mhòid Nàiseanta. A' phris, 1/3. N.B.—"Tha fiosrachadh mu gach earrann a thaghadh air a chlò-bhualadh gach bliadhna an leabhran fa leth."

1957. Gaelic and English on facing pages.

Ibid. Still in use; reprinted as required, with similar title page but with additions and emendations to the text.

[Collation] 27–36 p. 1910–56; 40–4 p. 1957–. 250 mm.

Comunn Gaidhealach. [*National Mod.*] Syllabus and Prize-List. (Supplement.) Glasgow 1957–.

An Comunn Gaidhealach. Ainmean gach earrann de Rosg is Bàrdachd agus na h-Orain a thaghadh air son an leth-cheudamh Mòd 's a ceithir a tha ri chumail an Inbhirnis bho'n 30mh latha de'n t-Sultainn gus an 4mh latha de'n Damhar, 1957. Gabhar ri ainmean gu ruig a' cheud latha de'n Og-mhios. A' phrìs sia sgillinn. Faic clàr-iomairt a' Mhòid air son fiosrachadh mu na co-fharpaisean, na duaisean agus na riaghailtean. (A' phrìs, 1/3).

The Highland Association. Names of prescribed Prose, Poetry and Songs selected for the Fifty-Fourth Mod to be held in Inverness from 30th September until 4th October 1957. Mod entries close on 1st June. Price sixpence. For particulars of competitions, prizes and rules refer to Mod Syllabus, price 1/3, including postage.

Gaelic and English on facing pages.

Ibid. 1957–73. PC.

[Collation] 4–8 p. 250 mm.

Comunn Gaidhealach. [*National Mod.*] N.B.—Also many sheets, with words and music, mostly reprinted from earlier publications; usually without name of competition. Most music for National Mod competitions was published in staff and sol-fa versions.

Comunn Gaidhealach. [Reports.] Inverness, 1967–.

Annual Report 1966–7. An Comunn Gaidhealach.

Ibid. 1968–.

[Collation] *c.* 50 p. 240 mm.

[Note] Gaelic with English translation. Previous Reports contained little Gaelic.

Comunn Gaidhealach. *Scottish Gaelic as a Specific Subject.* See *Scottish Gaelic as a Specific Subject.*

Comunn Gaidhealach. *Sruth.* See *Sruth.*

Comunn Gaidhealach. [War Literature.] Glasgow, n.d.

An Comunn Gaidhealach. [Illus.] Le deagh dhùrachd dhaibh-san a tha a' dion ar dùthcha cho curanta. Combaiste a' Mharaiche.

... curanta. Spioradalachd nan Gaidheal.

... curanta. Seasmhachd nan Gaidheal.

... curanta. An Impireachd agus na Gaidheil.

... curanta. Cogadh mor na Saorsa.

... curanta. Litir o'n Tigh.

[4] p per leaflet. 260 mm. NLS.

Reprints from *An Gaidheal*, issued to soldiers; re-issued in *Am Feachd Gaidhealach.* Reviewed in *An Gaidheal* in 1942.

Comunn Gaidhealach. See *Airgiod an Righ.*

Comunn Gaidhealach. See *Am Measg nam Bodach.*

Comunn Gaidhealach. See *Coisir a' Mhoid.*

Comunn Gaidhealach. See *Coisir na Cloinne.*

Comunn Gaidhealach. See *An Cuairtear*.

Comunn Gaidhealach. See *Dain Thaghte*.

Comunn Gaidhealach. See *An Deo-Greine*.

Comunn Gaidhealach. See *An Feachd Gaidhealach*.

Comunn Gaidhealach. See *An Gaidheal*.

Comunn Gaidhealach. See MacKinnon, Lachlan. [*Baird a' Chomuinn*.]

Comunn Gaidhealach. See *Orain Caraid*.

Comunn Gaidhealach. See *Scottish Gaelic as a Specific Subject*.

Comunn Gaidhealach. See *Seirbhis a' Chruin*.

Comunn Gaidhealach. See *Sruth*.

Comunn Gaidhealach. See *Uirsgeulan Gaidhealach*.

Comunn Gaidhealach. See also Clann an Fhraoich.

Comunn Gaidhealach. See also Comunn na h-Oigridh.

Comunn Gaidhealach, North of England Branch. *Leabhran*. Newcastle, 1972–.
An Comunn Gaidhealach. Leabhran Meur Taobh Tuath Shasuinn.
c. 24 p per issue. 260 mm.
Irregular Gaelic/English periodical. First seen No. 4, Summer 1972.

Comunn Gaidhealach Leodhuis. See *Eilean Fraoich*.

Comunn Gaidhlig Ghlaschu. See Gaelic Society of Glasgow.

Comunn Gaidhlig Inbhirnis. See Gaelic Society of Inverness.

Comunn Gaidhlig Oil-Thigh Obar-Dheadhain. See Crann.

Comunn na Gaidhlig an Lunnainn. See Gaelic Society of London.

Comunn na h-Oigridh. [*Clar-Eagair*.] Glasgow, n.d.
An Comunn Gaidhealach. Comunn na h-Oigridh. Clàr-eagair obair nam feachd.
7 p. 190 mm. PC.

Comunn na h-Oigridh. [*Obair agus Riaghailtean-Earalachaidh*.] Glasgow, 1935.
Gearr-Iomradh air Obair agus Riaghailtean-earalachaidh Comunn na h-Oigridh. A
brief preliminary note on the new Youth Movement in the Gaidhealtachd.
S. E. Marjoribanks, Am Faoilleach, 1935. G. E. Marjoribanks, January 1935.
11 p. 220 mm. PC.
Gaelic and English on facing pages.

Comunn na h-Oigridh. [*Riaghailtean agus Clàr-obrach*.] Glasgow, 1955.
An Comunn Gaidhealach. Comunn na h-Oigridh. Riaghailtean agus Clàr-obrach.
A. Learmonth & Son, Printers, 9 King Street, Stirling. 1955.
14 p; illus. 220 mm. PC.
Gaelic and English on facing pages. Comunn na h-Oigridh is a youth organisation
founded by Clann an Fhraoich, an all-Gaelic group within an Comunn Gaidhealach.
Leaders of Comunn na h-Oigridh have included George Marjoribanks, Hector
MacDougall and Kay Matheson.

Comunn na h-Oigridh. See *Clann an Fhraoich*.

Comunn na h-Oigridh. See *An Gaidheal Og*.

Comunn na h-Oigridh, Feachd Phortrigh. See *An Cabairneach*.

Comunn na h-Oigridh, Feachd Thobarmhoire. See *Na-h-Uibhean Priseil*.

Comunn na Albannach. [*Brosnachadh do na Gaidheil.*] London, n.d.
(Na h-Albannaich.) Comunn nan Albannach (The Scots National League), Lunnainn.
Headquarters: The Reform Hall, 4 Fumival Hall, London. Earrann I: Brosnachadh do
na Gàidheil. Part II: A manifesto to the Scots people. Kensington: Kenneth Mac-
Kenzie, The Booklovers' Resort. Price twopence.
16 p. 160 mm. GU:CL, SS.

Comunn nan Gaidheal. [*Deas-Ghnath.*] Sydney, C.B., 1928.
Deas-ghnàth Comunn nan Gaidheal, Sidni, C.B. Clò-bhuailte fo ùghdarras an Ard
Chomuinn. 1928.
28 p. 190 mm. Xavier.

Confession of Faith. See [*Westminster Confession of Faith.*]

Connor, R. D., *b.* 1855. [*Gaelic Poems.*] Stirling, [Pref. 1928].
Gaelic Poems by R. D. Connor, with some English translations. Published by friends.
61 p. 190 mm. PC.
  Preface by Connor; "Editor's Note" signed "D. A. M'P."
  Printed at *The Observer Press*, Stirling.
  Gaelic poems on pp 1–44; English 45–61.

Cook, Archibald, *c.* 1788–1865. [*Searmoinean Gaelic.*] Inverness, 1916.
Searmoinean Gaelig leis an Urr. Arch. Cook, a bha an Deimhidh. Inverness: printed
by the Northern Counties Newspaper and Printing and Publishing Company, Limited.
1916.
vi, 352 p. 200 mm. AU, BM, CoS, NLS.
  Preface signed by the editor, John R. MacKay.

—— [*Searmoin Ghaidhlig.*] Glasgow, 1946.
Searmoin Ghàidhlig Leis an Urr Gilleasbuig MacCuaig, a bha an Deimhidh. Gaelic
Sermons by the Rev. Archibald Cook. Glascho: Alasdair MacLabhruinn 's a Mhic, 268
Sràid Earraghaidheal, C.2.
First published 1916. Second edition 1946.
vii, 352 p. 190 mm. Stornoway Public Library.
  Stornoway Public Library.

—— [*Searmon.*] Inverness, 1916.
Searmon leis An Urr. Arch. Cook, a bha an Deimhidh. Inbhirnis. 1916.
[1], 23 p. 180 mm. FC.

—— [*Sermons (Gaelic and English).*] Glasgow, 1907.
Sermons (Gaelic and English). By the late Rev. Archibald Cook, Daviot. Edited, with
an introduction by Rev. John R. MacKay, M.A., Inverness. Glasgow: John M'Neilage, 65 Great Western Road. 1907.
xxxii, 315 p; plate. 190 mm. Mit., PC.
  Gaelic sermons, pp 1–234.

—— [*Tiodhlac do-Labhairt.*] Inverness, 1915.
An Tiodhlac Do-labhairt. A Gaelic Sermon preached by the late Rev. Archibald Cook,
Free Church, Daviot. Inverness: printed by Robert Carruthers & Sons. 1915. Price
threepence.
16 p. 180 mm. FC.
  1st ed. 1868, of which this is a reprint.

Craig, K. C., *d.* 1963 (ed.). See Campbell, John F. [*Gille nan Cochall Chraiceann.*]

—— See Campbell, John F. [*Leigheas cas o Cein.*]

—— See MacDonald, Duncan, of South Uist. [*Sgialachdan Dhunnchaidh.*]

—— See MacDonald, Duncan, of South Uist. [*Sgialachdan Eile o Uibhist.*]

—— See MacDonald, Duncan, of South Uist. [*Sgialachdan o Uibhist.*]

—— See MacDonald, Mary. [*Orain Luaidh.*]

Crann. Aberdeen, n.d.
  Crann. Iris 1. Comunn Gàidhlig Oil-thigh Obar-dheadhain.
  [20] leaves; illus. PC.
    Reproduced photographically; print on one side of leaf only.

Creideamh na Baha'i. See National Spiritual Assembly of the Baha'is of the British Isles.

Creighton, Helen. [*Gaelic Songs in Nova Scotia.*] Ottawa, 1964.
  National Museum of Canada Bulletin No. 198. Anthropological Series No. 66. Gaelic
  Songs in Nova Scotia. By Helen Creighton and Calum MacLeod. Issued under the
  authority of The Honourable Maurice Lamontagne, P.C., M.P., Secretary of State.
  Department of the Secretary of State, Canada. 1964.
  xii, 308 p; illus. 250 mm. Mit.
    Music in staff notation.

Croga an Oir. Glasgow, n.d.
  Croga an Oir. Adapted from Próca an Oir. (With grateful acknowledgements to The
  McCaig Trust and to Brown & Nolan, Limited.) Printed in the Republic of Ireland.
  An Comunn Gaidhealach.
  32 p; col. illus. 190 mm.
    c. 1958. Translated from Irish by Donald Grant.

Crois Tara. Glasgow, 1938–9.
  Crois Tara. Tir agus Canain. Uimhir 1. An t-Iuchar, 1938. Gach mios 2 sgillinn.
  [Colophon] Air a chur a mach le Dionnasg Gaidhlig na h-Alba aig 183 Sràid Dheòrsa,
  Glaschu. Clo-bhuailte le MacSheumais agus Rothach, Struibhle.
  . . . Leabhar 2. Uimhir 3. An Sultuine, 1939. [Last number.]
  [Frequency] Monthly.
  [Collation] 4 p. 380 mm.
  [Locations] Mit.
  [Note] In Gaelic and English. Replaced in 1946 by *An Ceum* as the magazine of the
  Gaelic League of Scotland.

Crois Tara. See also *An Ceum.*

Cuairtear, An. Glasgow, 1934.
  An Cuairtear. [Illus.] A' phrìs, trì sgillinn. An Comunn Gaidhealach, 212 West
  George Street, Glasgow. 1934.
  24 p. 190 mm. PC.
    Readings in verse and prose for schools and night-classes; mostly prizewinning pieces
    from National Mod Competitions.
    Printed Sinclair, Glasgow.

Cumadh agus Ordugh na Seirbhis Airson a bhi a Cuir air Leth Ceisdeir. See Church of
  Scotland. *Liturgy and Ritual.* [A Cuir air Leth Ceisdeir.]

Cumha Barraich. Glasgow, 1923.
  Cumha Barraich.
  A. MacLean & Sons, Printers, 360 Argyle Street.
  1 p. 270 mm.
    No music.

D.M.N.C. See Sinclair, Donald.

Dain Thaghte. Glasgow, 1906.
  Dàin Thaghte, a chum feum an sgoilean na Gaidhealtachd. Fo ùghdarras A' Chomuinn
  Ghaidhealaich. [Illus.] Air a chur am mach le Aonghas Mac Aoidh, 43 Murray Place,
  Struibhle. 1906. 3d.
  47 p, [1] p Clàr-innsidh. 190 mm. AU.

Dain Thaghte Ghaidhlig. Glasgow, n.d.
Dàin Thaghte Ghàidhlig. Selected Gaelic Poetry for reading and recitation. Glasgow: Alex. MacLaren & Sons, Argyle Street, C.2. Sixpence.
32 p. 180 mm. BM, PC.
    Post-1936.

Dana Oisein Mhic Fhinn. Edinburgh, 1902.
The Poems of Ossian. Edinburgh: John Grant, 31 George IV Bridge. 1902.
Dàna Oisein Mhic Fhinn, air an cur amach airson math coitcheannta muinntir na Gaeltachd. The Poems of Ossian. Dun-Eidin: John Grant, 31 George IV Bridge. 1902.
xvi, 344 p. 160 mm. AU.
    Contains "Editor's Preface" signed, "Thomas McLauchlan, 1859". 1st ed. 1818.

Daoine Sidhe. See Parker, Winifred. [*Na Daoine Sidhe.*]

Dealbh-Chluich-Ciuil Chloinne. [Prize-winning plays at the 1925 Mod.] See:
MacCormick, John. [*Am Ceol-Sithe.*]
MacFarlane, Malcolm. [*An Mosgladh Mor.*]
MacLeod, Christina. [*Na Raithean.*]

Dealbh-Chluichean an Gaidhlig. [Series of plays, translated from English, published by An Comunn Gaidhealach, *c.* 1950.] See:
Brandane, John. [*The Change-House.*]
Cocker, W. D. [*The Miller's Wooing.*]
Ferguson, J. A. [*The Scarecrow.*]
Francis, J. O. [*The Poacher.*]
Gregory, Lady. [*The Rising of the Moon.*]
MacPhail, M. S. [*The Eagle's Claw.*]
Malloch, G. R. [*The Grenadier.*]
Milton, J. C. [*Winds for Sale.*]
Ready, Stuart. [*Down to the Seas.*]
Stewart, Kenneth. [*The Five-Year Plan.*]
Synge, John. [*Riders to the Sea.*]

Dean of Lismore. See MacGregor, James, Dean of Lismore.

Deas-Ghnath Comunn nan Gaidheal. See Comunn nan Gaidheal. [*Deas-Ghnath.*]

Deo-Greine, An. Glasgow, 1905–23.
An Deo-Ghréine. The Monthly Magazine of An Comunn Gaidhealach. Volume I. Oct. 1905, to Sept. 1906, inclusive. Eneas MacKay, 43 Murray Place, Stirling.
An Deo-Gréine. The Monthly Magazine of An Comunn Gaidhealach. Volume II. Oct. 1906 to Sept. 1907, inclusive. . . .
. . . Volume V. Oct. 1909 to Sept. 1910, inclusive. An Comunn Gaidhealach, 108 Hope Street, Glasgow.
    Address changes to "114 West Campbell Street, Glasgow" in Vol. XVIII, 1922–3.
. . . Volume XVIII. Oct. 1922 to Sept. 1923, inclusive. An Comunn Gaidhealach, 114 West Campbell Street, Glasgow.
[Last Vol. Nos. 4–12 titled "Gàilig".]
[Continued as *An Gaidheal.*]
    [Frequency] Monthly.
    [Collation] *c.* 16 p per no. 260 mm.
    [Location] BM, Mit.
    [Editors] Malcolm MacFarlane, 1905–6; Rev. Malcolm MacLennan (Gaelic) and Rev. D. MacGillivray (English), 1906–8; Duncan Reid, 1908–12; Donald MacPhie, 1912–22; Neil Shaw, 1922; Neil Ross, 1923.
    [Printers] Archibald Sinclair, Glasgow, 1905–20; Scott, Allan & Learmonth, Stirling, 1921; Scott & Learmonth, Stirling, 1921–3.

Deo-Greine, An. See also *An Gaidheal.*

Dewar, Daniel, 1788–1867 (joint ed.). See MacLeod, Dr. Norman, Minister of St. Columba's Church, Glasgow. [*Dictionary of the Gaelic Language.*]

Dewar, John, *c.* 1801–72 (comp.). See Campbell, John F. [*Blar Traigh Ghruinneaird.*]

Dewar, Rev. John, –1919. [*Reminiscence of the War in South Africa.*] Edinburgh, n.d.
A Reminiscence of the War in South Africa. Sermon preached in Kilmartin Parish Church after the funeral of Queen Victoria by Rev. John Dewar, B.D.
24 p. 190 mm. Mit.
Gaelic Sermon, pp 13–24.

Dick, Lachlan, 1935–. [*Bardachd gu a Mineachadh.*] Inverness, 1972.
Bàrdachd gu a mìneachadh. Lachlainn Dick. Còmhlan Comhairle na Gàidhlig aig an E.I.S.
Air ullachadh air sgàth Còmhlan Comhairle na Gaidhlig aig an E.I.S. le: Màiri NicLeòid, Ard Sgoil Mhic Neacail; Lachlainn Dick, An Acadamaidh Rìoghail, Inbhirnis; Iain Steele, Ard Sgoil Phortrìgh. Air a dheasachadh do 'n chlò-bhuaileadair le Lachlainn Dick. Air fhoillseachadh an 1972 leis A' Chomunn Ghaidhealach. Clò-bhuailte le Eccleslitho, Inbhirnis.
[2], 115 p. 220 mm.

—— [*Leasain Ghaidhlig.*] Inverness, n.d.
[Cover] Leasain Ghaidhlig. Gaelic Lessons.
Learn Gaelic. Fichead leasan Gaidhlig. Twenty Gaelic lessons. Edited by Lachlan F. Dick, M.A. [and] Murdo MacLeod, M.A., B.A. Published for An Comunn Gaidhealach by Toradh, An Comunn Productions, Abertarff House, Inverness. Printed by John G. Eccles, 28 High Street, Inverness.
100 p; illus. 240 mm.
  1966. Issued with 10 L.P. records. Foreword by D. J. MacKay, the then President of An Comunn Gaidhealach.

Dieckhoff, Henry C., 1869–1950. [*Pronouncing Dictionary of Scottish Gaelic.*] Edinburgh, 1932.
A Pronouncing Dictionary of Scottish Gaelic, based on the Glengarry dialect according to oral information obtained from natives born before the middle of last century. By Henry Cyril Dieckhoff, O.S.B. [Illus.] W. & A. K. Johnston, Limited, Edinburgh and London. 1932.
With examples in the phonetic alphabet.

Dilworth, Anthony. [*Mainland Dialects of Scottish Gaelic.*] Fort Augustus, 1972.
Mainland Dialects of Scottish Gaelic. By Anthony Dilworth. 1972. Published by the Abbey Press, Fort Augustus.
[11] p; map. 240 mm. PC.

Dingwall Academy. See School Magazines.

Dioghluim o Theagasg nan Aithrichean. Glasgow, 1900.
Dioghluim o Theagasg nan Aithrichean. Earailean aig bord communachaidh, & c., leis na h-Urramaich Alasdair MacAdam, Raoghal Ban, agus Lachlan MacCoinnich. Air ùr chlo-bhualadh. Glasgow: John M'Neilage, 65 Great Western Road. 1900.
22 p. 190 mm. Mit.
1st ed. 1868.

Dionnasg Gaidhlig na h-Alba. See:
Ceol nam Beann.
Ceum, An.
Crois Tara.
Gaelic Community Song Sheet.

Domhnull Cam Macdhughaill. Stornoway, [Fore., 1965].
Dòmhnull Cam Macdhùghaill. Le Sgoil Bhaltois.
19 p. 240 mm. PC.
Printed by the *Stornoway Gazette.*

Domhnallach, Domhnall. See MacDonald Donald.

Domhnullach, Eoghan. See Dwelly, Edward.

Domhnullach, Eoin. See MacDonald, Rev. Dr. John.

Domhnullach, Iain. See MacDonald, Rev. Dr. John.

Domhnullach, Ruairidh. See MacDonald, Roderick.

Domhnallach, Tormod. See MacDonald, Rev. Norman.

Do'n Olla Shasgunnach. Oban, (1907?)
"Oran connsachaidh no riasanachaidh. Ratiocinating song with the English Doctor."
2 p.
A reprint of part of "Da Oran Oirdheirc, Do'n Olla Shasgunnach; agus Aon Oran do
Mhinisdeir Liosmor, Mr Domhnul Macneacail" of 1781. Not seen. Described in
TS-G.

Dorlach Sil. Edinburgh, 1931.
Dòrlach Sìl. Searmoinean le caochla mhinisteirean. Dun-Eideann: Comunn Clò-
bhualaidh na h-Eaglaise Saoir. 1931.
128 p. 200 mm. Mit., PC.
Foreword signed, "Donald MacLean, Fear-deasachaidh". Printed Turnbull &
Spears, Edinburgh.

Douglas, Katherine, 1893–1965. [*Pein-Ora.*] Dunvegan, 1972.
"Pein-Ora." Dealbhan-cluich, le an cuid ceòl, òrain agus òraidean freagarrach airson na
cloinne, gu h-uile le Catriona Dhùghlas, a' bhana-bhàrd Sgiathanach, a bha ann an
"Pein-Ora", Cille Mhoire An Eilean Sgiathanaich, 1893–1965. Fear-deasachaidh
Dòmhnall Budge, "Ceann follairt", Dunbheagain. Clò-bhuailte le John Blackburn Ltd.,
Leeds. 1972.
[Cover] . . . Deasaichte agus foillsichte le Dòmhnall Budge, Dunbheagan, An t-Eilean
Sgiathanach. 1972.
16 p. 280 mm.
Music in both notations.

——— [*Sar-Orain.*] Dunvegan, 1971.
Sar-Orain. Le Catriona Dhughlas. Na h-òrain is an ceòl gu h-uile le Catriona Dhùghlas,
bana-bhàrd Throdairnish an Eilean Sgiathanach, 1893–1965. Clo-bhuailte le John
Blackburn Ltd., Leeds. *c.* Dòmhnall Budge.
[Cover] . . . Deasaichte agus foillsichte le Dòmhnall Budge, Dunbheagan, An t-Eilean
Sgiathanach. 1971.
Music in both notations.

Dow, William, 1799–1855. [*The Resurrection.*] Edinburgh, 1915.
An Aiseirigh. Edinburgh: John Grant, 31 George IV Bridge. 1915.
39 p. 140 mm. FC, PC.
Translated by Rev. Hector MacAulay. Printed Oliver & Boyd, Edinburgh.

Drummond, Peter. [*Gaelic Series, by Bishop Ryle.*] Stirling, n.d.
Naigheachd Mhaith Do'n Chiontach;
C'aite am bheil Do Pheacaidhean?;
Am Bheil Thu 'n ad Chadal?;
Comasach air Tearnadh;

Dealbh no Cridhe?;
An Duine Iosa Criosd;
Am bheil Thu Saor?;
An Dachaidh.
1 p each.
    8 translated tracts published by Drummond's Tract Depot, Stirling. Advertised in
    An Deo-Greine 1906.

—— [*Mar so Deir an Tighearna.*] Stirling, n.d.
Mar so deir an Tighearna. Creid agus bithidh tu beo. Gaelic Series, No. 1. Peter
Drummond, Stirling. 4d per 100.
Mar so deir an Tighearna. Beannaichidh mi thu. Gaelic Series, No. 12. . . .
1 p each. 190 mm. NLS.
    A series of 12.

——[*Floral Scripture Leaflets.*] Stirling, n.d.
50 Floral Scripture Leaflets in Gaelic, for distribution in Sabbath Schools and general
circulation. Price Sixpence. Stirling: John MacFarlane, Manager, Drummond's Tract
Depot.
1 p each. 92 mm. NLS.
    Floral design and Scripture quotations.

Duilleagan Gaidhlig. [Gaelic Supplement of *Life and Work.*] See *Life and Work.*

Duncan, Angus (ed.). See MacLeod, Murdo, "Murchadh a' Cheisteir". [*Laoidhean agus
    Orain.*]

Dundee Highland Society. [*Year Book/Celtic Annual.*] Dundee, 1911–18.
    Dundee Highland Society (Branch of An Comunn Gaidhealach) Year Book. Session
    1910–11. [Illus.] Compiled and edited by Malcolm C. MacLeod, Hon. Treasurer of
    the Society. Dundee: printed by Campbell & Meldrum Ltd., Fairmuir Press.
39 p; illus. 210 mm. AU.
    Contains little Gaelic.
Second Year of Issue. The Celtic Annual. Year Book of Dundee Highland Society
(Branch of An Comunn Gaidhealach). [Illus.] Edited by Malcolm C. MacLeod.
Dundee: printed by John Long & Co., Bank Street. Published by Dundee Highland
Society. 1911.
64 p; illus. 250 mm. AU, NLS.
    NLS copy has [47]–64 p of Advertisements; AU copy contains 46 p.
Third Year of Issue . . . 1913.
62 p; illus. 250 mm. AU.
    Approx. half in Gaelic. AU copy lacks advertising pages.
Fourth Year of Issue. Dundee: printed by John Leng & Co., Ltd., Bank Street.
Published by Dundee Highland Society. Glasgow: Alex. MacLaren & Son, Argyle
Street. 1914.
96 p; illus. 250 mm. AU, EPL.
    Advertisements, pp 79–96, in EPL copy. AU copy has 78 p.
Fifth Year of Issue. 1915.
ii, 138 p; illus. 250 mm. AU, NLS.
    Gaelic Supplement, pp 79–112; advertisements (NLS copy), pp 113–38.
Sixth Year of Issue. Edited by Malcolm C. MacLeod. Dundee: Malcolm C. MacLeod,
188 Blackness Road. Glasgow: Alex. MacLaren & Son, 360–362 Argyle Street. 1918.
iv, 60 p; illus. 250 mm. NLS.
    [49]–60 p of advertisements. Approx. half Gaelic from 1913.

Dunnchadh mac Dhomhnaill ac Dhunnchaidh. See MacDonald, Duncan, of South Uist,
    1883–1954.

Dwelly, Edward, 1864–1939. [*Coinneamh Ghaidhlig.*] Herne Bay, 1905.
Coinneamh Ghàidhlig. A Gaelic Meeting. (Reprinted from "Faclair Gàidhlig le Dealbhan".) Camus a' Chorra (Herne Bay): E. MacDonald & Co., The Gaelic Press. 1905.
16 p. 105 mm. GU:CL.

—— [*Coinneamh Ghaidhlig.*] Glasgow, 1914.
Coinneamh Ghàidhlig. A Gaelic Meeting. A number of phrases and expressions grouped together for the first time. They will be useful as an aid in the conducting of all routine business at all Gaelic meetings. A' phrìs – 3 sgillinnean. Alasdair Mac-Labhruinn agus a Mhac, 360 Sràid Earraghaidheal, Glascho.
Second edition 1914.
16 p. 97 mm. PC.

—— [*Faclair Gaidhlig.*] Lyminge/Herne Bay, n.d.
Earrann 1. Faclair Gàidhlig, le dealbhan, anns am bheil na facail Ghàidhlig uile 's na leabhraichean a leanas: Faclair Armstrong, Faclair a' Chomuinn Ghaidhealaich, Faclair MhicAilpein, Faclair MhicBheathainn, Faclair MhicEachairn, Faclair MhicLeòid & Deòir, Ainmean Gàidhlig Eòin (MacFhearghais), Ainmean Gàidhlig Ghalair (Mac-Ghill'Ios'), Ainmean Gàidhlig Lusan (Camshron), agus iomadh leabhar eile. [Illus.] Sràid-na-cloiche: air a chur a mach le E. Dòmhnullach 's a Chuideachd, aig a' Chlòdh-Chlàr Ghàidhlig, Ardmór. Lyminge: (Kent). Published by E. MacDonald & Co., at the Gaelic Press, Ardmór.
Earrann 1 was issued in 2 sizes – 200 mm and 230 mm.
Ibid. Earrann 2–7.
230 mm.
Earrann 8 . . . Herne Bay (Camus a' Chorra): published by E. MacDonald & Co., The Gaelic Press.
Ibid. Earrann 9–32.
Earrann 33. "This is the concluding part of Faclair Gàidhlig."
xv, 1037, [1] p; illus. 230 mm. Mit., PC.
    Issued between 1902 and 1911. The Mitchell Library holding bears the "Herne Bay" imprint from No. 1, indicating that they were bound later than the PC copies (title page is on the covers). The parts were bound in three volumes with volume title pages issued by the publisher: see below.

—— [*Faclair Gaidhlig.*] Herne Bay, 1902–[11].
Faclair Gàidhlig air son nan sgoiltean, le dealbhan, agus a h-uile facal anns na faclairean Gàidhlig eile, le iomadh ceud nach fhaighear an gin dhiubh, ach a chaidh a thional bho luchd-bruidhinn agus sgoilearan na Gàidhlig anns gach cearn. Camus-a'-Chorra: air a chur a mach le E. Dòmhnullach 's a chd., aig a' Chlòdh-Chlàr Ghàidhlig. 1902–.
A Gaelic Dictionary specially designed for beginners and for use in schools. Profusely illustrated, and contains every Gaelic word in all the Dictionaries hitherto published, besides many hundreds collected from Gaelic-speakers and scholars all over the world, and now printed for the first time. Herne Bay: published by E. MacDonald & Co., at The Gaelic Press. 1902–.
. . . Volume 2. Herne Bay: published by E. MacDonald & Co., at The Gaelic Press. 1902–.
. . . Volume 3. Herne Bay: published by E. MacDonald & Co., at the Gaelic Press 1902–.
[4], xv, 1037, [1] p; illus. 220 mm. BM, GU, GU:CL.
    Vols. 2 and 3 have English title page only. The parts were bound by the libraries rather than by the publisher: in GU, Vols. 1 and 2 end on pages 409 and 744, respectively; in GU:CL, on pages 312 and 664.

—— [*Faclair Gaidhlig.*] Herne Bay, 1911.
The Illustrated Gaelic Dictionary. Specially designed for beginners and for use in

schools. Including every Gaelic word in all the other Gaelic dictionaries and printed books, as well as an immense number never in print before. By Edward Dwelly, F.S.G. Vol. 1. Revised Edition. Herne Bay: printed and published by the author, single-handed, at his publishing office in Mill Lane. 1911. Sole Agent: A. H. Mayhew, 56 Charing Cross Road, London, W.C.
... Volume 2.... 1911.
... Volume 3.... 1911.
[Cover] Faclair Gàidhlig.
[6], xiv, [2], 1037, [1] p; plate; illus. 220 mm. BM, GU:CL.

—— [*Faclair Gaidhlig*.] Fleet, 1918.
... By Edward Dwelly. Vol. 1. Revised Edition. Fleet, Hants: printed and published by the author single-handed, at his Genealogical Office in King's Road. 1918.
... Volume 2. ... 1918.
... Volume 3.... 1918.
[Cover] Faclair Gàidhlig.
[6], xiv, 1037 p; plate; illus. 220 mm. AU.

—— [*Faclair Gaidhlig*.] Fleet, 1930.
The Illustrated Gaelic Dictionary. Containing every Gaelic word and meaning given in all its predecessors, and a great number never in print before, with 675 illustrations, to which is prefixed a Concise Gaelic Grammar. Compiled by Edward Dwelly, F.S.A. (Scot.), F.S.G., Hon. Life Member of the Gaelic Society of London, Hon. Life Member of An Comunn Gaidhealach. Great Britain: printed and published by the compiler at Kenilworth Road, Fleet, Hants., and sold by Alex. MacLaren & Sons, 360–362 Argyle Street, Glasgow, C.2. and Miss J. MacDonald, MacDonald Music Store, Antigonish, Nova Scotia, Canada. MCMXXX.
[Cover] Faclair Gàidhlig.
[2], xiv, 1037, [2] p; plate; illus. 220 mm. Moray and Nairn County.
    The first 1 vol. ed. Referred to in later eds. as the "1929 edition".

—— [*Faclair Gaidhlig*.] Glasgow, 1949.
Ibid.
Fourth edition 1941.
[Cover] Faclair Gàidhlig.
[4], xiv, 1034 p; plate; illus. 220 mm. PC.
    Lacks the "List of Subscribers" of earlier eds.

—— [*Faclair Gaidhlig*.] Glasgow, 1949.
Ibid.
Fifth edition 1949.
[4], xiv, 1034 p; 3 plates; illus. 220 mm. PC.

—— [*Faclair Gaidhlig*.] Glasgow, 1967.
Ibid.
Sixth edition 1967.
[2], xiv, 1034 p; illus. 220 mm. PC.

—— [*Faclair Gaidhlig*.] Glasgow, 1971.
... Gairm Publications (incorporating Alex. MacLaren & Sons), 29 Waterloo Street, Glasgow, C.2.
Seventh edition 1971.
[Cover] Faclair Gàidhlig gu Beurla le dealbhan. Dwelly's Illustrated Gaelic to English Dictionary.

—— [*Faclair Gaidhlig*.] Glasgow, 1973.
Ibid.
Eighth edition 1973.
[2], xiv, 1034 p; 3 plates; illus. 220 mm.

Last revised edition 1918. Dwelly refers, in his Preface to the 1930 ed., to a supplement of *c.* 100 p: this has not been published. "Eoghan Dòmhnullach" was the pseudonym of Edward Dwelly.

Dwelly, Edward. See *Am Feillire.*

Earrann na h-Oigridh. See Comunn Gaidhealach. [*National Mod.*] Earrann na h-Oigridh.

Educational Institute of Scotland, Central Gaelic Committee. See Thomson, Donald. [*Poems for Interpretation.*]

Educational Institute of Scotland, Gaelic Advisory Panel. See Dick, Lachlan. [*Bardachd gu a Mineachadh.*]

E.G.M.F. See MacKinnon, Jonathan G.

Eaglais Aonaichte Chanada. See United Church of Canada.

Eaglais Chaluim Chille. See St. Columba Church Hymnary.

Eaglais na h-Alba. See Church of Scotland.

Eaglais Shaor agus an Eaglais ur. See Free Church of Scotland. [*An Eaglais Shaor agus an Eaglais ur.*]

Eaglais Shaor Aonaichte na h-Alba. See United Free Church of Scotland.

Eaglais Shaor na h-Alba. See Free Church of Scotland.

Earail do Bhuill a' Chomuinn. See Comunn Gaidhealach. *Earail.*

Edinburgh University Highland Society. [*Year Book* 1964–5.] Edinburgh, 1964.
Edinburgh University Highland Society Year Book 1964–5. Price 1/6.
44 p; illus. 240 mm. PC.
Editorial signed, "Roderick MacLeod, September, 1964". *c.* 11 p of Gaelic: poems, features and a story. Printed by Grosvenor Dupli-Type Services, Edinburgh. No more published.

Eilean a' Cheo. See Glasgow Skye Association. [*Eilean a' Cheo.*]

Eilean Fraoich. Stornoway, 1938.
Eilean Fraoich. Lewis Gaelic Songs and Melodies. Comunn Gaidhealach Leòdhais. Price 3/6.
Stornoway: printed at the *Gazette* Office. 1938.
[8], 111 p. 220 mm. BM, NLS, PC.
Preface signed by James Thomson and Duncan MacDonald. Music in sol-fa. In 4 parts: "Published Songs", "Unpublished Songs", "Orain Luaidh", "Puirt-a-Beul".

Eilean mo Ghaoil. Edinburgh, 1945.
Cogadh na Saorsa. Eilean mo Ghaoil. [Illus.] Printed by Oliver and Boyd, Edinburgh, for The Church of Scotland, The Free Church of Scotland. 1945.
88 p. 140 mm.
Gaelic sermons and essays. Published for distribution to soldiers.

Eileanach, An t-. Bernera, 1970–.
An t-Eileanach. [Illus.] Aireamh 1. Am Faoilleach, 1970. Leabhran Miosail Eaglais Bheàrnaraigh.
[Continuing]
[Frequency] Monthly, No. 1–24 (Dec. 1971); bi-monthly, No. 25–30 (Nov.–Dec. 1972); monthly, No. 31–.
[Collation] 8 p, No. 1; 12 p, No. 2–19 (July 1971); 8 p, No. 20–24 (Dec. 1971); 16 p, No. 25–27 (May–June, 1971); 20 p, No. 28; 12 p, No. 29–30 (Nov.–Dec. 1972); 4 p, No. 31, 200 mm; No. 1–30; 300 mm, No. 31–.
[Editor] Rev. Roderick MacLeod, Minister of Bernera, Harris.

Erskine, The Hon. Stuart Ruaraidh, of Marr, 1869–. [*Air Eachdraidh.*] Glasgow, n.d.
  The Ceilidh Books. Leabhraichean nan Ceilidh. Aireamh 15. Peiteag Ruaidh, Sgeul.
  Air Eachdraidh, le Ruaraidh Arascainn is Mhàirr. [Illus.] A' phrìs, trì sgillinnean. 3d.
  Alasdair Mac Labhruinn agus a Mhic, 360–362 Sràid Earraghaidheal, Glascho.
  [237]–267 p. 230 mm. PC.
    Reprinted from *Guth na Bliadhna*, XI.2, Summer 1914.

Erskine, The Hon. Stuart Ruaraidh, of Marr, 1869–. See *Am Bard*.

—— (ed.) See *Guth na Bliadhna*.

—— (ed.). See Scupoli, Lorentzo. [*Combattimento Spirituale.*]

Facal do na Gaidheil. See An Comunn Gaidhealach. [*Facal do na Gaidheil.*]

Faclair Gaidhlig. See Dwelly, Edward. [*Faclair Gaidhlig.*]

Faire agus Urnuigh. Edinburgh, [Intro. 1916].
  Cogadh mór na h-Eòrpa. Faire agus Urnuigh. [Illus.] Printed by Oliver and Boyd,
  Edinburgh, for The Church of Scotland, The United Free Church of Scotland, and
  The Free Church of Scotland.
  xii, 123 p. 140 mm. NLS.
    Issued to soldiers in the First World War.

—— *Faire agus Urnuigh.* Edinburgh, 1941.
  Cogadh na Saorsa. Faire agus Urnuigh. [Illus.] Printed by Oliver and Boyd, Edinburgh, for The Church of Scotland, The Free Church of Scotland. 1941.
  viii, 123 p. 140 mm. PC.
    One of a series of religious booklets issued for distribution to Highland soldiers in the
    Second World War.

Farquharson, Archibald. [*Laoidhean Shioin.*] Glasgow, 1924.
  Laoidhean Shioin. Le Gilleasbuig Farcharson. Glasgow: printed by Archibald Sinclair,
  47 Waterloo Street. 1924.
  119 p, [2] "An Clar-Innsidh." 170 mm. PC.
    1st ed. 1870.

Feachd Gaidhealach, Am. Glasgow, 1944.
  Am Feachd Gaidhealach. [Illus.; Quotation.] An Comunn Gaidhealach, 131 Sràid Iar
  Regent, Glaschu, C.2. 1944.
  320 p. 180 mm. EPL, NLS.
    Foreword by Malcolm MacLeod, President of An Comunn Gaidhealach. Dis-
    tributed to Highland soldiers. Comprises the extracts from *An Gaidheal* previously
    published in *Airgiod an Rìgh* (1942), *Seirbhis a' Chrùin* (1943) and leaflets ("Duill-
    eagan air leth").

Feachd Gaidhealach. See also *Airgiod an Righ*.

Feachd Gaidhealach. See also *Seirbhis a' Chruin*.

Feachd Phortrigh (Comunn na h-Oigridh). See *An Cabairneach*.

Feachd Thobarmhoire (Comunn na h-Oigridh). See *Na h-Uibhean Priseil*.

Fear na Butha. Glasgow, 1970.
  Fear na Bùtha. Le còmhlan a thainig cruinn aig Cruinneachadh an Luchd-teagaisg
  Ghàidhlig an Inbhirnis, 1968. Dealbhan le Cailean Spencer. Gairm. Glaschu. 1970.
  Fear na Bùtha. Sreath na Sgoile (air fhoillseachadh an co-bhoinn ri Coimitidh nan
  Leabhraichean-sgoile), Leabhar 6. Clò-bhualaidhean Gairm, Leabhar 19.
  [12] p; illus. 210 mm.

Fear na Ceilidh. [Sydney, C.B.], 1928–30.
Fear na Ceilidh. Miosachan Gàilig. Naigheachd, Sgeulachd, Eachdraidh, Bardachd. "Sgeul ri aithris air am o aois". Vol. I. March 1928. No. 1.
. . . Volume II. June 1930. No. 9. [Last seen.]
[Frequency] Monthly, Vol. I.1–Vol. I.10 (Dec. 1928); quarterly, Vol. I.11–12; monthly, Vol. II.1 (Aug. 1929)–Vol. II.6 (Jan. 1930); monthly, Vol. II.7 (April 1930)–Vol. II.9 (June 1930).
[Collation] *c.* 10 p each number, Vol. I; 12 p, Vol. II. 240 mm.
[Locations] AU, NLS (incomplete holding).
[Editor] Jonathan G. MacKinnon.
[Note] All-Gaelic magazine, published in Sydney, Cape Breton, Nova Scotia.

Fear nam Fiaclan. Glasgow, 1971.
Fear nam Fiaclan. Le còmhlan de luchd-teagaisg a thainig cruinn aig Cruinneachadh an luchd-teagaisg Ghàidhlig an Inbhirnis, 1968. Dealbhan le Cailean Spencer. Gairm. Glaschu. 1969.
Fear nam Fiaclan. Sreath na Sgoile (air fhoillseachadh an co-bhoinn ri Coimitidh nan Leabhraichean-sgoile), Leabhar 10. Clò-bhualaidhean Gairm, Leabhar 27.
[12] p; illus. 210 mm.

Fear-Smalaidh, Am. Glasgow, 1971.
Am Fear-Smàlaidh. Le còmhlan a thainig cruinn aig Cruinneachadh an Luchd-teagaisg Ghàidhlig an Inbhirnis, 1968. Dealbhan le Cailean Spencer. Gairm. Glaschu. 1971.
Am Fear-Smàlaidh. Sreath na Sgoile (air fhoillseachadh an co-bhoinn ri Coimitidh nan Leabhraichean-sgoile), Leabhar 11. Clò-bhualaidhean Gairm, Leabhar 28.
[12] p; illus. 210 mm.

Fear-Tathaich Miosail. See Monthly Visitor.

Feill a' Chomuinn Ghaidhealaich. See Comunn Gaidhealach.

Feill a' Chomuinn Ghaidhealaich, Buth nan Ealdhain. See An Comunn Gaidhealach.

Feill Cookery Book. Glasgow, 1907.
The Feill Cookery Book. [Illus.] Glasgow: M'Naughton & Sinclair, 29 Cadogan Street. 1907.
248 p. 190 mm. PC.
Recipes in Gaelic, pp 225–8.

Feillire. [Dwelly Version.] Lyminge/Herne Bay, 1901–8.
Am Féillire, agus Leabhar Pòca Gaidhealach. 1901. Sràid na Cloiche, Ceannd, Sasunn: air a chlòdh-bhualadh aig a' Chlòdh-Chlàr Ghàidhlig, agus air a reic le E. Dòmhnullach, Ardmór, Lyminge.
84 p. 99 mm. EU, PC.
. . . Lyminge: air a chur amach le E. Dòmhnullach 's a Chuideachd, aig a' Chlòdh-Chlàr Ghàidhlig, Ardmór.
80 p. 110 mm. EU, PC.
1903. [Not seen.]
Am Féillire, agus Leabhar-Pòca Gaidhealach, 1904. Lyminge: air a chur a mach le E. Dòmhnullach 's a Chuideachd, aig a' Chlòdh-Chlàr Ghàidhlig.
87 p. 110 mm. EU, PC.
. . . 1905. Camus a' Chorra (Herne Bay): air a chur a mach le E. Dòmhnullach 's a Chuideachd, aig a' Chlòdh-Chlàr Ghàidhlig.
87 p. 110 mm. EU, PC.
Ibid. 1906.
88 p. 110 mm. EU, PC.
An Ochdamh bliadhna. 1907.

88 p. 110 mm. EU, PC.
An Naoidheamh bliadhna. 1908.
96 p. 110 mm. EU, PC.
"Eoghan Dòmhnullach" was the pseudonym of Edward Dwelly.

Feillire. [MacLaren Version.] Glasgow, 1938–40.
Am Féillire agus Leabhar-Poca Gaidhlig. 1938. Glascho: Alasdair Mac Labhruinn 's a
Mhic, 268 Sràid Earra-Ghaidheal, C.2.
96 p. 103 × 69 mm. PC.
... 1939. An Dara Bliadhna.
4 ff, 96 p. 103 × 69 mm. PC.
... 1940. An Treas Bliadhna.
96 p. 103 mm. PC.

Feillire. [Mac-Talla Version.] Sydney, C.B., 1900.
Gaelic Almanac, 1900. Price 6c leis a' phost gu aite sam bith. Am Féillire agus
Leabhar Pòca Gaidhealach, 1900. Le "Creag an Fhithich". Sydney, Cape Breton:
Mac-Talla Printing and Publishing Co., Ltd., 1900.
32 p. 160 mm. AU, BM, Mit.

Ferguson, Archibald (ed.) See *A' Choisir-Chiuil*.

Ferguson, Calum, 1929–. [*Sath*.] Glasgow, n.d.
Leabhar 1. A transcript of the seventy lessons of Sàth, the Gaelic Teaching Course.
Copyright. Printed in Scotland. Written and devised by Calum Ferguson, M.A.
Printed by Tiumpan Developments, Ltd., produced by Gaelfonn Recording Co., and
distributed by Caledonian Music Co. Ltd., 59 St. Vincent Crescent, Glasgow, C.3.
Leabhar 2. The lesson-by-lesson vocabulary of Sàth, the Gaelic Teaching Course.
Written and devised by Calum Ferguson, M.A.
Leabhar 3. A brief account of Gaelic grammar, followed by lesson-by-lesson notes on
idioms, sentence construction, etc., of Sàth, the Gaelic Teaching Course. Written and
devised by Calum Ferguson, M.A.
Leabhar 4. Glossary. The words to be found in the seventy lessons of Sàth, the Gaelic
Teaching Course. Written and devised by Calum Ferguson, M.A.
[1], xii, 200 p; vii, 83 p; xii, 167 p; ii, 28 p. 260 mm.
Published 1969. Supplementary to 4 LP records. A deluxe edition was also issued.

Ferguson, Finlay. [*Orain Ghaidhlig*.] Glasgow, n.d.
Orain Ghàidhlig le Fionngladh Mac Fheargais (Eilean a' Cheò). Oran do Oigridh a'
Chéilidh; Oran na Gruaige (Bobbed Hair); Moladh na Gruaige (In Praise of the Un-
Bobbed). Glasgow: Alex. MacLren & Son.
7 p. Mit.
Advertised 1929; *MacLaren* gives date of publication as March 1926.

Ferguson, J. A., 1873–. [*Campbell of Kilmhor*.] Glasgow, n.d.
Caimbeulach na Cille Móire. Dealbh-chluich an aon sealladh. Gaelic translation of the
one-act play, "Campbell of Kilmhor", by J. A. Ferguson. Air eadar-theangachadh le
Dòmhnall MacDhòmhnaill, Eirisgeidh. An Comunn Gaidhealach, 131 West Regent
Street, Glasgow.
16 p. 220 mm.
English original first published 1915.

Ferguson, J. A., 1873–. [*The Scarecrow*.] Glasgow, 1951.
Dealbh-chluichean an Gàidhlig. Am Bodach-ròcais. Dealbh-chluich an aon sealladh.
Gaelic translation of the one-act play, *The Scarecrow*, by J. A. Ferguson. Air eadar-
theangachadh le Lachlann MacFhionghuin. An Comunn Gaidhealach, 131 West
Regent Street, Glasgow. 1951.
18 p. 190 mm.
English original first published 1922.

Ferguson, Roderick. [*Marbhrann Do'n Urramach Domhnull Domhnullach.*] See
MacFarlane, Donald. *The Rev. Donald Macdonald.*

Festival of Britain, 1951. [*20th Century Scottish Books.*] Glasgow, 1951.
   Festival of Britain, 1951. Catalogue of an Exhibition of 20th Century Scottish Books
   at the Mitchell Library, Glasgow. Published by the Scottish Committee of the Festival
   of Britain. 1951.
   x, 310 p. 200 mm. GU.
   "Gaelic Language and Literature", pp 77–82.

Fhianuis, An. Glasgow, [1893]–1903.
   (Air. 101.) An Fhianuis. Ianuaraidh, 1900. Eaglais Shaor na h–Alba. [Illus.]
   Deasaiche, An t-Urr. Iain Deòrsa MacNeill, Chaladair. . . . Gilleasbuig Mac-na-
   Ceàrdadh, Clò-bhuailtear Gàilig, Glaschu. [To No. 104.]
   Ianuaraidh, 1901. An Fhianuis. Eaglais Shaor Aonaichte na h-Alba. [Illus.] Deasaiche,
   An t-Urr. Iain Deòrsa MacNeill, Chaladair. Gilleasbuig Mac na Ceàrdadh, Clò-
   bhuailtear Gàelig, Glaschu.
   October, 1903. . . . [Last number.]
      [Frequency] Quarterly.
      [Collation] 24 p per number. 260 mm.
      [Locations] EU.
      [Note] Replaced "Iomradh air Craobhsgaoileadh an t-Soisgeil leis an Eaglais Shaoir"
      (1875–92) in 1893 as the Gaelic magazine of the Free Church of Scotland. Replaced
      as Free Church Gaelic magazine in 1901 by a Gaelic supplement in the "Free Church
      Monthly Record". A United Free Church of Scotland publication, 1901–03;
      replaced 1904 as Gaelic magazine of the United Free Church by "An Fhianuis
      Ghaidhealach", a Gaelic supplement in "The Highland Witness of the United Free
      Church of Scotland".
      English section has separate title page.
      Gaelic content *c.* 15 p per number.

Fhianuis Ghaidhealach, An. Glasgow/Edinburgh, 1904–29.
   An Fhianuis Ghaidhealach. Clàr-innsidh. . . .
      [Frequency] Monthly.
      [Collation] 6 p, No. 1 & 2; 8 p thereafter. 260 mm.
      [Editor] Rev. Malcom MacLennan, 1908–29.
      [Note] In "The Highland Witness of the United Church of Scotland . . . Archibald
      Sinclair, Printer and Publisher, 'Celtic Press', 47 Waterloo Street, Glasgow" from
      Jan. 1904 to Dec. 1907, after which "The Highland Witness" was incorporated into
      "The Missionary Record of the United Free Church of Scotland . . . Edinburgh".
      "An Fhianuis Ghaidhealach" appeared as a supplement to "The Missionary Record"
      from Jan. 1908 to Dec. 1913 (it had been an integral part of "The Highland Wit-
      ness"). "The Missionary Record" was renamed "The Record of the Home and
      Foreign Mission Work of the United Free Church of Scotland" in 1914; on the
      Union of the two churches in 1929, "An Fhianuis Ghaidhealach" and the Gaelic
      supplement of the Church of Scotland's "Life and Work" were amalgamated into a
      new 8 page supplement in "Life and Work".

Filidh Nam Beann. Glasgow, n.d.
   Filidh nam Beann: the Mountain Songster. The choicest collection of original and
   selected Gaelic songs now known. [Quotation.] Glasgow; Robert M'Greggor & Co.,
   wholesale and export stationers and publishers, India Buildings, 45 Bridge Street.
   iv, 92 p. 170 mm. PC.
   Possibly mid-19th century. Also an earlier ed. by M'Gregor & Co., with different
   address (22 Glassford Street).

Filidh nam Beann. Glasgow, n.d.
   . . . Glasgow: Watt & Stewart, 76 Queen Street. (Entered in Stationers' Hall.)
   iv, 92 p. 170 mm. GU:CL.

Filidh nam Beann. Glasgow, n.d.
... Glasgow: Archibald Sinclair, Gaelic Printer and Publisher, Celtic Press, 47 Waterloo Street.
iv, 92 p. 170 mm. AU, BM, PC.
    Contains a selection of Gaelic folk songs; no music. *c.* 1900.

Fionn (pseud). See Whyte, Henry.

Fionn ann an Tigh a' Bhlair-Bhuidhe. [Dwelly edition.] Herne Bay, n.d.
Uirsgeulan na Feinne. Cuid a h-Aon. Fionn ann an Tigh a' Bhlàir-Bhuidhe gun chomas suidh no éirigh, agus Sealg Bheinn-eidir. Herne Bay, England: published by E. MacDonald & Co., "The Gaelic Press", Mill Lane. Printed on paper made in Scotland.
43 p, 4 plates. 190 mm. AU.
    English translation on facing page. First advertised 1908.

Fionn ann an Tigh a' Bhlair Bhuidhe. [MacLaren edition.] See MacLaren, James. [*Fionn ann an Tigh a' Bhlair Bhuidhe.*]

First Communion Catechism. See Catholic Church. *Catechism.* [First Communion Catechism.]

Flavell, John, 1630?–1691. [*The Lord's Supper.*] Glasgow, n.d.
Mìneachadh air Suipeir an Tighearna, agus còmhradh càirdeil eadar ministeir agus Criosduidh amharusach, mu dheighinn Sacramaid Suipeir an Tighearn. Leis an Urramach Eoin Flabhal. Air 'adar-theangaichte gu Gaelig le Seumas MacGilliosa, Ministeir na h-Eaglaise Saoire ann an Cill-beri. Glasgow: Printed by Wm. Gilchrist, 64 Howard Street.
23 p. 160 mm. GU.
    Probably 19th century. Gaelic translations of other books by John Flavell were published in 1828, 1849, 1862.

Fletcher, Alexander, 1862–1921. [*Luinneagan Reobais.*] Glasgow, 1929.
Luinneagan Reòbais. Duannagan Gaoil is Orain Dùthcha le Alasdair Mac an Fhleisteir (nach maireann), Cill-Mheanaidh, Ile. Glascho: Gilleasbaig Mac-na-Ceàrdadh, 27a Sràid Cadogan, 1929.
27 p. 190 mm. Mit.
    Foreword by Neil Shaw.

Folklore Institute of Scotland. See Campbell, John L. [*Gaelic Folksongs from the Isle of Barra.*]

Forbes, Alexander R. [*Gaelic Names of Beasts.*] Edinburgh, 1905.
Gaelic names of beasts (mammalia), birds, fishes, insects, reptiles, etc. In two parts. I: Gaelic-English. II: English-Gaelic. Part I contains Gaelic names or terms for each of the above, with English meanings. Part II contains all the English names for which the Gaelic is given in Part I, with Gaelic, other English names, etymology, Celtic lore, prose, poetry, and proverbs referring to each, thereto attached. All now brought together for the first time by Alexander Robert Forbes, Edinburgh (formerly of Sleat, Skye). Edinburgh: Oliver and Boyd, Tweeddale Court; Norman MacLeod, George IV Bridge. 1905.
xx, 424 p, plate. 240 mm. AU, BM, GU, Mit., NLS.

Forbes, John (tr.). See Baxter, Richard. [*The Saints' Everlasting Rest.*]

Forbes, M. C. (tr.). See Murray, William. [*We Are Busy.*]

Forbes, Mabel C. (joint ed.). See "Sop As Gach Seid".

Francis, J. O., 1882–. [*Birds of a Feather.*] Glasgow, n.d.
Breac a Linne. Dealbh-chluich an aon sealladh. Gaelic translation of the one-act comedy, "Birds of a Feather", by J. O. Francis. Air eadar-theangachadh le Ailean Mac Gill-Eathain. An Comunn Gaidhealach, West Regent Street, Glasgow.
19 p. 220 mm.
    c. 1950. English original first published 1927.

Francis, J. O., 1882–. [*The Poacher.*] Glasgow, 1951.
Dealbh-chluichean an Gàidhlig. Am Poidsear. Dealbh-chluich àbhachdach an aon sealladh. Gaelic translation of the one-act comedy, "The Poacher", by J. O. Francis. Air eadartheangachadh le Dòmhnall Mac Gille Mhoire. An Comunn Gaidhealach, 131 West Regent Street, Glasgow. 1951.
29 p. 190 mm. English original first published 1910.
    Printed Learmonth, Stirling.

Fraochan is Peasan. Glasgow, 1969.
Fraochan is Peasan. Le còmhlan a thainig cruinn aig Cruinneachadh an Luchd-teagaisg Ghàidhlig an Inbhirnis, 1968. Dealbhan le Cailean Spencer. Gairm. Glaschu. 1969. Fraochan is Peasan. Sreath na Sgoile (air fhoillseachadh an co-bhoinn ri Coimitidh nan Leabhraichean-sgoile), Leabhar 2. Clò-bhualaidhean Gairm, Leabhar 11.
19, [1] p; illus. 210 mm.

Fraser, Alexander, of Dunvegan. [*Oran.*] Canada, n.p., n.d.
"Oran, le Alasdair Friseal, Dunbheagan, Gleann-garradh, Canada. 4 p. 8 vo."
Not seen. Information from *Dunn, T. S-G.*

Fraser, Alexander, Ontario Archivist, 1860–1936. [*Canain.*] Toronto, 1901.
"Canain agus Cliu ar Sinnsearan. Toronto, 1901."
Not seen. Information from *Clare, Dunn.*

—— [*Gaelic Folk Songs of Canada.*] Ottawa, 1903.
From the Transactions of the Royal Society of Canada. Second Series – 1903–1904. Volume IX, Section II. English history, literature, archaeology, etc. The Gaelic Folk Songs of Canada. By Alexander Fraser, Toronto. For sale by J. Hope & Sons, Ottawa; The Copp-Clark Co., Toronto; Bernard Quaritch, London, England. 1903.
[49]–60 p. 250 mm. NLS.

—— [*An Gaidheal ann an Canada.*] N.p., n.d.
"An Gaidheal ann an Canada."
Not seen. *Clare, Dunn.*

—— [*Gathering of the Clan MacDonald Society of Canada.*] Toronto, 1901.
The following words were spoken at the first Gathering of the Clan MacDonald Society of Canada, on Dominion Day (1st July) 1901, at Alexandria, County of Glengarry, Canada, and are republished from the press reports of a few friends who believe it to be the bounden duty of every Highlander to work unceasingly for the preservation of the language of the Gael. Alexander Fraser. Toronto, 15th July, 1901.
16 p. 200 mm. Harv.

—— [*Geàrr-sgeòil air Sir Seòras Uilleam Ros.*] Toronto, 1915.
Geàrr-sgeòil air Sir Seòras Uilleam Ros, agus air mar a thuinich na Gaidheil ann an Canada Uachdrach. Leis an Ollamh Alasdair Friseal. Toronto, 1915.
58 p. 200 mm. NLS.

—— [*Linn nan Aigh.*] N.p., n.d.
"Linn nan Aigh. Oissian is MacMhaighstir Alasdair."
Not seen. Information from *Clare, Dunn.*

—— [*Orain Duthcha nan Eilean.*] N.p., n.d.
"Orain Dùthcha nan Eilean."
Not seen. Information from *Clare, Dunn.*

—— [*Practical Lessons in Gaelic Grammar.*]
Practical Lessons in Gaelic Grammar.
Not seen.

—— [*Sir S. MacChoinnich.*] N.p., n.d.
"Sir S. MacChoinnich, am Fear-Tagraidh Fuileachdach."
Not seen. Information from *Clare, Dunn.*

Fraser, John, 1882–1945 (ed.). See MacGregor, James, Dean of Lismore. [*Poems from the Book of the Dean of Losmore.*]

Free Church of Scotland. [*An Eaglais Shaor agus an Eaglais Ur.*] Edinburgh, 1929.
[Illus.] An Eaglais Shaor agus an Eaglais Ur.
Air a chur amach le Comunn Clòdhbhuailidh Eaglais Shaor na h-Alba. Free Church Offices, 15 North Bank Street, Edinburgh, 31st August 1929.
4 p. 270 mm. NLS.

Free Church of Scotland. [*An Fhianuis.*] See *An Fhianuis.*

Free Church of Scotland. [*Fuinn nan Salm Ghaidhlig.*] See Free Church of Scotland. *Liturgy and Ritual.* Fuinn nan Salm Ghaidhlig.

Free Church of Scotland. [*Litir Aodhaireal.*] Glasgow, 1901.
"Litir Aodhaireal air a cur a mach le Ughdarras Ard-Sheanadh Eaglais Shaor na H-Alba. Glasgow, 1901."
Not seen. Information from *T S-G.*

Free Church of Scotland. *Liturgy and Ritual.* [Fuinn nan Salm Ghaidhlig.] Edinburgh, 1932.
[Illus.] Eaglais Shaor na h-Alba. Fuinn nan Salm Ghàidhlig. (Gaelic Psalmody.) Clòdh-bhuailte le h-ùghdarras Ard Sheanadh Eaglais Shaoir na h-Alba. (Published by authority of the General Assembly of the Free Church of Scotland.) Edinburgh: H. & J. Pillans & Wilson, 20 Bernard Terrace. 1932.
vii, 48 p. 200 mm. AU, Mit.
> Music in sol-fa notation. Contains: pp 1–24, 23 tunes; pp 25–38, T. L. Hately's "Seann Fhuinn nan Salm" of 1862 (with original title page); pp 39–48, F. W. Whitehead's "The Sutherlandshire version of the six Long Gaelic Psalm Tunes" (with original title page). *MacLaren* refers to "a later edition containing only the Long Tunes collected by Whitehead" but this has not been traced: Whitehead's "The Six Long Gaelic Psalm Tunes" was first published *c.* 1910. T. L. Hately's "Seann Fhuinn nan Salm" was republished in 1931.

Free Church of Scotland. *Liturgy and Ritual.* [Fuinn nan Salm Ghaidhlig.] See also:
Hately, T. L. [*Seann Fhuinn nan Salm.*]
Whitehead, F. W. [*The Six Long Gaelic Psalm Tunes.*]

Free Church of Scotland. [*Monthly Record.*] Glasgow/Edinburgh, 1900–.
[Masthead] The Monthly Record of the Free Church of Scotland . . . [Illus.] No. 1. Vol. 1. December, 1900. Price one penny.
December, 1903. The Monthly Record of the Free Church of Scotland. [Illus.] Printed and published by John M'Neilage, 65 Great Western Road, Glasgow.
The Monthly Record of the Free Church of Scotland. [Illus.] . . . Published by Authority, under supervision of the Publications Committee, at the Offices of the Church, The Mound, Edinburgh. One penny. 1907. January.
January 1949. The Monthly Record of the Free Church of Scotland. Contents. . . . [Continuing.]
> [Frequency] Monthly.
> [Pagination] *c.* 16 p per number, 1900–26; *c.* 25 p, 1927–42; *c.* 16 p, 1943–46; *c.* 20 p, 1947.

[Size] 280 mm.
[Locations] Mit.
[Note] "The Monthly Record" replaced "The Free Church of Scotland Monthly" in December 1900. The Gaelic pages replaced "An Fhianuis", which continued as an United Free Church of Scotland publication from 1901. The Gaelic section has at times carried a separate title – e.g. "Gaelic Supplement", "Na Duilleagan Gàidhlig", "An Earrainn Ghàidhlig". Between 1914 and 1917, the Gaelic section had separate pagination. *c*. 2 p of Gaelic per issue.

Free Church of Scotland. [*Monthly Record.*] See also An Fhianuis.

Free Church of Scotland (joint sponsors). See Cogadh Mor Na H-Eorpa. [For cross-references to individual titles in this series.]

Free Church of Scotland (joint sponsors). See Cogadh Na Saorsa. [For cross-references to individual titles in this series.]

Free Church of Scotland. See The Shorter Catechism.

Free Church of Scotland. See Westminster Confession of Faith.

Free Presbyterian Church of Scotland. [*Magazine and Monthly Record.*] Glasgow, [1895]–.
The Free Presbyterian Magazine and Monthly Record. (Issued by a Committee of the Free Presbyterian Synod.) Editor . . . [Quotation]. Vol. IV – 1899–1900. Glasgow: N. Adshead & Son, Printers, 11 & 92 Union Street. [Imprint varies.]
[Frequency] Monthly.
[Collation] *c*. 40 p per number, 1900–39; *c*. 20 p, 1940–50; *c*. 35 p, 1951–. 210 mm.
[Printers] N. Adshead & Son, Glasgow, Vol. IV-XXVI (1900–22); R. Carruthers, "Courier" Office, Inverness, Vol. XXVII-XXXV (1922–31); N. Adshead, Glasgow, Vol. XXXVI-LXVI (1931–62); Bennet & Thomson, Dumbarton, Vol. LXVII– (1962–).

Friseal, Alasdair. See Fraser, Alexander.

Fuinn nan Salm Ghaidhlig. See Free Church of Scotland. *Liturgy and Ritual.* [Fuinn nan Salm Ghaidhlig.]

Gaelic and Scots Folk Tales [etc.]. See School of Scottish Studies. [*Gaelic and Scots Folk Tales and Folk Songs and Scottish Music.*]

Gaelic Books Council. [*Leabhraichean Gaidhlig.*] Glasgow, 1971.
Leabhraichean Gàidhlig. Gaelic Books Council Exhibition, National Mod, Stirling, 1971.
16 p. 330 mm.

Gaelic Books Council. [*Exhibition, National Mod, 1972.*] Glasgow, 1972.
Gaelic Books Council. Exhibition. National Mod, Inverness, 1972.
38 p. 220 mm.

Gaelic Books Council. [*Clar Leabhraichean.*] Glasgow, 1973.
Clàr Leabhraichean. A Gaelic Book List. Comunn Leabhraichean Gàidhlig.
September 1973.
ii, 24 p. 340 mm.
[Preface]: "This list of Gaelic books in print was compiled for distribution at the Comunn Leabhraichean Gaidhlig Exhibition, in the Carrick Halls, Ayr, at the National Mod 1973."

c

Gaelic Community Song Sheet. [Glasgow], n.d.
Cha n-fhois gu buaidh. Dionnasg Gaidhlig na h-Alba (The Gaelic League of Scotland).
["Objects of The League: . . ."] Price 3d. Gaelic Community Song Sheet. . . .
43 p. 290 mm. PC.
An early version of "Ceol nam Beann".

Gaelic Community Song Sheet. See also Ceol nam Beann.

Gaelic Key. Glace Bay, N.S., n.d.
Second Edition. The Gaelic Key. Price 50 cents. Monotyped and printed by Brodie
Printing Company, Limited, Glace Bay, N.S.
16 p. 88 mm. Xavier.
1st ed. not seen.

Gaelic League of Scotland. See:
Ceol nam Beann.
Ceum, An.
Crois Tara.
Gaelic Community Song Sheet.

Gaelic Orthography, Recommended Forms. See Comunn Gaidhealach. [*Gaelic Ortho-graphy.*]

Gaelic Society of Glasgow. [*Leabhar an Ard-Fheis.*] Glasgow, 1937.
Comunn Gàidhlig Ghlaschu (Gaelic Society of Glasgow), Headquarters – The Highlanders' Institute. Leabhar an Ard Fhéis. Jubilee Brochure. 1887–1937. [Quotation.]
Glasgow: Archd. Sinclair, Celtic Press, 27A Cadogan Street. 1937.
24 p; illus. 230 mm. PC.

Gaelic Society of Glasgow. [*Transactions.*] Volume III. Glasgow, 1908.
The Old Highlands. Being papers read before the Gaelic Society of Glasgow, 1895–
1906. With an introduction by Neil Munro. Glasgow: Archibald Sinclair. MCMVIII.
xii, 351 p. 220 mm. AU, GU, Mit.
Vol. III of the Society's Transactions. Contains two papers in Gaelic.

Gaelic Society of Glasgow. [*Transactions.*] Volume IV. Glasgow, 1934.
The Active Gael. Being papers read before the Gaelic Society of Glasgow. With
introduction by Peter MacDougall, M.A., F.E.I.S. Glasgow: Archibald Sinclair.
MCMXXXIV.
xvi, 253p, 2 plates. 220 mm. AU. [Volume IV.]

Gaelic Society of Glasgow. [*Transactions.*] Volume V. Glasgow, [pref. 1958].
Volume V of The Transactions of The Gaelic Society of Glasgow.
222 p. 220 mm. GU, Mit.
1 article and text of 1 poem in Gaelic. Printed Learmonth, Stirling.

Gaelic Society of Inverness. [*Report.*] Inverness, [1946].
Comunn Gàidhlig Inbhir-nis. Gaelic Society of Inverness (Instituted 1871). Report
of the Proceedings at the Dinner on 12th April 1946, and at the cairn, Culloden, in
celebration of the bi-centenary of the Battle of Culloden on 16th April 1746. Chief:
Vice-Admiral Sir R. R. MacGregor, K.C.B., D.S.O. Honorary Secretary: Professor
W. J. Watson, LL.D., D.Litt.Celt., Edinburgh University. Secretary and Treasurer:
Alex. N. Nicolson, 28 Queensgate, Inverness. Chronicle, Inverness.
44, [3]p, plate. 200 mm. PC.

Gaelic Society of Inverness. [*Transactions.*] Inverness, [1872]–.
Transactions of The Gaelic Society of Inverness. Volume XXII, 1897–8. "Clann na
Gaidheal an Guaillean a Chéile". Inverness: The Gaelic Society of Inverness. 1900.
Ibid. 1902, 1904, 1907, 1910, 1915, 1918.

Comunn Gàidhlig Inbhir-nis. Transactions of the Gaelic Society of Inverness. Volume XXIX, 1914–19. "Clann nan Gaidheal ri Guaillean a' Chéile". Printed for the Society by the Northern Counties Newspaper and Printing and Publishing Company, Limited, Inverness. 1922.
Ibid. 1924, 1927, 1929, 1932, 1935, 1939, 1941, 1946.
Vol. XXXIV (1935) contained "Indexes to contents of Volumes I to XXXIV of the Transaction of the Society, 1871 to 1928".
... Volume XLI, 1951–2. Coronation Year Issue. With index ... 1953.
Vol. XLI was issued out of sequence. Sir Denys Lowson, Chief of the Gaelic Society in 1951–2, financed the publication of a volume containing the papers delivered during his year of office. The transactions for the intervening years (1937–50) were published later, as and when money became available: Vol. XXXVIII (1937–41) was published in 1962 and Vol. XXXIX/XL (1942–50) in 1963.
... Volume XXXVIII, 1937–41 ... Printed for the Society by The Highland Printers Limited, Diriebught Road, Inverness. 1962.
... Volume XXXIX/XL, 1942–50 ... Printed for the Society by A. Learmonth & Son, 9 King Street, Stirling. 1963.
Ibid. 1965, 1966, 1967, 1972.
[Collation] Pagination ranges from 340 p to 540 p. 220 mm.
[Locations] AU, BM, EU, GU.
[Contents] A selection of the papers read to the Society on historical, literary and linguistic topics relating to the Highlands.

Gaelic Society of London. [*Annual Report.*] London.
Comunn na Gàidhlig an Lunnainn. The Gaelic Society of London (founded 1777). 130th Annual Report and List of members. December 1907.
36 p. 180mm. Mit.
Reports for 1907 and 1933 only seen. Contain little Gaelic.

Gaelic Supplement of Life and Work. See *Life and Work: Na Duilleagan Gaidhlig.*

Gaidheal, An. Glasgow, 1923–67.
An Gaidheal. (Formerly "An Deo-Gréine".) The Monthly Magazine of An Comunn Gaidhealach. Volume XIX, Oct. 1923 to Sept. 1924, inclusive. An Comunn Gaidhealach, 114 West Campbell Street, Glasgow.
Number 1 of this vol. entitled "Gàilig". Address changes to "131 West Regent Street, Glasgow" from Vol. XXX, 1934–5.
... Volume XLIV (New Series). January 1949, to December 1949, inclusive. An Comunn Gaidhealach, 131 West Regent Street, Glasgow.
Vol. XLIV ran to December 1948, contained 15 numbers. Address changes to "65 West Regent Street, Glasgow" from Vol. XLV, 1950.
... Volume LXII. [Number 3, March 1967.]
[Replaced by *Sruth*, a fortnightly newspaper.]
[Frequency] Monthly.
[Collation] 16 p per no., 1923–39; *c.* 10 p, 1940–62; 12 p, 1963–7. 260 mm.
[Locations] BM, Mit.
[Editors] Neil Ross, 1923–36; Rev. Malcolm MacLeod, 1936–46; Rev. T. M. Murchison, 1946–58; James Thomson, 1958–62; Donald Grant, 1962–4; Roderick MacKinnon, 1964–7.
[Printers] Learmonth, Stirling, 1923–49; Caledonian Press, 1950–67.
[Note] Formerly "An Deo-Gréine".

Gaidheal, An. Reprints from "An Gaidheal". See:
Airgiod an Righ.
An Cuairtear.
An Feachd Gaidhealach.

Gaidheal, An. See also An Deo-Gréine.

Gaidheal, An. See also An Gaidheal Og.

Gaidheal, An. See also Sruth.

Gaidheal Og, An. Glasgow, 1949–60.
An Gaidheal Og. Miosachan Comunn na h-Oigridh. Leabhar I. Am Faoilleach, 1960. Aireamh 1. [Last seen.]
[Frequency] Monthly.
[Collation] *c.* 4 p per issue, 1949–54; *c.* 2 p, 1955–60.
[Locations] BM, Mit.
[Note] Supplement to "An Gaidheal".

Gailig. See An Deo-Greine.

Gailig. See An Gaidheal.

Gairm. Glasgow, 1952–.
Gairm. 112 Bath Street, Glaschu, C.2. Aireamh 1. Am Foghar, 1952.
Gairm. Aireamh 13. Am Foghar, 1955. 227 Bath Street, Glaschu, C.2.
Gairm. Aireamh 45. An Geamhradh, 1963. 227 Sràid Bhath, Glaschu, C.2. Fir-deasachaidh: Ruaraidh MacThómais agus Fionnlagh I. MacDhòmhnaill. Luchd-urrais: Fionnlagh I. MacDhòmhnaill agus Ruaraidh MacThómais. Rùnaire: Dòmhnall Iain MacIlleathain. Sanasan-reic (Advertisements): R. Ferguson, 227 Bath Street, Glasgow, C.2.
Gairm. (Stéidhichte 1951.) Aireamh 65. An Geamhradh, 1968 . .
Address changes to "29 Sràid Waterloo, Glaschu, C.2" from No. 71, Summer 1970. Editor statement varies: see note below.
[Continuing.]
[Frequency] Quarterly; also issued as bound volume of 4 numbers.
[Pagination] 94 p in each of the first 4 numbers [separately paginated]; 384 p per yearly vol. thereafter, with the exception of Vol. 8 (368 p) and Vol. 11 (440 p). Illus.
[Size] 210 mm.
[Locations] AU, EU, GU, Mit.
[Editors] Derick S. Thomson, 1952–; joint editor: Finlay J. MacDonald, 1952–64; asst. editor: Donald J. MacLeod, 1966–.
[Contents] An all-Gaelic literary magazine.
[Printers] Learmonth, Stirling.

Gairm. A selection from "Gairm". See MacDonald, John A. [*Criochan Ura.*]

Garioch, Robert, 1909– (joint author). See MacLean, Sorley. [*Seventeen Poems for Sixpence.*]

Gathan Greine. Edinburgh, n.d.
Gathan Gréine air son cridhe dhaoine, air an tarruing bho fhacal Dhé féin. Le ùgh-darras Iain H. Bell, 119 Sràid Sheòrais, Duneideann, d'am buin e.
16 p. 140 mm. Mit.
Advertised from 1929. Printed Turnbull & Spears, Edinburgh.

Gearr-Iomradh air Obair agus Riaghailtean-Earalachaidh Comunn na h-Oigridh. See Comunn na h-Oigridh. [*Obair agus Riaghailtean-Earalachaidh.*]

Geddes, Arthur, 1895–. [*Songs of Craig and Ben.*] Volume II. Glasgow, 1961.
The Songs of Craig and Ben. Lays, Laments, Love Songs and Lilts of the Mountaineers and Craigsmen of the Highlands and Islands, with their melodies and stories gathered and mainly translated by Arthur Geddes. Volume II: Songs of Farewell, Love and Laughter. Introduction. William Maclellan, 240 Hope Street, Glasgow. 1961.
xxxvi, [2], 90 p. 220 mm. Mit., NLS.
Mostly English translations of Gaelic songs, with some originals.

General Assembly Reading Book. See Church of Scotland, General Assembly. [*An Ceathramh Leabhar.*]

Gilbert, Bernard, 1882–. [*The Old Bull.*] Glasgow, n.d.
An Seann Tarbh. Dealbh-chluich an aon sealladh. Gaelic translation of the one-act play, "The Old Bull" by Bernard Gilbert. Air eadar-theangachadh le Seumas Mac-Thómais. An Comunn Gaidhealach, 131 West Regent Street, Glasgow.
20 p. 220 mm.
   c. 1950. Printed by the Caledonian Press, Glasgow.

Gillies, H. Cameron. [*Elements of Gaelic Grammar.*] London, 1902.
The Elements of Gaelic Grammar. Based on the work of the Rev. Alexander Stewart, D.D. By H. Cameron Gillies, M.D. Second Edition. With Appendix. London: published by David Nutt, 57–59 Long Acre. 1902.
xiv, 186 p. 190 mm. AU, GU.
   1st ed. 1896. 1st ed. of Stewart's Grammar was in 1801: the last ed. was in 1901. Printed by T. & A. Constable, Edinburgh.

—— [*Elements of Gaelic Grammar.*] See also Stewart, Alexander. [*Elements of Gaelic Grammar.*]

Gillies, James (tr.). See Flavel, John. [*The Lord's Supper.*]

Given, Jennie. [*Clarsach a' Ghlinne.*] Glasgow, [1925].
Clàrsach a' Ghlinne. Coig òrain air fhichead le'm fuinn agus teud-cheol simplidh le Seonaid Given. The Harp of the Glen. Twenty-five Gaelic songs arranged with simple accompaniments by Jennie Given, A.R.C.M. Price 3/–. Cloth 5/–. Paterson's Publications Ltd.; Glasgow: 152 Buchanan St.; London: 95 Wimpole Street, W.1.
36 p. 270 mm. Mit.
   1925 Foreword signed, "C. M'P, Gaelic Editor" [i.e. Malcolm MacFarlane]. In both notations, with harp accompaniments.

—— [*Clarsach a' Ghlinne.*] Glasgow, 1927.
A reprint; not seen.

—— [*Clarsach a' Ghlinne.*] Glasgow, 1936.
Alex. MacLaren & Son, Gaelic Printers and Publishers, 268 Argyle Street, Glasgow, C.2. First published 1925. Reprinted 1927 and 1936.
36 p. 270 mm. PC.
   In paper and cloth binding.

Glasgow Gaelic Society. See Gaelic Society of Glasgow.

Glasgow Highland Mission. See MacColl, Duncan. [*Laoidhean Soisgeulach.*]

Glasgow Skye Association. [*Eilean a' Cheo.*] Glasgow, 1921.
Eilean a' Cheò. Glasgow Skye Association. Souvenir Book of the Jubilee Gathering, St. Andrew's Halls, Glasgow, Friday, 2nd December 1921. Published by Glasgow Skye Association. Printed by Archibald Sinclair, "Celtic Press", Waterloo Street, Glasgow.
144 p; illus. 220 mm. PC.
   Contains one Gaelic article, "Seanna Chleachdaidhean an Eilein" by Colin Mac-Pherson. Foreword by John A. Nicolson.

Glasgow Skye Association. [*The Skye: One Hundred Years.*] Glasgow, [1965].
The Skye: One Hundred Years, 1865–1965.
84 p; illus. 220 mm. PC.
   Contains one Gaelic article, "Sgeul nam Bàrd" by John A. MacDonald. Printed by Tweeddale Press, Hawick.

Glasgow University. See Leabhraichean ura Gaidhlig Oilthigh Ghlascho.
[For cross references to individual titles in the series.]

Glasgow University Ossianic Society. See Ossian.

[*God Save the King*.] N.P., n.d.
    L. M. Doxology . . . "Gu'm bu fada beò an rìgh".
    1 p. 130 mm. PC.
        A card.

[*God Save the King*.] N.p., n.d.
    Laoidh na Rìoghachd. The National Anthem . . . Ead. le K. W. G.
    1 p. 200 mm. PC.
        Translation by Katherine Whyte Grant.

[*God Save the King*.] Edinburgh, 1911.
    Laoidh na Rìoghachd. The National Anthem, with music. Translated into Gaelic by
    the Rev. D. MacKintosh, M.A., St. Kentigern's, Lanark. As accepted by his late
    Majesty King Edward VII. Second edition. Edinburgh: John Grant, 31 George IV
    Bridge. 1911. Price 2d.
    [3] p. 220 mm. PC.
        Music in staff and sol-fa. 1st ed. not seen. English original first published 1742.

Grannd, Padruig. See Grant, Peter.

Grant, Donald, 1903–70. [*Tir an Aigh*.] Glasgow, 1971.
    Tìr an Aigh. Taghadh de na sgrìobhaidhean aig Dòmhnall Grannd. Gairm, Glaschu
    1971.
    Clò-bhualaidhean Gairm, Leabhar 29.
    243 p, plate. 210 mm.
        Foreword by John A. MacDonald, editor; tribute to Donald Grant by T. M.
    Murchison. In paperback and hardback.

—— (joint ed.). See Cainnt agus Facail Iomchuidh air son Coinnimh.

—— (tr.). See:
    Andersen, Hans Christian. [*The Snow Queen*.]
    Andersen, Hans Christian. [*Thumbelina*.]
    Bideau, Georges. [*The Dog with Bootees*.]
    Bideau, Georges. [*Robin Redbreast and His Friends*.]
    Croga an Oir.
    Grimm, Jacob & Wilhelm. [*Rosewhite and Rosered*.]
    Tir nam Blath.
    Tir na Meala.
    Tir nan Og.
    Tir nan Seud.

Grant, Katherine Whyte, 1845–. [*Aig Tigh na Beinne*.] Oban, 1911.
    Aig Tigh na Beinne. Le K. W. G. Oban: Hugh MacDonald, Bookseller, Esplanade.
    Glasgow: Alex. McLaren & Son, 360 and 362 Argyle St. 1911.
    283 p. 190 mm. AU, EU, GU, Mit., NLS.
        Printed by *The Oban Times*. Stories and reminiscences.

—— [*Dusgadh na Feinne*.] Paisley, 1908.
    Dùsgadh na Féinne. Dealbh-chluich air son na cloinne. Le K. W. G. J. and R.
    Parlane, Paisley. John Menzies and Co., Edinburgh and Glasgow. Madgwich,
    Houlston and Co., Ltd., London. 1908.
    16 p. 220 mm. PC.
        A musical playlet. A proposal to publish a revised ed. was advertised by Alex.
    MacLaren & Son in 1927; *MacLaren* states that this was in manuscript in 1945 and
    that it was their intention to publish it.

—— [*An Fheadag.*] [1913?].
"Translation of 'The Whistle'."
Not seen. Information from Lachlan MacBean's "Celtic Who's Who" (Kirkcaldy, 1921). The translation was published in *An Gaidheal* in 1963, from a manuscript presented to Mrs. Morag Edgar by Katherine Whyte Grant.

—— [*An Sgoil Bheag agus a' Mhaighdean-mhara.*] [1910?].
"An Sgoil Bheag agus a' Mhaighdean-mhara. Cluich airson clann-sgoile. Le K. W. G."
Not seen. Referred to in 1927 edition. The play was first published in *An Sgeulaiche*, Spring, 1910 (pp 79–89). The above possibly refers to an offprint.

—— [*An Sgoil Bheag agus a' Mhaighdean-mhara.*] Glasgow, 1927.
An Sgoil Bheag agus a' Mhaighdean-mhara. Cluich airson na clann-sgoile. Le Catriona Nic Ghille-bhàin Ghrannd (K. W. G.). Glascho: Alasdair Maclabhruinn 's a Mhic, 360–362 Sràid Earraghaidheal, C.2. 6d net.
First printed in *An Sgeulaiche*, 1910. Second edition, 1910. Third edition, 1927.
10 p. 190 mm. EPL, Mit., NLS.

—— (tr.). See [God Save the King].

Grant, Peter, 1783–1867. [*Dain Spioradail.*] Edinburgh, 1904.
Dàin Spioradail le Pàdruig Grannd, an Strathspey, Sgìreachd Aberneich. [Quotation.] Twentieth Edition. Edinburgh: John Grant, 31 George IV Bridge. 1904.
160 p. 140 mm. Mit.
Grant's poems were first published in 1818. The 1926 ed. refers to the above as the 19th ed. and dates it 1903, as does T S-G.

—— [*Dain Spioradail.*] Edinburgh, 1912.
Twentieth Edition. Edinburgh: John Grant, 31 George IV Bridge. 1912.
160 p, plate. 170 mm. AU, GU:CL.

—— [*Dain Spioradail.*] Glasgow, 1926.
Dàin Spioradail le Pàdruig Grannd, an Strath Spé, Sgìreachd Aberneich. Fo làimh Eachainn Mhic Dhùghaill. [Quotation.] Glascho: Alasdair Mac Labhruinn 's a Mhic, 360–362 Sràid Earraghaidheal.
Spiritual Songs by Rev. Peter Grant, Strathspey. Edited by Hector MacDougall.
Biographical sketch of the Author by Annie Grant Robinson and J. A. Grant Robinson.
Glasgow: Alexander Maclaren & Sons, 360-362 Argyle Street, C.2.
New large type edition, revised and corrected, 1926.
167 p, plate. 200 mm. BM, GU:CL, Mit.
A "23rd ed." was advertised, but no trace has been found of it or of a 22nd.

Graves, Alfred P., 1846–1931. [*The Celtic Song Book.*] [London], 1928.
The Celtic Song Book. Being representative folk songs of the six Celtic nations. Chosen by Alfred Preceval Graves, Litt.D., F.R.S.L., author of "The Irish Song Book", "The Irish Fairy Book", "Irish Doric", etc. 1928. Ernest Benn Limited.
[4], 332 p. 220 mm. BM, GU, Mit., NLS.
Contains [123]–135 p Scottish Gaelic songs with English translations by Francis Tolmie and Kenneth MacLeod, from whose collections the songs were drawn. Staff.

Greene, David, 1915– (joint ed.). See Carney, James. [*Celtic Studies.*]

Gregory, Lady Isabella Augusta, 1852–1932. [*The Rising of the Moon.*] Glasgow, 1950.
Dealbh-chluichean an Gàidhlig. An t-Airgiod-Cinn. Dealbh-chluich an aon sealladh. Gaelic translation of the one-act play, "The Rising of the Moon', by Lady Gregory. Air eadar-theangachadh le Lachlann MacFhionghuin. An Comunn Gaidhealach, 131 West Regent Street, Glasgow. 1950.
13 p. 190 mm.
English original first published in *Samhain*, December 1904; first performed 1907.

Griasaiche Bhearnaraidh.   See MacLeod, Allan, of Bernera. [*Griasaiche Bhearnaraidh.*]

Grieve, Norman. See Campbell, G. Murray. [*Edward VII, King of Scots.*]

Grimm, Jacob, 1785–1863 & Wilhelm, 1786–1859. [*Rosewhite and Rosered.*], Glasgow, n.d.
Leabhraichean a' Chomuinn. Ròsbhan is Ròsdhonn. Air innse le Grimm. Air a chur an Gàidhlig le Domhnall Grannd. [Illus.] Dealbhan le Françoise J. Bertier. Clò-bhuailte le Bias am Paris mar a dh'iarr An Comunn Gaidhealach.
[24] p; col. illus. 190 mm.
    1967. An elementary school-book; illus. Translated from French.

—— [*The Three Bears.*] Glasgow, n.d.
Leabhraichean A' Chomuinn. Na Trì Mathain. Le Grimm. Am Frangais le Claire Audrix. [Illus.] Dealbhan le Pierre Leroy. Clo-bhuailte le Bias am Paris mar a dh'iarr An Comunn Gaidhealach.
[24] p; col. illus. 190 mm.
    1969. An elementary school reader, translated from French by Donald Grant.

Guth na Bliadhna. [P. varies], 1904–25.
Guth na Bliadhna. The Voice of the Year. Leabhar 1. An Geamhradh. Aireamh 1. Clàr-amais . . . James Thin, 54 and 5 South Bridge, Edinburgh. [1904.]
    . . . Leabhar 1. An t-Earrach, 1904. Aireamh 2. Clàr-amais . . . The Aberdeen University Press, Limited. Published quarterly.
    The English title is dropped and "Published quarterly" replaced by "Air a chur a mach uair san ràidhe" from Vol. IV.
    . . . Leabhar V. An t-Earrach, 1908. Aireamh 2. Clàr-amais . . . Milne, Tannahill & Methven, The Mills, Horse Cross, Perth. [List of Principal Agents, which varies in detail thereafter.] Air a chur a mach uair san ràidhe.
Guth na Bliadhna. Leabhar XII. An-t-Earrach, 1915. Aireamh 1. Clàr-amais . . . Glaschu: Alasdair Mac Labhruinn is a Mhic, 360 Sràid Earraghaidheal.
    . . . Guth na Bliadhna. Ràidheachan a tha coisrighte do shaorsa na h-Albann, agus do na h-uile ceist a tha an crochadh ris a' chuspair sin. Leabhar XIII. An t-Earrach 1916. Aireamh 1. Clàr-amais . . . Glaschu: Alasdair Mac Labhruinn is a Mhic, 360 Sràid Earraghaidheal.
Leabhar XVI. Aireamh 3. Am Foghar, 1919. Tasdan agus sè sgillinn. Guth na Bliadhna. Ràitheachan a tha coisrigte do shaorsa na h-Albann, agus do na h·uile ceist eile a tha an crochadh ris a' chuspair sin. Giorra-bhrìghe . . . Seòladh an fhir-dhea-sachaidh: 12–14 Sràid a' Mhuilinn, Baile Pheirt, Albainn. Càin-leughaidh: aon bhliadhna, 6/– no $1.50 cents, saor leis a' phost. Foillsichearan: Alasdair MacLabhrainn is a Mhic, 360 Sràid Earraghaidheal, Glascho. Albainn Nodha: luchd-riarachaidh – The MacDonald Music Store, Antigonish.
Guth na Bliadhna. Uimhir 67. An t-Earrach 1921. Glaschu: Alasdair Mac Labh-rainn agus a Mhic, 360 Sràid Earraghaidheal. Càin-leughaidh Bhliadhnail, 6/– no 1 dollar 50 cents, saor leis a' phost.
    This style of title page was retained until No. 70, Winter 1921, after which there was a lapse in the publication of *Guth na Bliadhna* until 1923 [see immediately below].
Leabhar XIX. Uimhir 1. Clò-bhualadh ùr. Tasdan is sè sgillin. Guth na Bliadhna. An Geamhradh 1923. [Contents.] Glaschu: Alasdair Mac Leabhrainn agus a Mhic, 360 Sràid Earraghaidheal.
Leabhar XX. Uimhir 2. . . . An t-Earrach 1925 . . . [last no.].
    [Frequency] Quarterly. Lapse in publication between Spring 1921 and Winter 1923.
    [Collation] *c.* 100 p per quarterly no., 1904–11; *c.* 120 p, 1912–15; *c.* 100 p, 1916–21; 28 p, 1923–25. 220 mm, 1904–21; 310 mm, 1923–25.
    [Locations] Mit.
    [Editor] The Hon. Roderick Erskine of Mar.

[Contents] Approx. half in Gaelic at beginning; the amount of Gaelic increases; all-Gaelic from 1919. Contains current affairs articles, literary criticism, stories, poems and plays.

Guth na Bliadhna. See Leabhraichean na Ceilidh. [Numbered series of offprints, chiefly from *Guth na Bliadhna* and *An Sgeulaiche.*]

Guthrie, William, 1620–1665. [*The Christian's Great Gain.*] Glasgow, 1924.
Buannachd Mhor a' Chriosduidh le Uilleam Guthrie (1620–65). Glascho: Alasdair Mac Labhruinn 's a Mhic, 360–362 Sràid Earraghaidheal, C.2. 1924.
8 p. 120 mm. FC, PC.
A catechism.

—— [*The Christian's Great Interest.*] Edinburgh, 1912.
The Christian's Great Interest, in two parts, by William Guthrie, minister of the Gospel. [Quotation.] Edinburgh: John Grant, 31 George IV Bridge. 1912.
Còir Mhór a' Chriosdaidh, ann an dà earrainn, le Uilleam Guthrie, ministear an t-Soisgeil. [Quotation.] Edinburgh: John Grant, 31 George IV Bridge. 1912.
viii, 258 p. 170 mm.
1st ed. 1783; the above is a reprint of the 1845 ed. English original first published 1763.

Hall, [Christopher] Newman, 1816–1902. [*Come to Jesus.*] Stirling, n.d.
Thig gu Iosa. Le Numan Hall, LL.B., D.D. Eadar-theangaichte leis an Urr. I. D. MacNeill, Chaladair. Drummond's Tract Depot, Stirling. Price One Penny.
63 p. 140 mm. FC.
Published *c.* 1900 [poss. 1895]. Gaelic translation by Angus Macintyre published 1883. English original first published 1848.

Hardy, Thomas, 1840–1928. [*The Three Strangers.*] Edinburgh, 1944.
An Triùir Choigreach. Le Tomas Hardy. Air a thionndadh gu Gàidhlig na h-Alba le Eòin G. MacFhionghuin (a bha roimhe 'na fhear-deasachaidh Mac Talla). Fo laimh Iain Latharna Caimbeul. Chaidh an leabhar so a chlò-bhualadh ann an Albainn le T. agus A. Constable agus an Cuideachd, ann an Dun Eideann, gu feum an fhir-deasachaidh, anns a' bhliadhna 1944. Tha an leabhar so air a chur amach 'sa Ghàidhlig le cead Churtis Brown agus an Cuideachd.
The Three Strangers. By Thomas Hardy. Scottish Gaelic translation by J. G. MacKinnon (formerly editor and publisher of the Gaelic weekly, *Mac Talla*). Prepared for publication in Scotland by John Lorne Campbell. Printed by T. & A. Constable Ltd., Edinburgh, 1944. Gaelic translation published by permission of Messrs. Curtis Brown Ltd., London.
First printed 1944.
31 p. 220 mm. Mit., PC.
English original first published 1883.

Harp of Caledonia. Glasgow, n.d.
The Harp of Caledonia. A collection of popular Gaelic songs. Clàrsach na h-Alba: no, Orana Taghta Gaidhealach. [Quotation.] Glasgow: Archibald Sinclair, Celtic Press, 47 Waterloo Street.
63 p, [1] "An Clàr". 130 mm. Mit., PC.
1st ed. pre-1876; *MacLaren* describes the Sinclair ed. as later than 1908. Contains no music.

Hately, Thomas L., 1815–67. [*Seann Fhuinn na Salm.*] Glasgow, 1931.
Seann Fhuinn na Salm mar a tha iad air an seinn anns a' Ghaeltachd mu thuath; or, the old Gaelic psalm tunes as sung in the congregations of the Free Church of Scotland in the North Highlands. Taken down by T. L. Hately, precentor to the General

Assembly of the Free Church of Scotland. Glasgow: Alex. MacLaren & Sons, 360–362 Argyle St., C.2. Reprinted 1931.
[2], 21 p. 210 mm. Mit.
  1st ed. 1845 (14 p). Contains six tunes; two versions of "Stilt" and "French". Staff notation, pp 3–10; sol-fa, pp 11–21.

—— [*Seann Fhuinn nan Salm.*] See also:
Free Church of Scotland. [*Fhuinn nan Salm Ghaidhlig.*]
Whitehead, F. W. [*The Six Long Gaelic Psalm Tunes.*]

Havenhand, I. & J. [*The Life-boat.*] Inverness, 1974.
Am Bàta-Teasairginn. Le I. & J. Havenhand. Na dealbhan le John Berry. Air eadar-theangachadh le Fionnlagh MacNèill. Foillsichearan: An Comunn Gaidhealach, Inbhirnis. © Ladybird Books Ltd., Loughborough. Air a chlò-bhualadh an Sasunn, 1974.
Leabhar-leughaidh Ladybird Sreath 606B.
51 p; col. illus. 180 mm.

Hay, George Campbell, 1915–. [*Fuaran Sleibh.*] Glasgow, [Fore. 1947].
Fuaran Sléibh. Rainn Ghàidhlig le Deòrsa Caimbeul Hay. Uilleam Mac Gill' Fhaolain, 240 Sràid an Dòchais, Glaschu, Alba.
66 p. 250 mm. AU, BM, GU, Mit.
  c. 1948. Contains English prose translations of the poems.

—— [*O Na Ceithir Airdean.*] Edinburgh, 1952.
O Na Ceithir Airdean. Le Deòrsa Caimbeul Hay. Oliver and Boyd: Tweedale Court, Edinburgh; 98 Great Russell Street, London, W.C.
First published 1952.
viii, 71 p. 230 mm. AU, BM, Mit.
  Contains English translations in prose and translations into Gaelic from other languages. Printed The Central Press, Aberdeen.

—— (joint author). See MacLean, Sorley. [*Four Points of a Saltire.*]

Hay, James MacDonald. See MacGaraidh, Seumas.

Henderson, Angus, 1866–1937. [*Achd an Fhearainn.*] Glasgow, n d.
The Ceilidh Books. Leabhraichean nan Céilidh. Aireamh 43. Achd an Fhearainn. Le Aonghas Mac Eanruig. [Illus.] A' phrìs, trì sgillinnean. Alasdair Mac Labhruinn agus a Mhic, 360–2 Sràid Earraghaidheal, Glascho.
[113]–150 p. 210 mm. PC.
  Reprinted from *Guth na Bliadhna*, IX.2, Spring 1912.

—— [*Aicheamhail Eagalach.*] Glasgow, n.d.
The Ceilidh Books. Leabhraichean nan Céilidh. Aireamh 19. Aicheamhail Eagalach, no, Mar a dh'éirich do mhurtairean na Ceapaich. Le Aonghas Mac Eanruig. [Illus.] A' phrìs, trì sgillinnean. 3d. Alasdair Mac Labhruinn agus a Mhic, 360–2 Sràid Earraghaidheal, Glascho.
[401]–432. 210 mm. PC.
  Reprinted from *An Sgeulaiche*, I.5, January 1910.

—— [*Ceard is Cainnt.*] Glasgow, n.d.
The Ceilidh Books. Leabhraichean nan Céilidh. Aireamh 33. Siubhal air Falbh Impireachd. Ceàrd is Cainnt, le Aonghas Mac Eanruig. [Illus.] A' phrìs, trì sgillinnean. 3d. Alasdair Mac Labhruinn agus a Mhic, 360–2 Sràid Earraghaidheal, Glascho.
[251]–300 p. 220 mm. PC.
  Reprinted from *An Sgeulaiche*, X.3, Summer 1913.

—— [*Ceist nan Taighean.*] Glasgow, n.d.
The Ceilidh Books. Leabhraichean nan Céilidh. Aireamh 41. Ceist nan Taighean.
Le Aonghas Mac Eanruig. [Illus.] A' phrìs, trì sgillinnean. 3d. Alasdair Mac
Labhruinn agus a Mhic, 360–2 Sràid Earraghaidheal, Glascho.
[269]–286 p [also a version, [269]–310 p]. 220 mm.
From *Guth na Bliadhna*, XI.3, Autumn 1914.

—— [*Cogadh no Sìth.*] Glasgow, n.d.
The Ceilidh Books. Leabhraichean nan Céilidh. Aireamh 46. Cogadh no Sìth. Le
Aonghas Mac Eanruig. [Illus.] A' phrìs, trì sgillinnean. 3d. Alasdair Mac Labhruinn
agus a Mhic, 360–2 Sràid Earraghaidheal, Glascho.
[389]–404 p. 220 mm. PC.
Reprinted from *Guth na Bliadhna*, IX.4, Autumn 1912.

—— [*Am Fearann agus Cisean.*] Glasgow, 1911.
Am fearann agus cìsean. Le A. M. E. (Air ath-chlòdh bho "Ghuth na Bliadhna".)
The Taxation of Land Values. (Reprinted from *Guth na Bliadhna*.) Price One Penny.
Published for the United Committee for the Taxation of Land Values, Broad Sanctuary
Chambers, 20 Tothill Street, Westminster, by "Land Values" Publication Department,
67 West Nile Street, Glasgow, and 376–7 Strand, London, W.C. 1911.
22 p. 220 mm. FC.
Appeared in *Guth na Bliadhna*, VIII.1, Winter 1911.

—— [*Mar a Fhuair Mac-Bheatha 'na Righ.*] Glasgow, n.d.
The Ceilidh Books. Leabhraichean nan Céilidh. Aireamh 17. Mar a fhuair Mac-
Bheatha 'na Rìgh. Le Aonghas Mac Eanruig. [Illus.] A' phrìs, trì sgillinnean. 3d.
Alasdair Mac Labhruinn agus a Mhic, 360–2 Sràid Earraghaidheal, Glascho.
[223]–246 p. 210 mm. PC.
Reprinted from *An Sgeulaiche*, II.3, Autumn 1910.

—— [*Mar Gu'n Eireadh Neach o na Mairbh.*] Glasgow, n.d.
The Ceilidh Books. Leabhraichean nan Céilidh. Aireamh 25. Mar gu'n éireadh neach
o na mairbh. Le Aonghas Mac Eanruig. [Illus.] A' phrìs, trì sgillinnean. 3d. Alasdair
Mac Labhruinn agus a Mhic, 360–2 Sràid Earraghaidheal, Glascho.
[59]–101 p. 220 mm. PC.
Reprinted from *An Sgeulaiche*, I.1, September 1909.

—— [*Sgoiltean agus Oilean.*] Glasgow, n.d.
The Ceilidh Books. Leabhraichean nan Céilidh. Aireamh 42. Sgoiltean agus Oilean.
Le Aonghas Mac Eanruig. Cor, Còir agus Coirich. Le Aonghas Mac Dhonnachaidh.
[Illus.] A' phrìs, trì sgillinnean. 3d. Alasdair Mac Labhruinn agus a Mhic, 360–2
Sràid Earraghaidheal, Glascho.
[250]–276 p. 220 mm. PC.
Reprinted from *Guth na Bliadhna*, IX.3, Summer 1912.

—— [*Spealgadh nan Glasan.*] Glasgow, n.d.
The Ceilidh Books. Leabhraichean nan Céilidh. Aireamh 44. Ceist nan Ceistean.
Spealgadh nan Glasan, le Aonghas Mac Eanruig. [Illus.] A' phrìs, trì sgillinnean. 3d.
Alasdair Mac Labhruinn agus a Mhic, 360–2 Sràid Earraghaidheal, Glascho.
[393]–424 p. 220 mm. PC.
Reprinted from *Guth na Bliadhna*, X.4, Autumn 1913.

—— (ed.). See Alba [Newspaper].

—— (joint author). See An Solaraiche.

Henderson, George, 1866–1912. [*The Gaelic Dialects.*] N.p., n.d.
The Gaelic Dialects. George Henderson, Manse of Edderachillis, Scourie, Sutherland.
123 p. 230 mm. Mit., PC.
Reprint from *Zeitschrift für celtische Philologie*, IV & V, Halle an S. 1903 & 1905.

—— (ed.). See Campbell, John F. [*The Celtic Dragon Myth.*]

—— (ed.). See MacLeod, Dr. Norman, Minister of St. Columba's Church, Glasgow. [*The Highlanders' Friend: Second Series.*]

Highland Association. See Comunn Gaidhealach.

Highland Village Association. [*Leabhar a' Chlachain.*] Glasgow, 1911.
Leabhar a' Chlachain. Home Life of the Highlanders, 1400–1746. Printed for the Highland Village Association, Limited, Scottish Exhibition of National History, Art and Industry, Kelvingrove, Glasgow, by Robert Maclehose & Co., Limited, at the University Press, Glasgow. 1911.
viii, 148 p. 220 mm. EU:CL.
Edited by David W. MacKay. In Gaelic, "An Clachan a bh'ann" by Kenneth MacLeod, pp 135–45.

Highland Village Association. [*Souvenir: An Clachan.*] [Glasgow, 1911.]
Souvenir: an Clachan (the Highland Village). [Illus.] Printed by Wm. Ritchie & Sons, Ltd., Edinburgh, for A. MacLaren & Son, The Clachan.
[12 plates.] 111 mm. PC.
12 loosely bound photos with captions in Gaelic and English.

Highland Witness. See An Fhianuis Ghaidhealach.

Highlands and Islands of Scotland. See National Book League.

Hodge, Archibald, 1823–86. [*The Atonement.*] Edinburgh, [Intro. 1916].
Cogadh mór na h-Eòrpa. An Reite. Hodge. [Illus.] Printed by Oliver and Boyd, Edinburgh, for The Church of Scotland, The United Free Church of Scotland, and The Free Church of Scotland.
xii, 99 p. 140 mm. NLS.
Introduction dated 1916. One of a series of religious booklets issued to soldiers in World War I. English original first published 1867 (parts published in *Presbyterian Banner*, 1866–7).

Hogan, Edmund, 1831–1917. [*Luibhleabhran.*] Dublin, 1900.
Luibleabran: Irish and Scottish Gaelic Names of herbs, plants, trees, etc. By F. Edmund Hogan, S.J., F.R.U.I., D.Litt.; John Hogan, B.A.; John C. Mac erleam, S.J. Dochum Gloire De agus Onóra na hEireann. Dublin: M. H. Gill and Son, O' Connel Street. David Nutt, 57–59 Longacre, London. Oliver and Boyd, Edinburgh. 1900. (All rights reserved.)
xii, 137 p. 190 mm. AU, BM, GU:CL, CoS.

Holmer, Nils M., 1904–. [*The Gaelic of Arran.*] Dublin, 1957.
The Gaelic of Arran. By Nils M. Holmer. Dublin: The Dublin Institute for Advanced Studies, 64–5 Merrion Square. 1957.
viii, 211 p. 230 mm. GU.
Printed Thom, Dublin.

—— [*The Gaelic of Kintyre.*] Dublin, 1962.
The Gaelic of Kintyre. By Nils M. Holmer. Dublin: The Dublin Institute for Advanced Studies, 64–5 Merrion Square. 1962.
[6], 160 p. 230 mm. GU.
Printed Thom, Dublin.

—— [*Studies on Argyllshire Gaelic.*] Uppsala, 1938.
Skrifter utgivna av K. Humanisticka Vetenskaps-Samfundet i Uppsala, 31:1. Studies on Argyllshire Gaelic, by Nils M. Holmer. [Illus.] Uppsala: Almqvist & Wiksells Boktrycheri-A.-B. Leipzig: Otto Harrassowitz. Uppsala 1938.
231 p. 240 mm. BM, GU.

Holy Spirit Association. [*Ath-Bheothachadh.*] Thornton Heath, Surrey, n.d.
[Cover] Tha ath-bheothachadh mór bho Chorea air tighinn do'n bhaile.
[Back cover] . . . Air fhoillseachadh le Co-Chomunn an Spioraid Naoimh airson Aonadh Criosdachd an t-Saoghail, 28 Liverpool Road, Thornton Heath, Surrey.
Tel.: 01-653 8508.
6 p. 300 mm.
    1972. Published by the Holy Spirit Association for the Unification of World Christianity. Translated by Hamish Robertson.

Homer. [*Iliad.*] See MacLachlan, Ewen. [*Gaelic Verse.*]

Horan, Ellamay. See Catholic Church. *Catechism.* [First Communion Catechism.]

Hosking, Clement. [*Fine Song for Singing.*] Sydney, n.d.
Fine Song for Singing. A Celtic Oddyssey. By Clement Hosking.
Illustrated by Edith Lanser. Sydney: G. M. Dash.
230 p, plate; map [on lining papers]; illus. 190 mm.
    1950.

Hymnaries. See:
Church of Scotland. *Liturgy and Ritual.* [Laoidheadair Gaidhlig.]
MacBean, Lachlan. [*The Songs and Hymns of the Gael.*]
[*St Columba Church Hymnary.*]

Iain (pseud.). See Whyte, John.

Iain Beag Fhionnlaigh. See Smith, John.

Iain Mac Fhearchair. See MacCodrum, John.

Iain Og Ile (pseud.). See Campbell, John F.

Iasgair, An t-. Glasgow, 1969.
An t-Iasgair. Le còmhlan de luchd-teagaisg a thainig cruinn aig Cruinneachadh an Luchd-teagaisg Ghàidhlig an Inbhirnis, 1968. Dealbhan le Cailean Spencer. Gairm, Glaschu. 1969.
An t-Iasgair. Sreath na Sgoile (air fhoillseachadh an co-bhoinn ri Coimitidh nan Leabhraichean-sgoile), Leabhar 4. Clo-bhualaidhean Gairm, Leabhar 13.
[12] p. 210 mm.

Interlinear Gaelic Reader. See MacLaren's Interlinear Gaelic Reader.

Inverness Gaelic Society. See Gaelic Society of Inverness.

Inverness Royal Academy. See School Magazines.

Irisleabhar Ceilteach. Toronto, 1952–4.
Irisleabhar Ceilteach. Fir Deasachaidh/Eagarthoirí – Iain MacAoidh, 343 Belsize Drive, Toronto 12; Pádraig O Broin, 52 Derwyn Road, Toronto 6; Iain MacGhille-Mhaoil. Alba – Breiz – Cymru – Eire – Ellan Vannin – Kernow. I.1. Deire Fómhair – An Dàmhar 1952.
    Iain MacGhilleMhaoil dropped from list of editors after I.3; Ioan Ap Siencyn added, II.3. Minor changes in title page for virtually every issue.
Brezounek Cymraeg Kernewek Gaeilge Gàidhlig Gailck. Irisleabhar Ceilteach (Y Goelcert). Iain M. MacAoidh; Padraig O Broin; Ioan Prys Ap Siencyn: 343 Belsize Drive, Toronto 12, Canada. Guthan: HU.9-0535. Ráitheachán – luach bliadhnail (táille bhliana) $2.00. Iml. II, uimh. 4. Foghmhar, 1954. [Last seen.]
    [Frequency] Quarterly.
    [Collation] 112 p in Vol. I; 96 p in Vol. II. 220 mm.
    [Locations] BM, NLS.
    [Contents] A Pan-Celtic magazine, of miscellaneous content.

Iul A' Chriostaidh. See Catholic Church. *Liturgy and ritual.* [Iul A' Chriostaidh.]

Jackson, Kenneth H., 1909–. [*The Gaelic Notes in the Book of Deer.*] Cambridge, 1972.
The Osborn Bergin Memorial Lecture 1970. The Gaelic Notes in the Book of Deer.
Kenneth Jackson, Professor of Celtic in the University of Edinburgh. Cambridge: at
the University Press. 1972.
> xv, 164 p. 220 mm.
>> Introduction, pp 1–16; Texts and Translation, pp 17–36; Notes on the Texts,
>> pp 37–84; Historical Commentary, pp 85–124; Orthography and Language,
>> pp 125–52; Glossarial Index, pp 153–62; Index of Names, pp 163–4.

Jackson, Kenneth H. (joint ed.). See Campbell, John F. [*More West Highland Tales.*]
Volume Two.

John, Evan, 1901–. [*Strangers' Gold.*] Glasgow, n.d.
Or Choigreach. Dealbh-chluich an aon sealladh. Gaelic translation of the one-act play,
"Strangers' Gold", by Evan John. Air eadar-theangachadh le Lachlann Mac Fhionghuin. Glasgow: Brown, Son & Ferguson, Ltd., Publishers, 52–58 Darnley Street.
23 p. 190 mm.
> English original first published 1936. "Evan John" is the pseudonym of Evan John
> Simpson.

Johnson, Dr. Samuel, 1704–84. See Do'n Olla Shasgunnach.

Johnston, Annie (tr.). See Bartlett, Samuel. [*Braid Air a' Bhraid.*]

——— (joint comp.) See Campbell, John L. [*Gaelic Folksongs from the Isle of Barra.*]

Johnston, Duncan. [*Ceist nan Ceist.*] See Ceithir Comhraidhean.

Johnston, Duncan, 1881–1947. [*Cronan nan Tonn.*] Glasgow, 1938.
Crònan nan Tonn. Le Donnachadh Mac Iain. (The Croon of the Sea.) By Duncan
Johnston. With Foreword by Dr. Archd. N. Currie, M.A., M.B., Ch.B., D.Sc.,
Medical Inspector of Factories for Scotland. Glasgow: Archd. Sinclair, Celtic Press,
27a Cadogan Street. 1938.
64 p. 260 mm. Mit.
> Music in staff notation; piano accompaniment. English translations.

Journal of the Folk-Song Society, No. 16. London, 1911.
Journal of the Folk-Song Society. No. 16. Being the Third Part of Vol. IV. All
versions of songs and words published in this Journal are the copyright of the contributor supplying them, and are printed in this Journal on behalf of that contributor,
whose permission must be obtained for any reproduction thereof. London: 19 Berners
Street, W. Printed privately for the members of the Society by Robert Maclehose & Co.
Ltd., at the University Press, Glasgow. December, 1911.
xiv, 143–278, ix p. 210 mm. AU, BM, FC, PC.
> Contains: [143]–149 p "Notes and Reminiscences by Francis Tolmie"; [150]–156 p
> "Notes on the Modal System of Gaelic Tunes by Annie G. Gilchrist" and "Notes
> on the Gaelic Scale System, by Lucy E. Broadwood"; [157]–276 p of Gaelic Folk
> Songs edited by Francis Tolmie; Index of titles. Contains some English translations;
> music in staff notation. The songs are divided into six sections: Songs of Rest and
> Recreation; Songs of Labour; Ancient Heroic Lays; Songs to Chiefs and others;
> Laments; Love Lyrics, etc. Vol. IV published, as bound volume, 1914.

K.W.G. See Grant, Katherine W.

[*Kelp Industry.*] Oban, 1914.
The Kelp Industry. Reprint of two articles on the Industry from "The Oban Times",
the first appearing on 25th November 1914, with Gaelic translation thereof.
Obair a' Chelp. An gabh i cur air bonn diongmhalta?
4 p [English], 3 p [Gaelic]. 260 mm. GU:CL.
> The two are stapled together.

Kennedy, Dr. John, 1819–84. [*Searmon agus Oraid.*] Edinburgh, n.d.
Cogadh mór na h-Eòrpa. Searmon agus Oraid. An Dr. Ceanaideach. [Illus.] Printed by Oliver and Boyd, Edinburgh, for The Church of Scotland, The United Free Church of Scotland, and The Free Church of Scotland.
56 p. 140 mm. NLS.
    One of a series especially published for distribution to soldiers in the First World War.

Kennedy-Fraser, Marjory, 1857–1930. (joint ed.) [*Four Hebridean Love Lilts.*] London, n.d.
Low Voice. Medium Voice. High Voice. Four Hebridean Love Lilts. Collected and arranged by Marjory Kennedy-Fraser and Kenneth Macleod. Price 3/6 net. Boosey & Co.: 295 Regent Street, London, W.; 9 East 17th Street, New York; and 229 Yonge Street, Toronto. These songs may be sung in public without fee or licence. The public performance of any parodied version, however, is strictly prohibited. Copyright by Boosey & Co.
[4], 19 p, [1] "Appreciation" [4]. 310 mm. Mit.
    With English verse translations. Staff notation; piano accompaniment.
    Mitchell Library copy acquired 1922.

—— (joint ed.). [*From the Hebrides.*] Glasgow, [Intro. 1925].
From the Hebrides. Further Gleanings of Tale and Song. By M. Kennedy-Fraser and Kenneth Macleod. Paterson's Publications Ltd.: 52 Buchanan Street, Glasgow; 95 Wimpole Street, London.
xxiii, 131, [2] p, plate. 320 mm. AU, Mit.
    Introduction signed, "Marjorie Kennedy-Fraser, Edinburgh, 1st October 1925." Contains: Gaelic originals; English; verse translations; music in staff notation; piano accompaniment.

—— [*More Songs of the Hebrides.*] London, n.d.
More Songs of the Hebrides. Collected, edited, translated and arranged for voice and pianoforte by Marjory Kennedy-Fraser. Price 7/6 net. Boosey & Co., Ltd., 295 Regent Street, London, W.1., and Steinway Hall, 111–113, West 57th Street, New York. Copyright by Boosey & Co., Ltd. Printed in England.
viii, 55, [1] p, plate. Mit.
    With English translations. Music in staff notation; arranged for piano.

—— (joint ed.). [*Sea Tangle.*] London, [*c.* 1913].
Sea Tangle. Some more Songs of the Hebrides. Collected, edited, translated, and arranged for voice and pianoforte by Marjorie Kennedy-Fraser and Kenneth Macleod. Price 5/– net. Boosey & Co.: 295 Regent Street, London, W.; 9 East Seventh Street, New York. Copyright 1913 by Marjory Kennedy-Fraser.
44 p. 320 mm. AU.
    As above.

—— (joint ed.). [*Seven Songs of the Hebrides.*] London, n.d.
Seven Songs of the Hebrides by M. Kennedy-Fraser and Kenneth Macleod sung by Kenneth McKellar (on Decca LK. 4399). Birlinn of White Shoulders; An Eriskay Love Lilt; Heart of Fire Love; Sleeps the Noon in the Deep Blue Sky; Land of Heart's Desire; Peat Fire Flame; Bens of Jura. [Illus.] Boosey & Hawkes.
22 p. 310 mm. NLS.
    Music in Staff and Sol-fa.

—— (joint ed.). [*Songs of The Hebrides.*] First Volume. London, [*c.* 1909].
Songs of the Hebrides and Other Celtic Songs from the Highlands of Scotland. Some Collected and all arranged for voice and pianoforte by Marjory Kennedy-Fraser. Gaelic Editor – Kenneth Macleod. Price One Guinea. Boosey & Co.: 295 Regent Street, London, W.; and 9 East Seventeenth Street, New York. Copyright 1909 by Marjory Kennedy-Fraser.
[4], xxix, [5], 163 p. 320 mm. AU, GU, Mit.

—— (joint ed.). [*Songs of The Hebrides.*] First Volume. London, [*c.* 1922].
First Volume, Songs of the Hebrides. Collected and arranged for voice and pianoforte, with Gaelic and English words, by Marjory Kennedy-Fraser and Kenneth Macleod. Boosey & Co.: 295 Regent Street, London, W.; 9 East 17th Street, New York. Copyright 1909, by Marjory Kennedy-Fraser. New Edition, Copyright 1922 by Boosey & Co.
xxxviii, [2], 168 p; plate. Mit.
    Contains English verse translations. Music in staff notation; arranged for piano.

—— (joint ed.). [*Songs of The Hebrides.*] Second Volume. London, [*c.* 1917].
Second Volume, Songs of the Hebrides. Collected and arranged for voice and pianoforte, with Gaelic and English words, by Marjory Kennedy-Fraser and Kenneth Macleod. Boosey & Co.: 295 Regent Street, London, W.; and 9 East 17th Street, New York. Copyright 1917 by Boosey & Co.
[1], xx, 242, [1] p, 4 plates. 330 mm. GU, Mit.
    As above.

—— (joint ed.). [*Songs of The Hebrides.*] Third Volume. London, [*c.* 1921].
Third Volume, Songs of the Hebrides. Collected and arranged for voice and pianoforte, with Gaelic and English words, by Marjory Kennedy-Fraser and Kenneth Macleod. Boosey & Co.: 295 Regent Street, London, W.; 9 East 17th Street, New York; and 384 Yonge Street, Toronto. Copyright 1921 by Boosey & Co.
[1], xxiv, 185, [1] p; plate. 320 mm. Mit.
    As above. Most of the songs from the three volumes of "Songs of the Hebrides" were also sold separately.

—— (joint ed.). [*Songs of The Hebrides for Schools.*] London, n.d.
M. Kennedy-Fraser. Kenneth Macleod. Songs of the Hebrides for Schools. Vocal Score. Boosey & Hawkes.
21 p. 270 mm. PC.
    With English translations; music in staff notation; piano accompaniment.

—— [*Ten Selected Songs of The Hebrides.*] London, n.d.
Ten selected songs of the Hebrides (from Vols. I, II and III) for unison singing in schools. Arranged by M. Kennedy-Fraser. Edition with words and voice parts (in Old Notation and Tonic Sol-fa). Boosey & Hawkes, Ltd., 295 Regent Street, London, W.1. Printed in England.
23 p. 190 mm. PC.

—— (joint ed.). [*Twelve Selected Songs of the Hebrides.*] From Volume One. London, [Fore. 1914].
Twelve Selected Songs of the Hebrides, collected, edited, translated and arranged for voice and pianoforte by Marjory Kennedy-Fraser and Kenneth Macleod. Price 5/– net. Boosey & Co.: 295 Regent Street, London, W.; New York: 9 East 17th Street; and, Toronto: 229 Yonge Street. These songs may be sung in public without fee or licence. Copyright by Marjory Kennedy-Fraser.
[6], 50, [3] p; plate. 310 mm. Mit.
    The songs are from Volume I.

—— (joint ed.). [*Twelve Selected Songs of the Hebrides.*] From Volume Two. London, n.d.
From Volume Two. Twelve selected songs of the Hebrides. Collected, edited, translated and arranged for voice and pianoforte by Marjory Kennedy-Fraser and Kenneth Macleod. Price 7/6 net. Boosey & Co. Ltd. Sole Selling Agents: Boosey & Hawkes, Ltd., 295 Regent Street, London, W.1.; New York, Los Angeles, Sydney, Cape Town, Toronto, Paris. All rights reserved. Printed in England.
60 p. 310 mm. PC.

—— (joint ed.). [*Twelve Selected Songs of the Hebrides.*] From Volume Three. London, n.d.
From Volume Three . . . [as above].
60 p. 340 mm. PC.

Kerr, Judith. [*Mog The Forgetful Cat.*] Inverness, 1973.
Mog an cat diochuimhneach. An sgeulachd agus na dealbhan le Judith Kerr. Air a chur an Gàidhlig le A. M. MacDhòmhnuill. Club Leabhar. Inbhirnis.
c. Na dealbhan Judith Kerr 1970. *c.* Sgeulachd Club Leabhar 1973. Air fhoillseachadh agus clò-bhuailte ann am Beurla an 1970 le William Collins, Sons & Co. Ltd., London and Glasgow. An sgeulachd Ghàidhlig air fhoillseachadh an 1973 le Club Leabhar, Inbhirnis, IV1 2HJ.
[40] p; col. illus. 270 mm.

Knox's Liturgy. See Church of Scotland. *Liturgy and Ritual.* [Book of Common Order.]

La Bhruinn, Ailghinn. [*Machraichean Mora Chanada.*] Ottawa, 1907.
Machraichean Mora Chanada: Dorus Fosgailte do'n Ghaidheal. Aithris air mar a dh'àiticheadh Canada le sluagh na h-Alba; na cothroman a tha, an diugh, a' feitheamh air daoine na Gaidhealtachd a thig gu Canada-an-iar: air an cur fa chomhair an leugh-adair le Ailghinn La Bhruinn. [Quotation.] Air a chur am mach le ùghdarras Ard-Uachdaranachd Chanada, ann an Ottawa, 1907.
56 p; illus. 180 mm. PC.

La na Cloinne. See Nisbet, Jessie T. D. [*La na Cloinne.*]

Laing, Hugh, 1889–. [*Gu Tir mo Luaidh.*] Stornoway, [Pref. 1964].
Gu Tìr mo Luaidh (Dàin Eilthireach, Sgeulachdan agus Eachdraidh). Le Uisdean Laing.
Air a chlò-bhualadh agus air a chur a mach le: Paipear-Naigheachd Steòrnabhaigh, 10 Sràid Fhrangain, Steòrnabhagh, Eilean Leòdhuis.
71 p. 230 mm.
"Facal bho charaid" signed, "Ruaraidh MacThomais, Oilthigh Ghlaschu, 29:12:64".
Mostly Gaelic translations of poetry from other languages.

—— [*An Sealgair Naomh agus Dain Eile.*] Bernera, 1974.
An Sealgair Naomh agus Dàin Eile. Saor-eadartheangaichte le Uisdean Laing. Thug "An t-Eileanach" an leabhar seo am follais ann an 1974. Chaidh an leabhar ullachadh airson a' chlò le Ruairidh MacLeòid, agus bha e air a chlò-bhualadh le Cuideachd Sankey, Nelson, Lancs. Tha sinn fo fhiachan do Chomunn nan Leabhraichean Gàidhlig, a thug tiodhlac airgid seachad.
[2], 16 p. 210 mm.
Gaelic translation of: Sections I, II & V of "The Hound of Heaven" by Francis Thompson; poems by W. B. Yeats, Gerald Manley Hopkins, William Drummond, John Donne, George Herbert; 6 original poems.

Laithean Ceisde ann an Leodhas. Stornoway, n.d.
Làithean Ceisde ann an Leòdhas mu'n a' bhliadhna 1880. Published by Donald M. Campbell and printed by Stornoway Gazette Ltd., 10 Francis Street, Stornoway, Isle of Lewis.
48 p; illus. 220 mm. PC.
A recent publication. Introduction signed: "S.B., Dail o Dheas, Leodhas, Mios a' Mhàirt, 1881".

Lamont, Donald, 1874–1958. [*Prose Writings.*] Edinburgh, 1960.
Prose Writings of Donald Lamont (1874–1958). Edited by Thomas M. Murchison.

Published by Oliver & Boyd for the Scottish Gaelic Texts Society. Edinburgh. 1960.
Scottish Gaelic Texts. Volume Six.
xxxii, 212 p. 230 mm.
  Text, pp 1–170; Notes, pp 171–81; Vocabulary, pp 183–206; Index of Places, pp 207–12. Printed Cunningham, Alva.

—— (ed.). See Church of Scotland. [*Life and Work: Gaelic Supplement.*]

[Lang, Andrew.] See Whyte, Henry. [*Naidheachdan Firinneach.*] [Note.]

Laoide, Seosamh. See Lloyd, Joseph.

Laoidh-Dhiann Aithreachais. See MacFarlane-Barrow, James. [*Laoidh-Dhiann Aith-reachais.*]

Laoidheadair [Gaidhlig]. See Church of Scotland. *Liturgy and Ritual.* [Laoidheadair Gaidhlig.]

Laoidhean Gaidhlig. See Church of Scotland. *Liturgy and Ritual.* [Laoidhean Gaidhlig.]

Laoidh na Rioghachd. See [God Save the King.]

Leabhar a' Cheasnachaidh. See [Westminster Confession of Faith].

Leabhar a' Chlachain. See Highland Village Association. [*Leabhar a' Chlachain.*]

Leabhar Aideachaidh a' Chreidimh. See [Westminster Confession of Faith].

Leabhar Aithghearr nan Ceist. See [The Shorter Catechism].

Leabhar Cheist na Cloinne Bige. See Catholic Church. *Catechism.* [First Communion Catechism.]

Leabhar-Fhaclan nan Oran Gaidhlig a Sheinneadh 's a' Ghreis-Labhrais le Ruairidh MacLeoid. See MacLeod, Roderick, of Inverness. [*Leabhar-Fhaclan.*]

Leabhar Laoidhean Eaglais Chaluim Chille. See [St. Columba Church Hymnary].

Leabhar na Feinne. See Campbell, John F. [*Leabhar na Feinne.*]

Leabhar na h-Ard-Fheise. See Ceilidh nan Gaidheal. [*Leabhar na h-Ard-Fheise.*]

Leabhar Urnaigh. See Catholic Church. *Liturgy and Ritual.* [Christine Doctrine.]

Leabhraichean a' Chomuinn. [A series of school readers, translated from French.] See:
  Anderson, Hans Christian. [*The Snow Queen.*]
  Andersen, Hans Christian. [*Thumbelina.*]
  Bideau, Georges. [*The Dog with Bootees.*]
  Bideau, Georges. [*Robin Redbreast and His Friends.*]
  Grimm, Jacob and Wilhelm. [*Rosewhite and Rosered.*]

Leabhraichean Gaidhlig Oilthigh Obar-Dheadhan [fo stiùireadh Dhòmhnaill Mhic-Amhlaigh]. See:
  1. MacLeod, Finlay. [*Na Balaich air Ronaidh.*]

Leabhraichean Leughaidh. See MacKinnon, Lachlan. [*Leabhraichean Leughaidh.*]

Leabhraichean nan Ceilidh. See:
  Bhean Nighe, a'.
  Blar na Saorsa.
  Campbell, John F. [*Clann an Righ fo Gheasaibh.*]
  Campbell, John F. [*Fear a' Bhratain Uaine.*]
  Campbell, John F. [*Mogan Dearg Mac Iachair.*]
  Ceist nan Ceistean.
  Erskine, The Hon. Ruaraidh of Mar. [*Air Eachdraidh.*]

Henderson, Angus. [*Achd an Fhearainn.*]
Henderson, Angus. [*Aicheamhail Eagalach.*]
Henderson, Angus. [*Ceard is Cainnt.*]
Henderson, Angus. [*Ceist nan Taighean.*]
Henderson, Angus. [*Cogadh no Sith.*]
Henderson, Angus. [*Mar a Fhuair Mac-Bheatha 'na Righ.*]
Henderson, Angus. [*Mar Gu'n Eireadh Neach o na Mairbh.*]
Henderson, Angus. [*Sgoiltean agus Oilean.*]
Henderson, Angus. [*Spealgadh nan Glasan.*]
MacCormick, John. [*Eilean Dideil.*]
MacCormick, John. [*Thall's a Bhos.*]
MacDougall, Hector. [*A' Bhraisd Lathurnach.*]
MacFarlane, Malcolm. [*Mairi Nighean Alasdair Ruaidh.*]
MacFarlane, Malcolm. [*An Sgeul Goirid.*]
Peiteag Ruaidh.
Robertson, Angus. [*Cor, Coir agus Coirich.*]
Sinclair, Donald. [*A' Mhor-Roinn agus am Fearann.*]
Siubhal air Falbh Impireachd.
Whyte, Henry. [*Mar a Dh'Eirich Cuid de na Sean-Fhacail.*]
   A numbered series of off-prints from "Guth na Bliadhna" and "An Sgeulaiche".
   Published by Alex. MacLaren & Son, Glasgow, *c.* 1930.

Leabhraichean Sgoile Gaidhlig. See Watson, W. J. (gen. ed.). See also MacKinnon,
   Lachlan. [*Leabhraichean Leughaidh.*]

Leabhraichean ura Gaidhlig Oilthigh Ghlaschu [fo stiùireadh Ruairidh MhicThomais].
   See:
   1. MacLeod, Murdo. [*Laithean Geala.*] [Sreath na Sgoile, Leabhar 1.]
   2. Smith, Iain C. [*An Dubh is an Gorm.*]
   3. MacAskill, Alex. J. (ed.). [*Rosg nan Eilean.*] [Sreath na Sgoile, Leabhar 2.]
   4. MacDonald, Kenneth D. (ed.). [*Briseadh na Cloiche.*]
   5. MacKenzie, Colin N. [*Mar Sgeul a Dh'Innseas Neach.*]
   6. MacKenzie, Colin N. [*A' Leth Eile.*]
   7. MacKenzie, Colin N. [*Nach Neonach Sin.*]

Leabhraichean ura Gaidhlig Oilthigh Obar-Dheadhain [fo stiùireadh Ruairidh Mhic-
   Thomais]. See:
   1. MacLeod, Murdo. [*Laithean Geala.*] [Sreath na Sgoile, Leabhar 1.]
   2. Smith, Iain C. [*An Dubh is an Gorm.*]

Leabhran Meur Taobh Tuath Shasuinn. See Comunn Gaidhealach, North of England
   Branch. *Leabhran.*

Learning Gaelic. [First Series.] Wembley, 1949.
   British Broadcasting Corporation. Learning Gaelic. Ten elementary broadcast lessons.
   Scottish Home Service (391.1 metres). Mondays: 6.45 p.m.–7.00 p.m. 17th October–
   19th December 1949.
   Published by the British Broadcasting Corporation, The Grammar School, Scarle Road,
   Wembley. Printed by R. & R. Clark, Ltd., Edinburgh. No. 2430.
   23 p; illus. 220 mm. EPL, Mit.

Learning Gaelic. [First Series.] [London], 1956.
   British Broadcasting Corporation. Learning Gaelic. Ten elementary broadcast lessons.
   Scottish Home Service, 371 metres, 809 Kc/s; 93.1 Mc/s VHF. Tuesdays, 10 to
   10.15 p.m. 9th October–11th December 1956.
   Printed by R. & R. Clark, Edinburgh.
   23 p; illus. 210 mm. PC.
      The first ten lessons were repeated; the 1956 booklet is therefore a reprint of that of
   1949.

Learning Gaelic. [Second Series.] Wembley, 1950.
British Broadcasting Corporation. Learning Gaelic. The second series of broadcast lessons. Scottish Home Service (391.1 metres). Mondays: 6.45 p.m.–7.05 p.m. 16th January–10th April 1950. Repeated Fridays 10.15 p.m.–10.35 p.m.
Published by the British Broadcasting Corporation, The Grammar School, Scarle Road, Wembley. Printed by R. & R. Clark, Ltd., Edinburgh. No. 2472.
31 p; illus. 210 mm. NLS, PC.

Learning Gaelic. [Third Series.] London, 1950.
British Broadcasting Corporation. Learning Gaelic. The third series of broadcast lessons. Scottish Home Service (371.1 metres). Wednesdays: 6.50 p.m.–7.10 p.m. Repeated Fridays 10.15–10.35 p.m.
[Cover] B.B.C. Scottish Home Service. 18th October to 27th December 1950.
Published by the British Broadcasting Corporation, 35 Marylebone High Street, London, W.1. Printed by R. & R. Clark, Ltd., Edinburgh. No. 2611.
31 p; illus. 210 mm. NLS, PC.

Learning Gaelic. [Fourth Series.] London, 1951.
British Broadcasting Corporation. Learning Gaelic. The fourth series of broadcast lessons. Scottish Home Service (371.1 metres). Wednesdays. Repeated Fridays.
[Cover] B.B.C. Scottish Home Service. 3rd January to 21st March 1951.
Published by the British Broadcasting Corporation, 35 Marylebone High Street, London, W.1. Printed by R. & R. Clark, Ltd., Edinburgh. No. 2649.
31 p; illus. 210 mm. PC.
The lessons were devised by Edward Pursell and Hugh MacPhee; the narrators were John Bannerman and Archie Hendry; the programmes were produced by Hugh MacPhee.

Lees, J. Cameron, 1834–1913. [*Life and Conduct*.] Edinburgh, [Intro. 1916].
Cogadh mór na h-Eòrpa. Beatha agus Caitheamh-Beatha. Camaran Lees. [Illus.] Printed by Oliver and Boyd, Edinburgh, for The Church of Scotland, The United Free Church of Scotland, The Free Church of Scotland.
xi, 72 p. 140 mm. NLS.
Introduction by N. MacLean, dated 1916.
English original first published 1890.

Lever, William Hesketh, 1st Viscount Leverhulme, 1851–1925. [*Adhartas an Latha 'n Diugh*.] Port Sunlight, [1919].
Twentieth Century Development in Lewis and Harris. An address by Lord Leverhulme to the Philosophical Institution, Edinburgh, 4th November 1919.
Adhartas an latha 'n diugh an Leòdhas 's na Hearradh. Oraid a chaidh a thoirt seachad leis a' Mhorair Leverhulme an Talla nam Feallsanach, Dunéideann, an 4mh là de'n t-Samhuinn, 1919.
Port Sunlight: printed by Lever Brothers Limited.
22 p [English], 22 p [Gaelic]. 200 mm. PC.

Lhuyd, Edward, 1660–1709. [*Edward Lhuyd in the Scottish Highlands*.] Oxford, 1963.
Edward Lhuyd in the Scottish Highlands, 1699–1700. By J. L. Campbell, M.A. (Oxon.), LL.D. (Antigonish), and Derick Thomson, M.A. (Aberdeen), B.A. (Cantab.), Reader in Celtic at Aberdeen University. Oxford, at the Clarendon Press. 1963.
xxxii, 319 p; map. 230 mm. BM, GU.
Contents: Part I: "The Folklore and Gaelic Manuscript Survey", pp 1–87; Part II: "The Scottish Gaelic translation of John Ray's Dictionariolum Trilingue", pp 89–231; Part III: "Indexes".

Life and Work: Na Duilleagan Gaidhlig. Edinburgh, [1880]–.
Aireamh 1. [Illus.] 1900. [Na Duilleagan Gàidhlig.]
[Continuing]

[Frequency] Monthly.
[Collation] 4 p, 1900–29, 8 p per number thereafter.
260 × 240 mm.
[Editors] Donald Lamont, 1907–50; Thomas M. Murchison, 1950–.
[Note] Gaelic supplement of *Life and Work, A Parish Magazine* (latterly subtitled *The Church of Scotland Magazine and Record* and *The Record of the Church of Scotland*). *Life and Work* was first published 1879; the Gaelic supplement began in 1880.

Lindsay, Maurice, 1918–. [*Modern Scottish Poetry.*] London, 1946.
Modern Scottish Poetry. An Anthology of the Scottish Renaissance, 1920–45. Edited by Maurice Lindsay. Faber and Faber Limited, 24 Russell Square, London.
First published in MCMXLVI by Faber and Faber Limited.
145 p. 200 mm. BM, Mit.

—— [*Modern Scottish Poetry.*] London, 1966.
. . . First published in MCMXLVI. Second edition, revised and entirely reset, published in MCMLXVI.
200 p. 210 mm. Mit.
Contains Gaelic poems by George Campbell Hay, Sorley MacLean, Donald Sinclair and Derick Thomson.

—— (joint ed.). See Bruce, George. [*Scottish Poetry, Number One* and *Scottish Poetry, Number Three.*]

Linguistic Survey of the Gaelic Dialects of Scotland. See:
Borgström, Carl Hj. [*The Dialects of Skye and Ross-shire.*]
Borgström, Carl Hj. [*The Dialects of the Outer Hebrides.*]
Oftedal, Magne. [*The Gaelic of Leurbost.*]

Lismore. See MacGregor, James, Dean of Lismore.

Lloyd, Joseph (ed.). [*Alasdair Mac Colla.*] Dublin, 1914.
Alasdair Mac Colla. Sain-eolus ar a ghniomharthaibh gaisge. Seosamh Laoide do chuir le chéile. Déantùsai o Eoin Mhac Néill agus o Niall Mac Mhuireadhaigh sa leabhar so.
[Quotation.] Clódhanna, Teo.: ar n-a chur amach do Chonnradh na Gaedhilge i mBaile Atha Cliath. 1914.
viii, 76 p. 180 mm. PC.
Contains an essay on Alasdair Mac Colla by Eoin MacNeill and an excerpt from the MacDonald History in the Book of Clanranald by Neil MacMhuirich.

Lochaber High School [Fort William]. See School Magazines.

Lochran an Anma. See Catholic Church. *Liturgy and Ritual.* [Lochran an Anma.]

Lon Dubh. See Mac Farlane, Malcolm. [*An Lon Dubh.*]

London Gaelic Society. See Comunn na Gaidhlig an Lunnainn.

Low, T. S. [*Homage to John MacLean.*] Berwick, 1973.
Homage to John MacLean. Edited by T. S. Low. Berwick: The John MacLean Society. 1973.
48 p. 220 mm.
Contains three Gaelic poems by Sorley MacLean, Derick Thomson, William Neill.

Lucas Heywood. Edinburgh, n.d.

Lucas Heywood. Edinburgh, n.d.
Lucas Heywood. Edinburgh: Andrew Stevenson. "Luke Heywood". One penny.
6/– per 100.
31 p. 107 mm. FC.

Luideag-an-Uillt. See A' Bhean Nighe.

Luinneagan Taghte. Glasgow, n.d.
An luach, dà sgillinn (Price, 2d).
Luinneagan Taghte (Choice Lyrics in Gaelic).
Printed and published by Archd. Sinclair, Celtic Press, 27a Cadogan Street, Glasgow, C.2.
4 p. 260 mm. PC.
29 songs. No music.

Mac Mhaighstir Alasdair, Alasdair. See MacDonald, Alexander, *c.* 1690–1770.

MacAdam, Alexander, 1749–1817 (joint author). See Dioghluim o Theagasg nan Aithrichean.

MacAdam, Donald M. [*Gaelic Sermon.*] N.p., n.d.
"Gaelic Sermon." In "Centenary of the first landing of a Catholic Bishop on the shores of the Bras d'Or Lakes, Cape Breton, 1815–1915."
Clare. Dunn. Not seen.

—— [*Teagasg Chriost.*] Antigonish, N.S., n.d.
Teagasg Chriost air son Cloinne Bige. Casket Printing Company, Antigonish, N.S.
20 p. 150 mm. *Xavier.*

Mac a' Ghobhainn, Coinneach Iain. See Smith, Kenneth John.

Mac a' Ghobhainn, Iain. See Smith, Iain C.

MacAlpine, Neil, 1786–1866. [*Pronouncing Gaelic Dictionary.*] Edinburgh, 1903.
A Pronouncing Gaelic Dictionary, to which is prefixed a concise but most comprehensive Gaelic Grammar. By Neil M'Alpine. [Quotation.] Twelfth edition. Edition.
Edinburgh: John Grant. 1903.
iii–lix, 549 p. 200 mm. PC.
   Contains the English-Gaelic section, which was edited by John MacKenzie, as well as the Gaelic-English first part, edited by MacAlpine. The latter first appeared in 1832, the former in 1845.

—— [*Pronouncing Gaelic Dictionary.*] Edinburgh, 1906.
[Ibid.]
iii–lix, 549 p. 200 mm.

—— [*Gaelic-English and English-Gaelic Dictionary.*] Glasgow, 1971.
Gaelic-English and English-Gaelic Dictionary. Compiled by Neil MacAlpine and John MacKenzie. Gairm Publications, 29 Waterloo Street, Glasgow. 1971.
[Part 1] Pronouncing Gaelic-English Dictionary. Compiled by Neil MacAlpine. Gairm Publications, 29 Waterloo Street, Glasgow. 1971.
[Part 2] English-Gaelic Dictionary. Compiled by John Mackenzie. (This work formed Part II of MacAlpine's Pronouncing Gaelic Dictionary.) Gairm Publications, 29 Waterloo Street, Glasgow. 1971.
vi, 281 p, 269 p. 230 mm.

—— [*Pronouncing Gaelic-English Dictionary.*] Glasgow, 1929.
A Pronouncing Gaelic-English Dictionary. By Neil MacAlpine. Glasgow: Alexander Maclaren & Son, 360–362 Argyle Street, C.2.
Maclaren's New Edition 1929.
iii–xvi, 281 p. 200 mm.
   Without the English-Gaelic section.

—— [*Pronouncing Gaelic-English Dictionary.*] Glasgow, 1934, 1936, 1941, 1948, 1955, 1957, 1962.
[Ibid.]
iii–xvi, 281 p. 200 mm.
The English-Gaelic section was bound with the edition of 1962, but without overall title page.

—— [*Pronouncing Gaelic-English Dictionary.*] Glasgow, 1971.
Pronouncing Gaelic-English Dictionary. Compiled by Neil MacAlpine. Gairm Publications, 29 Waterloo Street, Glasgow. 1971.
vi, 281 p. 230 mm.
Photolithographic reprint. Printed Maclehose, Glasgow.

—— [*A Pronouncing Gaelic Dictionary.*] For separate editions of Part II see MacKenzie, John. [*An English-Gaelic Dictionary.*]

—— [*A Pronouncing Gaelic Grammar.*] Edinburgh, 1901.
A Pronouncing Gaelic Grammar. By Neil McAlpine. Edinburgh: 31 George IV Bridge. 1901.
[1] t.p.; xv–lix p. 190 mm. AU.
Originally formed the Introduction to MacAlpine's "Gaelic Dictionary".

MacAmhlaigh, Domhnall. See MacAulay, Donald.

Mac Fhleisteir, Alasdair. See Fletcher, Alexander.

Mac An Rothaich, Niall. See Munro, Neil.

Mac-An-t-Saoir, Alasdair. See MacIntyre, Alexander.

Mac-An-t-Saoir, Donnachadh Ban. See MacIntyre, Duncan.

MacAoidh, Ruairidh. See MacKay, Roderick.

MacAoidh, Uilleamina. See MacKay, Williamina.

MacAoidh, W. P. See MacKay, William P.

MacArthur, Bessy J. B. [*The Clan of Lochlann.*] Glasgow, n.d.
Clann Righ Lochlainn. Dealbh-chluich le Beitidh Nic Artair. Air eadartheangachadh o'n Bheurla le Dòmhnall MacDhòmhnuill. Choisinn an dealbh-chluich, Clann Rìgh Lochlainn, an aon duais a bha Comunn Radio Albann a' tairgsinn ré na bliadhna 1926–1927 air son comhfharpaisean dhealbh-chluichean. Chaidh an dealbh-chluich so a chraobh-sgaoileadh air son a' cheud uair, trìd an Radio, le Luchd-cluiche Dùthchail Albann, air a' cheud là ar fhichead de'n Ghiblein anns a' bhliadhna 1927. [Illus.]
Glascho: Alasdair Mac Labhruinn 's a Mhic, 268 Sràid Earraghaidheal, C.2.
16 p. 190 mm. EPL, Mit.
Advertised as "new Gaelic play" in *An Gaidheal*, 1934; MacLaren's address changed from 360–362 to 268 Argyle Street, *c.* 1930. English original first published 1928.

MacAskill, Alex. J., 1921–. [*Rosg nan Eilean.*] Glasgow, 1966.
Rosg nan Eilean. Deasaichte le Alasdair I. MacAsgaill. Roinn nan Cànan Ceilteach, Oilthigh Ghlaschu. 1966. iii.
Leabhraichean ùra Gàidhlig Oilthigh Ghlaschu (fo stiùireadh Ruairidh Mhic Thomais), Aireamh 3. Sreath na Sgoile, Leabhar 2.
viii, 250 p; illus. 220 mm.
Prose anthology for schools, with exercises.

—— (ed.). See Murray, Murdo. [*Luach na Saorsa.*]

MacAskill, I. (tr.). See Murray, William. [*Boys and Girls.*]

MacAskill, Iain Archie, 1898–1933. [*An Ribheid Chiuil.*] Stirling, 1961.
An Ribheid Chiùil. Being the Poems of Iain Archie MacAskill, 1898–1933, Bard of
Berneray, Harris. Edited with Introduction and Notes by Alick Morrison, M.A.
(Hons.), Principal Teacher of History in Knightswood and Riverside Secondary
Schools, Glasgow; Author of *The Clan Morrison*; Editor, *Orain Chaluim*. Stirling:
printed for the Editor by A. Learmonth & Son, 9 King Street. 1961.
124 p; 4 plates. 220 mm.

MacAskill, M. A. (joint author). See Mo Leabhar I: Leabhar-Leughaidh/Leabhar-
Oibreach; and Mo Leabhar II: Leabhar-Leughaidh.

MacAskill, Malcolm, 1825–1903. [*Orain Chaluim.*] Glasgow, n.d.
Orain Chaluim. Being the poems of Malcolm MacAskill, bard of Berneray, Harris.
Edited by Alick Morrison, M.A. (Hons.), Principal Teacher of History in Knightswood Sen. Sec. School and Riverside Sen. Sec. School, Glasgow, author of *The Clan
Morrison*. Glasgow: Alexander MacLaren & Sons, 268 Argyle Street, C.2.
81 p. 220 mm.
[70]–81 p of Notes. First advertised 1965.

MacAulay, Donald, 1930–. [*Seobhrach as a' Chlaich.*] Glasgow, 1967.
Seobhrach as a' Chlaich. Ceithir fichead dàn agus eile a sgrìobh Dòmhnall MacAmh-
laigh. Gairm. Glaschu. 1967.
Clò-bhualaidhean Gairm, Leabhar 6.
107 p. 230 mm.
Contains English prose translations of a number of the poems.

MacAulay, Rev. Hector (tr.). See Dow, William. [*The Resurrection.*]

MacBain, Alexander, 1855–1907. [*Etymological Dictionary of the Gaelic Language.*]
Stirling, 1911.
An Etymological Dictionary of the Gaelic Language. By Alexander MacBain, LL.D.
Stirling: Eneas MacKay. 1911.
xxxvi, 412 p, [8] p, plate. 220 mm. BM, GU, Mit.
1st ed. 1896; revised by Malcolm MacFarlane, who provides an "Editorial Note".
Printed by the Northern Counties Newspaper and Printing and Publishing Company,
Limited, Inverness.

—— [*Etymology of Gaelic Names.*] Stirling, 1911.
Etymology of the principal Gaelic national names, personal names and surnames. To
which is added a disquisition on Ptolemy's Geography of Scotland. By the late Alexander MacBain, M.A., LL.D. Eneas Mackay, Stirling. 1911.
50 p. 230 mm. BM.
Extracted from his *Etymological Dictionary*. The paper on Ptolemy was originally
read to the Gaelic Society of Inverness.

—— [*Higher Grade Readings.*] Inverness, 1905.
Higher Grade Readings with Outlines of Grammar and all the King's Scholarship
Examination papers in Gaelic (1888 to 1904). For King's Scholarship and Leaving
Certificate Examinations. Edited by Alexander MacBain, LL.D., author of *An Etymological Dictionary of the Gaelic Language*. Inverness: The *Northern Chronicle* Office.
1905.
xxxi, 106 p, [1] 'Index.' 190 mm. AU, BM, GU, Mit., NLS.

—— [*Gaelic Reader.*] Inverness, 1919.
Gaelic Reader with Outlines of Grammar for use in Higher Classes of schools in the
Highlands. Alexander MacBain, LL.D., author of *An Etymological Dictionary of the
Gaelic Language*, etc. New edition. Inverness: *The Northern Chronicle* Office. 1919.
xxxv, 98 p. 180 mm. Mit.
Printed *Northern Counties*, Inverness.

—— [*Gaelic Reader.*] Inverness, 1920.
. . . Third edition. Inverness: The *Northern Chronicle* Office. 1920.
xxxv, 99 p. 180 mm. AU.
  Contains the Preface to the 1905 and 1919 eds. Printed by *Northern Counties,* Inverness.

—— (joint author). [*How to Learn Gaelic.*] Inverness, 1902.
How to Learn Gaelic. Orthographical instructions, grammar and reading lessons. By Alexander MacBain, LL.D., and John Whyte. Third edition. Inverness: The *Northern Chronicle* Office. 1902.
[8], 76 p. 190 mm. AU, Mit.
  Printed *Northern Counties,* Inverness.

—— [*How to Learn Gaelic.*] Inverness, 1906.
. . . Fourth edition. Inverness: The *Northern Chronicle* Office. 1906.
[8], 76 p, 20 p "Vocabulary". 190 mm. GU:CL, Mit.
  First ed. (1897) was named "How to Read Gaelic". The "Vocabulary", by John Whyte, was published separately in 1906.

—— (joint author). [*How to Learn Gaelic.*] See also Whyte, John. [*Vocabulary for How to Learn Gaelic.*].

—— [*Outlines of Gaelic Etymology.*] Stirling, 1909.
Outlines of Gaelic Etymology. By the late Alexander MacBain, M.A., LL.D. Eneas MacKay: Stirling. 1909.
[4], xxxvii, a-c "Supplement", [1] p. BM. Corrigenda, 1 plate. 230 mm.
  Originally formed the Introduction to MacBain's *Etymological Dictionary of the Gaelic Language.*

MacBean, Jean. [*Duan Molaidh.*] Oban, n.d.
Duan Molaidh air Alasdair MacArtair, a Bharbhric, Taobh Lochodha. Le Sine Nic Bheathain, banntrach Dhomhnuill Chaimbeil, am Barrantuim. Printed by the *Oban Times,* Oban.
7 p. 170 mm. PC.

MacBean, Lachlan, 1853–1931. [*Elementary Lessons in Gaelic.*] Stirling, 1901.
Elementary Lessons in Gaelic. Reading, Grammar and Construction, with a Vocabulary and Key. By L. MacBean. Fifth edition. Stirling: Eneas MacKay, Murray Place. 1901.
[4], 62 p. 190 mm. GU:CL, Mit.

—— [*Elementary Lessons in Gaelic.*] Stirling, 1908.
. . . Sixth edition. Stirling: Eneas MacKay, Murray Place. 1908.
68 p. 190 mm. BM, EPL, NLS.
  1st ed. 1876.

—— [*Guide to Gaelic Conversation.*] Stirling, 1901.
Guide to Gaelic Conversation and Pronunciation. With dialogues, phrases, letter forms, and vocabularies. By L. MacBean, author of *Elementary Lessons in Gaelic, Songs and Hymns of the Gael,* etc. Stirling: Eneas MacKay, 43 Murray Place. 1901.
116 p. 180 mm. AU.
  Printed John Noble, Inverness.

—— [*Guide to Gaelic Conversation.*] Stirling, 1905.
Second edition. Stirling: Eneas MacKay, Murray Place. 1905.
116 p. 190 mm. BM, CoS, EPL, Mit.
  1st ed. 1884. The above is actually the 4th ed.

—— [*Psalmody.*] Stirling, 1910.
Gaelic Psalmody, in staff and sol-fa, with English translations. By Lachlan MacBean.
Stirling: Eneas MacKay, 43 Murray Place. 1910.
69–86 p. 280 mm. Mit.
> Bound with the 1900 ed. of MacBean's *Songs and Hymns,* of which the Psalmody is
> Part III. 1st ed., late 19th century.

—— [*Songs and Hymns of the Gael.*] Stirling, 1900.
The Songs and Hymns of the Gael. With translations and music and an introduction.
By L. MacBean. Stirling: Eneas MacKay, 43 Murray Place. 1900.
xvi, [68] p. 290 mm. AU, Mit.
> The *Songs and Hymns* were first published as separate parts in the 1880's, being first
> issued as one bound volume in 1888.

—— [*Songs of the Gael.*] Stirling, n.d.
Songs of the Gael. MacBean. Eneas MacKay, Publisher, Stirling.
[32] p. 240 mm. NLS.
> Part I of *Songs and Hymns of the Gael.* 1st ed., late 19th century. Present edition
> advertised in the press and acquired by NLS in 1921.

MacCaig, Norman, 1910–. [*Honour'd Shade.*] Edinburgh, [*c.* 1959].
Honour'd Shade. An Anthology of New Scottish Poetry to mark the bi-centenary of
the birth of Robert Burns. Selected and edited by Norman MacCaig. W. & R.
Chambers Ltd., Edinburgh and London.
1959 (*c.*). The Arts Council of Great Britain.
136 p. 210 mm.
> Printed T. & A. Constable, Edinburgh. Contains 8 Gaelic poems by Donald
> MacAulay, Sorley MacLean, Derick Thomson; with English translations.

—— [*Contemporary Scottish Verse.*] London, 1970.
The Scottish Library. Contemporary Scottish Verse 1959–69. Edited by Norman
MacCaig and Alexander Scott. Calder & Boyers. London.
First published in Great Britain 1970.
271 p. 210 mm.
> Includes Gaelic poems by Donald MacAulay, Sorley MacLean, Iain Smith and
> Derick Thomson; with English translations.

McCallum, Archibald (ed.). See McCallum, John. [*Iain Wesley.*]

MacCallum, Donald, 1849–1929. [*Dan Crunaidh.*] N.p., n.d.
Dan Crùnaidh do Righ Imhear. Leis An Urr. Dòmhnull MacCalum.
1 p, 1 p [English translation]. [*c.* 1902.] PC.

—— [*Domhnullan.*] Glasgow, 1925.
Dòmhnullan. Dàn Ceithir Earrannan. Leis an Urr. Dòmhnull Mac Chalum, ministear
aosda Sgìre na Loch an Leòdhas. Le dealbh an Ughdair. Glascho; Alasdair Mac-
Labhruinn 's a Mhic, 360 Sràid Earra-Ghaidheal. 1925.
xiv, 59 p, 2 plates. 190 mm. BM, GU:CL, Mit.
> Introduction by J. N. MacLeod. An English verse translation of the first "Canto"
> was published in 1927.

—— [*Sealg na Pairce.*] [1907?]
Sealg na Pàirce.
> Not seen. Referred to in Lachlan MacBean's *The Celtic Who's Who* (1921).

McCallum, John, 1844–1910. [*Iain Wesley.*] Glasgow, 1911.
Cùnntas Aithghearr air Iain Wesley agus sgrìobhaidhean eile, leis an Urr. Iain Mac
Calum nach maireann. Glaschu: Gilleasbuig Mac-na-Ceàrdadh, 47 Sraid Waterloo.
1911.

Memorial Papers of the Rev. John McCallum, Ardeonaig. Edited by the Rev. Archibald McCallum, North Knapdale. Glasgow: Archibald Sinclair, 47 Waterloo Street. 1911.
xii, 115 p; plate. 170 mm. AU, GU:CL, Mit.

MacCalmain, Thomas. See Murchison, Thomas M.

McCheyne, R. M., 1813–43. [*Guth mo Ghraidh.*] Edinburgh, n.d.
Cogadh mòr na h-Eòrpa. Guth mo Ghràidh (agus searmoinean eile). McCheyne. [Illus.) Printed by Oliver and Boyd, Edinburgh, for The Church of Scotland, The United Free Church of Scotland, and The Free Church of Scotland.
61 p. 140 mm. NLS.
    Translated by Rev. A. Sinclair. Issued to soldiers in the First World War.

——— [*Life and Sermons.*] Glasgow, 1939.
Beatha agus Searmoinean an Urramaich R. M. McCheyne, maille ri litrichean agus laoidhean. Ead. le Ailean Mac na Ceàrdaidh, Ceannmhòr. Glascho: Alasdair Mac Labhruinn agus a Mhic, 268 Sràid Earraghaidheal, C.2. 1939.
viii, 364 p. 200 mm. Mit., PC.
    Foreword by Donald Matheson. 1st ed. 1865, of which this is a reprint.

Mac-Choinnich, Iain. See MacKenzie, John.

MacCodrum, John, c. 1693–1779. [*Songs.*] Edinburgh, 1938.
The Songs of John MacCodrum, Bard to Sir James MacDonald of Sleat. Edited by William Matheson. Published by Oliver & Boyd for the Scottish Gaelic Texts Society. Edinburgh. 1938.
Scottish Gaelic Texts, Volume Two.
lii, 382 p. 230 mm. AU, BM, GU, Mit.
    Translation on facing pages.

——— [*Orain Iain Mhic Fhearchair.*] Edinburgh, 1939.
Orain Iain Mhic Fhearchair, a bha 'na bhàrd aig Sir Seumas Mac Dhòmhnaill. Air an deasachadh le Uilleam MacMhathain. Oliver & Boyd. Dùn-éideann. 1939.
xxiii, 108 p. 220 mm. GU:CL.
    A paper-covered edition, without English translations, issued for the use of schools. Introduction in Gaelic.

MacCoinnich, Cailein T. See MacKenzie, Colin N.

MacCoinnich, Domhnull. See MacKenzie, Donald.

MacCoinnich, Lachlan. See MacKenzie, Lachlan.

MacCoinnich, Uilleam. See MacKenzie, William.

MacColl, Duncan. [*Laoidhean Soisgeulach.*] Glasgow, 1913.
Laoidhean Soisgeulach air an tional le Iain Caimbeul agus air an cur a mach le Donnachadh MacColla, Ceann Suidhe Comunn Soisgeulach Gaidhealach Ghlascho. Glasgow: Archibald Sinclair, Celtic Press, 47 Waterloo Street; Alex. MacLaren & Son, Gaelic Booksellers, 360 Argyle Street. 1913.
128 p. 140 mm. GU, Mit.

——— [*Laoidhean Soisgeulach.*] Glasgow, 1922.
. . . 1922.
128 p. 140 mm. Mit.

——— [*Laoidhean Soisgeulach.*] Glasgow, 1957.
. . . Reprinted 1957. Glasgow: Alex. MacLaren & Son, Gaelic Booksellers, 268 Argyle Street. 1922.
128 p. 140 mm. PC.
    1st ed. 1899 (viii, [7]–126 p). Mostly translations; no music.

MacColl, Evan, 1808–98. [*Clarsach nam Beann.*] Glasgow, 1937.
Clàrsach nam Beann. Le Eoghan Mac Colla. An ceathramh clò-bhualadh, meudaichte agus ath-leasaichte. Published by The Evan MacColl Memorial Committee. Glasgow: Archibald Sinclair, 27a Cadogan Street. 1937.
vii, 171 p; plate. 220 mm. BM, Mit., NLS.
1st ed. 1836.

McConochie, J. Norman. [*Ghaidhlig a' Gairm.*] Glasgow, n.d.
Gaelic Calling. "Ghàidhlig a' Gairm." Contents: 16 popular Gaelic Songs. English and Gaelic words. English words and musical arrangements by J. N. McConochie. Staff and sol-fa. 2/– net. Mozart Allan, 84 Carlton Place, Glasgow, C.5.
34 p. 280 mm. Mit.
Mitchell Library copy acquired 1952; advertised and reviewed 1946.

—— [*Orain is Puirt-a-Beul.*] Glasgow, [*c.* 1930.]
Something New! Sing a song to your dance. Orain is Puirt-a-Beul. A' Cho-Sheirm le I. Tormod Mac Dhonnchaidh, Ceòlraidh Ghàidhlig Glaschu. Gaelic Songs and Dance Tunes. Arranged for Choral Singing by J. Norman McConochie, M.A., Conductor of the Glasgow Gaelic Musical Association. [List of Contents.] "This booklet is dedicated to the members of the G.G.M.A., for whom the arrangements were originally composed. Two of the numbers were prepared for the Choir's appearances at Annual Gatherings of the Lewis and Harris Association, and all have been given at the Choir's public appearances. The booklet is issued in the sincere hope that it may provide acceptable additions to the repertoires of other Gaelic choirs." J. N. McC. Staff notation. Price 1/6 net. Also published in sol-fa notation, 1/– net. Copyright 1930. Printed and published by Alex. MacLaren & Sons, 360–364 Argyle Street, Glasgow, C.2.
13 p. 250 mm. Mit., PC.
McConochie also edited sheet music with Gaelic words.

MacCormick, Donald. [*Hebridean Folksongs.*] Oxford, 1969.
Hebridean Folksongs. A Collection of Waulking Songs by Donald MacCormick in Kilphedir in South Uist in the year 1893. Some of them translated by the late Fr. Allan McDonald. Completed and edited by J. L. Campbell. Tunes transcribed, from recordings, by Francis Collinson. Oxford: at the Clarendon Press. 1969.
Seann-Orain Innse-Gall. Comh-chruinneachadh do dh'Orain Luadhaidh le Dòmhnall Mac Cormaic an Cille Pheadair an Ceann-a-deas Uibhist anns a' bhliadhna Ochd Ciad Ceithir Fichead 's a trì diag. Feadhainn dhiubh air an eadar-theangachadh le Mgr. Ailein Dòmhnallach. Air an criochnachadh 's air an deasachadh le Iain L. Caimbeul. Na fuinn air an sgrìobhadh le Francis Collinson. Atha-nan-Damh: Clò-Phreas Chlarendon. 1969.
xv, 375. 230 mm.
Text with translations, pp 43–159; Notes on the Text, pp 160–94; Music, pp 195–344; Bibliography, 345–50; Glossarial Index, pp 351–72; Index of Persons and Places, pp 373–75.

MacCormick, John, 1860–1947. [*An t-Agh Odhar.*] Glasgow, 1931.
Dealbh-Chluich Ghàidhlig. An t-Agh Odhar. Le Iain Mac Cormaic, F.S.A. The Dun Heifer. A Humorous Gaelic Sketch. Glascho: Alasdair Mac Labhruinn 's a Mhic, 360–2 Sràid Earraghaidheal, C.2. 1931. 1/–.
26 p. 190 mm. BM, EPL, Mit.
First published in *An Sgeulaiche*, 1910.

—— [*An Ceol-Sithe.*] Glasgow, n.d.
An Comunn Gaidhealach. Dealbh-chluich-ciùil Cloinne. An Ceòl-Sìthe. (A' Cheud duais, Mod 1925.) Le Iain Mac Cormaig. A' phrìs, se sgillinn. An Comunn Gaidhealach, 114 Sràid West Campbell, Glascho.

14 p, [1], "Ceol nan Oran" [sol-fa].
220 mm. Mit.
Reviewed in *An Gaidheal*, April 1926.

—— [*Domhnull mor agus Cailean Taillear*.] See MacCormick, John. [*Peigi Bheag*.]

—— [*Dun-Aluinn*.] Paisley, 1912.
Dunaline, or The Banished Heir. By John Mac Cormick. Edited by M. Mac Farlane.
[Illus.] Paisley: Alexander Gardner, Publisher by Appointment to the late Queen
Victoria.
Dùn-àluinn, no An t-Oighre 'na Dhìobarach. Le Iain Mac Cormaic. Fo làimh
Chaluim Mhic Phàrlain. [Illus.] Pàislig: Alasdair Gardner, Clòdh-bhuailtear do 'n
Bhan-rìgh Victoria nach maireann.
London: Simpkin, Marshall, Hamilton, Kent & Co., LMD. Alexander Gardner,
Printer, Paisley. 1912.
267 p. 190 mm. AU, BM, GU:CL, Mit.

—— [*Dun-Aluinn*.] Glasgow, n.d.
Dun-Aluinn, no An t-Oighre 'na Dhìobarach. Le Iain Mac Cormaig, F.S.A. Fo
làimh Chaluim Mhic Phàrlain. Glascho: Alasdair Mac Labhruinn 's a Mhic, 360–364
Sràid Earraghaidheal, C.2.
Dunaline, or The Banished Heir. By John Mac Cormick, F.S.A. Edited by Malcolm
MacFarlane. Glasgow: Alexander Maclaren & Sons, 360–362 Argyle Street.
267 p. 200 mm. PC.
2nd ed.; *c.* 1920. The first Gaelic novel. Parts of it had previously appeared in the
People's Journal; serialised in *The Celtic Monthly*, 1913–14.

—— [*Eilean Dideil*.] Glasgow, n.d.
The Ceilidh Books. Leabhraichean nan Céilidh. Aireamh 10. Eilean Dideil. Le Iain
Mac Cormaic. [Illus.] A' phrìs, trì sgillinnean. 3d. Alasdair Mac Labhruinn agus a
Mhic, 360–362 Sràid Earraghaidheal, Glascho.
[203]–222 p. 220 mm. PC.
Reprinted from *An Sgeulaiche*, II.3, Am Foghar 1910.

—— [*Am Fear a Chaill a Ghaidhlig*.] Glasgow, 1925.
Am Fear a Chaill a Ghàidhlig (Dealbh-Chluich). Le Iain MacCormaig, Glascho.
Calum is Bantrach Tharmaid (Còmhradh). Le Iain Mac-an-Aba, Cillemhoire. A'
phrìs, se sgillinn. An Comunn Gaidhealach, 114 Sràid West Campbell, Glascho.
1925.
27 p. 190 mm. Mit.
Calum is Bantrach Tharmaid, pp 20–7.

—— [*Gaol air a Dhearbhadh*.] Glasgow, n.d.
Gaol air a Dhearbhadh. Dealbh-chluich le Iain Mac Cormaig, F.S.A. The Test of
Love. A Humorous Gaelic Play. Fo làimh Eachainn Mhic Dhùghaill. Glascho:
Alasdair MacLabhruinn agus a Mhic, 360–362 Sràid Earraghaidheal, C.2.
20 p. 190 mm. BM, GU:CL, Mit., NLS.
Prize-winning piece at the 1913 Mod. First advertised 1929. BM – 1931.

—— [*Gu'n d'Thug I Speis Do'n Armunn*.] Stirling, 1908.
Gu'n d'thug i Spéis do'n Armunn. Sgeul le Iain Mac Cormaig. Fo làimh Chalum
Mhic Phàrlain. Aonghas Mac Aoidh, 43 Murray Place, Struibhle. 1908.
117 p. 200 mm. AU, BM, GU:CL.

—— [*Gu'n d'Thug I Speis Do'n Armunn*.] [Glasgow, 1929].
Gu'n d'thug i Spéis do'n Armunn.
Not seen. Described in *MacLaren* as, "Second Thousand: Alex. Maclaren, 1929".

——[*Maolagan Mor.*]
Not seen. Advertised in the second edition of Dun-Aluinn as, "Other work by
MacCormick . . . Seann Sgeul . . . Edited by Malcolm MacFarlane." Appeared in
Guth na Bliadhna, IX.4–XI.1, 1912–14.

—— [*Oiteagan O'n Iar.*] Paisley, 1908.
Breezes from the West. By John Mac Cormick. Edited by M. Mac Farlane. [Illus.]
Paisley: Alexander Gardner, Publisher by Appointment to the late Queen Victoria.
1908.
Oiteagan o'n Iar. Le Iain Mac Cormaig. Fo làimh Chaluim Mhic Phàrlain. [Illus.]
Pàislig: Alasdair Gardner, Clòdh-bhuailtear do'n Bhan rìgh Victoria nach maireann.
1908.
149 p. 200 mm. AU, GU:CL, Mit.

—— [*Peigi Bheag.*] Glasgow, 1925.
Peigi Bheag (Dealbh-Chluich). Le Iain MacCormaig, Glascho. Dòmhnull Mór agus
Cailean Tàillear (Còmhradh). Le Iain MacCormaig, Glascho. A' phrìs, se sgillinn.
An Comunn Gaidhealach, 114 Sràid West Campbell, Glascho. 1925.
31 p. 190 mm. AU, EPL, Mit.
Mod prize-winning pieces.

—— [*Rath-Innis.*] Glasgow, 1924.
An Comunn Gaidhealach. [Illus.] Rath-Innis. Dealbh-chluich Gaidhealach. Le Iain
MacCormaig, Glascho. Choisinn a' Chluich so an dara duais (£50) aig Mòd Ghlascho,
1921. A' phrìs, aon tasdan. An Comunn Gaidhealach, 114 Sràid West Campbell,
Glascho. 1924.
45 p. 220 mm. AU.
Another edition bound with "Mairead" by Archibald MacCulloch [*q.v.*].

—— [*Rath-Innis.*] See also MacCulloch, Archibald. [*Mairead.*]

—— [*An Reiteachadh Rathail.*] [?]
An Reiteachadh Rathail.
[51]–85 p. 190 mm.
Not seen. One of a number of plays advertised in *An Deo-Greine*, X: 3 (Dec. 1914)
by Alex. MacLaren & Sons. First published in MacCormick's *Oiteagan o'n Iar*
(1908), from which the above bibliographical data was derived: probably an
offprint. *MacLaren* refers to an edition of 1914 but this entry is demonstrably
inaccurate in another detail (describing first publication as in *An Sgeulaiche*, 1910).
See detailed note under Donald Sinclair: "*Suiridhe Raoghail Mhaoil*".

—— [*An Reiteachadh Rathail.*] Glasgow, 1929.
Dealbh-Chluich Ghàidhlig. An Reitheachail Rathail. Mock Trial by Sheriff and Jury.
A Humorous Gaelic Sketch by John Mac Cormick, F.S.A. Glascho: Alasdair Mac
Labhruinn 's a Mhic, 360–362 Sràid Earraghaidheal, C.2. 1929.
[51]–85 p. 190 mm. BM, PC.
From MacCormick's *Oiteagan o'n Iar*, 1908.

—— [*Seanchaidh na h-Airigh.*] Stirling, 1911.
Seanchaidh na h-Airigh. Le Iain Mac Cormaic. Fo làimh Chaluim Mhic Phàrlain.
[Quotation.] Struibhle: Aonghas Mac Aoidh, 43 Murray Place. 1911.
61 p. 200 mm. AU, BM, GU:CL, Mit., SS.

—— [*Seanchaidh na Traghad.*] Stirling, 1911.
Seanchaidh na Tràghad. Le Iain Mac Cormaic. Fo làimh Chaluim Mhic Phàrlain.
[Quotation.] Struibhle: Aonghas Mac Aoidh, 43 Murray Place. 1911.
64 p. 190 mm. AU, BM, GU:CL, Mit., SS.

——[*Thall 's a Bhos.*] See MacFarlane, Malcolm. [*An Sgeul Goirid.*]

MacCowan, Roderick. [*The Men of Skye.*] Glasgow, 1902.
The Men of Skye. By Roderick MacCowan. [Quotations.] Glasgow: John Mac-
neilage, 65 Great Western Road. Edinburgh: Norman MacLeod, 25 George IV
Bridge. Portree: John Maclaine. 1902.
xix, 230 p. 200 mm. Mit.
Mainly in English. Appendix of Gaelic poems, pp 213–30.

MacCuaig, Gilleasbuig. See Cook, Archibald.

MacCuinn, E. See MacQueen, E[wen].

Mac Cuis, D. I. See MacCuish, Donald J.

MacCuish, Donald J. [*Ceit Mhor agus Maighstir Lachlunn.*] Dundee, 1917.
Ceit Mhòr agus Maighstir Lachlunn (Loch-carain); maille ri Trì Naidheachdan
Uidhisteach. Le D. I. Mac Cuis. Dundee: Malcolm C. MacLeod, Bookseller and
Publisher, 183 Blackness Road. 1917.
32 p. 170 mm. BM, NLS.
Advertisements on pp 28–32.

—— [*Ceit Mhor agus Maighstir Lachlunn.*] [Glasgow, 1942].
Ceit Mhór agus Maighstir Lachlunn.
Not seen. *MacLaren* states that an edition (32 p) was published by Alex. MacLaren &
Son in 1942.

—— [*Eachdruidh air Aonghas MacCuis.*] Inverness, 1911.
Eachdruidh air Aonghas MacCuis, "An Ceisteir", agus air na "h-urramaich" ann an
Uidhist-a-Tuath. (Memoir of Angus McCuish, "Catechist", and the North Uist
Worthies.) By Donald John McCuish, a native of Sollas, North Uist, now at Redcastle.
[Quotation.] Inverness: Robert Carruthers & Sons. 1911.
[4], 88 p. 200 mm. AU, Mit.

MacCulloch, Archibald, –1923. [*Mairead.*] Glasgow, 1924.
Dà Dhealbh-Chluich Gaidhealach. "Mairead", le Gilleasbaig MacCullaich. "Raith-
Innis", le Iain MacCormaig. A' phris – dà thasdan. An Comunn Gaidhealach, 114
Sràid West Campbell, Glasgow. 1924.
[2], 101 p. 220 mm. PC.

—— [*Mairead.*] Glasgow, n.d.
An Comunn Gaidhealach. [Illus.] "Mairead". Dealbh Chluich an ceithir earrannan.
Le Gilleasbaig MacCullaich. A' phrìs, aon tasdan. An Comunn Gaidhealach, 114
Sràid West Campbell, Glascho.
56 p. 220 mm. EPL.
This edition probably published in 1924 also. "Mairead" was awarded the first prize
in a competition for a Gaelic play at the 1921 National Mod.

MacDhomhnaill, Coinneach D. See MacDonald, Kenneth D.

MacDhomhnaill, Iain A. See MacDonald, John A.

MacDhomhnuill, T. D. See MacDonald, T. D.

Mac Dhonnachaidh, Aonghas. See Robertson, Angus.

MacDhonnchaidh, I. Tormod. See McConochie, J. Norman.

MacDhughaill, Ailean. See MacDougall, Allan.

MacDhughaill, Eachann. See MacDougall, Hector.

MacDiarmid, Alexander, 1853–1930. [*Urnuigh an Tighearna.*] Oban, 1921.
Urnuigh an Tighearna: Mìneachadh Sìmplidh leis An Urramach Alasdair Mac-
Dhiarmaid, 's a' Mhorairne. [Illus.] An t-Oban: air a chlòdh-bhualadh le Eoghan
Dòmhnullach. 1921.
The Lord's Prayer: A Plain Exposition by The Reverend Alexander MacDiarmid,
Morvern. [Illus.] Oban: Hugh MacDonald, Bookseller and Printer. 1921.
108 p. 190 mm. EPL, NLS, PC.

MacDiarmid, James, *d.* 1930. [*Mac Tighearn Aird-Eonaig.*] Inverness, 1901.
Mac Tighearn Aird-Eonaig agus Taibhse Fhionna-Ghlinn. Le Seumas MacDhiar-
maid, Cill-Fhinn. Inverness: printed at The Highland News Printing Works. 1901.
12 p. 190 mm. PC, SS.

MacDonald, Alexander, "Alasdair Mac Mhaighstir Alasdair", *c.* 1690–*c.* 1720. [*Birlinn
Chlann Raghnaill.*] See MacLeod, Angus. [*Sar Orain.*]

—— [*Poems.*] Inverness, 1924.
The Poems of Alexander MacDonald (Mac Mhaighstir Alasdair). Edited with translations, glossary and notes by Rev. A. MacDonald, Minister of Killearnan, joint author
of *The Clan Donald*, etc., and Rev. A. MacDonald, D.D., Minister of Kiltarlity, joint
author of *The Clan Donald*, etc. Inverness: printed by the Northern Counties Newspaper and Printing and Publishing Company, Limited. 1924.
xliv, 408 p; illus. [facsimile]. 270 × 180 mm. AU, BM, EU, GU, Mit.
English verse translation.

MacDonald, Alexander, of Inverness, *d.* 1928. [*Story and Song from Loch Ness-side.*]
Inverness, 1914.
Story and Song from Loch Ness-side. Being principally sketches of olden-time life in
the valley of the Great Glen of Scotland, with particular reference to Glenmoriston and
vicinity. By Alexander MacDonald, Inverness. [Quotation.] Inverness: printed by the
Northern Counties Newspaper and Printing and Publishing Company, Limited.
1914.
v, [1], 330 p; 2 plates. 200 mm. BM, NLS.
Contains some Gaelic.

MacDonald, Alistair M. (tr.). See Kerr, Judith. [*Mog The Forgetful Cat.*]

McDonald, Fr. Allan, 1859–1905. [*Bardachd Mhgr Ailein.*] Edinburgh, 1965.
Bàrdachd Mhgr Ailein. Air a dheasachadh le Iain L. Caimbeul ("Fear Chanaidh").
The Gaelic Poems of Fr. Allan McDonald of Eriskay (1859–1905). Prepared for
publication, with some translations, by John Lorne Campbell, D.Litt., LL.D. Air an
clò-bhualadh le T. & A. Constable, Dùn-Eideann. 1965.
136 p; plate. 230 mm.

—— [*Ceathramhan a Rinneadh do Dh'Eirisgeidh.*] N.p., n.d.
Ceathramhan, a rinneadh do dh' Eirisgeidh.
1 p. 320 mm. NLS.
A photo-copy. The NLS copy is described by J. L. Campbell as "a photograph of
what appears to have been the first printing of the poem now called 'Eilean na h-Oige',
either as a broadsheet or as an offprint, not a reprint from *Am Bolg Solair* (1908)".

—— [*Eilean na h-Oige.*] N.p., n.d.
Eilean na h-Oige. Leis an Athair Urramach Ailean Mac Dhòmhnaill.
[8]. 230 mm. *Xavier.*
Canadian in origin. The poem was first published in *Guth na Bliadhna*, I, 1904.

—— [*Gaelic Words and Expressions from South Uist and Eriskay.*] Dublin, 1958.
Gaelic Words and Expressions from South Uist and Eriskay collected by Rev. Fr. Allan
McDonald of Eriskay (1859–1905). Edited by J. L. Campbell, M.A. (Oxon.),

Hon. LL.D. (Antigonish). Dublin Institute for Advanced Studies, 64–5 Merrion Square. 1958.
[4], 301 p; plate. 230 mm. AU, BM, GU, Mit.
Printed Colm o Lochlainn, Dublin.

——— [*Gaelic Words and Expressions from South Uist and Eriskay.*] Oxford, 1972.
. . . Oxford University Press. 1972.
Second edition with supplements.
[5], 317 p; plate. 230 mm.
See Campbell, John L. [*Fr. Allan MacDonald of Eriskay.*]

MacDonald, Alphonse. [*Cape Breton Songster.*] Sydney, N.S., n.d.
Cape Breton Songster: A Book of Favorite English and Gaelic Songs. Sydney, *c.* 1935.
70 p [Gaelic songs, pp 51–70].
Not seen. Information from *Clare.*

MacDonald, Rev. Angus, 1860–1937. [*The MacDonald Collection of Gaelic Poetry.*]
Inverness, 1911.
The MacDonald Collection of Gaelic Poetry. By the Rev. A. MacDonald, Minister of Killearnan, joint author of *The Clan Donald*, etc., and Rev. A. MacDonald, Minister of Kiltarlity, joint author of *The Clan Donald*, etc. Inverness: The Northern Counties Newspaper and Printing and Publishing Company Ltd. 1911.
xcii, 408 p. 270 mm. AU, BM, GU, Mit.
Pagination in *TS-G* differs.

——— (joint ed.). See MacDonald, Alexander, "Alasdair Mac Mhaighstir Alasdair."
[*Poems.*]

MacDonald, Rev. Archibald, Minister of Kiltarlity, 1853–1948 (tr.). See Boulton, Harold. [*An Unrecorded Miracle of St. Columba.*]

——— (joint ed.). See MacDonald, Alexander, "Alasdair Mac Mhaighstir Alasdair."
[*Poems.*]

——— (joint ed.). See MacDonald, Rev. Angus. [*The MacDonald Collection of Gaelic Poetry.*]

——— (tr.). See Munro, Neil. [*The Lost Pibroch.*]

MacDonald, Archibald, of New Boston. [*Laoidhean.*] Sydney, n.d.
"Na Laoidhean Ghilleasbuig 'ic Dhòmhnuill Oig ann an New Boston. Sydney, *c.* 1900?"
Clare. Dunn. Not seen.

MacDonald, Catherine M. (tr.). See Peach, L. Du Garde. [*Florence Nightingale.*]

MacDonald, Donald, "Dòmhnall Ruadh Chorùna," 1887–1967. [*Domhnall Ruadh Choruna.*] Glasgow, 1969.
Dòmhnall Ruadh Chorùna. Orain is dàin le Dòmhnall Dòmhnallach á Uibhist a Tuath.
Gairm. Glaschu. 1969.
Clò-bhualaidhean Gairm, Leabhar 10.
101 p; plate. 230 mm.
Edited by John A. MacPherson. Foreword by Fred MacAulay.

MacDonald, Donald, of Barvas, 1861–1916. [*Dain, Orain is Sgeulachdan.*] Glasgow, 1920.
The Barvas Bard. Songs, Poems, Stories, and Sketches. By Donald MacDonald, Songsmith of Barvas, Lewis. Now first published. Glasgow: Alexander MacLaren & Sons, Gaelic Printers and Publishers, 360–362 Argyle Street. 1920.

D

Bàrd Bharabhais. Dàin, Orain is Sgeulachdan. Le Dòmhnull MacDhòmhnuill, Gobha ann an Barabhas. Glaschu: Alasdair Mac Labhruinn is a Mhic, 360–362 Sràid Earraghaidheal. 1920.
[6], 87, [3] p; plate. 190 mm. AU, BM, Mit., SS.
Printed Milne, Tannahill & Methven, Perth.

MacDonald, Donald, of Eriskay, 1912– (tr.). See Brandane, John. [*The Change-House.*]

—— (tr.). See Ferguson, J. A. [*Campbell of Kilmhor.*]

—— (tr.). See MacArthur, Bessy J. [*The Clan of Lochlann.*]

—— (tr.). See Milton, J. C. [*Winds for Sale.*]

MacDonald, Donald John, 1919–. [*Sguaban Eorna.*] Inverness, 1973.
Sguaban Eòrna. Bàrdachd Ghàidhlig is Dàin le Dòmhnall Iain MacDhòmhnaill. Uidhist a Deas. Club Leabhar—Inbhirnis.
Air fhoillseachadh le Club Leabhar Ltd., Inbhirnis, 1973.
151 p. 190 mm.
Foreword by William Matheson; cover illustration by Frank Thomson. Printed Eccles, Inverness.

MacDonald, Duncan, of South Uist, 1883–1954. [*Fear na h-Eabaid.*] N.p., n.d.
International Conference held at Stornoway, October 1953, under the auspices of the University of Glasgow and the British Council. Fear na h-Eabaid: the man with the habit. A folk tale related by Duncan MacDonald, Peninerine, South Uist (Donnchadh Mac Dhòmhnaill Mhic Dhonnchaidh), and recorded by John Lorne Campbell, Esq., LL.D., of Canna, at Loch Boisdale, 14th February 1950. Transcribed and translated by Angus Matheson and Derick Thomson. (The Tale was recorded from the same source by K. C. Craig in 1944, and published in his book, Sgialachdan Dhunnchaidh. To facilitate comparison the paragraphing of the version printed here follows that book as closely as possible.)
31 p. 220 mm. PC.

—— [*Sgialachdan Dhunnchaidh.*] Glasgow, [1944].
Sgialachdan Dhunnchaidh. Seann sgialachdan air an gabhail le Dunnchaidh Mac Dhomhnaill ac Dhunnchaidh, Uibhist a Deas, mar a chual e aig athair fhéin iad. 1944. Air an sgrìobhadh le K. C. Craig. Printed and published for K. C. Craig by Alasdair Matheson & Co. Ltd., Glasgow.
[6], 72 p. 220 mm. EPL, EU, GU.
No introduction or notes.

—— [*Sgialachdan Eile o Uibhist.*] [Dublin, 1949.]
Sgialachdan Eile ó Uibhist.
[134]–151 p. 220 mm. NLS.
Editorial Note, "Duncan MacDonald, aged 65, crofter and mason of Peighinn nan Aoghairean, South Uist, is the narrator of these (and other) tales which I wrote down in his hospitable home several years ago: K. C. Craig." Offprint from *Bealoideas/The Journal of the Folklore of Ireland Society*, XIX, 1949 (1950).

—— [*Sgialachdan o Uibhist.*] [Dublin, 1947.]
Sgialachdan ó Uibhist.
[231]–250 p. 220 mm. NLS.
Editorial Note, "The two tales in Scottish Gaelic here published were recorded by Mr K. C. Craig in April 1946 from the recital of Duncan MacDonald, mason, of Peighinn nan Aoghairean, South Uist, in the Hebrides." Offprint from *Bealoideas/ The Journal of the Folklore of Ireland Society*, XVII, 1947 (1949).

MacDonald, Duncan of Stornoway. [*Anna Bhan an Glascho.*] See Tri Comhraidhean.

—— [*Coinneach Beag agus Domhnull Ban.*] See Ceithir Comhraidhean.

—— [*Foirfich Nodha.*] See Tri Comhraidhean.

—— [*Gaelic Idioms and Expressions.*] Glasgow, 1932.
Gaelic Idioms and Expressions. With free translations. Compiled by Duncan Mac-Donald, Headmaster, Sandwickhill Public School, Stornoway. An Comunn Gaidhealach, 212 West George Street, Glasgow. 1932.
[8], 124 p. 190 mm. AU, Mit., PC.
Printed Learmonth. Based on MacDonald's earlier *Gnàthasan Cainnte Gàidhlig.* See immediately below.

—— [*Gnathasan Cainnte Gaidhlig.*] Stornoway, 1927.
Gnàthasan Cainnte Gàidhlig. Gaelic idioms and expressions. Compiled by Duncan MacDonald (President, Lewis Branch of An Comunn Gaidhealach, 1926-7). Published for the Great Féill. Printed at the *Gazette* Office, Stornoway. 1927.
32 p. 220 mm. CoS, Mit., PC.
This is in effect – though not formally – the first edition of the above.

—— (joint ed.). See Eilean Fraoich.

MacDonald, Ewen. See Dwelly, Edward.

MacDonald, Finlay J., 1925– (joint ed.). See Gairm.

—— (tr.). See Wright, Gordon. [*Love Lingers On.*]

MacDonald, Gilbert (tr.). See [Westminster Confession of Faith].

MacDonald, Iain Lom. See MacDonald, John, seventeenth century poet, *c.* 1624–*c.* 1707.

MacDonald, John, "An Dall," Eighteenth Century Poet. [*Laoidhean.*] Oban, 1902.
Laoidhean agus Dain Spioradail. Le Iain Dòmhnullach, an Dall. Oban: printed at the *Oban Times* Office. 1902.
31 p. 190 mm. PC.

MacDonald, John, Lecturer in Celtic in Aberdeen University (ed.). See MacLachlan, Ewen. [*Gaelic Verse.*]

—— (ed.). See Scottish Gaelic Studies.

MacDonald, Rev. Dr. John, of Ferintosh, 1779–1849. [*Leabhar Aithghearr nan Ceist.*] See *The Shorter Catechism.*

—— [*Marbhrainn.*] Edinburgh, 1912.
Marbhrainn a rinneadh air Diadhairibh Urramach nach maireann, agus Dàna Spioradail eile. Le Dr. Iain Dòmhnullach, Ministeir na h-Eaglais Saoire 's an Tòisidheachd. An Seathamh mìle. Edinburgh: John Grant, 31 George IV Bridge. 1912.
202 p. 170 mm. EPL.
1st ed. 1848.

—— [*Marbhrainn.*] Glasgow, n.d.
. . . Le Dr. Iain Dòmhnullach, Ministear na h-Eaglais Saoire 's an Tòisidheachd. Glasgow: Alex. MacLaren & Sons, 268 Argyle Street, C.2.
202 p. 180 mm. Stornoway Public Library.
After 1931.

MacDonald, John, Schoolmaster, 1886–. [*Voices From the Hills.*] Glasgow, 1927.
Voices from the Hills. (Guthan o na Beanntaibh.) A Memento of the Gaelic Rally, 1927. Edited by John MacDonald, M.A. [Illus.] Published by An Comunn Gàidhealach (The Highland Association). 1927.
xv, 304 p; 28 plates; illus. 260 mm. AU, EU, GU, NLS.
Illustrated with line drawings and photographs. A miscellany of poetry and prose in Gaelic and English. Printed Archibald Sinclair, Glasgow.

—— (ed.). See Watson, William J. (general ed.). [*Leabhraichean Sgoile Gaidhlig, An Ceathramh Leabhar Leughaidh.*]

MacDonald, John, Seventeenth Century Poet, *c.* 1624–*c.* 1707. [*Orain Iain Luim.*] Edinburgh, 1964.
Orain Iain Luim. Songs of John MacDonald, Bard of Keppoch. Edited by Annie M. MacKenzie, M.A., Ph.D., Lecturer in the Department of Celtic, University of Aberdeen. Published by Oliver & Boyd for the Scottish Gaelic Texts Society. Edinburgh. 1964.
Scottish Gaelic Texts, Volume Eight.
xlvii, [1] "Table of Sources" [350 × 420 mm], 439 p; maps (on lining papers). 220 mm. English translation on facing pages. Text, pp 1–229; Notes, pp 230–327; Variant Readings, pp 328–375; Metres and Airs, pp 376–382; Appendices, pp 382–425; Vocabulary, pp 426–439.

—— [*Orain Iain Luim.*] Edinburgh, 1964.
. . . Abridged edition. 1964.
xliii, 130 p. 220 mm. PC.
A special paperback edition for schools; lacks the English translation. An edition of MacDonald's poems by A. MacLean Sinclair was published in 1895.

—— [*Orain Iain Luim.*] Edinburgh, 1973.
. . . Published by the Scottish Academic Press for the Scottish Gaelic Texts Society, Edinburgh.
First published 1964. Reprinted 1973.
xlvii, [1], "Table of Sources", 439 p; maps (on lining papers). 220 mm.

MacDonald, [Mrs. John], [*Orain.*] N.p., n.d.
Orain le Bean Iain Dòmhnullaich a Bréanish Uig, Leódhas, a tha 'n diugh an Sgire Shléite anns an Eilean Sgitheanach. (All rights reserved.)
36 p. 180 mm. PC.
Some music in sol-fa.

MacDonald, John A., 1920–. [*Ceum air Cheum.*] Inverness, [Pref. 1968].
Ceum air Cheum. A New Approach to Gaelic. By John A. MacDonald. Air a chlò-bhualadh le Eccles, Inbhirnis.
[2], 28 p. 250 mm.

—— [*Ceum air Cheum.*] Inverness, 1970.
. . . Reprinted 1970. Air a chlò-bhualadh le Eccles, Inbhirnis.
[2], 28 p. 250mm.
Reprinted from *An Gaidheal*, 1964–5. Published by An Comunn Gaidhealach.

—— [*Criochan Ura.*] Glasgow, 1958.
Criochan Ura. Trusadh de rosg is de bhàrdachd o'n ràitheachan Gairm, air a chur ri chéile le Iain A. MacDhòmhnaill. Gairm: 227 Bath Street, Glaschu, C.2. 1958.
Gairm Publications, Vol. I.
150 p; illus. 220 mm. AU, GU.
Contains Vocabulary. Printed Learmonth, Stirling.

—— (ed.). See Grant, Donald. [*Tir an Aigh.*]

MacDonald, Keith Norman, 1835–1913. [*In Defense of Ossian.*] [Oban], 1906.
In defense of Ossian. Being a summary of the evidence in favour of the authenticity of the poems. By Keith Norman MacDonald, M.D. (Reprinted from the *Oban Times.*) 1906.
[4], 73 p, iv, plate. 220 mm.

—— [*MacDonald Bards from Mediaeval Times.*] Edinburgh, 1900.
MacDonald Bards from Mediaeval Times. By Keith Norman MacDonald, M.D. (Reprinted from the *Oban Times.*) Edinburgh: Norman MacLeod, 25 George IV Bridge. 1900.
[6], 126 p. 210 mm. BM, Mit.

—— [*MacDonald Bards from Mediaeval Times.*] Glasgow, 1929.
MacDonald Bards from Mediaeval Times. By Keith Norman MacDonald, M.D. Glasgow: Alex. MacLaren & Sons, 360–362 Argyle Street, C.2.
First published 1900. Re-issued 1929.
[6], 126 p. 210 mm. PC.

—— [*Puirt-a-Beul.*] [Oban], 1901.
Puirt-a-beul—Mouth-tunes: or, Songs for dancing as practised from a remote antiquity by the Highlanders of Scotland. Collected and arranged by Keith Norman Mac-Donald, M.D., and reprinted from the *Oban Times.* 1901.
[1], viii, [3]–54 p. 210 mm. Mit., SS.
    Music in sol-fa.

—— [*Puirt-a-Beul.*] Glasgow, 1931.
Collected and arranged by Keith Norman MacDonald, M.D. Glasgow: Alex Mac-Laren & Sons, 360–362 Argyle Street, C.2.
Reprinted 1931.
[2], viii, [3]–54, [1] p. 210 mm. Mit., PC.

MacDonald, Kenneth. [*An Ealdhain Ur.*] See Ceithir Comhraidhean.

MacDonald, Kenneth D., 1937–. [*Briseadh na Cloiche.*] Glasgow, 1970.
Briseadh na Cloiche, agus sgeulachdan eile. Deasaichte le Coinneach D. Mac-Dhòmhnaill. Roinn nan Cànan Ceilteach, Oilthigh Ghlaschu. 1970.
Leabhraichean ùra Gàidhlig Oilthigh Ghlaschu (fo stiùireadh Ruairidh Mhic Thomais), Aireamh 4.
A selection of the short stories entered for a B.B.C. radio competition in 1968.

MacDonald, Mary, *c.* 1854–. [*Orain Luaidh.*] Glasgow, [Intro. 1949].
Orain Luaidh Màiri Nighean Alasdair. Air an cruinneachadh le K. C. Craig. Published for K. C. Craig by Alasdair Matheson & Co., Ltd., 37 Miller Street, Glasgow, C.1.
[4], 124 p. 190 mm. EU, GU, PC.

MacDonald, Morag. [*Na Fasain Ura.*] See Tri Comhraidhean.

MacDonald, Neil. [*Eachann agus an Tarbh.*] [Glasgow], n.d.
Eachann agus an Tarbh. By Neil MacDonald.
36 p, [10] "Vocabulary." 200 mm. Mit., NLS.
    Mitchell Library copy acquired 1954.

—— [*Eachunn agus an Tarbh.*] [Glasgow], 1973.
Eachunn agus an Tarbh. By Neil MacDonald.
Second edition February 1973.
51 p. 190 mm.
    Foreword by John Paterson, Publications Editor of the Gaelic League of Scotland.
    Printed Learmonth, Stirling.

MacDonald, Norman, of Lewis, 1927–. [*Creach Mhor nam Fiadh.*] Stornoway, 1973.
Creach Mhór nam Fiadh. Le Tormod Dòmhnallach. Na dealbhan le Diana de Vere Cole.
Air a chlò-bhualadh agus air a chur a mach an 1973 le Gasaet Steòrnabhaigh, 10 Sràid Fhrangain, Steòrnabhagh, Eilean Leódhuis.
80 p; illus. 210 mm. PC.

MacDonald, Rev. Norman of Skye, 1904–. [*MacAidh Thiridhe.*] Stirling, n.d.
MacAidh Thiridhe. Leis an Urr. Tormod Dòmhnallach Air a chlòdh-bhualadh do'n Urramach Tormod Dòmhnallach, Ministear Charinis, Uidhist a Tuath, le A. Learmonth agus a Mhac, Sràid an Rìgh, Sruighlea.
[2], 36 p; plate. 190 mm.
  Not seen. 1964.

—— [*Macaidh Thiridhe.*] Stirling, n.d.
MacAidh Thiridhe. Leis an Urr. Tormod Dòmhnallach. (An dara clòdh-bhualadh, le beagan leasachaidh.)
[2], 36 p; plate. 190 mm. PC.
  1970.

MacDonald, R. C. [*Feasgar Trang's an Osd-Thigh.*] [Glasgow], 1949.
Feasgar Trang 's an Osd-Thigh. Dealbh-Chluich an aon sealladh le R. T. Mac-Dhòmhnaill. Printed for An Comunn Gaidhealach by Eneas MacKay, Stirling. 1949.
21 p. 190 mm. EU, GU:CL.

MacDonald, Roderick. [*Gleann an Deoir.*] Glasgow, n.d.
Gleann an Deòir. Dàin Spioradail le Ruairidh Dòmhnullach, Feidigearraidh, Leodhas. Fo làimh Eachainn Mhic Dhùghaill. Songs and Poems by Roderick MacDonald, Fidigarry, Lochs, Stornoway. Glascho: Alasdair MacLabhruinn 's a Mhic, 360–362 Sràid Earra-Ghaidheal, C.2. (All rights reserved.)
31 p. 190 mm. NLS, PC.
  Advertised 1929.

MacDonald, Sileas, c. 1660–c. 1729. [*Bardachd Shilis na Ceapaich.*] Edinburgh, 1972.
Bàrdachd Shìlis na Ceapaich (c. 1660–c. 1729). Air a dheasachadh le Colm O Baoill. Air fhoillseachadh le Comunn Litreachas Gàidhlig na h-Alba. Dun-éideann. 1972.
Poems and Songs by Sileas MacDonald (c. 1660–c. 1729). Edited by Colm O Baoill. Published by The Scottish Academic Press for The Scottish Gaelic Texts Society. Edinburgh. 1972.
Scottish Gaelic Texts, Volume Thirteen. Bàrdachd Shilis na Ceapaich.
lxvii, 271 p. 230 mm.
  Text and Translation, pp 1–122; Notes, pp 123–82; Sources and Readings, pp 183–221; Metres and Tunes, pp 223–47; Appendices, pp 249–61; Index of Names, pp 263–64; Glossary, pp 265–71. Printed R. & R. Clark.

MacDonald, T. D., 1864–1937. [*An Deidh a' Chogaidh.*] Glasgow, [Fore., 1921].
An Déidh a' Chogaidh. Le T. D. MacDhomhnuill. Ughdaire: "Dàin is Dealbhan-fhacail an am a' Chogaidh", etc. Published by Archibald Sinclair, The Celtic Press, Waterloo Street, Glasgow; Hugh MacDonald, Bookseller, Oban; and printed by The Celtic Press as above.
34 p. 190 mm. PC.
  Foreword dated 1921.

—— [*Celtic Dialects.*] Stirling, 1903.
Celtic Dialects: Gaelic, Brythonic, Pictish, and some Stirlingshire place-names. Paper read before the Gaelic Society of Stirling, 31st March 1903, by T. D. MacDonald. Stirling: Eneas Mackay, 43 Murray Place. 1903.
46 p, [2] "The Gaelic Society of Stirling."
200 mm. BM, EU, Mit.

—— [*Dain agus Dealbhan-Fhacail.*] Glasgow, n.d.
Dàin agus Dealbhan-fhacail an am a' Chogaidh. Le T. D. MacDhòmhnuill, Ughdar: "Dàin Eadar-theangaichte", "Puirt mo Sheanmhair", "Celtic Dialects", "The Lords of Lochaber", "War-Time Verses", "Appin and its Neighbourhood", etc. Glasgow: Archibald Sinclair, Celtic Press, 47 Waterloo Street.
64 p. 190 mm. BM, Mit., NLS, PC.
Advertised as "now ready" in *An Deo-Greine*, February 1919.

—— [*Dain Eadar-Theangaichte.*] Stirling, 1903.
Dàin Eadar-Theangaichte. Le T. D. MacDhòmhnuill. Air an clò-bhualadh le Aonghas MacAoidh, Struidhla. 1903.
95 p, [1] "Errata". 200 mm. AU, BM, Mit., NLS, SS.
Printed Jamieson & Munro, Stirling.
Includes 9 poems by Robert Burns.

—— [*Gaelic Proverbs.*] Stirling, [Intro. 1926].
Gaelic Proverbs and Proverbial Sayings. With English translation. T. D. MacDonald, author of "The Lords of Lochaber", "Celtic Dialects", "Dàin Eadar-theangaichte", "Dàin an am a' Chogaidh", "Dàin an déidh a' Chogaidh", etc. Eneas MacKay, Stirling.
156, [3] p. 190 mm. BM, GU, SS.
Printed Jamieson & Munro, Stirling.

—— (ed.) See *Puirt mo Sheanmhar*.

MacDougall, Alexander, 1837–1919. [*Laoidh air Fulangais Chriosd.*] Oban, n.d.
Laoidh air fulangais Chriosd. Words by Alexander MacDougall. Music from "The Celtic Lyre".
3 p. 220 mm. Mit.
Printed *Oban Times*, Oban. *TS-G* gives date of publication as 1902. Music in sol-fa.

—— (tr.). See Owen, John. [*The Glory of Christ.*]

MacDougall, Allan, *fl.* 1873–1928. [*Laoidhean Molaidh.*] Glasgow, n.d.
Laoidhean Molaidh. Leis an Urramach Ailean Mac Dhùghaill, An Caolas, Tirithe. Fo làimh Eachainn Mhic Dhùghaill. Glasco: Alasdair Mac Labhruinn 's a Mhic, 360–362 Sràid Earraghaidheal, C.2.
64 p. 190 mm. BM, PC, SSG.
c. 1928.

MacDougall, Dugald G., 1845–1914. [*Braiste Lathurna.*] Glasgow, 1959.
Bràiste Lathurna. (The Brooch of Lorn.) A memorial volume of Gaelic Poems and Songs by the late Dugald Gordon MacDougall, Bard of the Clan MacDougall. Compiled and edited with biographical sketch by Somerled MacMillan. Printers: K. & R. Davidson, Ltd., 205–207 West George Street, Glasgow. 1959.
174 p; 2 plates. 220 mm. GU, Mit.

MacDougall, Hector, 1880–1954. [*A' Bhraisd Lathurnach.*] Glasgow, n.d.
The Ceilidh Books. Leabhraichean nan Céilidh. Aireamh 4. A' Bhràisd Lathurnach. Le Eachann Mac Dhùghaill. [Illus.] A' phrìs, se sgillinnean. 6d. Alasdair Mac Labhruinn agus a Mhic, 360–362 Sràid Earraghaidheal, Glascho.
[177]–206 p. 220 mm. PC.
Reprinted from "Guth na Bliadhna", XI.2, Summer 1914.

—— [*Cath-Chuairt Eideirt Bhruis an Eirinn.*] Glasgow, n.d.
Cath-chuairt Eideirt Bhruis an Eirinn. Le Eachann Mac Dhùghaill, ùghdar "An Gaol a bheir Buaidh", "Somhairle Mór MacGhille Bhrìde", etc. Le Roimh-radh, bho pheann Ruaraidh Arascainn is Mhàirr. A' phrìs – aon tasdan. Alasdair Mac Labhrainn is a Mhic, 360 Sràid Earraghaidheal, Glascho.
iv, 60 p; plate. 220 mm. BM, NLS, PC, SS.
Reviewed in "An Deo-Greine", April 1919; advertised in "An Deo-Greine" and "Guth na Bliadhna" 1919.

—— [*Dealbh-Chluichean Gaidhlig.*] Glasgow, n.d.
Dealbh-chluichean Gàidhlig. Le Eachann Mac Dhùghaill. Gaelic Plays. Còir
Samhna air Leannan. Glascho: Alasdair MacLabhruinn is a Mhic, 360–362 Sràid
Earraghaidheal, C.2.
31 p. 190 mm. BM, NLS, PC.
    Contains also "Mar a dh'aisigeadh dhi a' Ghàidhlig", pp 21–31. Reviewed in
"An Gaidheal", January 1925; dated 1924 in *MacLaren*.

—— [*An Gaol a Bheir Buaidh.*] Glasgow, 1912.
An Gaol a Bheir Buaidh. Dealbh-chluich le Eachann M. Mac Dhùghaill. Gilleasbuig
Mac-na-Ceàrdadh, Clo-bhualadair, 47 Waterloo Street, Glascho. 1912.
19 p. 230 mm. GU-CL, PC.

—— [*Smeorach nan Cnoc 's nan Gleann.*] Glasgow, 1939.
Smeòrach nan Cnoc 's nan Gleann. Comh-chruinneachadh bàrdachd a chaidh a
dheanamh am Màrgairi an Iar-dheas, Ceap Breatuinn. Roimh-radh leis an Oll. P. I.
Mac Neacail. Fo làimh Eachainn Mhic Dhùghaill. Glascho: Alasdair Maclabhruinn
agus a Mhic, 268 Sràid Earraghaidheal, C.2.
The Songster of the Hill and the Glen. A collection of Gaelic poetry. Foreword by
the Rev. Dr. P. J. Nicholson, Antigonish, Nova Scotia. Edited by Hector MacDougall.
Glasgow: Alexander MacLaren & Sons, 268 Argyle Street, C.2.
First published 1939.
xii, 148 p; plate. 190 mm. BM, Mit., NLS.
    Another foreword by Donald MacFarlane.

—— [*Somhairle Mor Mac Ghille-Bhride.*] [Glasgow, n.d.]
Somhairle Mór Mac Ghille-Bhrìde. Eachann Mac Dhùghaill.
[191–218] p. 220 mm.
    Referred to in "Cath-chuairt Eideirt Bhruis an Eirinn" as one of MacDougall's
publications: not seen. Presumably a reprint from "Guth na Bliadhna" in the
Leabhraichean nan Ceilidh series (published by Alex. MacLaren, Glasgow); it
appeared in "Guth na Bliadhna", Leabhar X.2, Spring 1913: the collation above is
derived from that source.

—— [*Tri Orain Eireannach.*] [?]
Tri Orain Eireannach air an cur an Gàidhlig Albannaich: "Dàn Moladh na Gaedhilge",
"Eibhlin a Rùin", "Páistin Fionn". 1911.
    Not seen. Information from a list of MacDougall's publications by T. M. Murchi-
son. "Gairm", Vol. 8, Summer 1954.

—— (joint author). See *Comhraidhean Gaidhlig*.

—— (ed.). See Grant, Peter. [*Dain Spioradail.*]

—— (ed.). See MacCormick, John. [*Gaol air a Dhearbhadh.*]

—— (ed.). See MacDonald, Roderick. [*Gleann an Deoir.*]

—— (ed.). See MacDougall, Allan. [*Laoidhean Molaidh.*]

—— (ed.). See MacKay, Roderick. [*Oiteagan a Tir nan Og.*]

—— (ed.). See MacKenzie, William. [*Cnoc Chusbaig.*]

—— (ed.). See MacLennan, John. [*Duanagan agus Sgeulachdan Beaga.*]

—— (ed.). See MacNiven, Duncan (joint author). [*Baird Chill-Chomain.*]

—— (ed.). See Matheson, Jessie. [*Gleann na h-Irioslachd.*]

—— (ed.). See Matheson, John. [*Fiosrachadh Mu'n Bhiobull.*]

—— (ed.). See Morrison, Angus, of Barvas. [*An Gradh-Bhuan.*]

—— (ed.). See Nicolson, Nicol. [*An t-Urramach Iain Mac Rath.*]

—— (ed.). See Sinclair, A. MacLean. [*Clarsach na Coille.*]

—— (ed.). See Smith, Dr. John. [*Urnuighean air son Theaghlaichean.*]

—— (ed.). See Willison, John. [*Mother's Catechism.*]

MacDougall, James, 1833–1906. [*Folk Tales and Fairy Lore.*] Edinburgh, 1910.
  Folk Tales and Fairy Lore in Gaelic and English. Collected from oral tradition by Rev.
  James MacDougall, sometime Minister of Duror, author of *Craignish Tales*, and *Folk
  and Hero Tales*. Edited with introduction and notes by Rev. George Calder, B.D.,
  Minister of Strathfillan, author of *The Irish Aeneid*, Honorary Member of the Caledonian Medical Society. Edinburgh: John Grant, 31 George IV Bridge. 1910.
  xv, 328 p; plate. 230 mm. BM, GU, Mit., NLS.
    The English and Gaelic are on facing pages. Printed Archibald Sinclair, Glasgow.

MacEacharn, Domhnull. See MacKechnie, Donald.

MacEachen, Ewen, 1769–1849. [*Faclair Gaidhlig is Beurla.*] Inverness, 1902.
  Faclair Gàidhlig is Beurla le Eobhan Mac-Eachainn. MacEachen's Gaelic-English
  Dictionary. Second edition Revised and enlarged by Alexander MacBain, LL.D.,
  and John Whyte. Inverness: *The Highland News* Office. 1902.
  viii, 406 p. 190 mm. AU, GU, Mit.
    1st ed. (with 402 p) was in 1842.

—— [*Faclair Gaidhlig is Beurla.*] Inverness, 1906.
  . . . Third edition. Revised and enlarged by Alexander MacBain, LL.D., and John
  Whyte. Inverness: Taylor and Bain. 1906.
  x, 407 p. 190 mm. AU, BM.

—— [*Faclair Gaidhlig is Beurla.*] Inverness, 1922.
  . . . Fourth edition. Revised and enlarged. Inverness: The Northern Counties Newspaper and Printing and Publishing Company, Limited. 1922.
  xi, [1], 475 p. 170 mm. PC.
    This edition revised by R. Barron and Dr. Donald James MacLeod.

—— [*Faclair Gaidhlig is Beurla.*] Inverness, 1936.
  . . . Fifth edition. Revised and enlarged. The Northern Counties Newspaper and
  Printing and Publishing Company, Limited. 1936.
  xi, [1], 321 p. 190 mm. BM, NLS.

—— [*Faclair Gaidhlig is Beurla.*] Inverness, 1948.
  Ibid.
  xi, [1], 321 p. 190 mm.

—— [*Faclair Gaidhlig is Beurla.*] Inverness, 1960.
  . . . Fifth edition. Revised and enlarged. Highland Printers, Limited, Inverness. 1960.
  xi, [1], 321 p. 190 mm. EPL.

—— [*Faclair Gaidhlig is Beurla.*] Inverness, 1968, 1970.
  Ibid.
  xi, [1], 321 p. 190 mm.
    With imprints, "Second impression" and "3rd impression", respectively.

—— (tr.). See Scupoli, Lorentzo. [*Combattimento Spirituale.*]

Mac Eanruig, Aonghas. See Henderson, Angus.

MacEchern, Dugald, 1867–1947. [*Clarsach nan Gaidheal*.] Inverness, 1904.
Clàrsach nan Gàidheal (Harp of the Gael). With English translations. By Rev. Dugald
MacEchern, M.A., B.D., Bard to the Gaelic Society of Inverness. Printed by per-
mission of The Comunn Gaidhealach, being the Society's Mod Poem, awarded the
Prize of the Highland Society of London.
Inverness: printed by T. M. Thomson, 5 Chapel Street. 1904.
26 p. 150 mm. PC.
    Gaelic original, pp 4–12; English translation, pp 13–26.

MacErlean, John C. (joint ed.). See Hogan, Edmund. [*Luibhleabhran*.]

MacFadyen, John, 1850–1935. [*Companach na Cloinne*.] Stirling, 1912.
[Cover] Companach na Cloinne. Leabhran Sgoil anns am bheil sgeòil thaitneach.
[Illus.] Aonghas Mac Aoidh, 43 Murray Place, Stirling. 1912.
[Title page] Companach na Cloinne. Le Iain Mac Phaidein. Fo làimh Chaluim Mhic
Phàrlain.
84 p, [1] "An Clar-amais". 190 mm. AU, BM, GU:CL, Mit.

—— [*An t-Eileanach*.] Glasgow, 1921.
The Islander. Original Gaelic Songs, Poems and Readings. By John MacFadyen,
Glasgow. Second edition. Glasgow: Alex. MacLaren & Sons, 360 Argyle Street.
1921.
An t-Eileanach. Dàin, Orain agus Sgeoil-aithris. Le Iain Mac Phaidein, Glascho. An
dara clò-bhualadh. Glascho: Alasdair Mac Labhrainn agus a Mhic, 360 Sràid Earra-
Ghaidheal. 1921.
xii, 314 p; plate. 190 mm. AU, BM, GU:CL, Mit.
    1st ed. 1890 (303 p).

—— [*Sgeulaiche nan Caol*.] Glasgow, 1902.
Sgeulaiche nan Caol. Original Gaelic Readings, Sketches, Poems and Songs. By John
MacFadyen, Glasgow, author of "An t-Eileanach". [Illus.] Glasgow: Archibald
Sinclair, "Celtic Press", 47 Waterloo Street. 1902.
xiv, 296 p; plate. 190 mm. AU, BM, GU, Mit., SS.
    Some music, in sol-fa.

MacFarlane, Alexander (ed.). See MacLennan, Malcolm. [*Handbood of Gaelic Phrases
    and Sentences*.]

MacFarlane, Angus. [*Gaelic Names of Plants*.] Inverness, 1928.
Gaelic Names of Plants: Studies of their Uses and Lore. By the Rev. Angus Mac-
Farlane, F.S.A. (Scot.). Reprinted from the "Transactions of the Gaelic Society",
Vol. XXXII. Inverness: printed at the *Northern Chronicle* Office. 1928.
48 p. 220 mm. AU.

MacFarlane, Donald. *The Rev. Donald MacDonald*. Glasgow, 1903.
Memoir and remains of the Rev. Donald MacDonald, Shieldaig, Ross-shire. By the
Rev. Donald MacFarlane (late of Raasay), minister of the Free Presbyterian Church,
Dingwall. [Quotation.] Glasgow: John M'Neilage, 65 Great Western Road. 1903.
vi, 224 p. 220 mm. Mit.
    Mostly in English; Gaelic elegy on Rev. Donald MacDonald, by Roderick Ferguson,
    pp 222–4.

MacFarlane, Malcolm, 1853–1931. [*Binneas nam Bard*.] Stirling, 1908.
Binneas nam Bàrd. Leabhar anns am bheil dàin, òrain is duanagan nan Gaidheal
Albannach air am foillseachadh maille ri'm fuinn. Le Calum Mac Phàrlain. Leabhar
a h-Aon. Earrann a h-Aon. Struibhle: Aonghas Mac Aoidh, 43 Murray Place. 1908.
Bardic Melody. A book in which the poems, songs and ditties of the Scottish Gaels are

exhibited along with their airs. By Malcolm Mac Farlane. Book 1, Part 1. Stirling: Eneas MacKay, 43 Murray Place. 1908.
x, 112 p. 220 mm. AU, BM, GU:CL, Mit., NLS., SS.
    Printed Archibald Sinclair, Glasgow. 9 parts were proposed; according to "The Celtic Who's Who" (Kirkcaldy, 1921; edited Lachlan MacBean), MacFarlane "edited first and second numbers of *Binneas nam Bard*"; but a second part has not been traced and only Part 1 appears in the School of Scottish Studies Library, which contains MacFarlane's own private library.

—— [*Am Bru-Dhearg.*] Stirling, 1909.
Am Brù-Dhearg. Fo làimh Chaluim Mhic Phàrlain. Air a chur am mach le Aonghas Mac Aoidh, 43 Murray Place, Struibhle. 1909.
The Robin. Edited by Malcolm Mac Farlane. Music by C. H. MacKay. Stirling: Eneas MacKay, 43 Murray Place. 1909.
24 p. 180 mm. Mit., NLS, PC, SS.
    2-part harmony; sol-fa.

—— [*Am Bru-Dhearg.*] Stirling, 1913.
Am Brù-dhearg. 3d net. [Illus.] Fo laimh Chaluim Mhic Phàrlain. Air a chur am mach le Aonghas Mac Aoidh, 43 Murray Place, Struibhle. 1913.
The Robin. 3d net. [Illus.] Edited by Malcolm Mac Farlane. Music by C. H. MacKay. Stirling: Eneas MacKay, 43 Murray Place. 1913.
24 p. 190 mm. PC.

—— [*Am Comh-Threoraiche.*] Stirling, 1911.
[Cover] An Comh-threòraiche. Leabhran Sgoil a chum feum na cloinne. [Illus.] Aonghas Mac Aoidh, 43 Murray Place, Stirling. 1911.
[Title page] An Comh-threòraiche. Le Calum Mac Phàrlain.
64 p; illus. 200 mm. BM, GU:CL, SS.

—— [*An Lon Dubh.*] Part I. Paisley, n.d.
Part I. An Lòndubh (The Blackbird). A collection of Twenty Gaelic Songs, with music, in two-part harmony. Intended for use in the schools of the Highlands; but all the songs are suitable for adults. J. and R. Parlane, Paisley; John Menzies and Co., Edinburgh and Glasgow; Houlston and Sons, London. 2d. net.
16 p. 190 mm. PC.
    The first advertisement seen was in 1905; *TS-G* suggests, "*c.* 1908".

—— [*An Lon Dubh.*] Part I. Paisley, n.d.
. . . J. and R. Parlane, Paisley; John Menzies and Col, Edinburgh and Glasgow; Madgwick, Houlston and Co. Ltd., London. 2d. net.
24 p. 190 mm. AU.
    Advertised as "just out", 1908.

—— [*An Lon Dubh.*] Part I. Dundee, n.d.
. . . suitable for adults. Malcolm C. MacLeod, 183 Blackness Road, Dundee.
24 p. 190 mm. PC.
    Gaelic editor Malcolm MacFarlane; musical arrangements by R. D. Jameson and Neil Orr. Music in sol-fa notation.

—— [*An Lon Dubh.*] Part II. Paisley, n.d.
Part II. An Lòn Dubh (The Blackbird). [Illus.] A collection of twenty-six Gaelic songs, with music, in two-part harmony. Intended for use in the schools of the Highlands; but all the songs are suitable for adults. J. and R. Parlane, Paisley; John Menzies and Co., Edinburgh and Glasgow; Madgwick, Houlston and Co., Ltd., London. 2d. net.
24 p. 190 mm. AU.

—— [*An Lon Dubh.*] Part II. Dundee, n.d.
. . . suitable for adults. Malcolm C. MacLeod, 183 Blackness Road, Dundee.
24 p. 190 mm. PC.
    Gaelic editor Malcolm MacFarlane. Musical arrangements by R. D. Jameson and
Neil Orr.

—— [*Mairi Nighean Alasdair Ruaidh.*] Glasgow, n.d.
The Ceilidh Books. Leabhraichean na Céilidh. Aireamh 36. Màiri Nighean Alasdair
Ruaidh.
Le Calum Mac Phàrlain. A' phrìs, trì sgillinnean. 3d. Alasdair MacLabhruinn agus
a Mhic, 360–362 Sràid Earraghaidheal, Glascho.
[17]–36 p. 220 mm. PC.
    Reprinted from *Guth na Bliadhna*, XI.1, Spring, 1914.

—— [*Am Mosgladh Mor.*] [?]
Am Mosgladh Mor.
[136]–8, [156]–9, [171]–4. 240 mm.
    Not seen. One of a number of plays advertised in "An Deo-Greine", X:3–6 (Dec.
1914–March 1915) by Alex. MacLaren & Sons. First published in *The Celtic
Monthly*, Vol. XXII, 1914, from which the above collation is derived: presumably
an offprint. See detailed note under Donald Sinclair: "Suiridhe Raoghail Mhaoil".

—— [*Am Mosgladh Mor.*] Glasgow, n.d.
An Comunn Gaidhealach. [Illus.] Dealbhchluich-ciùil Cloinne. Am Mosgladh Mór
(An Dara duais, Mod 1925). Le Calum Mac Phàrlain. A' phrìs, se sgillinn. An
Comunn Gaidhealach, 114 Sràid West Campbell, Glascho.
16 p. 220 mm. AU, Mit., PC.
    Advertised as "New Publication" in *An Gaidheal*, XXI.7, April 1926. Music in
sol-fa.

—— [*The Phonetics of the Gaelic Language.*] Dundee, n.d.
The Phonetics of the Gaelic Language, with an exposition of the current orthography
and a system of phonography. By Malcolm MacFarlane. [Quotation.] Dundee:
Malcolm C. MacLeod.
95 p; illus. 190 mm. PC.
    Printed Geo. E. Findlay, Dundee. 1st ed. 1889 of which this is a reprint.

—— [*The School Gaelic Dictionary.*] Stirling, 1912.
The School Gaelic Dictionary. Prepared for the use of learners of the Gaelic language.
By Malcolm MacFarlane. Eneas MacKay, Bookseller, 43 Murray Place, Stirling.
1912.
Am Briathrachan Beag. Air a dheasachadh a chum feum luchd-ionnsachaidh na
Gàidhlig le Calum Mac Phàrlain. Aonghas Mac Aoidh, Leabhar-reiceadair, 43 Murray
Place, Struibhle. 1912.
viii, 189 p, [2] Exs. of proof correcting. 200 mm. AU, BM, GU, Mit., NLS.

—— [*The School Gaelic Dictionary.*] Stirling, n.d.
. . . Eneas MacKay, Stirling.
. . . Aonghas Mac Aoidh, Struibhle.
vii, 189 p, [2] Exs. of proof correcting. 190 mm. NLS.

—— [*Gaelic-English Dictionary.*] Stirling, n.d.
Gaelic-English Dictionary. Prepared for the use of students of the Gaelic language.
By Malcolm MacFarlane. Eneas MacKay, Stirling.
[4], 189 p, [1] Exs. of proof correcting. 190 mm. EPL.
    This edition is dated "1948" in the Edinburgh Public Library catalogue; no evidence
for this dating is traceable in the copy itself. Otherwise the relationship of the above
editions is not clear.

—— [*An Sgeul Goirid.*] Glasgow, n.d.
The Ceilidh Books. Leabhraichean nan Ceilidh. Aireamh 2. An Sgeul Goirid, le Calum Mac Phàrlain. Thall 's a Bhos, le Iain Mac Cormaic. [Illus.] A' phrìs, se sgillinnean. 6d. Alasdair Mac Labhruinn agus a Mhic, 360–362 Sràid Earraghaidheal, Glascho.
64 p. 220 mm. PC.
Reprinted from *An Sgeulaiche*, III.1, Spring, 1911.

—— [*An Smeorach.*] Stirling, n.d.
An Smeòrach. [Illus.] Fo làimh Chaluim Mhic Phàrlain. Air a chur am mach le Aonghas Mac Aoidh, Struibhle. Price sixpence.
The Mavis. Edited by Malcolm Mac Farlane. Music by C. H. MacKay. Eneas MacKay, Stirling.
24 p. 180 mm. Mit., PC.
First advertised in *An Deò-Greine*, III.2, Nov. 1907.

—— [*An Smeorach.*] Stirling, 1911.
. . . Air a chur am mach le Aonghas Mac Aoidh, 43 Murray Place, Struibhle. 1911.
. . . Stirling: Wneas MacKay, 43 Murray Place. 1911.
24 p. 200 m. AU, SS.

—— [*An Smeorach.*] Stirling, 1920.
. . . 1920.
24 p. 180 mm. PC.
Music in sol-fa notation; two-part harmony.

—— *Songs of the Highlands.*] Inverness, n.d.
Songs of the Highlands. The Gaelic and English Words arranged by Malcolm Mac Farlane. The Symphonies and Accompaniments by Fr. W. Whitehead. Inverness: Logan & Company, 59 Church Street; also, Aberdeen, Elgin, Nairn, and Dingwall.
vii, 201 p. 360 mm. AU, BM, GU, Mit.
First advertised in *Am Bard*, 1902; notice in *TGSJ*, 1902. Music in both notations.

—— [*An Treoraiche.*] Stirling, 1903.
An Treòraiche. Leabhran sgoil air son na cloinne. Air a chur a mach le Aonghas Mac Aoidh, Leabhar-reiceadair, 43 Murray Place, Struibhle. 1903. 3d.
Bha an leabhran so air a chur ri chéile le Calum Mac Phàrlain; agus air a chur a mach le còmhnadh o Chéilidh nan Gaidheal am Baile Ghlascho.
40 p; illus. 190 mm. PC.

—— [*An Treoraiche.*] Stirling, 1906.
. . . 1906.
An dara clò-bhualadh.
40 p; illus. 190 mm. PC.

—— [*An Treoraiche.*] Stirling, 1911.
An Treòraiche. Leabhran sgoil a chum feum na cloinne. Air a thoirt a mach le Aonghas Mac-Aoidh, Leabhar-reiceadair, 43 Murray Place, Struibhle. 1911. 3d.
An Treòraiche. Le Calum Mac Phàrlain. An treas clò-bhualadh.
40 p; illus. 190 mm. AU, GU:CL, SS.
All editions printed by Jamieson & Munro, Stirling.

—— [*An Uiseag.*] Glasgow, n.d.
The Lark. Second edition. An Uiseag. Leabhran-ciùil air son sgoilean. Air a chur a mach le Calum Mac Phàrlain agus Eanraig Mac Gille-bhàin. Gaelic songs for schools, in two-part harmony. Archibald Sinclair, 47 Waterloo Street, Glasgow. 3d.
16 p. 160 mm. FC.

—— [*An Uiseag.*] Glasgow, n.d.
The Lark. Third edition. An Uiseag.
16 p. 160 mm. GU:CL.

—— [*An Uiseag.*] Glasgow, n.d.
The Lark. Fourth edition. An Uiseag.
16 p. 160 mm. Mit., PC.
    Sinclair's address changed to 27a Cadogan Street, Glasgow, in this edition. "An Clàr-Innsidh" on inside back cover. Music in sol-fa notation. First edition 1894.

—— (Gaelic ed.). See Given, Jennie. [*Clarsach a' Ghlinne.*]

—— (rev. ed.). See MacBain, Alexander. [*Etymological Dictionary of the Gaelic Language.*]

—— (ed.). See MacCormick, John. [*Seanchaidh na h-Airigh.*]

—— (ed.). See MacCormick, John. [*Seanchaidh na Traghad.*]

—— (ed.). See MacFadyen, John. [*Companach na Cloinne.*]

—— (ed.). See MacLean, Lachlan. [*Uilleam Uallas, Iain Knox agus Rob Ruadh.*]
(ed.). See MacRae, Duncan. [*Fernaig Manuscript.*]

—— (ed.). See *Uirsgeulan Gaidhealach.*

MacFarlane, Murdo, 1901–. [*An Toinneamh Diomhair.*] Stornoway, n.d.
An Toinneamh Diomhair. Na h-Orain aig Murchadh MacPhàrlain, Bàrd Mhealaboist. Air a chlò-bhualadh agus air a chur a mach le Gasaet Steòrnabhaigh, 10 Sràid Fhrangain, Steòrnabhagh, Eilean Leódhuis.
102 p; plate. 220 mm.
    Published 1973. Foreword by A. J. MacAskill.

MacFarlane-Barrow, James, 1880–1943. [*Laoidh-Dhiann Aithreachais.*] [1919?]
Laoidh-dhiann Aithreachais.
    Not seen. Referred to in "The Celtic Who's Who" (ed. Lachlan MacBean; Kirkcaldy, 1921).

—— [*Urnuighean Sonruichte ann an am Cogaidh.*] [1915?]
Urnuighean sònruichte ann an ám cogaidh.
    Not seen. Information from "The Celtic Who's Who" (1921).

—— (comp.). See Urnuighean Airson na Cloinne.

Mac Fheargais, Fionnladh. See Ferguson, Finlay.

Mac Fhionghain, Alasdair. See MacKinnon, Alexander.

Mac Fhionghain, Domhnall. See MacKinnon, Donald.

Mac Fhionghain, Ruairidh. See MacKinnon, Roderick.

MacFhionghuin, Lachlann. See MacKinnon, Lachlan.

MacGaraidh, Seumas, 1885–1966. [*The Bracken Ablaze.*] London. n.d.
The Bracken Ablaze. Being Fugitive Verses in Gaelic and English by Seumas MacGaraidh. With Introduction by Compton MacKenzie. London: Arthur H. Stockwell, Limited, 29 Ludgate Hill, E.C.4.
96 p; plate. 180 mm. NLS.
    Contains 15 Gaelic poems. Printed in John Drew, Ltd., Aldershot. *c.* 1941. "Seumas MacGaraidh" was the pseudonym of James MacDonald Hay.

Mac Ghill Eathain, Somhairle. See MacLean, Sorley.

Mac Ghille Mhoire, Aonghas. See Morrison, Angus.

MacGilleathain, Ailean Caimbeul. See MacLean, Allan Campbell.

MacGilleathain, Gilleasbuig. See MacLean, Archibald.

Mac Gill-Eathain, Lachlann. See MacLean, Lachlan.

MacGilleathain, Niall. See MacLean, Neil.

MacGillemhicheil, Alasdair. See Carmichael, Alexander.

Mac Gillfhaolain, Aonghas. See MacLellan, Angus.

MacGill-Fhinnein, Gordon. See MacLennan, Gordon.

MacGillivray, Angus, 1805–?. [*Our Gaelic Proverbs.*] Glasgow, 1928.
  Our Gaelic Proverbs. A Mirror of the Past. By Angus MacGillivray, C.M., M.D.,
  D.Sc., F.R.S.E., F.S.A.Scot. Reprinted from the *Caledonian Medical Journal*, January
  1928. Glasgow: printed by Alex. MacDougall, 70 Mitchell Street. 1928.
  20 p. 220 mm. EPL, PC.

MacGillivray, John (ed.). See MacLean, John. [*Oran do Mhac-Mhic-Alasdair Ghlinne-Garadh.*]

MacGreggor, Stuart (joint author). See MacLean, Sorley. [*Four Points of a Saltire.*]

MacGregor, Alexander, 1806–?. [*Songs.*] N.p., n.d.
  Songs of Alexander MacGregor. By Rev. Chas. M. Robertson.
  16 p. 220 mm. EU.
  No title page.

MacGregor, James, Dean of Lismore, *c.* 1480–1551. [*Heroic Poetry from the Book of the Dean of Lismore.*] Edinburgh, 1939.
  Heroic Poetry from the Book of the Dean of Lismore. Edited by Neil Ross, C.B.E.,
  D.D., D.Litt., Minister of Laggan. Published by Oliver & Boyd for the Scottish Gaelic
  Texts Society. Edinburgh. 1939.
  Scottish Gaelic Texts, Volume Three.
  xxxi. 306 p. 230 mm. AU, BM, GU, Mit.
    Text, pp 1–207; Notes, pp 208–53; Appendices, pp 254–80; Indexes, pp 285–306.

MacGregor, James, Dean of Lismore, *c.* 1480–1551. [*Poems from the Book of the Dean of Lismore.*] Cambridge, 1937.
  Poems from the Book of the Dean of Lismore, with a catalogue of the book and indexes
  by E. C. Quiggin, Late Fellow of Granville and Caius College, Cambridge. Edited by
  J. Fraser, Jesus Professor of Celtic in the University of Oxford. Cambridge: at the
  University Press. 1937.
  xii, 111 p, [1] "Index of Authors". 250 mm. BM, EU, GU:CL, Mit.

MacGregor, James, Dean of Lismore, *c.* 1480–1551. [*Scottish Verse from the Book of the Dean of Lismore.*] Edinburgh, 1937.
  Scottish Verse from the Book of the Ddan of Lismore. Edited by William J. Watson,
  LL.D., Litt.D.Celt., Professor of Celtic in the University of Edinburgh. Published by
  Oliver & Boyd for the Scottish Gaelic Texts Society. Edinburgh. 1937.
  Scottish Gaelic Texts, Volume One.
  xl. 335 p. 230 mm. AU, BM, GU, Mit., NLS.
    Text, pp 1–255; Notes, pp 257–300; Glossarial Index, pp 310–20; Index of Places,
    pp 321–7 List of Members, pp 329–35.

—— [*Scottish Verse from the Book of the Dean of Lismore.*] Edinburgh, 1937.
... 1937.
155 p. 220 mm. EU, PC.
Special edition for schools; no translation or notes.
Indexes to the Book of the Dean of Lismore, by T. F. O. Rahilly, published in
Scottish Gaelic Studies, Vol. IV.I.

MacGregor, Lt.-Col. John, 1848–1932. [*Luinneagan Luaineach.*] [?]
Luinneagan Luaineach.
This book was published in 1897; but it is included in a list of "just published" books
by Alex. MacLaren in 1929. There is no other evidence for a 20th century edition.

Mac Iain, Donnachadh. See Johnston, Duncan.

Mac Ille Mhoire, Murchadh. See Morrison, Murdo.

Mac 'Ill Fhialain, Aonghus. See MacLellan, Angus.

MacInnes, Duncan, d. 1903. [*Comhraidhean.*] Glasgow, 1938.
Còmhraidhean an Gàidhlig 's am Beurla. Conversations in Gaelic and English. By
Rev. D. MacInnes, author of "Folk and Hero Tales of Argyllshire". With introduction
by Professor Blackie. [Quotation.] New edition. Glasgow: Alex. MacLaren & Sons,
268 Argyle Street, C.2.
First edition 1880. Reprinted 1938.
64 p. 190 mm. EPL, PC.

MacInnes, John, of The School of Scottish Studies, Edinburgh University, 1930– (joint
ed.). See Campbell, John F. [*More West Highland Tales.*] Volume Two.

—— See School of Scottish Studies. [*Music from the Western Isles.*]

—— See School of Scottish Studies. [*The Waulking Songs of Barra.*]

MacInnes, John, of South Uist (comp.). See Campbell, John. [*Orain Ghaidhlig.*]

MacInnes, L. [*Dialect of South Kintyre.*] Campbeltown, n.d.
Dialect of South Kintyre. An interesting study by Mr. L. MacInnes. Reprinted from
The Campbeltown Courier.
A paper on the Dialect of S. Kintyre, submitted to the Kintyre Antiquarian Society, by
Mr. L. MacInnes.
29 p. 230 mm. GU:CL.
A study of the Scots dialect of Kintyre. "List of Gaelic words in the dialect of South
Kintyre", pp 10–13.

MacInnes, Malcolm, 1871–1951. [*Iseabail na h-Airigh.*] Glasgow, [*c.* 1933].
A Highland Musical Play Sgeul-òran le Fuinn. Iseabail na h-Airigh. Ishebel of the
Shealing. Introducing 33 original songs and melodies. The words in Gaelic and
English. The music in staff and sol-fa notations. Written and composed by Malcolm
MacInnes, M.A., LL.B. Glasgow: Alex. MacLaren & Sons, Publishers of Gaelic and
Scottish Literature, 268 Argyle Street, C.2. Copyright 1933.
[4], 38 p. 270 mm. PC.
First published, in parts, in *Am Bard*, 1901–2.

—— [*Songs of the Isle of Skye.*] Glasgow, [*c.* 1931].
Songs of the Isle of Skye. By Malcolm MacInnes, M.A., LL.B., Advocate. Gaelic and
English. With accompaniments by Malcolm Davidson. Copyright 1931. Price
5/– net. Glasgow: Alex. MacLaren & Sons, 360–2 Argyle Street, C.2.
[4], 18 p. 320 mm. PC.
Both notations.

—— [*Traditional Airs of Skye and the West*.] London, [Pref. 1942].
"Swallow-flights of song that dip / their wings in tears and skim away." Traditional Airs of Skye and the West. With Gaelic and English Words. By Malcolm MacInnes, M.A., LL.B., Author of Lilts from the Western Isles, Songs of the Isle of Lilts from the Western Isles, Songs of the Isle of Skye, Ishebel of the Shealing, Rory's Courting. Copyright. 4/– Bayley & Ferguson; London: 2 Great Marlborough Street, W.; Glasgow: 54 Queen Street, C.1.
[4], 26 p. 270 mm. AU.
    Both notations; piano accompaniments.

—— (rev. ed.). See Nicolson, Alexander, Advocate. [*Gaelic Proverbs*.]

MacInnes, Paul, 1928 (tr.). See MacLean, Allan C. [*Ribbon of Fire*.]

MacIntosh, Donald, 1743–1808. See Nicolson, Alexander, Advocate, 1827–93. [*Gaelic Proverbs*.]

MacIntyre, Alexander. [*Balaich an t-Sratha*.] Glasgow, 1946.
Balaich an t-Sratha. No, Iain beag agus a chuideachd. Leis an Lighiche, Alasdair Mac-an-t-Saoir, An Ard-Ruighe. (Dr. Alexander MacIntyre, Airdrie.) Price, 1/6. Glaschu: Alasdair Mac Labhruinn agus a Mhic, 268 Sràid Earraghaidheal. 1946.
48 p. 190 mm. GU:CL, PC.
    Foreword by Hector MacDougall.

MacIntyre, Angus. [*Cruachan Vistas*.] Glasgow, n.d.
Angus MacIntyre. Cruachan Vistas 1871–1931. Chiefly a collection of sonnets, songs, etc. (Fraoch Geal.) [Illus.] Glasgow: Angus MacIntyre. Edinburgh and Glasgow: John Menzies & Co., Ltd.
72 p; illus. 200 mm. AU, BM, Mit.
    Some music: in staff.
    Foreword by Angus Henderson. c. 1931.

MacIntyre, Donald, 1889–1964. [*Sporan Dhomhnaill*.] Edinburgh, 1968.
Sporan Dhòmhnaill. Gaelic Poems and Songs by the late Donald MacIntyre, The Paisley Bard. Compiled and edited by Somerled MacMillan. Published by Oliver and Boyd for the Scottish Gaelic Texts Society. Edinburgh. 1968.
Scottish Gaelic Texts, Volume Ten.
xxx, 418 p. 230 mm.
    Text, pp 1–341; Notes, Index, Glossary, pp 342–418.

MacIntyre, Duncan, 1724–1812. [*Beinn Dorainn*.] Stirling, 1949.
Duncan Ban MacIntyre. Beinn Dorainn. With English version and notes by John MacKechnie, M.A. Eneas MacKay, Stirling.
First published 1949.
68 p. 190 mm. BM, Mit., NLS.
    An English verse translation of Iain Chrichton Smith of this poem was published in *Akros* 3:9, January 1969, and reprinted by Preston Akros in March and June 1969.

—— [*Moladh Beinn Dobhrainn*.] See MacLeod, Angus. [*Sar Orain*.]

—— [*Orain Agus Dana*.] Edinburgh, 1901.
Orain agus Dana Gaidhealach, le Donnachadh Ban Mac-an-t-Saoir. Songs and Poems, in Gaelic, by Duncan Ban MacIntyre. Twelfth edition. With an English translation of *Coire Cheathaich* and *Ben Dorain*. Edinburgh: John Grant, 31 George IV Bridge. 1901.
233 p. 160 mm. AU.
    1st ed. 1768; the above is a reprint of that of 1871. Printed Oliver & Boyd, Edinburgh.

—— [*Orain agus Dana.*] Edinburgh, 1908.
... Thirteenth edition. ... Edinburgh: John Grant. 1908.
233 p. 180 mm. EPL, Mit.

—— [*Orain Ghaidhealach.*] Edinburgh, 1912.
Orain Ghaidhealach le Donnchadh Macantsaoir. Air an eadartheangachadh agus air an
cur a mach le Deòrsa Caldair. Dun-éideann: Iain Grannd, 31 George IV Bridge.
1912.
The Gaelic Songs of Duncan MacIntyre. Edited with translation and notes by George
Calder. Edinburgh: John Grant, 31 George IV Bridge. 1912.
xl, 535 p; 5 plates [1 folio]. 210 mm. AU, EU, GU, Mit.
Verse translations. Printed Oliver & Boyd, Edinburgh.

—— [*Songs.*] Edinburgh, 1952.
The Songs of Duncan Bàn MacIntyre. Edited with a translation, introduction and
notes by Angus MacLeod, M.A., B.Sc., F.E.I.S. Published by Oliver & Boyd for the
Scottish Gaelic Texts Society. Edinburgh. 1952.
Scottish Gaelic Texts, Volume Four.
xlvii, 581 p; 2 plates. 230 mm. BM.
Notes, pp 421–557; Glossarial Index, pp 565–81.

—— [*Vie, Etude, Citations, Traductions.*] Inverness, n.d.
Université de Rennes. Donnchadh Bàn Mac an t-Saoir (Duncan Bàn Mac Intyre)
1724–1812. Poète gaélique écossais. Vie, étude, citations, traductions. Thèse
présentée à la Faculté des Lettres pour le Doctorat par Donald James MacLeod, M.A.,
H.M.I.S., Inverness, Ecosse, Inspecteur de gaélique et de langues modernes, Scottish
Education Department. Printed by the Northern Counties Newspaper and Printing
and Publishing Company, Limited, Margaret Street, Inverness.
viii, 243 p, [1] Bibliography, 220 mm. AU, PC.
Text and French translation on facing pages.

MacIntyre, Dr. John, 1869–1947. See Brandane, John.

MacIntyre, Rev. John, 1794–1870. [*Translations and Original Gaelic Songs.*] Oban,
1916.
Translations into Gaelic Verse of some Jacobite and Scottish Songs and Original Gaelic
Songs. By the Rev. John MacIntyre, LL.D., of Kilmonivaig. With appendix. Also,
Article on the Clan Battle on the North Inch of Perth in 1396. Oban: printed at
The Oban Times Printing Works. 1916.
44 p, vii Appendix. 190 mm. EU.
The Clan Battle, etc., pp ii–v. English obituary on Lieut. Peter MacIntyre, vi–vii;
Gaelic elegy on John MacIntyre, vii.

MacIver, Colin. [*Orain Ghailig.*] Sydney, C.B., 1902.
Orain Ghàilig, le Cailean Mac-Iomhair, a rugadh ann am baile Bharabhais, Eilean
Leòghais, Siorrachd Rois, Alba, agus a tha chòmhnaidh an diugh am Milan, siorrachd
Compton, Quebec. Sydney, C.B.: Mac-Talla Publishing Company, Ltd. 1902.
35 p. 190 mm. *Xavier.*

MacIver, Donald, 1857–. [*Bilingual Text Book.*] Inverness, 1900.
Bilingual Text Book. By D. MacIver, F.E.I.S., Bayble School. Inverness: printed at
The Highland News Office. 1900.
[2], 90 p. 190 mm. Mit.
"The writer's objects in compiling this Class-Book is to facilitate the teaching of
English in the Upper Division of his own school."—Preface.

MacIver, Mary A., 1894–. [*Ceol agus Deoir.*] Stornoway, n.d.
Ceòl agus Deoir. Le Màiri A. MicIomhair.
Printed by Stornoway Gazette Ltd., 67–69 Kenneth Street, Stornoway.
40 p. 220 mm.

—— [*Cuimhneachan.*] Stornoway, [Fore. 1968].
Cuimhneachan air an t-Urramach Murchadh MacRath a bha ann an Ceann-Loch (Leodhas), agus air Murchadh Mairtainn a Sgìre a' Bhac. Le Màiri A. Nic Iomhair. Prìs 3/6.
Air a chlò-bhualadh le Gasaet Steornabhaigh, 10 Sràid Fhrangain, Steòrnabhagh.
24 p. 220 mm.
    Foreword by "J.M.C."

—— [*Marbhrann.*] Stornoway, n.d.
Marbhrann do Dhòmhnull MacIomhair. Le a phiuthar, Màiri A. Nic Iomhair. Prìs 1/6.
Printed by Stornoway Gazette Ltd., 10 Francis Street, Stornoway, Isle of Lewis.
8 p. 220 mm. PC.
    Published 1968.

MacKay, A. M. (ed.). See *Celtic Monthly*.

MacKay, Catherine. [*Laoidhean agus Orain.*] Edinburgh, 1917.
Laoidhean agus Orain. Le Catriona Thangaidh. Air an sgrìobhadh as a beul fhéin leis an Urr. Alasdair MacRath, M.A., Cill Chalum-an-Eala an Ceann-Tìre. Edinburgh: W. F. Henderson, 19 George IV Bridge. 1917.
38 p. 160 mm. FC.
    Printed Morrison & Gibb, Edinburgh.
    "Rugadh i ann an Tangaidh, baile beag air fearann-eaglais Bharabhais, far a robh a h-athair 'na bhuachaille aig a' mhinistear."—Foreword. Reprinted from *An Fhianuis Ghaidhealach*, 1917.

MacKay, D. T., 1878–. [*Cul-taic an t-Saighdeir.*] Dundee, 1919.
War Price 4½d. MacLeod's Gaelic Booklets No. 3. Cul-taic an t-saighdeir. (Tais-geadan furtachd do'n Churaidh Chriosdaidh, anns am bheil earrannan sònruichte de na Sgriobtuirean Naomha, a tha freagarrach do gach car, cor is cunnart a tha 'n leanmhuinn dreuchd an t-saighdeir, air an cur sios leth-taobh duilleige mu choinnimh gach latha 'sa mhios.) Leis an Urr. D. T. Mac Aoidh, (Ploc Loch Aillse). [Illus.] Calum Siosal Mac Leòid, Leabhar-reiceadair, Dùn-dé. An ceud clobhualadh. 1919.
[32]. 170 mm. GU:CL.

—— [*Leabhran oir nan Geallana.*] Oban, 1927.
Leabhran Oir nan Geallana. (Booklet of Gospel Promises.) By D. T. MacKay, Plockton (Late Tiree). Oban: printed and published by Hugh MacDonald. 1927.
44 p. 190 mm. PC.

—— (ed.). See Highland Village Association. [*Leabhar a' Chlachain.*]

MacKay, Donald J., 1930–. (ed.). See Mo Leabhar II: Leabhar-Oibreach.

MacKay, John, 1856?–1909. (ed.). See *The Celtic Monthly*.

MacKay, John G., 1848–1942. [*Gaelic Phrases and Sentences.*] Glasgow, 1946.
MacKay's Gaelic Phrases and Sentences. Easy Gaelic Syntax. The correct arrange-ment of Gaelic words in sentences. Popularly treated for beginners by J. G. MacKay. [. . .] Glasgow: Alex. MacLaren & Sons, 268 Argyle Street, C.2.
Copyright. First edition 1899. Second edition 1946.
iv, 57 p. 190 mm. EPL, GU:CL, PC.

—— [*The Tale of the Cauldron.*] Dundee, 1927.
Ancient Legends of the Scottish Gael. The Tale of the Cauldron. Gaelic and English. Arranged by J. G. MacKay. Sixteen paintings by Gordon Browne, R.I. Dundee: published by Malcolm C. MacLeod, 183 Blackness Road. 1927.
64 p. 210 mm. BM, NLS, PC.
    Printed George E. Findlay, Dundee.

—— (ed.). See Campbell, John F. [*Gille a' Bhuidseir.*]

—— (comp.). See Campbell, John F. [*More West Highland Tales.*] Volume One/ Volume Two.

—— (ed.). See Campbell, John F. [*Na se Bonnaich Bheaga.*]

MacKay, John M. (joint ed.). See Irisleabhar Ceilteach.

MacKay, John R. [*An Eaglais Phresbiterianach Shaor.*] N.p., [1906].
"An Eaglais Phresbiterianach Shaor agus an Eaglais Shaor a reir an lagha."
8 p.
Not seen. Information from *TS-G*.

—— (ed.). See Cook, Archibald. [*Searmoinean Gaelig.*]

—— (ed.). See Cook, Archibald. [*Sermons (Gaelic and English).*]

—— (ed.). See MacKenzie, Donald. [*Laoidhean Spioradail.*]

MacKay, Roderick, 1873–1949. [*Oiteagan o Tir nan Og.*] Glasgow, 1938.
Oiteagan o Tìr nan Og. Orain agus Dàin le Ruairidh Mac Aoidh, Loch-nam-Madadh.
Fo laimh Eachainn Mhic Dhùghaill. Glascho: Alasdair MacLabhruinn is a Mhic,
268 Sràid Earra-Ghaidheal, C.2.
Breezes from Tìr nan Og. Songs and Poems by Roderick MacKay, Illeray, Lochmaddy.
Edited by Hector MacDougall. Glasgow: Alexander MacLaren & Sons, 268 Argyle
Street, C.2.
First published 1938.
viii, 109 p. 200 mm. Mit., NLS.
Foreword by George MacKenzie.

MacKay, Thomas. [*Practical Hints on Cooking.*] Glasgow, 1905.
Practical Hints on Cooking and Baking. By Thomas MacKay, Largs, Ex-President,
Clan MacKay Society. Translated into Gaelic by Henry Whyte ("Fionn"). Glasgow:
Clan MacKay Society. 1905.
Seòlaidhean Feumail mu Chòcaireachd 's mu Fhuineadh. Eadair-theangaichte o'n
Bheurla le "Fionn". Glaschu: Comunn Chloinn Aoidh. 1905.
xiii, [2]–47 p. 170 mm. EU, Mit.
Gaelic and English on facing pages.

MacKay, William P. [*Grace and Truth.*] Glasgow, n.d.
Gaelic edition of *Grace and Truth*. Chap. 1, "There is No Difference. "An Gràs agus
an Fhìrinn" Fo Dha Shealladh Dheug. Le W. P. Macaoidh, M.A., Hull. [Quotation.]
Eadar-theangaichte o'n Bheurla. Glasgow: *The Witness* Office, 180 Buchanan Street,
Booksellers and Publishers of Christian Literature. Price 1d. 1s. per dozen. Post free.
24 p. 180 mm. AU, PC.
English original first published late 19th century.

MacKay, Williamina. [*Oran.*] N.p., n.d.
Oran o throm-inntinn a bhàird air suidheachadh na h-Eaglaisean. Williamina MacKay.
6 p. 260 mm. PC.

—— [*Teanntachd na h-Eaglais Aonaichte.*] N.p., n.d.
Teanndachd na h-Eaglais Aonaichte. Le Uilleamina Macaoidh.
7 p. 210 mm. PC.
Not in *TS-G*.

MacKechnie, Donald, 1836–1908. [*Am Fear-Ciuil.*] Glasgow, 1904.
Am Fear-Ciuil. Original Gaelic humorous sketches, poems, songs, and translations.
By Donald MacKechnie, Edinburgh. [Quotation.] Glasgow: Archibald Sinclair,
Celtic Press, 47 Waterloo Street. 1904.
Am Fear-Ciuil. Dàin agus Orain, etc. Le Domhnull MacEacharn, Duneideann.
[Quotation.] Glascho: Gilleasbuig Mac-na-Ceardadh, 47 Sraid Waterloo. 1904.
xvi, 225 p; plate. 200 mm. GU:CL, Mit., SS.

—— [*Am Fear-Ciuil.*] Edinburgh, 1910.
Am Fear-Ciùil. Dàin, òrain, òraidean, is sgeulachdan. Le Dòmhnull MacEacharn, an Dunéideann. An dara clò-bhualadh, le móran ris. [Quotation.] Dunéideann: Iain Grannd, Drochaid Dheòrsa IV. 1910.
Am Fear-Ciùil. Poems, songs, and translations, with prose sketches, grave and gay. By Donald MacKechnie, Edinburgh. Second edition, much enlarged. [Quotation.] Edinburgh: John Grant, George IV Bridge. 1910.
xvi, 336 p; illus. 200 mm. AU, GU, Mit.
  "Prefatorial Note" by Donald MacKinnon.

—— [*Am Fear-Ciuil.*] Stirling, [Fore. 1940].
Am Fear-Ciùil. Dàin, òrain, òraidean is sgeulachdan. Le Domhnull MacEacharn (nach maireann), Duneideann. [Quotation.] Clo-bhuailte fo ughdarras A' Chomuinn Ghaidhealaich le Aonghas MacAoidh, 44 Craigs, Sruighlea.
Am Fear Ciùil. Poems, songs, and translations, with prose sketches, grave and gay. By the late Donald MacKechnie, Edinburgh. [Quotation.] Published for An Comunn Gaidhealach, 131 West Regent Street, Glasgow, by Eneas MacKay, 44 Craigs, Stirling.
316 p. 200 mm. Mit.
  Printed Jamieson & Munro, Stirling.

MacKechnie, Elizabeth E. (ed.). See Stewart, John Roy. [*Poems.*]

MacKechnie, John, 1897–. [*Catalogue of Gaelic Manuscripts.*] Boston, 1973.
Catalogue of Gaelic Manuscripts in selected libraries in Great Britain and Ireland. Compiled by John MacKechnie, M.A., B.D., B.L., LL.B., Former Reader in Celtic Languages at King's College, Aberdeen, Scotland. Volume 1: Notes to the Manuscripts; Index of Initia. G. K. Hall & Co., 76 Lincoln Street, Boston, Massachusetts. 1973.
. . . Volume 2: Index to Notes on Manuscripts.
xi, 759 p; iii, 700 p. 370 × 270 mm. GU, NLS.

—— [*Gaelic Without Groans.*] Stirling, 1934.
Gaelic without Groans! In a series of twenty-nine lessons. By John MacKechnie, M.A. Eneas MacKay, Stirling.
First published 1934.
155 p; illus. 190 mm. AU, BM, Mit.

—— [*Gaelic Without Groans.*] Stirling, 1935, 1948.
ibid.
155 p; illus. 190 mm.

—— [*Gaelic Without Groans.*] Edinburgh, 1962.
Gaelic without Groans. John MacKechnie, M.A. Oliver & Boyd, Edinburgh and London.
First published (Eneas MacKay) 1934.
Second revised edition 1962.
124 p. 190 mm. Mit.

—— [*Gaelic Without Groans.*] Edinburgh, 1963, 1965, 1966, 1970, 1971.
ibid.
124 p. 190 mm.

—— [*The Owl of Strone.*] [Glasgow], 1946.
The Owl of Strone. Edited by John MacKechnie, M.A., B.L., B.D. Sgoil Eòlais na h-Alba. 1946.
36 p. 220 mm. GU Mit. SS.
  Printed The Caledonian Press Glasgow. With Notes.

—— [*The Owl Remembers.*] Stirling, 1933.
The Owl Remembers. Gaelic poems selected and edited with notes by John Mac-
Kechnie, M.A., B.D., F.S.A.(Scot.). Introduction and English versions by Patrick
McGlynn, M.A., D.Litt. Eneas MacKay, Stirling.
First published 1933.
110 p. 200 mm. BM, EPL, Mit., PC.
   Translations on facing pages.

—— (ed.). See MacIntyre, Duncan. [*Beinn Dorainn.*]

MacKellar, Mary, 1835–90. [*The Tourist's Handbook.*] Edinburgh, n.d.
The Tourist's Handbook of Gaelic and English Phrases, with pronunciation. By Mrs
Mary MacKellar, Bard to the Gaelic Society of Inverness. Edinburgh: John Grant,
31 George IV Bridge.
24 p. 106 mm. PC.
   1st ed. late 19th century, by MacLachlan & Stewart, Edinburgh. The above is
   probably the edition advertised in *Guth na Bliadhna* in 1919.

—— [*The Tourist's Handbook.*] Glasgow, n.d.
. . . Glasgow: Alex. MacLaren & Sons, Argyle Street, C.2.
24 p. 104 mm. GU:CL, Mit.
   Possibly the Jubilee Edition of 1929.

—— [*The Tourist's Handbook.*] Glasgow, 1935, 1940, 1953.
Ibid.
24 p. 104 mm.
   Mary MacKellar's *The Tourist's Handbook* was used by Malcolm MacLennan as the
   basis of his *Handbook of Gaelic Phrases and Sentences* (first edition 1930), revised by
   Alexander MacFarlane, 1939.

—— [*The Tourist's Handbook.*] See also MacLennan, Malcolm. [*Handbook of Gaelic
Phrases and Sentences.*]

MacKenzie, Anne. [*Amhrain Anna Sheumais.*] [Amersham], [*c.* 1973].
Amhrain Anna Sheumais.
c. 1973 Miss A. Mackenzie.
Processed and printed by Halstan & Co. Ltd., Amersham, Bucks., England.
[4], 26 p. 220 mm.
   Contains 26 songs, with music in both notations.

MacKenzie, Annie M. (ed.). See MacDonald, John, Seventeenth Century poet. [*Orain
Iain Luim.*]

MacKenzie, Archibald J. [*History of Christmas Island Parish.*] N.p., n.d.
History of Christmas Island Parish. By Archibald J. MacKenzie. With an Introduction
by Rev. Patrick Nicholson, Ph.D., Professor in St. F. X. College.
167 p. 220 mm. PC.
   Contains 18 Gaelic songs, pp 150–67.

MacKenzie, Colin N., 1917–. [*A' Leth Eile.*] Glasgow, 1971.
A' Leth Eile. Cailein T. MacCoinnich. Roinn nan Cànan Ceilteach, Oilthigh Ghlaschu.
1971.
Leabhraichean ùra Gàidhlig Oilthigh Ghlaschu (fo stiùireadh Ruairidh MhicThomais),
Aireamh 6.
115 p. 220 mm.
   Printed Learmonth, Stirling.

—— [*Mar Sgeul a Dh'Innseas Neach.*] Glasgow, 1971.
Mar sgeul a dh'innseas neach. Cailein T. MacCoinnich. Roinn nan Cànan Ceilteach, Oilthigh Ghlaschu. 1971.
Leabhraichean ùra Gàidhlig Oilthigh Ghlaschu (fo stiùireadh Ruairidh MhicThomais), Aireamh 5.
100 p. 220 mm.
 Printed Learmonth, Stirling.

—— [*Nach Neonach Sin.*] Glasgow, 1973.
Nach Neònach Sin. "A measg annasan is iongantais am t-saoghail uile, chan eil dad as iongantaiche na'n fhìrinn." Cailein T. MacCoinnich. Roinn nan Cànan Ceilteach, Oilthigh Ghlaschu. 1973.
Leabhraichean ùra Gàidhlig Oilthigh Ghlaschu (fo stiùireadh Ruairidh MhicThomais), Aireamh 7.
56 p. 220 mm.
 Printed Maclehose, Glasgow

—— [*Oirthir Tim.*] Glasgow, 1969.
Oirthir Tìm. Sgeulachdan le Cailein T. MacCoinnich. Gairm. Glaschu. 1969.
Clò-bhualaidhean Gairm, Leabhar 8.
176 p. 210 mm.

MacKenzie, Donald, 1768–1861. [*Laoidhean Spioradail.*] Inverness, 1909.
 Laoidhean Spioradail. Le Dòmhnull MacCoinnich, fear ceasnuichidh 'bh'ann an sgìre Assuint, an Cataobh. Air an deasachadh airson a' chlòdh-bhualaidh so leis An Urr. I. R. MacAoidh, M.A., Inbhirnis. Inverness: *Northern Chronicle* Office. 1909. Price ninepence.
47 p. 190 mm. EPL, FC, Mit.

MacKenzie, John, 1806–48. [*Eachdraidh a' Phrionnsa.*] Paisley, 1906.
 Eachdraidh a' Phrionnsa, no Bliadhna Theàrlaich: anns am bheil min-chunntas air Taisdeal a' Phrionnsa do dh' Albainn; Togbhail nam Fineachan Gaelach 'na Aobhar; agus Gach Teugbhail 'bha aca r'a Nàimhdean; maille ri Iomruagadh a' Phrionns' agus a Luchd-Leanmhuinn an déigh Latha Chuil-Fhodair, etc. Le Iain Mac-Choinnich, Ball Urramach de Chomunn Oisianach, Ghlascho; de Chomunn na Gàelig ann an Lunnainn, etc.; Fear-Sgrìobhaidh "Sàr-Obair nam Bàrd Gàelach", agus "Eachdraidh Beatha nam Bàrd", etc. Paislig: Alasdair Gardner, Clòdh-bhuailtear, le a deòin rìoghail fein, do'n Bhàn-Rìgh Victoria nach maireann. 1906.
199 p. 200 mm. BM, GU:CL, Mit.
 1st ed. 1844.

—— [*English-Gaelic Dictionary.*] Glasgow, 1930.
An English-Gaelic Dictionary. By John MacKenzie, author of *The Beauties of Gaelic Poetry*. Being Part Second to MacAlpine's Pronouncing Gaelic-English Dictionary. Glasgow: Alex. MacLaren & Sons, 268 Argyle Street, C.2.
MacLaren's New Edition. 1930.
v-x; 285–549 p. 190 mm.
 The above (without separate title page or pagination) appeared as part of the 1903 and 1906 editions of MacAlpine's Dictionary. The reprint of 1962 (see below) was bound with Part One, but had a separate title page. 1st ed. 1845.

—— [*An English-Gaelic Dictionary.*] Glasgow, 1936, 1943, 1950, 1956, 1962.
Ibid.
v-x, [285]–549 p. 190 mm.

—— [*English-Gaelic Dictionary.*] Glasgow, 1971.
English-Gaelic Dictionary. Compiled by John MacKenzie. (This work formed Part II of MacAlpine's Pronouncing Gaelic Dictionary.) Gairm Publications, 29 Waterloo Street, Glasgow. 1971.
269 p. 220 mm.

—— [*English-Gaelic Dictionary*.] See also MacAlpine, Neil. [*Gaelic-English and English-Gaelic Dictionary*.]

—— [*Sar-Obair nam Bard Gaelach*.] Edinburgh, 1904.
Sàr-Obair nam Bard Gaelach: or, The Beauties of Gaelic Poetry and the Lives of the Highland Bards; with historical and critical notes, and a comprehensive glossary of provincial words. By John MacKenzie, Esq., Honorary Member of the Ossianic Society of Glasgow, the Gaelic Society of London, etc. With an historical introduction containing an account of the manner, habits, etc., of the ancient Caledonians, by James Logan, Esq., F.S.A.S., Corresponding Member S.Ant.Normandy, author of the Scottish Gael, etc. New edition. Edinburgh: Norman MacLeod, 25 George IV Bridge. 1904.
lxvi, 408 p; plate. 260 mm. AU, EU, Mit.
> Printed Lorimer & Chalmers, Edinburgh. 1st ed. 1841; the 2nd ed. of 1865 had 408 p.

—— [*Sar-Obair nam Bard Gaelach*.] Edinburgh, 1907.
Sar-Obair nam Bard Gaelach. The Beauties of Gaelic Poetry and Lives of the Highland Bards. Edited by John MacKenzie. With an historical introduction containing an account of the manners, habits, etc., of the ancient Caledonians, by James Logan, F.S.A.S. Edinburgh: John Grant, 31 George IV Bridge. 1907.
[4], lxxii, 447 p. 230 mm. GU-CL, PC.

—— (ed.). See Buchanan, Dugald. [*Beatha agus Iompachadh, Maille ri Laoidhean*.]

—— (tr.). See Bunyan, John. [*Grace Abounding*.]

—— (tr.). See Bunyan, John. [*Pilgrim's Progress*.]

—— (tr.). See Bunyan, John. [*The World to Come*.]

—— (ed.). See Ross, William. [*Orain Ghaelach*.]

MacKenzie, Kenneth, "Coinneach Odhar". See Blair, Duncan B. [*Coinneach Odhar*.]

MacKenzie, Lachlan, 1754–1819. [*Additional Lectures, Sermons, and Writings*.]
> Inverness, 1930.
"The Rev. Mr. Lachlan" of Lochcarron. Additional Lectures, Sermons, and Writings of a famous Highland minister of the old school. Practically all hitherto unpublished. Supplementary to volume already published. Compiled and published by James Campbell, Inverness.
Inverness: Robt. Carruthers & Sons. 1930.
xvi, 442 p; illus. 220 mm. BM, Mit.
> Foreword by Rev. Ewen MacQueen, Inverness.

—— [*Lectures, Sermons, and Writings*.] Inverness, 1928.
"The Rev. Mr. Lachlan" of Lochcarron. Lectures, Sermons, and Writings of a famous Highland minister of the old school. Including some of his work which has never hitherto been published. Compiled and published by James Campbell, Inverness.
Robt. Carruthers & Sons. 1928.
xvi, 462 p. 220 mm. Mit.
> Foreword by D. Beaton, Wick. Mainly in English.

—— [*Ros o Sharon*.] Edinburgh, n.d.
Cogadh mòr h-Eorpa. Ròs o Sharon. MacCoinnich. [Illus.] Printed by Oliver and Boyd, Edinburgh, for the Church of Scotland, The United Free Church of Scotland, 61 p. 140 mm. NLS.
> An edition distributed to soldiers in the First World War.

—— [*Ros o Sharon.*] Glasgow, n.d.

Ròs o Sharon. Searmoin leis An Urr. Lachlan MacCoinnich a bha ann an Lochcarron. Alasdair Mac Labhruinn 's a Mhic, Reiceadairean Leabhraichean Gàidhlig, 268 Sràid Earra-Ghaidheal, Glascho, C.2. Price twopence.

16 p. 160 mm. Mit., PC.

MacLaren gives date as 1940. 1st ed. 1897 (33 p).

—— (joint author). See Dioghluim o Theagasg nan Aithrichean.

—— See MacCuish, Donald J. Ceit Mhor agus Maighstir Lachlunn.

MacKenzie, Morag (joint author). See MacLeod, Christine. [*Calum Cille.*]

—— (joint author). See MacLeod, Christine. [*Na Lochlannaich.*]

MacKenzie, Peggy (comp.). See MacKenzie, William, of Point, Lewis. [*Cnoc Chusbaig.*]

MacKenzie, William, of Point, Lewis, 1857–1907. [*Cnoc Chusbaig.*] Glasgow, 1936.

Cnoc Chùsbaig. Comh-Chruinneachadh de Orain agus Dàin le Uilleam Mac Coinnich, Siadar an Rudha Leódhais. Comh-Chruinneachadh le Peigi Nic Coinnich. Roimh-ràdh le Dòmhnull Mac Coinnich, A.M. Fo làimh Eachainn Mhic Dhùghaill. Glascho: Alasdair Mac Labhruinn 'sa Mhic, 268 Sràid Earra-Ghaidheal, C.2.

Cnoc Chùsbaig. A Collection of Songs and Poems by William MacKenzie, Shader Point, Lewis. Collected by Peggy MacKenzie. Foreword by Donald MacKenzie, M.A. Edited by Hector Mac Dougall. Glasgow: Alex MacLaren & Sons, 268 Argyle Street, C.2.

First published 1936. Copyright.

61 p. 190 mm. BM, Mit., PC.

Appendix, "Gaelic and English Poems" by Peggy MacKenzie, pp 49–61.

MacKenzie, William, of Skye. [*Old Skye Tales.*] Glasgow, 1934.

Old Skye Tales. Further traditions, reflections and memories of an octogenarian Highlander. William MacKenzie, Culnacnoc, author of "Skye: Iochdar-Trotternish and District". Illustrated. Glasgow: Alex. MacLaren & Sons, Argyle Street, C.2.

First published in November 1934.

xi, [1], 161 p; 12 plates. 190 mm. BM, NLS.

In English, with extensive quotation from Gaelic poetry.

—— [*Skye: Iochdar-Trotternish and District.*] Glasgow, 1930.

Skye: Iochdar-Trotternish and District. Traditions, reflections and memories. By William MacKenzie. Seventeen illustrations. Glasgow: Alex. MacLaren & Sons, 360–362 Argyle Street, C.2.

First published in August 1930.

xvi, 176 p; 17 plates. 190 mm. BM, NLS.

In English, with extensive quotation from Gaelic poetry.

MacKenzie, William, Secretary of Crofters' Commission. [*Gems of Highland Song, Book 1.*] Edinburgh, [*c.* 1923].

Gems of Highland Song. With the original Gaelic words, and a translation into English. By William MacKenzie. Arranged for solo voices, with accompaniment (and chorus *ad. lib.*) by J. A. Moonie Book 1. Price 1s. 6d. Edinburgh: Bruce, Clements & Co., Music Publishers, 128a George Street. Copyright 1923 by Bruce, Clements & Co. Full score and bound parts may be obtained from the publishers.

[4], 13 p. 280 mm. NLS.

According to *MacLaren* this is the 6th ed.

—— [*Gems of Highland Song.*] Book 2. N.p., n.d.

Gems of Highland Song.

Book 2 not seen. Described in *MacLaren* as containing 8 songs and published twice, the second edition being by Patersons, Glasgow in 1914. Not listed in B.M.

MacKinnon, Alexander. [*Dain agus Orain*.] Charlottetown, 1902.
Dàin agus Orain. Le Alasdair Mac-Fhionghain. Edited by the Rev. A. MacLean
Sinclair. [Illus.] Charlottetown: printed by Haszard and Moore. 1902.
48 p. 160 mm. EU:CL, Mit.
   "Notes", etc., pp 38–48.

MacKinnon, Donald, Free Church Minister. [*Domhnall Munro*.] N.p., n.d.
Dòmhnall Munro, An Dall, Snitheasort, anns An Eilean Sgitheanach. Le Dòmhnall
Mac Fhionghain, Port-rìgh. A' phrìs sia sgillinn.
12 p. 220 mm. PC.

—— [*The Gaelic Bible and Psalter*.] Dingwall, 1930.
The Gaelic Bible and Psalter. Being the story of the translation of the Scriptures into
Scottish Gaelic, with metrical versions of the Psalms and Paraphrases. By Rev. Donald
MacKinnon, F.S.A.(Scot.), Portree. Price 5/6. Dingwall: printed and published by
the Ross-shire Printing and Publishing Co. Ltd. 1930.
[7], 119 p, [6] "Index". 190 × 130 mm. BM, GU:CL, Mit.
   The discussion is in English, with Gaelic quotations.

—— [*An t-Ionad-fasgaidh*.] Edinburgh, 1951.
An t-Ionad-fasgaidh. Searmoinean air Isàiah XXXII: 2. Le Dòmhnall Mac Fhionghain.
Edinburgh: Lindsay & Co., Ltd., 17 Blackfriars Street. 1951.
[2], 78 p. 200 mm. PC.

—— (comp.). See Sguaban a Achaidhean nan Aithrichean.

MacKinnon, Donald, of Leurbost. [*Durachd mo Chridhe*.] Glasgow, [*c.* 1938].
Dùrachd mo Chridhe. Dàin Spioradail. Le Dòmhnull Mac Fhionghuin, Liùrabost,
Steòrnabhagh, Leodhas. Glascho: Alasdair MacLabhruinn 's a Mhic, 268 Sràid
Earra-Ghaidheal, C.2.
15 p. 190 mm. EPL, NLS.

MacKinnon, Donald, Professor of Celtic in Edinburgh University, 1839–1914. [*Gaelic
   Manuscripts*.] Edinburgh, 1912.
A descriptive catalogue of Gaelic manuscripts in the Advocates' Library Edinburgh, and
elsewhere in Scotland. By Donald MacKinnon, M.A., Professor of Celtic Languages,
etc., in The University of Edinburgh. Compiled at the instance of John, Fourth
Marquess of Bute, through whose liberality it is published. Edinburgh: printed by
T. and A. Constable, printers to His Majesty, and published by William Brown, 5
Castle Street. 1912.
xii, 348 p. 260 mm. BM, GU:CL, Mit., Etc.
   Index, pp 228–348.

—— [*Prose Writings*.] Edinburgh, 1956.
Prose Writings of Donald MacKinnon, 1839–1914, the first Professor of Celtic in the
University of Edinburgh. Edited by Oliver and Boyd for the Scottish Gaelic Texts
Society. 1956.
Scottish Gaelic Texts, Volume Five.
xxviii, 337 p. 230 mm. AU, GU, Mit.
   Text, pp 1–318; Notes, pp 319–20; Vocabulary, pp 321–30; "List of Members",
pp 331–7. See also his "Seanfhocail".

—— [*Reading Book*.] Part I. Edinburgh, 1906.
Reading Book for the use of students of the Gaelic class in the University of Edinburgh.
Part I. [Quotation.] Edinburgh: James Thin, Publisher to the University. 1906.
vii, 261 p. 190 mm. AU, CoS.
   1st ed. 1889, of which this is a reprint.

—— [*Reading Book.*] Part II. N.p., n.d.
[In pencil.] MacKinnon. Class Book II.
204 p. 190 mm. CoS, PC.
  Neither copy has a title page.

—— [*Seanfhocail.*] Edinburgh, 1956.
Seanfhocail. Prose Writings of Donald MacKinnon, 1839–1914, the first Professor of
Celtic in the University of Edinburgh. Edited by Lachlan MacKinnon, M.A., F.E.I.S.
Published by Oliver and Boyd for the Scottish Gaelic Texts Society. Edinburgh. 1956.
vii, 135 p. 220 mm. PC.
  Extracted from his "Prose Writings" for use in schools.

—— See *Celtic Review*.

MacKinnon, John (tr.). See Bell, J. J. [*Thread o' Scarlet.*]

MacKinnon, Jonathan G., 1870–1944. [*Na Gaidheil an Ceap Breatunn.*] See Vernon,
C. W. Cape Breton, Canada.

—— (comp.). [*The Pied Piper and Other Stories.*] Sydney, C.B., 1919.
Am Piobaire Breac agus dà sgeul eile. Eadartheangaichte o'n Bheurla le E. G. M. F.
Thainig na trì sgeulan beaga so a dùthchannan céin: a' cheud sgeul – le cead na cuideachd
– as a' Ghearmailt; an dara sgeul a Ruisia; agus an treas sgeul as a' Ghréig. Sydney,
C.B.: printed by Don. MacKinnon. 1919.
16 p. 210 mm. BM, *Xavier*.

—— (ed.). See Fear na Ceilidh.

—— (tr.). See Hardy, Thomas. [*The Three Strangers.*]

—— (ed.). See Mac Talla.

—— (tr.). See Tolstoi, Lev Nikolaevich. [*Where God is, Love is.*]

—— (tr.). See Van Dyke, Henry. [*The Three Strangers.*]

MacKinnon, Lachlan, 1903–. [*Baird a' Chomuinn.*] Glasgow, 1953.
Bàird a' Chomuinn. Comh-chruinneachadh de'n bhàrdachd a choisinn an crùn aig a'
Mhòd Nàiseanta o'n bhliadhna 1923 gu 1951. Air a dheasachadh le Lachlann Mac-
Fhionghuin, M.A., F.E.I.S. An Comunn Gaidhealach, 65 Sràid West Regent,
Glaschu, C.2. 1953.
[4], 100 p. 190 mm.
  Printed A. Sinclair, Glasgow. Contains brief biographies of the poets.

—— [*Cascheum nam Bard.*] Inverness, 1939.
Cascheum nam Bàrd. An Anthology of Gaelic Poetry. Selected and edited with
Vocabulary and Notes on the poets by Lachlan MacKinnon, M.A. Inverness: printed
by the Northern Counties Newspaper and Printing and Publishing Company, Limited.
1939.
vii, 170 p. 200 mm. BM, Mit, NLS.

—— [*Cascheum nam Bard.*] In 3 parts. Inverness, 1939.
. . . 1939.
vii, 37 p; vii, 39 p; vii, 54 p. 190 mm.
  "Earrann I/II/III" after editor's name in each part.

—— [*Cascheum nam Bard.*] In 3 parts. Inverness, 1952.
. . . Second edition. 1952.
[6], 41 p; [4], 43 p; iv, 63 p. 190 mm. PC.
  "Second edition" after sub-title.

—— [*Cascheum nam Bard.*] Inverness, 1953.
... Second edition. 1953.
vii, 184 p. 190 mm. EU.
"Second edition" imprint. In one volume.

—— [*Cascheum nam Bard.*] In 3 parts. Inverness, n.d.
Ibid.
[6], 41 p; [4], 43 p; [4] 63 p. 190 mm.
All the three-part editions lack the "Vocabulary and Notes".

—— [*Cascheum nam Bard.*] Earrann III only. Inverness, 1957.
Cascheum nam Bàrd. An Anthology of Gaelic Poetry. (Second edition.) Selected and
edited by Lachlan MacKinnon, M.A. Earrann III. Inverness: printed by the Northern
Counties Newspaper and Printing and Publishing Company, Limited. Reprinted 1957.
[4], 63 p. 180 mm. PC.

—— [*Leabhraichean Leughaidh, a' Cheud Cheum.*] Glasgow, n.d.
Leabhraichean Leughaidh. A' Cheud Cheum. Air a dheasachadh le Lachlann Mac-
Fhionghuin, M.A. [Illus.] Clòdh-bhuailte fo ùghdarras A' Chomuinn Ghàidhealaich
le Blackie agus a Mhac, Ltd., Glaschu.
80 p; illus. 180 mm. BM, PC.

—— [*Leabhraichean Leughaidh, Leabhar na Cloinne Bige.*] Glasgow, n.d.
Leabhraichean Leughaidh. Leabhar na Cloinne Bige. Air a dheasachadh le Lachlann
MacFhionghuin, M.A. [Illus.] Clòdh-bhuailte fo ùghdarras A' Chomuinn Ghàidhealaich le Blackie agus a Mhac, Ltd., Glaschu.
96 p; illus. 180 mm. BM, Mit.

—— [*Leabhraichean Leughaidh, Leabhar I.*] Glasgow, n.d.
Leabhraichean Leughaidh. Leabhar I. Air a dheasachadh le Lachlann MacFhionghuin,
M.A. [Illus.] Clòdh-bhuailte fo ùghdarras A' Chomuinn Ghàidhealaich le Blackie agus
a Mhac, Ltd., Glaschu.
112 p; illus. 180 mm. BM, Mit.

—— [*Leabhraichean Leughaidh, Leabhar II.*] Glasgow, n.d.
Leabhraichean Leughaidh. Leabhar II. Air a dheasachadh le Lachlann MacFhionghuin, M.A. [Illus.] Clòdh-bhuailte fo ùghdarras A' Chomuinn Ghàidhealaich le
Blackie agus a Mhac, Ltd., Glaschu.
160 p; illus. 180 mm. BM, GU:CL, Mit.

—— [*Leabhraichean Leughaidh, Leabhar III.*] Glasgow, n.d.
Leabhraichean Leughaidh. Leabhar III. Air a dheasachadh le Lachlann MacFhionghuin, M.A. [Illus.] Clòdh-bhuailte fo ùghdarras A' Chomuinn Ghàidhealaich le
Blackie agus a Mhac, Ltd., Glaschu.
176 p; illus. 180 mm. BM, GU:CL, Mit.

—— [*Leabhraichean Leughaidh, Leabhar IV.*] Glasgow, n.d.
Leabhraichean Leughaidh. Leabhar IV. Air a dheasachadh le Lachlann MacFhion-
ghuin, M.A. [Illus.] Clòdh-bhuailte fo ùghdarras A' Chomuinn Ghàidhealaich le
Blackie agus a Mhac, Ltd., Glaschu.
224 p; illus. 180 mm. BM, GU:CL, Mit.
Reviewed in "An Gaidheal", XLIV.1. January 1949. Based on "Leabhraichean
Sgoile Gàidhlig", published *c.* 1920, under the general editorship of W. J. Watson.

—— [*Leabhraichean Leughaidh.*] See also Watson, William J. [*Leabhraichean Sgoile
Gaidhlig.*]

—— [*An Seanachaidh.*] Glasgow, 1936.
An Seanachaidh. Leabhar Leughaidh Gaidhlig. Air a dheasachadh le Lachlann MacFhionghuinn, M.A. [Illus.] Clo-bhuailte fo ùghdarras A' Chomuinn Ghaidhealaich le Aonghas Mac Aoidh, 40 Craigs, Struibhle.
First published 1936.
163 p. 190 mm. EU, GU:CL, NLS.

—— [*An Seanachaidh.*] Glasgow, 1948.
Ibid.
First published 1936. Current reprint 1948.
160 p. 190 mm. GU:CL.
   Tales from J. F. Campbell's "Popular Tales of the West Highlands".
   Both editions printed by Jamieson & Munro, Stirling.

—— (tr.). See Ferguson, J. A. [*The Scarecrow.*]

—— (tr.). See Gregory, Lady Augusta. [*The Rising of the Moon.*]

—— (tr.). See John, Evan. [*Strangers' Gold.*]

—— (ed.). See MacKinnon, Donald, Professor of Celtic in Edinburgh University. [*Prose Writings.*]

—— (ed.). See MacKinnon, Donald, Professor of Celtic in Edinburgh University. [*Seanfhocail.*]

—— (joint ed.). See MacPhail, Malcolm C. [*Am Filidh Latharnach.*]

—— (tr.). See Malloch, G. R. [*The Grenadier.*]

MacKinnon, Mary A., 1880–. [*Airgiod Siusaidh.*] Glasgow, n.d.
Airgiod Siùsaidh. A Gaelic Play, in four acts. By Mary A. MacKinnon (Mrs. A. Campbell). [Illus.] Glasgow: printed by Archibald Sinclair, "Celtic Press", 27a Cadogan Street.
32 p. 220 mm. PC.
   First advertised 1930.

—— [*Beitidh.*] Glasgow, n.d.
"Beitidh". A Gaelic and English play, in three acts. By Mary A. MacKinnon. Written in aid of the Tiree Memorial Fund. Glasgow: printed by Archibald Sinclair, "Celtic Press", 47 Waterloo Street, Glasgow.
22 p. 220 mm. NLS.
   MacLaren gives date as 1916.

—— [*Beitidh.*] Glasgow, n.d.
Beitidh. Dealbh-chluich an Gàidhlig agus am Beurla. Le Màiri A. Chaimbeul. A Gaelic and English play, in three acts. Glascho: Alasdair MacLabhruinn 's a Mhic, 360–362 Sràid Earraghaidheal, C.2.
   Dated 1925 in *MacLaren*. Advertised first in *An Gaidheal*, 1927.

—— [*Posadh Seonaid.*] Glasgow, n.d.
Pòsadh Seònaid. A Gaelic and English play, in five acts. By Mary A. MacKinnon (Mrs. A. Campbell). Written in aid of the Feill 1927 Fund. [Illus.] Glasgow: printed by Archibald Sinclair, "Celtic Press", 47 Waterloo Street, Glasgow.
32 p. 220 mm. PC.

—— [*Ri Guaillibh a' Cheile.*] Glasgow, n.d.
"Ri Guaillibh a' Chéile." ("Shoulder to Shoulder.") By Mary A. MacKinnon (Mrs. A. Campbell). Glasgow: printed by Archibald Sinclair, "Celtic Press", 27a Cadogan Street.
20 p. 220 mm. Mit., PC.
   First advertised 1930; Mitchell Library copy acquired 1930.

MacKinnon, Roderick, of Bernera. [*Ar Slanuighear.*] Glasgow, [*c.* 1932].
Ar Slànuighear. Dàin Spioradail le Ruairidh Mac Fhionghain. Ten Spiritual Hymns
by Roderick MacKinnon, Bernera, Harris. Glascho: Alasdair Mac Labhruinn 's a
Mhic, 268 Sràid Earraghaidheal, C.2. Copyright, 1932.
20 p. 190 mm. PC.

MacKinnon, Roderick, of Skye, 1902–. [*Gaelic.*] London, 1971.
Teach Yourself Books. Gaelic. Roderick MacKinnon, M.A. Teach Yourself Books,
St. Paul's House, Warwick Lane, London, E.C.4.
First printed 1971.
xi, 324 p. 180 mm.

—— [*Gaelic.*] London, 1972.
Ibid.
First printed 1971. Second impression 1972.
xi, 324 p. 180 mm.

MacKinnon, Roderick, "Ruairi Iain Bhàin", 1864–1944. See Campbell, John L.
[*Gaelic Folksongs from the Isle of Barra.*]

MacKinnon, D. (tr.). See God Save the King.

MacLabhrainn, [Iain]. See MacLaurin, [John].

MacLachlan, Ewen, 1773–1822. [*Gaelic Verse.*] Aberdeen, 1937.
Aberdeen University Studies 114. Ewen MacLachlan's Gaelic Verse. Comprising a
translation of Homer's Iliad Book I–VIII and original compositions. Edited by John
MacDonald, M.A., Reader in Celtic in the University of Aberdeen. Printed for the
University of Aberdeen by R. Carruthers & Sons, Inverness. MCMXXXVII.
xv, 262 p. 260 mm. AU, BM, GU, Mit., NLS.

MacLagan, Robert C., 1839–. [*Games and Diversions of Argylleshire.*] London, 1901.
The Games and Diversions of Argylleshire. Compiled by Robert Craig MacLagan,
M.D. "Albainn bheadarrach!" London: published for the Folk-Lore Society by David
Nutt, 57–59 Long Acre. 1901.
Publications of the Folk-Lore Society XLVII (1900).
ci, [1] "Scheme of Classification", 270 p; 3 plates. 230 mm. AU, BM, Mit.
Discussion in English; contains Gaelic rhymes used in games. Some music, in both
notations. Printed Ballantyne, Hanson & Co., Edinburgh and London.

MacLaren, James, *d.* 1953. [*Fionn ann an Tigh a' Bhlair Bhuidhe.*] Glasgow, n.d.
Uirsgeulan Ghàidhlig. Fionn ann an Tigh a' Bhlàir Bhuidhe gun chomas suidhe no
éirigh. Fingal in the House of Blar Buidhe without the power of sitting down or getting
up. Glasgow: Alexander MacLaren & Son, Gaelic Publishers and Booksellers, 360–
362 Argyle Street.
[16] p. 190 mm. PC.
Notes signed, "J. M. L." Advertised in "An Deo-Greine", XI.2, Nov. 1915.

—— [*Fionn ann an Tigh a' Bhlair Bhuidhe.*] Glasgow, 1949.
[Cover.] MacLaren's Gaelic Publications. Fingal in the House of the Blar Buidhe.
A weird Highland tale with Gaelic and English on opposite pages. A boon to the
learner of Gaelic. Translated and edited by James MacLaren. Alex. MacLaren &
Sons, 268 Argyle Street, C.2. Ninepence.
Uirsgeulan Ghàidhlig. Fionn ann an Tigh a' Bhlàir Bhuidhe gun chomas suidhe no
éirigh. Fingal in the House of Blar Buidhe without the power of sitting down or rising
up. [...] Glasgow: Alex. MacLaren & Sons, 268 Argyle Street, C.2.
[16] p. 170 mm. PC.
English translation on facing pages; intended for learners of Gaelic.

—— [*Fionn ann an Tigh a' Bhlair Bhuidhe.*] See also Fionn ann an Tigh a' Bhlair Bhuidhe. [*Dwelly version.*]

—— (ed.). See MacLaren's Gaelic Interlinear Reader.

—— See MacLaren's Gaelic Self-taught.

MacLaren's Gaelic Self-taught.] Glasgow, 1923.
Suas leis a' Ghàidhlig. MacLaren's Gaelic Self-taught. Third edition – completely revised. Glasgow: Alex. MacLaren & Sons, Gaelic Publishers, Printers and Book-sellers, 360–362 Argyle Street.
[Verso] 1923.
viii, 184 p. 190 mm. BM, PC.
Based on "Introduction to Gaelic for Beginners" by J. W. MacLean. This is the first edition of "MacLaren's Gaelic Self-taught": the two editions of MacLean's "Introduction" are treated as earlier editions of "MacLaren's".

—— [*MacLaren's Gaelic Self-taught.*] Glasgow, 1935.
. . . Fourth edition – revised. Glasgow: Alex. MacLaren & Sons, Gaelic Publishers, Printers and Booksellers, 268 Argyle Street, C.2.
[Verso] 1935.
[2], viii, 184 p. 190 mm. BM.

—— [*MacLaren's Gaelic Self-taught.*] Glasgow, 1941, 1944, 1948, 1957, 1960, 1963, 1967.
Ibid.
viii, 184 p. 190 mm.
MacLaren address changes.

—— [*MacLaren's Gaelic Self-taught.*] Glasgow, 1970, 1971, 1974.
. . . Reprint of fourth (revised) edition. Gairm, Glasgow. 1970 [1971, 1974].
viii, 184 p. 190 mm.
Otherwise an exact reprint of the 4th ed. "Key to Exercises" (with separate t.p. and pagination) is bound with some of the above eds. and also issued separately: see immediately below.

—— See also MacLean, J. W. [*Introduction to Gaelic for Beginners.*]

—— [*Key to Exercises.*] Glasgow, 1923.
Key to exercises and answers to examination questions in MacLaren's Gaelic Self-taught, third edition. Also adapted as a Gaelic exercise book. Glasgow: Alex. MacLaren & Sons, 360–362 Argyle Street.
[Verso] 1923.
x, 40 p. 190 mm.

—— [*Key to Exercises.*] Glasgow, 1931, 1935, 1942, 1948, 1958, 1960, 1963, 1966, n.d.
Ibid.
x, 40 p. 190 mm.
Lacks the introductory pages when bound with "MacLaren's Gaelic Self-taught". Revised 1935. MacLaren address changes. Latest ["Gairm"] editions lack date and imprint.

MacLaren's Hebrides Collection of Scottish Songs. Glasgow, n.d.
MacLaren's Hebrides Collection of Scottish Songs No. . . .
4 p. 300 × 350 mm.
A series of 73 songs, with music in both notations; 20 of the songs are in English or Scots; all the Gaelic songs have versified English translations.

MacLaren's Interlinear Gaelic Reader. Glasgow, [*c.* 1935].
MacLaren's Interlinear Gaelic Reader. Gaelic with English translations. [Contents.]
Glasgow: Alex. MacLaren & Sons, 268 Argyle Street, C.2. Printed in Scotland on
Scottish paper. Copyright 1935.
32 p. 180 mm. EPL, Mit., PC.
Translations of the Bible and of an Aesop fable, poem by Neil MacLeod, etc.
Intended for learners of Gaelic.

MacLauchlan, Thomas (ed.). See Dana Oisein Mhic Fhinn.

MacLaurin, John. [*The Cross of Christ.*] Edinburgh, n.d.
Cogadh mór na h-Eòrpa. Crann-Ceusaidh Chriosd. Maclabhrainn. [Illus.] Printed
by Oliver and Boyd, Edinburgh, for The Church of Scotland, The United Free Church
of Scotland, and The Free Church of Scotland.
80 p. 140 mm. Mit., NLS.
Translated by Rev. Dugald MacPhail. Published for the use of soldiers in the First
World War. English original ("Glorying in the Cross of Christ") first published
1794.

MacLean, A. N. [*An Approach to Gaelic.*] Stirling, 1949.
An Approach to Gaelic. Part One. By A. N. MacLean, M.A. Published for An
Comunn Gaidhealach by Eneas Mackay, Stirling. 1949.
iv, 92 p; illus. 190 mm. EPL, GU:CL.
Printed Jamieson & Munro, Stirling.

MacLean, Alistair, 1885–1936. [*The Gaelic Phono-Grammar.*] Inverness, 1932.
The Gaelic Phono-grammar. A conversation grammar for the use of beginners. By
The Rev. Alistair MacLean, B.D. To be used with a set of gramophone records spoken
by Neil MacLean, M.A., B.Sc., and published for the Proprietors by The Parlophone
Company, Ltd. Price 3/6 net.; or with the 5 illustrative records, 18/–. Inverness:
printed by the Northern Counties Newspaper and Printing and Publishing Company,
Limited. 1932.
xvi, 136 p. 200 mm. Mit., NLS.
Introductions by Lady Elspeth Campbell and Compton MacKenzie.

MacLean, Allan (tr.). See Francis, J. O. [*Birds of a Feather.*]

—— (tr.). See Synge, John. [*Riders to the Sea.*]

MacLean, Allan Campbell, 1922–. [*Ribbon of Fire.*] Glasgow, 1967.
Teine Ceann Fòid. Le Ailean Caimbeul Macgilleathain. Eadar-theangaichte le Pòl
MacAonghais. Gairm. Glaschu. 1967.
Clò-bhualaidhean Gairm, Leabhar 5.
110 p. 220 mm.
Abridged and translated by Paul MacInnes. English original first published 1962.

MacLean, Ann. [*Cobhair as na Speuran.*] Glasgow, n.d.
"Cobhair as na Speuran." Dealbh-Chluich le Anna Nic Gilleathain, Glaschu. A' cheud
duais, Mod 1936. [Illus.] An Comunn Gaidhealach, 131 Sràid Iar Regent, Glaschu.
A' phrìs – sè sgillinn.
15 p. 220 mm. EPL, Mit.
Reviewed in "An Gaidheal", 1937.

MacLean, Archibald. [*Laoidhean Spioradail.*] Glasgow, n.d.
Laoidhean Spioradail, le Gilleasbuig Mac Gilleathain. Glascho: Gilleasbuig Mac na
Ceardadh, Clò-bhuailtear Gàidhlig.
23 p. 180 mm. EU, PC.
Dated 1901 in *TS-G.*

MacLean, C. (joint author). See Mo Leabhar I: Leabhar-Leughaidh/Leabhar-Oibreach; and Mo Leabhar II: Leabhar-Leughaidh.

MacLean, Calum I, 1915–60. [*The Charm of the Lasting Life*.] N.p., n.d.
A variant of the Charm of the Lasting Life from Uist. By Calum I. MacLean.
4 p. 250 mm. PC.
> Reprinted from "Saga Och Sed" (1954). Not seen.
> Information from John F. Campbell, Canna.

—— [*Conall Ulaban*.] Dublin, 1945.
Sgéalta as Albainn . . . Conall Ulaban, Mac Rìgh Cruachan.
[237]–246 p. 220 mm. PC
> Offprint from "Béaloideas", XV, Dublin, 1945.

—— (joint ed.). See School of Scottish Studies. [*Gaelic and Scots Folk Tales and Folk Songs*.]

MacLean, Donald, Minister of Dunvegan, 1856–1917. [*Typographia Scoto-Gadelica*.] Edinburgh, 1915.
Typographia Scoto-Gadelica. Or, Books Printed in the Gaelic of Scotland from the year 1567 to the year 1914. With bibliographical and biographical notes. By The Rev. Donald MacLean, Dunvegan, Skye. Edinburgh: John Grant, 31 George IV Bridge. 1915.
Only two hundred and fifty copies of this work have been printed, of which two hundred and forty copies, signed and numbered, are for sale in England and America. This copy is . . . [Signature.].
x, 372 p. 270 mm. AU, BM, GU, PC.
> Printed R. & R. Clark, Edinburgh.

—— [*Typographia Scoto-Gadelica*.] Shannon, 1972.
Typographia Scoto-Gadelica. Donald MacLean. Irish University Press. Shannon, Ireland. 1972.
Scottish Reprints. Typographia Scoto-Gadelica.
[1915 t.p. and limited edition statement, as above.]
[4], x, 372 p. 250 mm.
> First published with wider margins Edinburgh (John Grant) 1915. The third and fourth lines of the title, originally printed in red, have been reset somewhat smaller and printed in black: but this is in all other respects a photolithographic facsimile of the first edition.

MacLean, Donald, of Isleworth. [*Cuairtear nan Gaidheal*.] Glasgow, [*c*. 1949].
Cuairtear nan Gàidheal. Nine Gaelic songs and five songs in English. By Donald MacLean, Isleworth. Melodies and pianoforte accompaniments by Andrew J. Orr. Staff and sol-fa music. Glasgow: Alex. MacLaren & Sons, 268 Argyle Street, C.2. Copyright 1949. Price 3/6.
31 p. 260 mm. Mit., PC.
> Foreword in Gaelic and English by Hector MacDougall. Contains only eight Gaelic songs. Cover sub-title – "Eight Gaelic Songs".

MacLean, Donald, Professor in the Free Church College, Edinburgh, 1869–1943. See Buchanan, Dugald. [*Spiritual Songs*.]

—— (joint ed.). See Campbell, John F. [*More West Highland Tales*.] Volume One.

—— (joint ed.). See Cogadh mor na h-Eorpa. [For cross references to individual publications in this series.]

—— (ed.). See Dorlach Sìl.

E

MacLean, James W. [*Introduction to Gaelic for Beginners.*] [In 8 parts.] Glasgow, n.d.
Introduction to Gaelic for Beginners by one who has acquired the language. Jas. White
MacLean, formerly Teacher to the Celtic Union, The Edinburgh and Leith School
Boards. Glasgow: Alex. MacLaren & Son, Gaelic Booksellers, 229 and 360 Argyle
Street. Part I [to Part VIII].
128 p [16 p per part]. 190 mm.
MacLaren states that the 8 parts were issued between 1911 and 1914.

—— [*Introduction to Gaelic for Beginners.*] [Parts 1–4 only.] [Glasgow], n.d.
Introduction to Gaelic for Beginners by one who has acquired the language. Part I [to
Part IV].
48 p. 190 mm. Mit.
MacLaren states that Parts I–IV were revised by James MacLaren.

—— [*Introduction to Gaelic for Beginners.*] [1 vol.] Glasgow, n.d.
Introduction to Gaelic for Beginners by one who has acquired the language. Jas. White
MacLean, formerly Teacher to the Celtic Union, The Edinburgh and Leith School
Boards. Glasgow: Alex. MacLaren & Sons, Gaelic Booksellers, 360–362 Argyle Street.
[8], 128 p. 190 mm. GU:CL, NLS.
MacLaren gives July 1915 as date of publication but BM, GU:CL and NLS give
1916.

—— [*Introduction to Gaelic for Beginners.*] Glasgow, 1919.
Gaelic Self-taught. An Introduction to Gaelic for Beginners. With easy imitated
phonetic pronunciation. By James White MacLean, formerly Teacher to the Celtic
Union, Edinburgh and Leith School Boards and the Vancouver Gaelic Society. Second
and Revised Edition. Alexander MacLaren & Sons, 360–362 Argyle Street, Glasgow.
1919.
[5], 126 p. 180 mm. AU, PC.
Revised by James MacLaren and known hereafter as "MacLaren's Self-Taught".

—— [*Introduction to Gaelic for Beginners.*] For all subsequent editions see MacLaren's
Gaelic Self-Taught.

MacLean, John, "Bàrd Thighearna Cholla", 1787–1848. [*Oran do Mhac-Mhic-Alasdair
Ghlinne-Garadh.*] N.p., n.d.
Oran do Mhac-Mhic-Alasdair Ghlinne-Garadh. An ainm Bàrd Thighearna Cholla.
The Glengarry version of the song. Written from memory by John MacGillivray,
Oldground, Invergarry, December, 1913.
[4] p. 220 mm. PC.

—— See Sinclair, A. MacLean. [*Filidh na Coille.*]

MacLean, John, "Kaid", d. 1932. [*Book of Remembrance.*] Glasgow, 1939.
Book of Remembrance. John (Kaid) MacLean. Glasgow: Archd. Sinclair, Celtic
Press, 27a Cadogan Street. 1939.
64 p. 180 mm. PC.
Poems and songs; contains 2 pages of Gaelic.

MacLean, Lachlan, 1798–1848. [*Uilleam Uallas, Iain Knox, agus Rob Ruadh.*] Stirling,
1912.
Eachdraidhean-beatha nan Albannach Iomraiteach ud: Uilleam Uallas, Iain Knox agus
Rob Ruadh. Le Lachlann Mac Gill-Eathain nach maireann. Fo làimh Chaluim Mhic
Phàrlain. Aonghas Mac Aoidh, Leabhar-reiceadair, 43 Murray Place, Struibhle. 1912.
116 p; illus. 190 mm. AU, SS.
The above appeared originally as separate essays in periodicals.

—— (comp.). Campbell, John F. [*Leigheas Cas o Cein.*]

MacLean, Malcolm (joint ed.). [*Alba.*] Glasgow, 1948.
   Alba. A Scottish Miscellany in Gaelic and English. No. 1. Editors: Malcolm MacLean,
   T. M. Murchison. [Illus.] Published by William MacLellan, 240 Hope Street,
   Glasgow, C.2. for An Comunn Gaidhealach, 131 West Regent Street, Glasgow, C.2.
   [Cover] 1948.
   85 p; illus. 230 mm. AU, BM, EPL, GU:CL, Mit.
   No more issued.

MacLean, Mary M., 1921–. [*Gainmheach an Fhasaich.*] Inverness, [*c* 1971].
   Gainmheach an Fhàsaich. Màiri M. Nic Gill-Eathain. Club Leabhar Limited.
   Inbhirnis.
   c. Màiri M. Nic Gill-Eathain 1971.
   104 p. 190 mm.
   Printed Eccles, Inverness.

—— [*Lus Chrun a Griomasaidh.*] Inverness, [*c.* 1970].
   Lus Chrun a Griomasaidh. Sgeulachdan. Màiri M. Nic Gill-Eathain. Club Leabhar
   Limited, Tigh Obar Thairbh, Sràid na h-Eaglaise, Inbhirnis.
   c. Màiri M. Nic Gill-Eathain 1970.
   [8], 134 p. 190 mm.
   Printed Eccles, Inverness.

—— [*Sunbeams and Starlight.*] N.p., n.d.
   Sunbeams and Starlight. English and Gaelic Poems. By Mary M. MacLean, Black-
   point, Grimsay, North Uist. (This little booklet is affectionately dedicated to the tender
   memories that bind me irrevocably to the town of Oban. M. McL.)
   19 p. 180 mm. EPL.
   Gaelic poems, pp 16–19.

MacLean, Neil. [*Orain is Dain.*] N.p., n.d.
   Orain is Dàin le Niall MacGilleathain. Gaelic Songs and Poems by Neil MacLean.
   Arranged by Violet Mathieson, Dip.Mus.Ed., R.S.A.M.
   50 p. 260 mm. Mit., NLS.
   Foreword by T. M. Murchison. Music in both notations; arranged for piano.
   Reviewed in *An Gaidheal*, January 1950.

MacLean, Sorley, 1911–. [*Barran agus Asbhuain.*] Dublin, n.d.
   [Cover] Barran agus Asbhuain. Somhairle Mac Gill-Eain a' leughadh cuid de a dhàin
   fhéin. Poems by Sorley MacLean read by himself. Ceirnini Cladaigh.
   [Title page] Text of the poems with English translations. Faclan nan Dàn, agus Eadar-
   theangachadh orra gu Beurla.
   [15] p. 310 × 310 mm.
   1973. Transcript of an LP record of Sorley MacLean reciting his own poetry.
   Forewords by Iain C. Smith, Mairtinn O Direain, Hugh Macdiarmid. English
   translation of all the poems.

—— [*Dain do Eimhir.*] Glasgow, 1943.
   Dàin do Eimhir agus Dàin Eile. Le Somhairle Mac Ghill Eathain. Air an cur a mach le
   William MacLellan, 240 Hope St., Glaschu. MCMXLIII.
   103 p. 270 mm. AU, EU, GU, Mit., NLS.
   "Poems to Eimhir", English verse translations by Iain Chrichton Smith of a selection
   of poems from "Dàin do Eimhir" was published by Northern House, Newcastle on
   Tyne, in 1968 and 1971 [paperback] and by Victor Gollancz, London, in 1971
   [hardback].
   E*

—— [*Four Points of a Saltire.*] Edinburgh, [*c.* 1970].
Four Points of a Saltire. The poetry of Sorley MacLean, George Campbell Hay,
William Neill, Stuart MacGregor. Published by Reprographia, 23 Livingstone Place,
Edinburgh, EH9 1PD.
Copyright 1970.
[5]–165 p; illus. 240 mm.
  Preface by Tom Scott. Gaelic poems comprise: 17 by MacLean; 17 by Hay; 2 by
  Neill; all with English translation. Poems in English and Scots by Hay, Neill and
  MacGregor.

—— [*From the Height of the Cuilinn.*] Edinburgh, 1971.
Sorley MacLean. From the Height of the Cuilinn. Designed by Alasdair Hamilton.
Copyright Sorley MacLean 1943 and Alasdair Hamilton 1971. Printed in Great
Britain by Alexander Barr Ltd., 6 Sciennes Gardens, Edinburgh, EH9 1NR, Scotland.
1 p. 410 × 300 mm.
  Poster poem. Contains the Gaelic text of the poem, "An Uair a Labhras mi mu
  Aodann", with English translation.

—— [*Reothairt.*] Ashington, [1973].
Reothairt. Somhairle Macgill-eain. Midnag, Ashington, Northumberland. Poetry
Poster 25.
1 p. 680 × 500 mm.
  Poster poem. Gaelic text only. Published by Mid-Northumberland Arts Group.

—— [*Seventeen Poems for Sixpence.*] Edinburgh, 1940.
Seventeen Poems for Sixpence. By Somhairle Mac Ghill-eathain and Robert Garioch.
Edinburgh. The Chambers Press. 1940.
28 p. 200 mm. NLS.
  8 Gaelic poems by MacLean; 6 Scots and 2 English by Garioch; 1 Scots translation
  by Garioch of a poem by MacLean. Contains an extract from MacLean's long
  unpublished poem, "An Cuilthionn".

MacLellan, Angus, of Nova Scotia. [*Raonull ban Mac Eoghain Oig.*] Antigonish, n.d.
Raonull Bàn Eoghain Oig. Le Aonghas Mac Gillfhaolain. Casket Print, Antigonish.
26 p. 210 mm. PC.

MacLellan, Angus, of South Uist (1869–1966). [*Saoghal an Treobhaiche.*] Oslo, 1972.
Norsk Tidsskrift for Sprogvidenskap (Norwegian Journal of Linguistics). Edited by
Hans Vogt. Secretary Carl Hj. Borgström. Supplementary Volume X. Oslo. 1972.
Universiterforlaget.
Lochlann. A review of Celtic Studies. Edited by Magne Oftedal. Volume V. Oslo.
1972. Universitetforlaget.
Printed in Sweden by Almqvist and Wiksells, Boktrycheri Aktiebolag, Uppsala. 1972.
Saoghal an Treobhaiche. The autobiography of a Hebridean Crofter. Told by Angus
MacLellan, M.B.E. Tape-recorded, transcribed and annotated by John Lorne
Campbell.
[7], 234 p; plate. 260 mm.
  Lochlann is a supplement of *N.T.S.*

—— [*Saoghal an Treobhaiche.*] Inverness, 1972.
Saoghal an Treobhaiche. Le Aonghus Mac 'ill Fhialain, M.B.E. ("Aonghus Beag").
Air a recòrdadh 's air a asgrìobhadh le Fear Chanaidh. Club Leabhar. Inbhirnis.
Air a chlò-bhualadh anns an t-Suain le Almqvist and Wiksells, Boktrycheri Aktiebolag,
Uppsala. 1972.
[7], 234 p; plate. 230 mm.
  Gaelic original of "The Furrow behind me" (Routledge and Kegan Paul, London,
  1962). Recorded 1960–1. Introduction by J. L. Campbell, dated 1967. Contains
  Notes pp 209–23, Bibliography pp 224–5, Glossarial Index pp 226–34.

MacLellan, Robert, 1907–. [*The Cailleach.*] N.p., n.d.
A' Chailleach. Dealbh-chluich an aon sealladh. Gaelic translation of the one-act play, The Cailleach, by Robert MacLellan.
18 p. 190 mm. PC.
Copyright note, "Application to perform this play must be made to A. & J. Donaldson, Ltd., Publishers, 69 Ingram Street, Glasgow." English original first published 1940.

—— [*The Changeling.*] N.p., n.d.
An Tàcharan. Dealbh-chluich àbhachdach an aon sealladh. Gaelic translation of the one-act comedy, The Changeling, by Robert MacLellan. Air eadar-theangachadh le Iain M. MacMhathain.
19 p. 190 mm. GU:CL, PC.
Note, "Application to perform this play must be made to A. & J. Donaldson, Ltd., Publishers, 69 Ingram Street, Glasgow." English original first published 1935.

McLellan, Vincent A. [*Failte Cheap-Breatuinn.*] Sydney, C. B., 1933.
Fàilte Cheap Breatuinn. McNeil Edition. Including, the original Fàilte Cheap-Breatuin, together with, a supplementary of songs, stories, notes, and a biography of Mr V. A. McLellan, by James Hughie McNeil, Sydney, Cape Breton. A Bhealltain, 1933.
267 p. 230 mm. PC.
1st ed. 1891. "Only 8 type-written copies made of the above ed." – Prof. C. I. MacLeod, St. Francis Xavier University, Antigonish, Nova Scotia.

MacLellan, B. A. (tr.). See Murray, William. [*Things we Like.*]

MacLellan, Donald. [*Blasad Gaidhlig.*] Edinburgh, 1972.
[Cover] Blasad Gàidhlig. (A Taste of Gaelic.) A recorded cassette tape of Gaelic tuition for beginners with transcription booklet. Simple conversation spoken in Gaelic and translated. Written and recorded by Donald MacLennan. Published in Scotland by Reprographia, 23 Livingstone Place, Edinburgh, EH9 1PD.
[Title page] Blasad Gàidhlig. (A Taste of Gaelic.) By Donald MacLennan. Published by Reprographia, 23 Livingstone Place, Edinburgh, EH9 1PD, Scotland. 1972.
20 p. 220 mm.

MacLennan, Gordon. [*Gaidhlig Uidhist a Deas.*] Dublin, 1966.
Gàidhlig Uidhist a Deas. (Téacsleabhar.) Gordon Mac Gill-fhinnein a chuir le chéile. Institiùid Ard-leinn Bhaile Atha Cliath, 10 Bóthar Burlington, Baile Atha Cliath 4. 1966.
xiii, 139 p. 220 mm.
Printed Hely Thom Limited, Dublin.

MacLennan, John. [*Duanagan agus Sgeulachdan Beaga.*] Glasgow, 1937.
Duanagan agus Sgeulachdan Beaga. Le Iain Dubh Mac Dhòmhnuill 'ic Iain. [Quotation.] Fo làimh Eachainn Mhic Dhùghaill. Glascho: Alasdair MacLabhruinn 's a Mhic, 268 Sràid Earra-ghaidheal, C.2.
Poems and Storyettes. By John MacLennan, Brisbane. Edited by Hector Mac-Dougall. Glasgow: Alex. MacLaren & Sons, 268 Argyle Street, C.2.
First published 1937.
ix, 117 p. 200 mm. BM, EPL, GU:CL, Mit., NLS.

MacLennan, Malcolm, 1862–1931. [*Ceo na Moineadh.*] Edinburgh, 1907.
Ceò na Mòineadh (Peat Reek) á Luidhearan Dhuneidinn (from Edinburgh Chimneys) "Clanna nan Gàidheal 'an guaillibh a chéile". St. Columba's United Free Church. Edinburgh. Martinmas 1907.
24 p; plate. 220 mm. EU.
4 pages of Gaelic. 2 items signed by MacLennan; contains frontispiece portrait of MacLennan.

—— [*Handbook of Gaelic Phrases and Sentences.*] Edinburgh, 1930.
Handbook of Gaelic Phrases and Sentences. With pronunciations and English equivalents. Based on "The Tourist's Handbook" by Mrs. Mary MacKellar. New edition revised and enlarged by Malcolm MacLennan, D.D. Edinburgh: John Grant, 31 George IV Bridge. 1930.
63 p. 170 mm. BM, FC.
  Printed Oliver and Boyd, Edinburgh.

—— [*Handbook of Gaelic Phrases and Sentences.*] Edinburgh, 1939.
Based on "The Tourist's Handbook". By Malcolm MacLennan, D.D. New edition revised and enlarged by Alexander MacFarlane, M.A. Edinburgh: John Grant, 31 George IV Bridge. 1939.
64 p. 170 mm. CoS, GU:CL, Mit.

—— [*Handbook of Gaelic Phrases and Sentences.*] Edinburgh, 1949, 1962.
Ibid.
  Based on "The Tourist's Handbook" by Mary MacLellar.

—— [*Handbook of Gaelic Phrases and Sentences.*] See also MacKellar, Mary. [*The Tourist's Handbook.*]

—— [*MacLeod's Gaelic Reader.*] Edinburgh, 1909.
MacLeod's Gaelic Reader. With Notes and Vocabulary. Edited by Malcolm Mac-Lennan, Edinburgh. Edinburgh: Norman MacLeod. 1909.
66 p. 190 mm. GU:CL, Mit., NLS.
  Traditional tales.

—— [*The Gaelic Reader.*] Edinburgh, 1913.
The Gaelic Reader. With Notes and Vocabulary. Edited by Malcolm MacLennan. New and revised edition . Edinburgh: John Grant, 31 George IV Bridge. 1913.
80 p. 190 mm. AU, BM, PC.
  3 poems have been added.

—— [*Pronouncing and Etymological Dictionary*] Edinburgh, 1925.
A Pronouncing and Etymological Dictionary of the Gaelic Language. Gaelic-English, English-Gaelic. By Malcolm MacLennan, D.D. Edinburgh: John Grant, 31 George IV Bridge. 1925.
xvi, 613 p. 230 mm. AU, BM, EPL, Mit.
  Printed Oliver and Boyd, Edinburgh.

—— (tr.). See Bunyan, John. [*The Pilgrim's Progress.*]

—— (ed.). See Church of Scotland. [*Liturgy and Ritual.*] An Laoidheadair.

—— (joint ed.). See Cogadh mor na h-Eorpa. For cross-references to individual publications in this series.

—— (ed.). See MacLeod, Murdo, of Scalpay. [*Laoidhean agus Dain Spioradail.*]

—— (ed.). See Martin, Donald J. [*Teagasg nan Cosamhlachdan.*]

—— (ed.). See Monthly Visitor.

MacLeod, Alasdair, 1900–. [*Laoidhean.*] Inverness, [*c.* 1973].
Laoidhean. Alasdair Mac Leòid. Club Leabhar. Inbhirnis.
c. Alasdair Mac Leòid 1973.
[6], 33 p. 210 × 150 mm.
  Foreword by D. Gillies. Cover design by Mary Munro.

MacLeod, Allan, of Bernera, 1858–1939. [*Griasaiche Bhearnaraidh.*] Glasgow, n.d.
Griasaiche Bheàrnaraidh. A Bhàrdachd, le iomradh air. Le Niall Mac-an-Tuairneir.
Published by the Caledonian Press for Neil Turner, Drinishader, Harris, Inverness-
shire.
24 p. 220 mm. PC.
    Reviewed in "Life and Work", October 1953, in "An Gaidheal", March 1954.
Foreword by T. M. Murchison.

MacLeod, Allan, of Stornoway, 1840/1–1931. [*Cliu agus Cuimhneachan.*] Glasgow,
1931.
Cliù agus Cuimhneachan air cuid de na Criosdaidhean a chaidh dhachaidh. Le Ailean
MacLeòid, anns a' Ghleann-Ur, Steòrnabhagh, Leodhas. Glascho: Alasdair Mac-
Labhruinn agus a Mhic, 360–362 Sràid Earraghaidheal, C.2. 1931.
16 p. 190 mm. EPL, Mit., NLS.

MacLeod, Angus, ?–1960. [*Sar Orain.*] Glasgow, 1933.
Sar Orain. Three Gaelic Poems. Luinneag Mhic Leòid – Mary MacLeod, Màiri
Nighean Alasdair Ruaidh. Birlinn Chlann Raghnaill – Alexander MacDonald, Alasdair
MacMhaighstir Alasdair. Moladh Beinn Dobhrainn – Duncan MacIntyre, Donn-
chadh Bàn. Edited by A. MacLeod, M.A., B.Sc., F.E.I.S., Rector, Oban High School.
An Comunn Gaidhealach, 212 West George Street, Glasgow. 1933.
xv, 232 p. 190 mm. AU, GU:CL, Mit.
    Printed Learmonth, Stirling.

—— (ed.). See MacIntyre, Duncan. [*Songs.*]

MacLeod, Babi, 1902–. [*Gaelic Proverbs.*] Inverness, [*c.* 1973].
Gaelic Proverbs. Bàbi Nic Leòid. Club Leabhar. Inbhirnis.
c. Babi Nic Leòid 1973.
[9], 22 p; illus. 210 mm.
    Illus. by Margaret Thomson. Foreword by Angus Mackenzie, Lochinver. Printed
Eccleslitho, Inverness.

MacLeod, B. A. (joint author). See Mo Leabhar I: Leabhar-Leughaidh/Leabhar-
Oibreach; and Mo Leabhar II: Leabhar-Leughaidh.

MacLeod, C. A. (joint author). See Mo Leabhar I: Leabhar-Leughaidh/Leabhar-
Oibreach; and Mo Leabhar II: Leabhar-Leughaidh.

MacLeod, Calum I. N., 1913–. [*Bardachd a Albainn Nuaidh.*] Glasgow, 1970.
Bàrdachd a Albainn Nuaidh. Deasaichte le Calum Iain M. MacLeòid. Gairm.
Glaschu. 1970.
Clò-bhualaidhean Gairm, Leabhar 25.
108 p. 220 mm.
    Printed Learmonth, Stirling.

—— [*An t-Eilthireach.*] Glace Bay, N.S., 1952.
An t-Eilthireach. Original Gaelic Poems and Melodies. By Major C. I. N. MacLeod.
Printed by Brodie Printing Service Ltd., Glace Bay, Nova Scotia. 1952.
43 p. 220 mm. NLS.
    Music in staff. Foreword by Dr. D. J. MacLeod. Enclosed is a loose typed sheet,
"Glossary".

—— [*Scottish Gaelic for Beginners.*] Halifax/Glasgow, n.d.
[Script.] Scottish Gaelic for Beginners. Gàidhlig na h-Albann air son Luchd-
tòiseachaidh. Series No. 1.
[Record label.] Scottish Gaelic for Beginners. . . . A Simplified Course conducted by

Major Calum Iain MacLeod, Gaelic Advisor to the Province of Nova Scotia, and Mrs.
C. I. N. MacLeod.
12 p. 270 mm. PC.
> 1 L.P. record of Gaelic dialogue, with a script comprising 12 typed sheets stapled
> together. Issued *c.* 1955 by Rodeo Records, Halifax, N.S.; re-issued by Gaelfonn,
> Glasgow, Scotland, *c.* 1956.

—— [*Sgialachdan a Albainn Nuaidh.*] Glasgow, 1969.
Sgialachdan á Albainn Nuaidh. Air an cruinneachadh 's air an sgrìobhadh le Calum
Iain M. MacLeòid. Gairm. Glaschu. 1969.
Clò-bhualaidhean Gairm, Leabhar 15.
150 p. 200 mm.
> Eachdraidh nan Eilthireach, pp 9–23; Sgialachdan nan Eilthireach, pp 25–114;
> Sgialachdan á Albainn, pp 137–148; Seanchasan Eibhinn, pp 137–48.

—— [*Simplified Gaelic Lessons for Beginners.*] Glace Bay, N.S., 1950.
Simplified Gaelic Lessons for Beginners. By Major Calum I. N. MacLeod.
Printed by Brodie Printing Service, Ltd., Glace Bay, N.S. 1950.
16 p. 180 mm. PC.
> Not seen. "The stocks were bought and disposed of by the Nova Scotia School Book
> Bureau." – Prof. C. I. N. MacLeod.

—— (joint ed.). See Creighton, Helen. [*Gaelic Songs in Nova Scotia.*]

MacLeod, Christina, –1954. [*Ceolraidh Cridhe.*] Glasgow, [*c.* 1943].
Ceòlraidh Cridhe. Music from the Heart. Nine original Highland melodies with
Gaelic and English words. By Christina MacLeod. Some of the airs, the arrangement
and accompaniments by Kenneth I. E. MacLeod. Dedicated to all those brave men and
women from Lewis and the Hebrides who serve their country on the sea, on the land
and in the air. Glasgow: Alex. MacLaren & Sons, 268 Argyle Street, C.2. Printed in
Scotland.
Price 4/- net. Copyright, 1943.
[2], 26 p. 260 mm. Mit., PC.
> Music in both notations.

—— [*Na Raithean.*] Glasgow, n.d.
An Comunn Gaidhealach. [Illus.] Dealbhchluich-ciùil Cloinne. Na Ràithean. An
treas duais (ionann), Mod, 1925. Le Cairistiona NicLeòid. A' phrìs se sgillinn. An
Comunn Gaidhealach, 114 Sràid West Campbell, Glascho.
6 p, [2] "Ceol nan Oran". 220 mm. AU, Mit.
> Advertised in "An Gaidheal", 1926.

—— [*An Sireadh.*] Stirling, 1952.
An Sireadh. Le Chiorstai NicLeòid. Cuimhneachan air m'athair agus mo mhàthair.
[Quotation.] Air a chlòdhbhualadh le Aonghas MacAoidh, Struibhle. 1952. Printed
at the Observer Press, 40 Craigs, Stirling.
v, 74 p. 190 mm. Mit., PC.
> Foreword by J. N. MacLeod.

—— See MacLeod, Kenneth I. E. [*Music from the Heart.*]

MacLeod, Christine. [*Calum Cille.*] Inverness, 1972.
Calum Cille. Le Cairistiona NicLeòid agus Mòrag NicCoinnich. Dealbhan le Dòmhnall
MacLeòid. Eccleslitho. Inbhirnis. 1972.
35 p; illus. 210 mm.

—— [*Na Lochlannaich.*] Glasgow, 1970.
Na Lochlannaich. Le Cairistiona NicLeòid, Mórag NicCoinnich agus Dolìna Nic-
Fhearghais. Dealbhan le Dòmhnall MacLeòid. Gairm. Glaschu. 1970.
[2], 37 p; illus. 290 mm.
> Printed Eccleslitho, Inverness.

MacLeod, Donald James, 1879–1955. [*Standardisation of Gaelic Pronunciation.*] Inverness, 1932.
Inverness Gaelic Society. Address on The Standardisation of Gaelic Pronunciation, by D. J. MacLeod, M.A., D.Litt., Officier d'Academie. Printed by the Northern Counties Newspaper and Printing and Publishing Company, Limited, Margaret Street, Inverness. 1932.
21 p. 220 mm. PC.

—— (ed.). See MacIntyre, Duncan. [*Vie, Etude, Citations, Traductions.*]

—— (joint author). See An Solaraiche.

MacLeod, Donald John, 1943–. [*Dorcha tro Ghlainne.*] Glasgow, 1970.
Dorcha tro Ghlainne. Taghadh de sgeulachdan-goirid. Deasaichte le Dòmhnall-Iain MacLeòid. Gairm. Glaschu. 1970.
Clo-bhualaidhean Gairm, Leabhar 24.
150 p. 210 mm.
Printed Learmonth, Stirling.

—— [*An t-Eilean a Tuath.*] Glasgow, 1972.
An t-Eilean a Tuath. Orain agus bàrdachd á Leódhas agus Na Hearadh. Air a dheasachadh do Chomunn Leódhais agus Na Hearadh le Dòmhnall Iain MacLeòid. Comunn Leódhais agus Na Hearadh. Glaschu. 1972.
An t-Eilean a Tuath. Comunn Leódhais agus Na Hearadh. Leabhar I.
[8], 77 p. 220 mm.

—— (comp.). See Aberdeen University Library. [*Scottish-Gaelic Holdings.*]

MacLeod, Finlay. [*Na Balaich air Ronaidh.*] Aberdeen, 1972.
Na Balaich air Rònaidh. Dealbh-chluich airson réidio ann an sia earrainnean. Fionnlagh MacLeòid. Na deilbh le Dòmhnall Mac a' Ghobhainn. Roinn an Fhoghluim Cheiltich, Oilthigh Obar-Dheadhan. 1972.
Leabhraichean Gàidhlig Oilthigh Obar-Dheadhan (fo stiùireadh Dhòmhnaill Mhic-Amhlaigh), A' Cheud Leabhar.
142 p; illus. 220 mm.
The play was broadcast on B.B.C. radio 1966.

MacLeod, Fred T., 1872–. [*Eilean a' Cheo.*] Edinburgh, [Pref. 1917].
Eilean a' Cheò. Articles on Skye by Skyemen. Edited with an introduction by Fred. T. MacLeod, F.S.A.Scot. Printed and published by Gordon Wilson, 47 Thistle Street, Edinburgh.
xv, 133 p; plate. 190 mm. Mit.
Contains one Gaelic article, "Na h-Orduighean anns an Eilean", by Donald MacPhie, pp 67–71.

MacLeod, Iain, 1933–. [*Sraidean is Sleibhtean.*] Glasgow, 1971.
Sràidean is Sléibhtean. Sgeulachdan goirid le Iain MacLeod. Gairm. Glaschu. 1971.
Clò-bhualaidhean Gairm, Leabhar 30.
70 p. 220 mm.
Printed Learmonth, Stirling.

MacLeod, Ina (ed.). See MacLeod, Murdo, Murchadh a' Cheisteir, 1837–1914. [*Murchadh a' Cheisteir.*]

MacLeod, James. [*Cailinn Sgiathanach.*] Glasgow, [Fore., 1923].
Cailinn Sgiathanach. No, Faodalach na h-Abaid. Le Seumas MacLeòid. Glascho: Alasdair MacLabhruinn 's a Mhic, 360–362 Sràid Earra-Ghaidheal.
A Maid of Skye. Or, The Foundling of the Abbey. By James MacLeod. Glasgow: Alexander MacLaren & Sons, 360–362 Argyle Street.
[4], 364 p. 190 mm. AU, BM, GU:CL Mit.

MacLeod, John, "Iain Tholsta". [*Dain.*] N.p., n.d.
Dàin. Le Iain MacLeòid (Iain Tholsta) nach maireann.
11 p. 200 mm. PC.

MacLeod, John, "Iain Thormaid Bhig". [*Bardachd Ghaidhlig.*] Glasgow, n.d.
Bàrdachd Ghàidhlig. Le Iain MacLeòid (Iain Thormaid Bhig), Tom a' Ghlinne, Siabost.
32 p. 190 mm. PC.
Foreword signed "N. McA." "Tha 'n leabhar so air a chlò-bhualadh fo thaic Comunn Eilean Leòdhais, am baile Ghlaschu"; Foreword.

MacLeod, Rev. John, Minister of Barvas. [*Am Measg nan Lili.*] Inverness, 1948.
Am Measg nan Lili. Tormod Sona a bha 'n Siadair Bharabhais. Leis an Urr. Iain MacLeod, an Eaglais Shaor, Barabhas. A' phrìs 5/6. Inverness: The Highland News Office. 1948.
[4], xxiv, 146 p; plate. 190 mm. GU.

MacLeod, John, of Culkein-Store. [*Dain agus Orain.*] Edinburgh, 1900.
Poems and Songs. By John MacLeod, sometime professor of English Literature, etc., Garrick Chambers, London. Edinburgh: Norman MacLeod, 25 George IV Bridge. 1900.
Dàin agus Orain. Le Iain MacLeòid, Culkeinstorr. Dunéideann: Tormad MacLéòid, Drochaid Righ Deorsa IV. 1900.
32 p. 170 mm. NLS.
Printed Lorimer & Gillies, Edinburgh.

—— [*Dain agus Orain.*] Inverness, 1907.
. . . Inverness: printed by the Northern Counties Newspaper and Printing and Publishing Company, Limited. 1907.
. . . Inbhirnis: An Eachdraidh Thuathach. 1907.
48 p. 190 mm. CoS.

—— [*Dain agus Orain.*] Inverness, 1918.
. . . Second edition . . . 1918.
68 p. 180 mm. AU, Mit., NLS.
Poems in English, pp 52–68.

MacLeod, John, of Glendale, Skye. [*Ceolraidh Iain Mhic Leoid.*] [?].
Ceòlraidh Iain Mhic Leòid.
Advertisement by Alex. MacLaren's, 1930: "Ceòlraidh Iain Mhic Leòid, of Glendale, Skye. Collected by Rev. Donald MacCallum. To be published as soon as possible." Apparently not published.

MacLeod, John A., 1919–. [*Criomagan Ioma-Dhathte.*] Edinburgh, 1973.
Criomagan Ioma-Dhathte. Le Iain Aonghas MacLeoid. Techmac 'sa Chomunn. Duneideann. 1973.
116 p; illus. 220 mm.
Line drawings by Calum Ferguson.

—— [*Luinneagan Mhicleoid.*] Edinburgh, 1973.
Luinneagan MhicLeòid. Iain Aonghas Macleòid as na Hearadh, am Bàrd aig Mòd Nàiseanta a' Chomuinn Ghaidhelaich, Sruighlea 1971. Techmac 's a Chomunn. Duneideann. 1973.
59 p. 230 mm.
Contains 17 tunes, in sol-fa notation.

MacLeod, John N., 1880–1954. [*Bardachd Leodhais.*] Glasgow, 1916.
Bàrdachd Leodhais. Fo làimh Iain N. MacLeòid. [Illus.] Glaschu: Alasdair Mac Labhruinn agus a Mhic, 360–362 Sràid Earraghaidheal. 1916.
[2], xx, 275 p; 11 plates. 230 mm. AU, GU, Mit.
Some tunes in sol-fa notation. Printed Milne, Tannahill & Methven, Perth.

—— [*Bardachd Leodhais.*] Glasgow, [Fore. 1955].
Bàrdachd Leodhais. Fo làimh Iain N. MacLeoid. [Illus.] Glaschu: Alasdair Mac
Labhruinn agus a Mhic. 268 Sràid Earraghaidheal.
xx, 275 p; 11 plates. 230 mm. GU:CL, PC.
   Foreword by John MacKay for the Glasgow Lewis and Harris Association. Contains
   some tunes in sol-fa.

—— [*Fionghal a' Phrionnsa.*] Dingwall, 1932.
"Fionghal a' Phrionnsa". Dealbh-chluich Gàidhlig le Iain N. MacLeòid. Seòras
Griasaiche, Buth nan Leabhraichean, Inbhirpheofharain, agus Alasdair Mac Labhruinn
and a Mhic, Glaschu. 1932.
39 p. 200 mm. AU, EU.

—— [*Litrichean Alasdair Mhoir.*] Stornoway, 1932.
Litrichean Alasdair Mhóir. Le Iain N. MacLeòid. Oifis "Cuairtear Steornabhaigh",
18 Sràid Choinnich, Steòrnabhagh. 1932.
xv, 392 p. 190 mm. AU, GU:CL.
   Selection from MacLeod's weekly "diary" in the *Stornoway Gazette*, 1917–.

—— [*Posadh Moraig.*] Glasgow, 1916.
Pòsadh Móraig. (Dealbh-chluich Ghàidhlig.) Le Iain N. MacLeòid, ùghdar
"Reiteach Móraig". Glaschu: Alasdair Mac Labhruinn agus a Mhic, 360 Sràid
Earraghaidheal. 1916.
16 p. 230 mm. PC.
   Sequel to "Reiteach Móraig".

—— [*Reiteach Moraig.*] Glasgow, 1911.
Réiteach Móraig. Le Iain M. MacLeòid, Cinntàile. Le dealbh an ùghdair. Glaschu:
Gilleasbuig MacnaCeardadh, Clò-bhuailtear Gàidhlig. 1911.
[2], ii, 12 p; plate. 230 mm. Mit.

—— [*Reiteach Moraig.*] Glasgow, 1922.
Reiteach Móraig. Le Iain M. MacLeòid. An treas clò-bhualadh. Glaschu: Alasdair
MacLabhruinn agus a Mhic, 360 Sràid Earraghàidheal, Clò-bhuailtearan Gàidhlig.
1922.
[4], 12 p. 230 mm. PC.
   First published in "An Sgeulaiche", 1910.

—— (ed.). See Nicolson, Calum. [*Dain Spioradail.*]

MacLeod, Kenneth (joint ed.). See Kennedy-Fraser, Marjory. [*Four Hebridean Love
   Lilts.*]

—— (joint ed.). See Kennedy-Fraser, Marjory. [*From the Hebrides.*]

—— (joint ed.). See Kennedy-Fraser, Marjory. [*Sea Tangle.*]

—— (joint ed.). See Kennedy-Fraser, Marjory. [*Seven Songs of the Hebrides.*]

—— (joint ed.). See Kennedy-Fraser, Marjory. [*Songs of the Hebrides.*]

—— (joint ed.). See Kennedy-Fraser, Marjory. [*Songs of the Hebrides for Schools.*]

—— (joint ed.). See Kennedy-Fraser, Marjory. [*Twelve Songs of the Hebrides.*]

MacLeod, Kenneth I. E., 1912–. [*Music from the Heart.*] Leeds, [*c.* 1972].
   A Memorial Tribute. Music from the Heart. By Kenneth I. E. MacLeod. Being 15
   selected songs composed to poems by his mother, Christina MacLeod, and by Christian
   Curr, William Singer, Robert Burns, John S. Martin and John Masefield. Published
   by John Blackburn Ltd., Old Run Road, Leeds.
32 p. 280 mm.
      Copyright 1972. Gaelic content: 2 poems by Christina MacLeod, with English
      translations, and Gaelic translation of 1 poem by Christian Curr.

—— (arr.). See MacLeod, Christina. [*Ceolraidh Cridhe.*]

MacLeod, M. (joint author). See Mo Leabhar I: Leabhar-Leughaidh/Leabhar-Oibreach; and Mo Leabhar II: Leabhar-Leughaidh.

MacLeod, Malcolm, 1881–1946. [*An Iuchair Oir.*] Stirling, 1950.
The Golden Key. Gaelic Sermons by The Reverend Malcolm MacLeod, M.A. Edited with Gaelic Memoir and Biographical Sketch in English, by The Rev. T. M. Murchison, M.A. Stirling Tract Enterprise. 1950.
An Iuchair Oir. Searmoinean leis an Urramach Calum MacLeòid, M.A. Air an deasachadh le Iomradh air Beatha an Ughdair leis an Urramach T. M. MacCalmain, M.A. Comunn nan Trachdaichean, Sruighlea.
147 p; plate. 230 mm. BM, GU, NLS.
Printed Jamieson & Munro, Stirling.

—— (joint ed.). See Church of Scotland. *Liturgy and Ritual.* [An Laoidheadair.]

—— (ed.). See Am Feachd Gaidhealach.

—— (tr.). See Oldham, J. H. [*The Possibilities of Prayer.*]

MacLeod, Malcolm C. [*Modern Gaelic Bards.*] Stirling, 1908.
Modern Gaelic Bards. Edited by Malcolm C. MacLeod. Stirling: Eneas Mackay, 43 Murray Place. 1908.
243 p; 10 plates. 230 mm. AU, BM, Mit.
Music in sol-fa.

—— [*Modern Gaelic Bards: Second Series.*] Dundee, 1913.
Modern Gaelic Bards. Edited by Malcolm C. MacLeod. Second Series. Part 1. Dundee: John Leng & Co., Ltd., Bank Street. Glasgow: Alex. MacLaren & Son, Argyle Street. 1913.
iv, [1], 128 p; 6 plates. 220 mm. AU, BM, Mit., SS.

—— [*Modern Gaelic Bards: Second Series.*] Dundee, n.d.
Modern Gaelic Bards. Edited by Malcolm C. MacLeod. Second Series. Dundee: Malcolm C. MacLeod, 183 Blackness Road.
This Edition is limited to 100 copies, of which this is No. . . . [Signature of M. C. MacLeod.]
iv, [1], 128 p; 6 plates. 290 mm. GU:CL, Mit., SS.
Printed Leng, Dundee.

—— (ed.). See Dundee Highland Society. [*Year Book/Annual.*]

MacLeod, Mary, of Stornoway. (joint ed.). See Dick, Lachlan. [*Bardachd gu a Mineachadh.*]

MacLeod, Mary, Seventeenth Century Poetess, *c.* 1615–1705. [*Luinneag Mhic Leoid.*] See MacLeod, Angus. [*Sar Orain.*]

—— [*Orain agus Luinneagan Gaidhlig.*] London, 1934.
Gaelic Songs of Mary MacLeod. Edited with Introduction, Translation, Notes, etc., by J. Carmichael Watson. Blackie & Son, Limited, London and Glasgow. 1934.
Orain agus Luinneagan Gàidhlig le Màiri nighean Alasdair Ruaidh.
xxxiv, 158 p; plate. 190 mm. AU, BM, EU, GU, Mit.
Translation on facing pages. Text, pp 1–107; Notes, pp 109–46; Vocabulary, pp 147–58.

—— [*Orain agus Luinneagan Gaidhlig.*] Edinburgh, 1965.
Orain agus Luinneagan Gàidhlig le Màiri Nighean Alasdair Ruaidh.
Gaelic Songs of Mary MacLeod. Edited by J. Carmichael Watson. Published by Oliver & Boyd for the Scottish Gaelic Texts Society. Edinburgh. 1965.
Scottish Gaelic Texts Volume Nine.
xxxiv, 158 p. 230 mm.
Printed Robert Cunningham, Alva.

MacLeod, Murdo, H.M. Inspector for Schools, 1929–. [*Laithean Geala*.] Aberdeen, 1962.
Laithean Geala. Murchadh MacLeòid, M.A., B.A., Fear-stiùiridh na Gàidhlige an sgoiltean Siorrachd Inbhirnis. Na dealbhan le Aonghus Mac-a-phì, Ard-sgoil Inbhirnis. Oilthigh Obair-Dheadhain. 1962.
Leabhraichean ùra Gàidhlig Oilthigh Obair-Dheadhain (fo stiùireadh Ruairidh MhicThómais); Sreath na Sgoile, Leabhar 1. Làithean Geala, le Murchadh MacLeoid.
viii, 144 p; illus. 190 mm. PC.
    Printed by Blackie, Glasgow.

—— [*Laithean Geala*.] Aberdeen, 1965.
. . . An dara clò-bhualadh. Oilthigh Obair-Dheadhain. 1965.
viii, 144 p; illus. 190 mm.

—— [*Laithean Geala*.] Glasgow, 1972.
Làithean Geala. Murchadh MacLeòid, M.A., B.A. Na dealbhan le Aonghas Mac-a-phì, Ard-sgoil Inbhirnis. An treas clò-bhualadh. Oilthigh Ghlaschu. 1972.
Leabhraichean ùra Gàidhlig Oilthigh Ghlaschu (fo stiùireadh Ruairidh MhicThomais); Sreath na Sgoile, Leabhar 1. Làithean Geala. Le Murchadh MacLeòid.
viii, 144 p; illus. 190 mm.
    Printed Maclehose, Glasgow.

—— [*Seumas Beag*.] Glasgow, 1968.
Seumas Beag. Murchadh MacLeòid, Fear-stiùiridh na Gàidhlige an sgoiltean Siorrachd Inbhirnis. Na dealbhan le Gilleasbuig Friseal. Gairm. Glaschu. 1968.
Clò-bhualaidhean Gairm, Leabhar 7.
[4], 52 p; illus. 190 mm.
    Printed Learmonth Stirling.

—— (joint ed.). See Dick, Lachlan. [*Leasain Ghaidhlig*.]

MacLeod, Murdo, "Murchadh a' Cheisteir", 1837–1914. [*Laoidhean agus Orain*.] Edinburgh, 1962.
Bàrdachd Mhurchaidh a' Cheisdeir, Laoidhean agus Orain. Songs and hymns, by Murdo MacLeod (The Lewis Bard). Printed at The Darien Press, Ltd., Bristo Place, Edinburgh, 1962.
vi, 73 p; 3 plates. 230 mm.
AU, EPL, GU, Mit.

—— [*Laoidhean agus Orain*.] Edinburgh, 1965.
Bàrdachd Mhurchaidh a' Cheisdeir. Laoidhean agus òrain. Songs and hymns by Murdo MacLeod (The Lewis Bard). Second edition. Printed at The Darien Press Ltd., Bristo Place, Edinburgh. 1965.
[3], vi, 73 p; plate. 230 × 150 mm.
    Introduction signed, "A.D. [i.e. Angus Duncan], J.M.D. [i.e. Jane Mary Duncan, daughter of the poet]".

—— [*Murchadh a' Cheisteir*.] Stornoway, 1961.
Murchadh a' Cheisteir.
Stornoway Gazette, Lewis. 1961.
99 p; 5 plates. 230 mm. PC.
    Preface signed, "Mrs. Ina MacLeod, Edinburgh" [daughter of the poet].

MacLeod, Murdo, of Leurbost, 1886–1966. [*Laoidhean Gaidhlig*.] Stornoway, n.d.
Laoidhean Gàidhlig le Murchadh Macleoid, Liurbost.
Published by Mrs. A. J. MacKenzie, 16 Newton Street, Stornoway, and printed by Stornoway Gazette Ltd., 10 Francis Street, Stornoway.
20 p. 230 mm. PC.
    Foreword signed, "D. MacIlliosa". *c.* 1967.

MacLeod, Murdo, of Scalpay, 1881–1907. [*Laoidhean agus Dain Spioradail.*] Edinburgh, 1908.
  Laoidhean agus Dàin Spioradail. Le Murachadh MacLeòid (nach maireann), Scalpaidh na h-Earradh. Air a dheasachadh leis an Urr. Calum Mac 'Illinnein, B.D., an Dunéideann. Edinburgh: Norman MacLeod. 1908.
  xi, 83 p. 190 mm. AU, EPL, GU:CL, Mit.
    Printed Morrison & Gibb, Edinburgh. Foreword signed, "A.S.M., S.M."

—— [*Laoidhean agus Dain Spioradail.*] Edinburgh, 1966.
  . . . Sold and published by the Knox Press, 15 North Bank Street, The Mound, Edinburgh, 1. Reprinted by the Ross-shire Printing and Publishing Co., Dingwall, Rossshire, August, 1966.
  xiii, 48 p. 210 mm. PC.
    The Knox Press is The Free Church of Scotland's publishing agency.

—— [*Marbhrann.*] N.p., n.d.
  Marbhrann do Mhrs Iain Macleòid, Scalpaidh na h-earradh (nighean Iain Caimbeul, Tolstadh 'o thuath), nach maireann. (Le Murchadh Macleòid, Scalpaidh.) . . .
  [4] p. 180 mm. FC.

MacLeod, Neil, 1843–1913. [*Clarsach an Doire.*] Edinburgh, 1902.
  Clàrsach an Doire. Gaelic Poems, Songs, and Tales. By Neil MacLeod. Third edition – revised and enlarged. With portrait of the author. Edinburgh: Norman MacLeod, 25 George IV Bridge. 1902.
  Clàrsach an Doire. Dàin, Orain, is Sgeulachdan. Le Niall MacLeòid. [Verse.] An treas clò-bhualadh. Le dealbh an ùghdair. Dunéideann: Tormaid MacLeoid. 1902.
  xii, 268 p; plate. 200 mm. AU, BM, Mit.
    Printed Oliver & Boyd, Edinburgh.

—— [*Clarsach an Doire.*] Edinburgh, 1909.
  . . . Fourth edition – revised and enlarged . . . 1909.
  . . . An ceathramh clò-bhualadh . . . 1909.
  xii, 267 p; plate. 200 mm. EU:CL, Mit.

—— [*Clarsach an Doire.*] Glasgow, 1924.
  . . . Fifth edition . . . Glasgow: Alexander MacLaren & Sons, 360–362 Argyle Street, C.2.
  . . . An cóigeamh clò-bhualadh . . . Glascho: Alasdair Mac Labhruinn 's a Mhic, 360–362 Sràid Earraghaidheal, C.2.
  xiv, 274 p; plate. 200 mm. Mit., PC.
    1st ed. 1883.

MacLeod, Norman, "Am Bàrd Bochd", 1906–68. [*Bardachd a Leodhas.*] Glasgow. 1969.
  Bàrdachd a Leódhas. Air a cruinneachadh 's air a deasachadh le Tormod MacLeòid ("Am Bàrd Bochd"). Gairm. Glaschu. 1969.
  Clò-bhualaidhean Gairm, Leabhar 14.
  [8], 79 p. 220 mm.
    Introductory tribute to Norman MacLeod by Derick Thomson. Printed Learmonth, Stirling.

MacLeod, Norman, Gaelic Master of Glasgow High School, *d.* 1934 (ed.). See Reid, Duncan. [*Elementary Course of Gaelic.*]

MacLeod, Dr. Norman, Minister of St. Columba's Church, Glasgow, 1783–1862. [*Caraid nan Gaidheal.*] Edinburgh, 1910.
  Caraid nan Gaidheal. The Friend of the Gael. A choice selection of Gaelic writings by Norman MacLeod, D.D. Selected and edited by Rev. A. Clerk, LL.D., Minister

of Kilmallie. With a memoir of the author by his son, Norman MacLeod, D.D. Barony Parish, Glasgow. Edinburgh: John Grant, 31 George IV Bridge. 1910. xlviii, 792 p; plate. 230 mm. AU, Mit., PC.

―――― (joint ed.). [*Dictionary of the Gaelic Language.*] Edinburgh, 1901.
A Dictionary of the Gaelic Language, in two parts: I, Gaelic and English; II English and Gaelic. First part comprising a comprehensive vocabulary of Gaelic words, with their different significations in English; and the second part comprising a vocabulary of English words, with their various meanings in Gaelic. By the Rev. Dr. Norman Mac-Leod, minister of Campsie, and the Rev. Dr. Daniel Dewar, one of the ministers of Glasgow. Edinburgh: John Grant, 31 George IV Bridge. 1901.
vii, [1], 1005 p, [2] "Proper Names". 250 mm. GU.

―――― [*Dictionary of the Gaelic Language.*] Edinburgh, 1909.
. . . By the Rev. Dr. Norman MacLeod and the Rev. Dr. Daniel Dewar. Edinburgh: John Grant. 1909.
vii, [1], 1005 p, [2] "Proper Names". 250 mm. AU.
    1st ed. 1831, of which the editions of 1901 and 1909 are reprints (pagination of 1831 edition [4] 1005 p, [1] "Names".

―――― [*The Highlanders' Friend: Second Series.*] Edinburgh, 1901.
The Gaelic Classics, No. 1. The Highlander's Friend: second series. A further selection from the writings of the late Very Reverend Norman MacLeod, D.D., St. Columba's Church, Glasgow. Edited by Dr. George Henderson, Minister of Eddrachillis, Examiner in Celtic, Edinburgh University, and Hon. Scholar of Jesus College, Oxford. Edinburgh: Norman MacLeod, 25 George IV Bridge. 1901.
viii, 175 p. 200 mm. Mit.
    Printed Lorimer and Chalmers, Edinburgh.

―――― [*Leabhar nan Cnoc.*] Inverness, 1905.
Leabhar nan Cnoc. Comh-chruinneachadh de nithibh sean agus nuadh; airson oilean agus leas nan Gaidheal. Le Tormoid MacLeòid, D.D., Ministeir an t-Soisgeil ann an Campsie. [Quotation.] New edition. Inverness: "Northern Chronicle" Office. Edinburgh: Norman MacLeod, 25 George IV Bridge. 1898.
[Addendum to 1898 Prefatory Note.] N.B. – We have got the edition of 1898 reprinted without variation; because, while the former issue had become exhausted, a steady demand for the book still existed. Applicants for copies can now be supplied. Inverness, May, 1905.
xvi, 264 p. 190 mm. NLS.

―――― [*Leabhar nan Cnoc.*] Inverness, 1919.
    . . . 1898.
[Addendum to Prefatory Note of 1898.] N.B. – We have got the edition of 1898 reprinted without variation; because while the former issue had become exhausted, a steady demand for the book still existed. Inverness, 1919.
xvi, 264 p. 190 mm. AU, PC.
    First edition 1834.

―――― [*Long Mhor nan Eilthireach.*] N.p., n.d.
Long Mhor nan Eilthireach. By Norman MacLeod. (For the use of the Celtic Union Gaelic Classes.)
8 p. 210 mm. PC.

―――― (ed.). See Smith, Dr. John. [*Urnuighean air son Theaghlaichean.*]

MacLeod, Dr. Norman, of Inverness, 1838–1911. [*Ar Tigh Naomh agus Maiseach.*]
    Inverness, 1903.
"Ar Tigh Naomh agus Maiseach." Searmoin a rinneadh aig coisrigeadh Eaglais Uir ann an sgireachd Hionspuill an Eilean Thir-idhe air Sàbaid a' Chomanachaidh an 29

là de mhios Mhairt, 1903 leis an Urramach Tormoid Mac-leòid, D.D. Inverness: The
Northern Counties Printing and Publishing Company, Ltd. 1903.
24 p; plate. 210 mm. EU:CL, Mit.

MacLeod, Norman K. [*An Cogadh.*] N.p., n.d.
An Cogadh.
   Not seen. *Clare. Dunn.*

MacLeod, Robert. [*Moladh a Bhreacan.*] N.p., n.d.
"Moladh a Bhreacan." (Air a sgriobh le Rob. Macleoid.) . . .
[1] p. 190 mm. NLS.

MacLeod, Roderick, Minister of Bernera. [*Guthan o'n Chrann-Cheusaidh.*] Bernera.
   1972.
Guthan o'n Chrann-Cheusaidh. 25 p. Ruairidh MacLeòid.
Thug "An t-Eileanach" an leabhar seo am follais ann an 1972.
36 p. 210 mm.

MacLeod, Roderick, Minister of Bernera (ed.). See A' Charraig.

—— (ed.). See Edinburgh University Highland Society. [*Year Book.*]

—— (ed.). See An t-Eileanach.

MacLeod, Roderick, of Inverness, 1867–1934. [*Ceithir Orain Ghaidhlig.*] Glasgow, n.d.
Ceithir Orain Ghàidhlig eadar-theangaichte bho'n Bheurla, mar a sheinneadh iad le
Ruairidh Mac-Leòid, Inbhir-nis. [Illus.] Clò-bhuailte le Alasdair Mac Labhruinn 's a
Mhic, Glascho.
8 p. 180 mm. PC, SS.
   First advertised in "An Gaidheal", August 1924. Foreword by I. N. MacLeod.
   The songs are: "Lass o' Killiecrankie", "Stop your tickling, Jock", "Kate Dalrymple",
   "K.-K.-Katie".

—— [*Leabhar-Fhaclan.*] Glasgow, [Fore. 1923].
Leabhar-fhaclan nan Oran Gàidhlig a sheinneadh 's a' Ghreis-labhrais le Ruairidh
Mac-Leòid. Le dealbh an t-seinneadair. Gaelic Songs on the Gramophone, sung by
Roderick MacLeod. Glascho: Alasdair Mac Labhruinn 's a Mhic.
19 p; plate. 190 mm. Mit., SS.
   Music in sol-fa. Foreword signed, "Ruairidh Mac Leòid, 10 Sràid Dhruimin,
   Inbhir-nis, 2 de'n Ghearran, 1923."

MacLeod's Gaelic Booklets. See:
   MacCuish, Donald J. [*Ceit Mhor Agus Maighstir Lachlann.*]
   MacKay, David N. [*Cul-Taic an t-Saighdeir.*]
   Stewart, J. B. [*Chi Sinn Thall Thu.*]

MacLeoid, Alasdair. See MacLeod, Alexander.

MacLeoid, Calum. See MacLeod, Malcolm.

MacLeoid, Calum Iain M. See MacLeod, Calum Iain N.

MacLeoid, Domhnall Iain. See MacLeod, Donald John.

MacLeoid, Fionnlagh. See MacLeod, Finlay.

MacLeoid, Iain. See MacLeod, John.

MacLeoid, Iain Aonghas. See MacLeod, John A.

MacLeoid, Iain N. See MacLeod, John N.

MacLeoid, Murchadh. See MacLeod, Murdo.

MacLeoid, Niall. See MacLeod, Neil.

MacLeoid, Ruairidh. See MacLeod, Roderick.

MacLeoid, Seumas. See MacLeod, James.

MacLeoid, Tormod. See MacLeod, Norman.

Mac Mhathain, Eoin. See Matheson, John.

MacMhathain, Iain M. See Matheson, John M.

[MacMhuirich, Neil]. See Clanranald, Book of: The MacDonald History.

—— (joint author). See Lloyd, Joseph. [*Alasdair Mac Colla.*]

Mac Mhuirich, Ruaidhri. See Morison, Roderick.

MacMillan, Angus (tr.). See Brandane, John. [*Rory Aforesaid.*]

MacMillan, Fr. John, 1880–1951. [*Gaelic Folk Songs of the Isles of the West.*] Volume I.
    London, [*c.* 1930].
    Gaelic Folk Songs of the Isles of the West. Volume I. Six songs (traditional and original)
    by Father John MacMillan, with legends and translations by Dr. Patrick McGlynn
    (Glasgow University). Music arranged by Frank W. Lewis. Price 5/– net. Boosey &
    Co., Limited. [London, New York City, Paris and Sydney addresses of Boosey &
    Hawkes and associated companies.] Copyright, 1930, by Boosey & Co., Ltd. Printed in
    England.
    v, [2]–35 p. 330 mm. AU, PC.
        Staff notation.

—— [*Gaelic Folk Songs of the Isles of the West.*] Volume II. London, [*c.* 1930].
    Gaelic Folk Songs of the Isles of the West. Volume II. Six songs (traditional and
    original) by Father John MacMillan, with legends and translations by Dr. Patrick
    McGlynn (Glasgow University). Music arranged by Frank W. Lewis. Price 5/– net.
    Choral versions of these songs are published. Boosey & Co., Ltd., 295 Regent Street,
    London, W.1., and 111–113 West 57th Street, New York. Copyright, 1930, by
    Boosey & Co., Ltd. Printed in England.
    [6], 29 p. 310 mm. AU, Mit.
        Staff notation.

MacMillan, John M. [*Airgiod a' Chruaidh Fhortain.*] [?]
    Airgiod a' Chruaidh Fhortain.
        Alex. MacLaren, Glasgow, advertisement, 1937: "Airgiod a' Chruaidh Fhortain".
        New Gaelic play by John M. MacMillan. Not seen.

MacMillan, Somerled, 1909–. [*Peat-Reek.*] London, n.d.
    Peat-reek (Smùid Mòna). Foreword by Sir Hugh S. Roberton. Words and music by
    Somerled MacMillan (Bard of the Clan MacMillan). London: Bayley & Ferguson, 2
    Great Marlborough Street, W. Glasgow: 54 Queen Street.
    [4], 35 p. 280 mm. Mit.
        English translation interlinear. Both notations; piano accompaniament. Reviewed in
        "An Gaidheal", December 1949; acquired Mitchell Library, February 1950.

—— (ed.). See MacDougall, Dugald G. [*Braiste Lathurna.*]

—— (ed.). See MacIntyre, Donald. [*Sporan Dhomhnaill.*]

MacNab, John. [*Calum is Bantrach Tharmaid.*] See MacCormick, John. [*Am Fear a
    Chaill a Ghaidhlig.*]

Mac Na-Ceardadh, Domhnull. See Sinclair, Donald.

Mac Neacail, Alasdair. See Nicolson, Alexander.

MacNeacail, Calum. See Nicolson, Malcolm.

Mac Neacail Domhnull. See Nicolson, Donald.

Mac-Neacail, Neacal. See Nicolson, Nicol.

MacNeil, James. [*Gaelic Lessons for Beginners.*] Sydney, N.S., 1939.
  Gaelic Lessons for Beginners. James MacNeil. Published by Post Publishing Co., Ltd.,
  Sydney, N.S. 1939.
  72 p. 210 mm. PC.
    Not seen. Information from Dr. Donald MacLean Sinclair, Antigonish, Nova
    Scotia.

MacNeil, James H. (ed.). See MacLellan, Vincent A. [*Failte Cheap Breatuinn.*]

MacNeill, Eoin (joint author). See Lloyd, Joseph. [*Alasdair Mac Colla.*]

MacNeill, Finlay (tr.). See Havenhand, I. & J. [*The Life-Boat.*]

MacNeill, John G. [*Mallachd na Misg.*] Glasgow, n.d.
  Mallachd na Misg. Leis an Urramach Iain Deòrsa MacNeill, Sgìreachd Chaldair.
  To be had from G. Wallace Ross, Secretary Free Church Temperance Society, 2 Ailsa
  Terrace, Hillhead, Glasgow.
  4 p. 210 mm. NLS.
    Not in *TS-G.*

—— (tr.). See Hall, [Christopher] Newman. [*Come to Jesus.*]

MacNiven, Charles, *d.* 1944 (joint author). See MacNiven, Duncan. [*Baird Chill-Chomain.*]

MacNiven, Duncan (joint author). [*Baird-Chill-Chomain.*] Glasgow, 1936.
  Bàird Chill-Chomain. Orain agus Dàin le Donnchadh agus Teàrlach Mac Nimhein,
  Ile. Fo làimh Eachainn Mhic Dhùghaill. Roimh-Ràdh le Niall Mac Gille Sheath-
  anaich, Rùnair, An Comunn Gaidhealach. Glascho: Alasdair Mac Labhruinn 's a
  Mhic, 268 Sràid Earra-Ghaidheal, C.2.
  The Kilchoman Bards. The Songs and Poems of Duncan and Charles MacNiven,
  Islay. Edited by Hector MacDougall. Foreword by Neil Shaw, F.S.A.(Scot.), Sec-
  retary of An Comunn Gaidhealach. Glasgow: Alex. MacLaren & Sons, 268 Argyle
  Street, C.2.
  First published 1936.
  159 p. 190 mm. EU, GU:CL, Mit., NLS.

Mac Phaidein, Iain. See MacFadyen, John.

MacPhail, Donald, 1885– (joint comp.). See Cainnt agus Facail Iomchuidh air son
  Coinnimh.

—— (joint ed.). See MacPhail, Malcolm C. [*Am Filidh Latharnach.*]

MacPhail, Dugald, 1819–87 (tr.). See MacLaurin, John. [*The Cross of Christ.*]

MacPhail, John S., 1824–. [*Earail Dhurachdach.*] Edinburgh, n.d.
  Earail Dhùrachdach do mhàthraichean òga anns na ceàrnaidhean de'n Ghàidhealtachd
  's an robh e na mhinister. Le an caraide dìleas, Iain S. MacPhàil. Edinburgh: The
  Religious Tract and Book Society of Scotland, 99 George Street.
  39 p; plate. 16 mm. Mit.
    c. 1900. Printed Turnbull & Spears, Edinburgh.

—— [*Litir mu Theanntachd na h-Eaglais.*] Glasgow, 1904.
Litir mu theanndachd na h-Eaglais: do dh'òigridh Bheinn-na-Faola, Chillemhoire, agus Shléibhte, far an do shaothraich e mar mhinisteir ré leth-cheud bliadhna. Bho'n Urramach Iain S. MacPhàil. Gilleasbuig Mac-na-Ceàrdadh, Clò-bhuailtear Gàidhlig, Glaschu. 1904.
20 p; illus. 220 mm. EU, FC.

—— See Seolaidhean mu Shlainte.

MacPhail, M. S. [*The Eagle's Claw.*] Glasgow, 1950.
Dealbh-chluichean an Gàidhlig. Spuir na h-Iolaire. Dealbh-chluich an aon sealladh. Gaelic translation of the one-act play, The Eagle's Claw, by M. S. MacPhail. Air eadar-theangachadh le Dòmhnall MacThómais (An t-Oban). An Comunn Gaidhealach, 131 West Regent Street, Glasgow. 1950.
16 p. 190 mm. PC.
Printed Learmonth, Stirling.

MacPhail, Malcolm C., 1847–1913. [*Am Filidh Latharnach.*] Stirling, 1947.
Am Filidh Latharnach. Le Calum Caimbeul Mac Phàil, "Am Bard Latharnach". Air a chlòdh-bhualadh le Aonghas MacAoidh, Struibhle. 1947.
xi, 81 p. 190 mm. GU:CL, Mit.
Contains Preface of 1878; Editors' Preface signed, "Dòmhnall Mac Phàil (Mac a' Bhàird), Lachlann MacFhionghuin". 1st ed. 1878. Contains 7 tunes, in sol-fa.

MacPhail, Neil. [*Cumha.*] Glasgow, n.d.
Cumha do'n Urramach Niall Camshron a bha na Mhinistear na h-Eaglais Shaoir-Chléireil Ghlasachu air son sea bliadhna deug air fhichead agus a chaochail air an 9mh latha de'n Mhàrt 1932. Le Niall Mac Phàil. Eadartheangaichte gu Beurla le Caraid. Lament for the late Rev. Neil Cameron, who was Free Presbyterian Minister in Glasgow for thirty-six years, who died on 9th March 1932. Gaelic by Neil MacPhail, Glasgow. English translation by a Friend. English Foreword by Rev. James MacLeod, Greenock.
16 p. 190 mm. PC.
Gaelic poem, pp 7–11.

Mac Pharlain, Calum. See MacFarlane, Malcolm.

MacPharlain, Murchadh. See MacFarlane, Murdo.

MacPhater, Charles (tr.). See Burns, Robert. [*Poems and Songs.*]

MacPhee, Hugh, 1899– (joint author). See Learning Gaelic.

MacPherson, Alistair. [*Treubhantas na'n Gaidheal Albannach.*] N.p., n.d.
Treubhantas na'n Gaidheal Albannach. The Valour of the Scottish Gael. By Alistair MacPherson, F.I.B.P., National Reserve, Late XV The King's Hussars. Dedicated to Lady MacDonald of the Isles.
x, 64 p. 140 mm. PC.
Poems in Gaelic. *c.* 1902.

—— [*Welcome to Alexander Somerled Angus.*] Edinburgh, 1918.
Welcome to Alexander Somerled Angus, the Son of the Heir of MacDonald, Prince of the Western Isles, Chief of Clan Colla, Lord of the Race of Conn. By Alistair Mac-Pherson, F.I.B.P., National Reserve, Late XV The King's Hussars. Edinburgh: printed by T. and A. Constable, Printers to his Majesty. 1918.
10 p. 210 mm. AU, FC.

MacPherson, James, 1736–. See Dana Oisein Mhic Fhinn.

MacPherson, Janet. [*Cumha.*] N.p., n.d.
Cumha airson an Urramaich Mr. Alastair Mac-an-t-Saoir an déigh dha Eilean Phrionns
Eideard fhàgail. Le maighdinn òig dam b'ainm Seònaid Nic a' Phearsain, a chaidh a
dhùsgadh gu iomaguinn mu a cor siorruidh fo éisdeachd.
8 p. 220 mm. FC.

MacPherson, John, "The Coddy", 1876–1955. [*Tales of Barra.*] Edinburgh, 1960.
Tales of Barra told by the Coddy (John MacPherson, Northbay, Barra, 1876–1955).
With Foreword by Compton MacKenzie and Introduction and Notes by J. L. Campbell.
1960. Printed for the Editor by W. & A. K. Johnston and G. W. Bacon Ltd. Edinburgh.
214 p. 190 mm. PC.
Mainly in English; 2 songs and 1 story in Gaelic.

—— [*Tales of Barra.*] Told by the Coddy. Edinburgh, 1961.
. . 1961. Printed for the Editor by W. & A. K. Johnston and G. W. Bacon Ltd.
Edinburgh.
227 p; 2 plates. 190 mm. PC.
2 songs and 3 stories in Gaelic.

—— [*Tales of Barra.*] Edinburgh, 1973.
. . . 1973. Printed for the Editor by Morrison & Gibb, Ltd., Edinburgh.
228 p; 1 plate. 190 mm.

MacPherson, John A. (ed.). See MacDonald, Donald, "Dòmhnall Ruadh Chorùna".
[*Domhnall Ruadh Choruna.*]

MacPherson, John M. [*Gaelic and English Poems.*] Glasgow, n.d.
Gaelic and English Poems. By John M. McPherson. Glasgow: Archibald Sinclair,
Celtic Press, 27a Cadogan Street.
32 p. 190 mm. BM, PC.
Gaelic poems, pp 9–28. *c.* 1941.

MacPherson, Mary, 1821–98. [*Laoidhean Bean Torra Dhamh.*] Inverness, 1902.
Laoidhean Bean Torra Dhamh. Gaelic Hymns of Mrs. Clark, including three never
before published. Edited by Rev. Thomas Sinton, Dores. *Northern Chronicle* Office:
Inverness. 1902.
28 p. 190 mm. FC, Mit.

—— [*Bean Torra Dhamh: Her Poems and Life.*] Arbroath, n.d.
Mary MacPherson (Mrs. Clark). Bean Torra Dhamh. The religious poetess of
Badenoch. Her poems and Life. Edited by Rev. Alexander Macrae, author of *Kinloch-
bervie, The Fire of God among the Heather*, etc. Arbroath: The Herald Press, Brothock
Bridge.
72 p; 2 plates. 190 mm. AU, BM, EU, Mit., NLS.
Reviewed in "An Gaidheal" 1935, acquired BM, NLS, 1935.

—— [*Bean Torra Dhamh: Her Poems and Life.*] Glasgow, n.d.
. . . Illustrated. Glasgow: Alex. MacLaren & Sons, 268 Argyle Street, C.2.
64 p; illus. 190 mm. PC.
The "Life" is in English.

MacPherson, T. S., 1870–1947 (tr.). See Brandane, John. [*The Glen is Mine.*]

MacPhie, Donald, 1852–1922 (ed.). See Watson, William J. (general ed.). [*Leabhraichean Sgoile Gaidhlig.*]

MacQuarrie, Duncan (ed.). See Mu'n Cuairt an Cagailte.

MacQueen, Ewen. [*Searmoin.*] Inverness, n.d.
Searmoin leis an Urr. E. MacCuinn, Inbhirnis, air feasgar là Sàbaid a' Chomunnachaidh, June 1929. [Quotation.] Printed by Robert Carruthers & Sons, "Courier" Office, Inverness.
12 p. 210 mm. FC.

—— (ed.). See MacKenzie, Lachlan. [*Additional Lectures, Sermons and Writings.*]

McR., M. See McRitchie, Malcolm.

MacRae, Alexander (ed.). See MacKay, Catherine. [*Laoidhean agus Orain.*]

—— (ed.). See MacPherson, Mary. [*Bean Torra Dhamh: Her Poems and Life.*]

MacRae, Duncan H., 1640–93. [*The Fernaig Manuscript.*] Dundee, 1923.
Làmh-Sgrìobhainn Mhic Rath. "Dorlach Laoidhean do sgrìobhadh le Donnchadh Mac Rath, 1688" anns an dà leabharan a tha aig an am so an leabhar-lann Oilthigh Ghlascho; agus iad an so air an litreachadh an dà chuid a réir gnàths Dhonnchaidh agus gnàths coitcheann an latha 'n diugh, le Calum Mac Phàrlain. Dun-dé: Calum S. Mac Leòid, Blackness Road 183.
The Fernaig Manuscript. A Handful of Lays written by Duncan Mac Rae, 1688, in two booklets presently lying in the Library of the University of Glasgow; revealed here according to Duncan's own spelling and the standard spelling of the present day, by Malcolm Mac Farlane. Dundee: Malcolm C. MacLeod, 183 Blackness Road. 1923. xv, 345, [1] p; 12 plates. 260 mm. BM, PC.

—— [*The Fernaig Manuscript.*] Dundee, 1923.
. . . Dun-dé: Calum S. Mac Leòid, Blackness Road 183.
. . . Dundee: Malcolm C. MacLeod, 183 Blackness Road. 1923.
Cha deach os cionn ceud ceann gu leth de Leabhar Làmh-sgrìobhainn Mhic Rath a chur an clò mu choinnimh an fhroisidh so; agus is teisteas an t-ainm shios gur e so mac-samhail [No.] dhiubh. [Signature, "Calum S. Mac Leòid".]
xv, 345, [1] p; 12 plates. 260 mm. AU, GU, Mit., SS.
A more expensive production than the above (e.g. has wider margins). Both editions printed by Milne, Tannahill & Methven, Perth.

MacRitchie, J. A. (joint ed.). See Mo Leabhar I: Leabhar-Leughaidh/Leabhar-Oibreach; Mo Leabhar II: Leabhar-Leughaidh.

McRitchie, Malcolm, 1803–85. [*Gaelic Hymns.*] Stornoway, 1924.
Gaelic Hymns. By M. McR., F.C., Strathy. For the use of his congregation, chiefly his evening class for young people. Gazette Office, Stornoway. 1924.
62 p. 190 mm. FC.
Introduction by R. MacLeod, Free Church Manse, Garrabost. Printed at the *North Star* Office, Dingwall. 1st ed. 1863 (24 p); 2nd ed. 1864 (64 p).

MacRury, John. [*Mairnealachd.*] [Sydney, C.B. (?)]
Màirnealachd.
Dunn. Reprint from Mac-Talla?

Mac-Talla. Sydney, C. B., [1892]–1904.
Mac-Talla. "An Nì nach cluinn mi an diugh cha'n aithris mi màireach." Vol. I. Sidni, C. B., Di-Sathairne, Mai 28, 1892. No. 1.
. . . Vol. XII. Sidni, Ceap Breatunn, Di-Haoine, Iun 24, 1904. No. 26. [Last number.]
[Frequency] Weekly until Vol. X, No. 16, Oct. 1901; fortnightly thereafter.
[Pagination] 4 p per number in Vol. I, 8 p thereafter. 2 numbers were run together in Vols. IX and X, leaving both volumes 8 p short. Vol. XII has 208 p, not 200 p as indicated (Nos. 25 and 26 both have pages 193–200).

[Size] 330 mm [I–IV], 360 mm [V–VI], 400 mm [VII–XII].
[Locations] AU and NLS have microfilms of the complete set.
[Editor] Jonathan G. MacKinnon.
[Contents] A Gaelic newspaper.

Mac Thomais, Ruaraidh. See Thomson, Derick S.

MacThomais, Seumas. See Thomson, James.

Mair, William, 1830–1920. [*The Truth about the Church of Scotland.*] Edinburgh, n.d.
An Fhìrinn mu Eaglais na h-Alba. Leis an Urramach Uilleam Mair, D.D. Eadar-
theangaichte o'n Bheurla le Iain. Clòbhuailte le Uilleam Blackwood agus a Mhic an
Dun-Eideann agus a Lunainn.
80 p. 150 mm. FC, Mit.
    According to *TS-G* "translated by Rev. John MacRury, Snizort and published 1902".
    English original first published 1891.

Mairi Nighean Alasdair. See MacDonald, Mary.

Mairi Nighean Alasdair Ruaidh. See MacLeod, Mary, Seventeenth Century Poetess.

Mairi Tailleir. [*Rannan Eibhinn Cloinne.*] Glasgow, 1969.
Rannan Eibhinn Cloinne. Le Màiri Tàilleir (Bana-sgoilear Leódhasach). Dealbhan le
Dòmhnall R. MacThómais. Gairm. Glaschu. 1969.
Clò-bhualaidhean Gairm, Leabhar 16.
34, [1] p. 180 mm.
    Mairi Tailleir is a pseudonym.

Malloch, G. R. [*The Grenadier.*] Glasgow, 1950.
Dealbh-chluichean an Gàidhlig. Am Bàta-Luath. Dealbh-chluich an aon sealladh.
Gaelic translation of The Grenadier by G. R. Malloch. Air eadar-theangachadh le
Lachlann MacFhionghuin. Printed for An Comunn Gàidhealach by Eneas MacKay,
Stirling. 1950.
20 p. 190 mm. PC.
    English original first published 1930.

Mao, Tsê-Tung, 1893–197 . [*Three Constantly Read Articles.*] Edinburgh, 1969.
Mao Tsê-Tung. As leth an t-sluaigh. Mar chuimhneachan air Tormod Peutan. Am
bodach amaideach a ghluais na beanntan. Clò-bhuailte le Pairtidh Luchd-obrach na
h-Alba. Duneideann. 1969.
10 p. 220 mm.

Marbhrann. N.p., n.d.
Marbhrann do Mhrs Graham, bean Mhr Graham, ministeir na h-Eaglaise Saoire.
4 p. 170 mm. PC.
    Mrs. Graham died 1881.

Marjoribanks, George, *d.* 1940. [*A' Chlann fo Gheasaibh.*] Inverness, 1935.
A' Chlann fo Gheasaibh. Dealbh-chluich beag airson Comunn Na h-Oigridh. Le
Seòras Marjoribanks. Inverness: The *Northern Chronicle* Office. 1935.
8 p. 190 mm. PC.

—— [*Dealbh mo Sheanar.*] Glasgow, 1936.
Dealbh mo Sheanar. Dealbh-chluich beag ann an dà shealladh. Le Seòras Gallda.
1936. Alasdair MacLabhruinn 's a Mhic, 268 Sràid Earra-Ghaidheal, Glascho, C.2.
Copyright.
11 p. 190 mm. EPL, Mit., PC.

—— [*Mairi Bhan Ghlinn Freoin.*] Glasgow, [Fore. 1937].
Màiri Bhàn Ghlinn Freòin. Le Seòras Gallda. [Illus.] An Comunn Gaidhealach, 131
Sràid Iar Regent, Glaschu. A' phrìs – sè sgillinn.
16 p. 220 mm. EPL, Mit., PC.

—— [*Tea a Nasgaidh?*] Inverness, 1935.
Tea a Nasgaidh? Dealbh-chluich beag airson Comunn na h-Oigridh. Le Seòras
Marjoribanks. Inverness: The *Northern Chronicle* Office. 1935.
8 p. 190 mm. PC.

Marshall, Alexander. [*God's Way of Salvation.*] Glasgow, n.d.
Slàinte ann an Rathad Dhé. Gaelic edition of "God's Way of Salvation". Three
million copies issued. Eadar-theangaichte le Iain Camaron, F.E.I.S., Ullapul. Le
Alastair Marshall. Glasgow: Pickering and Inglis, 229 Bothwell Street. London:
Alfred Holness, 14 Paternoster Row, E.C. One Penny.
40 p. 150 mm. FC.
English original first published 1949.

Marshall, Walter, 1628–80. [*Sanctification.*] Edinburgh, [Intro. 1916].
Cogadh mór na h-Eorpa. Naomhachadh. Marshall [Illus.] Printed by Oliver and
Boyd, Edinburgh, for The Church of Scotland, The United Free Church of Scotland,
and The Free Church of Scotland.
xi, 99 p. 140 mm. NLS.
Introduction signed, "Norman MacLean, 1916." One of a series especially published
for soldiers in the First World War. English original ("The Gospel Mystery of
Sanctification") first published 1692.

Martin, Donald J., 1847–1913. [*Teagasg nam Miorbhuilean.*] Edinburgh, [Intro. 1916].
Cogadh mór na h-Eòrpa. Teagasg nam Miorbhuilean. Leis an Urramach Dòmhnull
Iain Màirtinn. [Illus.] Printed by Oliver and Boyd, Edinburgh, for The Church of
Scotland, The United Free Church of Scotland, and The Free Church of Scotland.
xi, 104 p. 140 mm. NLS.
Introduction signed, "Norman MacLean, 1916." First World War series.

—— [*Teagasg nam Miorbhuilean.*] Edinburgh, 1942.
Cogadh na Saorsa. Teagasg nam Miorbhuilean. Leis an Urramach Dòmhnull Iain
Màirtinn. [Illus.] Printed by Oliver and Boyd, Edinburgh, for The Church of
Scotland, The Free Church of Scotland. 1942.
vii, 104 p. 140 mm. PC.
Second World War series.

—— [*Teagasg nan Cosamhlachdan.*] Edinburgh, 1914.
Teagasg nan Cosamhlachdan. Leis An Urramach Dòmhnull Iain Màirtinn, M.A.
(nach maireann), a bha 'n a mhinisteir anns an Eaglais Shaoir Aonaichte ann an Stiòrna-
bhagh agus anns an Oban. Air a dheasachadh leis An Urramach Calum Macillinnein,
B.D., Ministeir Eaglais Shaor Aonaichte Chalumchille, an Dun-Eideann. Edinburgh:
John Grant, 31 George IV Bridge. 1914.
xxx, 197 p; 1 plate. GU.
Introductory appreciation of Martin by Malcolm Nicolson Munro, Taynuilt.
Printed Oliver & Boyd, Edinburgh.

Martin, Hugh, 1821–85. [*The Shadow of Calvary.*] Edinburgh, [Intro. 1916].
Cogadh mór na h-Eòrpa. Sgàil Chalbhari. Màirtinn. [Illus.] Printed by Oliver and
Boyd, Edinburgh, for the Church of Scotland, The United Free Church of Scotland,
and The Free Church of Scotland.
xi, 148 p. 140 mm. NLS.
Introduction dated 1916.
One of a series of religious booklets published for distribution to soldiers in the First
World War.

—— [*The Shadow of Calvary.*] Edinburgh, 1942.
Cogadh na Saorsa. Sgàil Chalbhari. Màirtinn. [Illus.] Printed by Oliver and Boyd, Edinburgh, for the Church of Scotland, the Free Church of Scotland. 1942.
vii, 148 p. 140 mm. PC.
Second World War series. English original first published 1875.

Mass, The. See Catholic Church. *Liturgy and Ritual.* [Mass.]

Matheson, Angus. [*Proverbs from Lewis.*] N.p., n.d.
Some proverbs and proverbial expressions from Lewis. Angus Matheson, Glasgow. Reprinted from *The Journal of Celtic Studies*, Vol. 1, No. 1, November 1949. Made in the United States of America.
[105]–115 p. 230 mm. PC.

—— (joint ed.). See Campbell, John F. [*More West Highland Tales.*] Volume Two.

—— (ed.). See Carmichael, Alexander. [*Carmina Gadelica.*] Volume V, VI.

—— (joint ed.). See MacDonald, Duncan. [*Fear na h-Eabaid.*]

Matheson, Isabella. [*Do'n Urramach Iain Friseal.*] N.p., n.d.
"Do'n Urramach Iain Friseal. (Isabella Matheson, 1909.)"
Dunn. Not seen.

Matheson, Jessie. [*Gleann-Dail.*] Glasgow, 1931.
Gleann-Dail. Dàin spioradail. Le Seònaid Nic Mhathain, Eilean a' Cheò. [Illus.] Glasgow: Alexander MacLaren & Sons, 360–362 Argyle Street, C.2. 1931.
16 p. 180 mm. Mit., NLS, PC.

—— [*Gleann na h-Irioslachd.*] Glasgow, n.d.
Gleann na h-Irioslachd. Dàin spioradail. Le Seònaid Nic Mhathain, Eilean a' Cheò. Spiritual Hymns by Mrs Jessie Matheson. Fo làimh Eachainn Mhic Dhùghaill. Glascho: Alasdair Mac Labhruinn 's a Mhic, 360 Sràid Earraghaidheal, C.2. 1/–.
20 p. 190 mm. BM, NLS, PC.
Music in sol-fa. MacLaren dates it 1927; advertised 1929.

Matheson, John, 1820–84. [*Fiosrachadh Mu'n Bhiobull.*] Glasgow, 1941.
Fiosrachadh mu'n Bhìobull. Le Eòin Mac Mhathain. Fo làimh Eachainn Mhic Dhùghaill. Glascho: Alasdair MacLabhruinn agus a Mhic, 268 Sràid Earra-ghaidheal, C.2.
First edition 1880. Second edition 1941.
32 p. 190 mm. PC.
Contains short biography of Matheson by Alex. MacLaren.

—— [*Fuinn nan Salm.*] [Glasgow, ?].
Fuinn nan Salm, mar 'tha iad air an seinn ann an Alba, maille ri priomh leasain air son luchdfoghluim. Le Eòin Mac-Mhathain.
1st ed. 1863. *MacLaren* and the introduction to the 1941 edition of Matheson's "Fiosrachadh mu'n Bhìobull" refer to "a new edition", published *c.* 1940, containing the original 40 tunes "and the long tunes". Possibly refer to the Free Church of Scotland's "Fuinn nan Salm Ghàidhlig" (1932), which contains T. L. Hately's and F. W. Whitehead's versions of the "long tunes".

—— [*Fuinn nan Salm.*] See also Free Church of Scotland. *Liturgy and Ritual.* [Fuinn nan Salm Ghaidhlig.]

Matheson, John M. [*Bha 'Ainm Anns an Fhearann.*] Glasgow, 1949.
Bha 'Ainm anns an Fhearann. Dealbh-chluich an aon sealladh. Le Iain M. Mac-Mhathain. Printed for An Comunn Gaidhealach by Eneas MacKay, Stirling. 1949.
15 p. 190 mm. EPL, EU, PC.

—— (tr.). See MacLellan, Robert. [*The Changeling.*]

Matheson, William (ed.). See MacCodrum, John. [*Songs.*]

—— (ed.). See Morison, Roderick. [*An Clarsair Dall: Orain.*]

Megaw, B. R. S. (ed.). See Scottish Studies.

Mil nan Dan. Edinburgh, n.d.
Cogadh mór na h-Eòrpa. Mil nan Dàn. [Illus.] Printed by Oliver and Boyd, Edinburgh, for The Church of Scotland, The United Free Church of Scotland, and The Free Church of Scotland.
112 p. 140 mm. NLS.
Issued to soldiers in the First World War. Selection of Gaelic poetry.

—— [*Mil nan Dan.*] Edinburgh, n.d.
Cogadh na Saorsa. Mil nan Dàn. [Illus.] Printed by Oliver and Boyd, Edinburgh, for The Church of Scotland, The Free Church of Scotland.
112 p. 140 mm. PC.
Second World War Series.

Milton, J. C. [*Winds for Sale.*] Glasgow, 1951.
Dealbh-chluichean an Gàidhlig. Gaothan ri'n Reic. Dealbh-chluich an aon sealladh. Gaelic translation of the one-act play, Winds for Sale, by J. Coleman Milton. Air eadar-theangachadh le Dòmhnall Mac Dhòmhnaill (Eirisgeidh). An Comunn Gaidhealach, 131 West Regent Street, Glasgow. 1951.
21 p. 180 mm. PC.
Printed Learmonth, Stirling. English original first published 1946.

Mitchell, George. [*Laoidhean.*] N.p., n.d.
Laoidhean le Sheòras Mitchell. [Illus.] Callanish Leodhas.
7 p. 210 mm. PC.

Mod. See An Comunn Gaidhealach.

Moffat, Alfred, 1866–1910. [*Ministrelsy of the Scottish Highlands.*] London, n.d.
The Ministrelsy of the Scottish Highlands. A Collection of Highland Melodies, with Gaelic and English Words. Selected, edited, and arranged by Alfred Moffat. London: Bayley & Ferguson, 2 Great Marlborough Street, W. Glasgow: 54 Queen Street.
[4], 135 p. 280 mm. AU, Mit.
Both notations; piano accompaniment in "An Deo-Greine", September 1910.

Moffat-Pender, Iain M., *d.* 1961. [*Is Ann.*] Glasgow, 1930.
Is Ann. A simple explanation of a conversational difficulty experienced by those learning the Gaelic Language. By I. M. Moffat-Pender. "A valuable Supplementary Chapter to all the Gaelic Grammars." – Eachann MacDhùghaill. Price Sixpence. Glasgow: Alex. MacLaren & Sons, Printers and Publishers, 360–362 Argyle Street, C.2. 1930. (Copyright.)
8 p. 190 mm. BM, GU:CL, Mit.

—— [*Litrichean Ghaidheal an Latha an Diugh.*] Stornoway, n.d.
[Title page.] Litrichean Ghaidheal an Latha an Diugh.
[Cover.] Address delivered by Iain MacAlasdair Moffat-Pender to Ceilidh nan Gaidheal, Glasgow, 23rd October 1926. Printed at the *Gazette* Office, Stornoway.
16 p. 220 mm. FC.

—— [*Lorna.*] Glasgow, 1954.
Lorna. I. M. Moffat-Pender, M.A. ("Mo mhac foghlama" – An t-Ollamh Maolmhuire Díolun) do scriobh. Do bhuaidh an chuid is mó de na h-agallmhaibh seo an chéad duais ag an Mhod (An t-Oireachtas) i n-Albain. Déanta agus clóbhuailte i n-Eirinn le Brun agus O Nualláin, Teór., An Cló Richview, Cluain Sceach. 1954. [In Irish script.]

Lorna. Le I. M. Moffat-Pender, M.A. ("Duine inbheach am measg mo sgoilear" – An t-Ollamh U. I. Mac Bhàtair). Baile Ghlaschu: Bell and Bain Limited. 1954.
[7], 83 p; 4 plates. 270 mm. PC.
> Plays. Scottish and Irish Gaelic on facing pages. They were distributed free to schoolchildren and bear the inscription: "Donated by I. M. Moffat-Pender to . . .".

—— [*Mo Nighean Donn Bhoidheach*.] Edinburgh, 1924.
Mo Nighean Donn Bhòidheach, agus Sgeulachdan Eile. Le Iain MacAlasdair Moffat-Pender. U. M. Urchardainn agus a Mhac, Dun-Eideann. 1924.
119, [1] p, plate; illus. 200 mm. BM, GU:CL, NLS.
> "An rathad chun nan Eilean", an account of a Highland walking tour, pp 48–119.

—— [*Sgeul Gaidhealach*.] Glasgow, [1923].
Sgeul Gaidhealach.
8 p. 250 mm. Mit., PC.
> Bound with a 4 p leaflet: pp 1–2 comprise a Comunn Gaidhealach circular; pp 3–4 give details of a competition for naming the above story. The circular is dated "1st June 1923"; the Mitchell Library copy of the two leaflets is bound with "An Gaidheal", Vol. XX, 1924–5.

—— (joint comp.). [See *Cainnt agus Facail Iomchuidh air son Coinnimh*.]

—— (ed.). See Cameron, Alexander. [*Orain, Sgriobhaidhean agus Litrichean*.]

Moireach, Iain. See Murray, John.

Moireach, Murchadh. See Murray, Murdo.

Moireasdan, Aonghas. See Morrison, Angus.

Mo Leabhar I: Leabhar-Leughaidh. Inverness, n.d.
Mo Leabhar I. Leabhar-leughaidh. Chaidh an leabhar so a dheasachadh an Leodhas le C. A. Mhoirreach, C. Nicilleathain, I. Nicruisnidh, C. A. Nicleòid, B. A. Nicleòid, M. Nicleòid, M. A. Nicasgaill. Rinn A. M. Màrtainn na dealbhan. An Comunn Gaidhealach, Tigh Obairthairbh, Inbhirnis. Air a chlò-bhualadh le Eccles, Inbhirnis.
[20]; col. illus. 230 mm.
> Recent.

Mo Leabhar I: Leabhar-Oibreach. Inverness, n.d.
Mo Leabhar I. Leabhar-oibreach. Chaidh an leabhar so a dheasachadh an Leodhas le C. A. Nicmhuirich, C. Nicilleathain, I. Nicruisnidh, C. A. Nicleòid, B. A. Nicleòid, M. Nicleòid, M. A. Nicasgaill. Rinn A. M. Nicmhartainn na dealbhan. An Comunn Gaidhealach, Tigh Obairthairbh, Inbhirnis. Air a chlò-bhualadh le Eccles, Inbhirnis.
[20] p; illus. 210 mm. PC.

Mo Leabhar II: Leabhar-Leughaidh. Inverness, n.d.
Mo Leabhar II. Leabhar-leughaidh. Dheasaicheadh an leabhar an Leodhas le C. A. Nicgille Mhoire, C. Nicilleathain, I. Nicruisnidh, C. A. Nicleòid, B. A. Nicleòid, M. Nicleòid, M. A. Nicasgaill. Rinn Coinneach Stiùbhart na dealbhan. An Comunn Gaidhealach, Tigh Obarthairbh, Inbhirnis. Air a chlò-bhualadh le Eccles, Inbhirnis.
[26] p; col. illus. 250 mm. PC.

Mo Leabhar II: Leabhar-Oibreach. Inverness, n.d.
Mo Leabhar II. Leabhar-oibreach. Chaidh na ceistean a thogail bho'n leabhar a chaidh a dheasachadh an Leodhas le C. A. Nicgille Mhoire, C. Nicilleathain, I. Nicruisnidh, C. A. Nicleòid, B. A. Nicleòid, M. Nicleòid, M. A. Nicasgaill. Rinn Coinneach Stiùbhart nan dealbhan. Dheasaich Dòmhnall I. MacAoidh na leasain oibreach. An Comunn Gaidhealach, Tigh Obarthairbh, Inbhirnis. Air a chlò-bhualadh le Eccles, Inbhirnis.
[26] p; col. illus. 250 mm. PC.
A series of elementary readers for schools, prepared by a panel of teachers.

[*Monthly Visitor.*] Edinburgh, 1904–31.
 Am Fear-Tathaich Miosail.
 4 p. 21 mm.
 Translations by Rev. Malcolm MacLennan, Edinburgh, of religious tracts issued
 monthly by The Scottish "Monthly Visitor" Tract Society, Edinburgh.

Moonie, J. A. (arr.). See MacKenzie, William, Secretary of the Crofters' Commission.
 [*Gems of Highland Song.*] Book L.

Morgan, Edwin, 1920– (joint ed.). See Bruce, George. [*Scottish Poetry.*] Number
 One/Three.

Morison, Duncan M., 1906–. [*Ceol Mara.*] London, [Fore. 1935].
 Ceol Mara. Songs of the Isle of Lewis. Collected and arranged by Duncan M. Morison.
 With a foreword and introduction by the Marchioness of Londonderry, D.B.E.
 Price 7/6 net. J. & W. Chester, Ltd., London: 11 Great Marlborough Street, W.1.
 France: Rouart, Levolle et cie, Paris. Belgium: Les Editions Modernes, Bruxelles.
 Switzerland: Foetisch Frères, Lausanne. Italy: A. & G. Carisch & Co., Milano.
 Germany: Hug & Co., Leipzig. Holland: Braekmans & Van Poppel, Amsterdam.
 Czecho-slovakia: Hudebri Matices, Prague. South America: Iriberri, Belloeg & cia.,
 Buenos Aires.
 [2], vii, [2], 38 p. 300 mm. Mit., NLS.
 Staff notations. 14 Gaelic songs, 7 with English translations; 3 English songs.

Morrison, Duncan M. (arr.), 1900–. See Robertson, Angus. [*Orain na Ceilidh.*]

Morison, Roderick, "An Clàrsair Dall", *c.* 1656–*c.* 1714. [*An Clarsair Dall: Orain.*]
 Edinburgh, 1970.
 An Clàrsair Dall. Orain Ruaidhri Mhic Mhuirich agus a chuid ciùil. Air an deasachadh
 le Uilleam Mac Mhathain. Air fhoillseachadh le Comunn Litreachas Gàidhlig na
 h-Alba. Dun-éideann. 1970.
 The Blind Harper. Songs of Roderick Morison and his music. Edited by William
 Matheson. Printed by R. & R. Clark, Ltd., for The Scottish Gaelic Texts Society.
 Edinburgh. 1970.
 Scottish Gaelic Texts, Volume Twelve. An Clàrsair Dall.
 lxxvi, 265 p. 230 mm.
 Text and Translation, pp 1–79; Notes, pp 95–148; Airs and Metres, pp 149–74;
 Appendices, pp 175–254; Indexes, pp 255–65.

Morrison, Alexander Campbell, 1860–1940. [*Gaelic and Other Poems.*] Edinburgh,
 1941.
 Gaelic and other poems. By Alexander Campbell Morrison, M.B., C.M. Oliver and
 Boyd; Edinburgh: Tweeddale Court; London: 98 Great Russell Street, W.C. 1941.
 viii, 140 p. 200 mm. PC.
 Section I: Poems in Gaelic, pp 1–70; Section II: English translations, pp 71–109;
 Section III: Poems in Scots, pp 111–140. Foreword by Neil Ross.

Morrison, Alick, 1911– (ed.). See MacAskill, Iain Archie. [*An Ribheid Chiuil.*]

—— (ed.). See MacAskill, Malcolm. [*Orain Chaluim.*]

Morrison, Angus, of Barvas, 1860–1940. [*An Gradh-Bhuan.*] Glasgow, 1946.
 An Gràdh-Bhuan. Dàin spioradail le Aonghas MacGhille Mhoire. Spiritual Songs by
 Angus Morrison. Edited by Hector MacDougall. Glascho: Alasdair MacLabhrainn is
 a Mhic, 268 Sràid Earraghaidheal, C.2. 1946.
 15 p. 190 mm. NLS.
 Foreword by "R.M." Printed Milne, Tannahill and Methven, Perth.

Morrison, Angus, of Edinburgh, 1866–1943. [*Dain agus Orain Ghaidhlig.*] Edinburgh,
[Pref. 1929].
Dàin agus Orain Ghàidhlig. Le Aonghas Moireasdan. Maille ri mìneachadh. Dun-
Eideann: An "Darien Press", 5 Aite Bristo.
Gaelic Poems and Songs. By Angus Morrison. With explanatory notes. Edinburgh:
The Darien Press, 5 Bristo Place.
xvi, 416 p. 220 mm. AU, BM, EU, GU, Mit., NLS.

—— [*Orain nam Beann.*] Part I. Glasgow, [Fore. 1913].
Orain nam Beann. (Songs of the Mountains.) A Collection of Gaelic Songs, containing
many airs not hitherto published. Selected, edited, and in part composed by Angus
Morrison. Music in both notations with pianoforte accompaniment. Part 1. Copyright. Price 5/– net. Glasgow: Aird & Coghill Ltd., 24 Douglas Street.
[2], 53 p. 310 mm. Woodside P.L., Glasgow.
> On some copies, the following is pasted over the publisher's imprint: "Glasgow:
> Alexander MacLaren & Sons, Gaelic Publishers, 268 Argyle Street, C.2. All Rights
> of Reproduction reserved by them." This indicates the purchase by MacLaren of
> the existing stock of this edition some time after 1931 (MacLaren's moved from
> 360–362 to 268 Argyle Street in 1931.)

—— [*Orain nam Beann.*] Part 1. Glasgow, [c. 1946].
. . . Music in both notations with pianoforte accompaniment by Charles R. Baptie.
Copyright. Price 6/– net. Alex. MacLaren & Sons, 268 Argyle Street, Glasgow, C.2.
[2], 53 p. 310 mm. AU, PC.
> Contains the 1913 Foreword but the first song bears a copyright imprint of 1946:
> clearly a reprint of that date.

—— [*Orain nam Beann.*] Part 1: New Series. [Glasgow, 1932?].
Orain nam Beann.
> *MacLaren:* "Orain nam Beann. Part 1. New Series. 3 songs, Gaelic and English.
> Methven Simpson. 1932." Advertised in MacLaren's catalogue, 1938: "Orain nam
> Beann. New Series. Book 1."

—— [*Oran a' Cheasar.*] Glasgow, 1916.
Oran a' Cheasar. Song on the Kaiser. Le A. M. [Illus.] Alex. MacLaren & Sons,
Gaelic Publishers and Booksellers, 360–362 Argyle Street, Glasgow. 1916.
8 p. 170 mm. PC.
> Cover note: "Sold in Aid of the Red Cross Fund". Reprinted in his "Dàin agus
> Orain Ghàidhlig", pp 34–7.

Morrison, C. A. (joint author). See Mo Leabhar: I: Leabhan-Leughaidh/Leabhar-
Oibreach: and Mo Leabhar II: Leabhar-Leughaidh/Leabhar-Oibreach.

Morrison, Donald (tr.). See Francis, J. O. [*The Poacher.*]

—— (tr.). See Ready, Stuart. [*Down to the Seas.*]

[Morrison], Duncan M. See Morison, Duncan M.

Morrison, F. M. [*Orain Uidhisteach.*] Glasgow, [c. 1933].
> Orain Uidhisteach. From Miss F. M. Morrison's Collection. All songs in this book are
> copyright, 1933. Published by Alex. MacLaren & Sons, 268 Argyle Street, Glasgow,
> C.2. Arranged and printed by T. Morrison, 6 Piershill Place, Edinburgh, 8.
> 15 p. 280 mm. PC.
> Both notations; piano accompaniment. Handwritten, reproduced photographically.

Morrison, John, 1790–1852. [*Dain Iain Ghobha.*] Edinburgh, n.d.
[Title page.] Dàin Iain Ghobha.
[Dust jacket.] The Poems of John Morrison. Edited by George Henderson. Knox Press.
[12], lxxv, 315 p; [2], xlvi, 350 p. 190 mm.
1967. Reprint – in one volume – of the 2 vol. ed. of 1893–6. Besides that edition's Preface, Memoir and Introduction, the present ed. contains a "Publisher's Preface", signed, "G. N. M. Collins (for the Knox Press, Edinburgh)". The Knox Press is the publishing agency of the Free Church of Scotland.

Morrison, Murdo, of Barvas, 1884–. [*Fear Siubhal nan Gleann.*] Glasgow, [Intro. 1923].
Fear Siubhal nan Gleann. Orain agus Dàin. Le Murchadh Mac-ille-Mhoire, Siadar Bharabhais. (Leth-bhreach air a thoirmeasg.) Glascho: Alasdair Mac Labhruinn 's a Mhic, 360–362 Sràid Earraghaidheal.
The Traveller of the Glens. Poems and Songs. By Murdo Morrison, Shader, Barvas. (Copyright.) Glasgow: Alexander MacLaren & Sons, 360–362 Argyle Street.
x, 86 p; plate. 190 mm. BM.

Morrison, Murdoch, of Cape Breton, 1842–. [*Orain Fuinn is Cladaich.*] Glasgow, 1931.
Orain Fuinn is Cladaich. Gaelic Poems and Songs. By Murdoch Morrison (Murchadh Choinnich Bhàin), Ferguson's Lake, Cape Breton. Printed for Alex. Finlayson, Grand River, C. B. Glasgow: Alexander MacLaren & Sons, 360–362 Argyle Street, C.2. 1931.
64 p. 190 mm. BM, GU:CL, Mit., NLS.

Morrison, Roderick (tr.). See Raspe, Rudolph E. [*The Adventures of Baron Munch-Hausen.*]

—— (tr.). See Stevenson, Robert L. [*Kidnapped.*]

—— (tr.). See Stevenson, Robert L. [*Treasure Island.*]

Morrison, William M. (tr.), 1866–1952. See Shakespeare, William. [*Julius Caesar.*]

Morrison./ See also Morison.

Mosgladh. Sydney/Antigonish, 1922–33.
Mosgladh. "The Awakening." Leabhar I. An t-Earrach, 1922. Aireamh 1. [Illus.] "Gloir Dhe agus math ar cinnidh." Scottish Catholic Society of Canada (organised 1st July 1919).
A new series began 1929.
Mosgladh. [Illus.] December 1933. Published by the Scottish Catholic Society of Canada. "Glòir Dhe agus math ar cinnidh." [Last seen.]
[Frequency] Quarterly.
[Collation] *c.* 50 p per issue. 260 × 300 mm.
[Locations] Harv., Xavier.
[Note] According to Prof. Calum I. N. MacLeod, of St. Francis Xavier University Antigonish, separate editions of "Mosgladh" were printed in Sydney, Cape Breton (260 × 180 mm) and in Antigonish (300 × 230 mm).

Mu'n Cuairt an Cagailte. Inverness, [*c.* 1972].
Mu'n cuairt an Cagailte. Sgeulachdan. Club Leabhar Limited. Inbhirnis.
c. Club Leabhar Limited, Inbhirnis. 1972.
98 p. 190 mm.
Prepared for the press by Duncan MacQuarrie. Printed Eccles, Inverness. A selection of stories submitted for a B.B.C. radio competition in 1968. See also MacDonald, Kenneth: "*Briseadh na Cloiche.*"

Munro, James, 1794–1870. [*Gaelic Primer.*] Edinburgh, 1902.
A New Gaelic Primer: containing elements of pronunciation; an abridged grammar; formation of words; a list of Gaelic and Welsh vocables of like signification: also, a copious vocabulary, with a figured orthoepy; and a choice selection of colloquial phrases on various subjects, having the pronunciation marked throughout. By James Munro, H.M.E.I., I.C. & O.S.G., etc. Seventh edition. Improved and enlarged. Edinburgh: John Grant, 31 George IV Bridge. 1902.
86 p, ii "Index". 180 mm. EPL.

—— [*A Gaelic Primer.*] Edinburgh, 1908.
... 1908.
86 p, ii "Index". 180 mm. AU, GU:CL, Mit.
Reprints of the 1854 ed.; 1st ed. 1828.

—— [*Gaelic Vocabulary and Phrase Book.*] Glasgow, n.d.
Munro's Gaelic Vocabulary and Phrase Book. Containing copious vocabularies and a choice selection of colloquial phrases on various subjects arranged under distinct heads, each having an imitated pronunciation marked. Glasgow: Alex. MacLaren & Sons, Argyle Street, C.2.
64 p. 190 mm. PC.
Originally formed part of Munro's "Gaelic Primer".

—— [*Gaelic Vocabulary and Phrase Book.*] Glasgow, n.d.
Munro's Gaelic Vocabulary and Phrase Book. Gairm Publications.
Gaelic Vocabulary and Phrase Book. By James Munro, H.M.E.I.
64 p. 180 mm. [1971.]

Munro, Neil, 1864–1930. [*The Lost Pibroch.*] Inverness, [Pref. 1913].
The Lost Pibroch and Other Shieling Stories. By Neil Munro, LL.D. Translated into Gaelic by Rev. Archd. MacDonald, Kiltarlity. Division 1. Price ninepence. Inverness: The *Northern Chronicle* Office. John Grant, 31 George IV Bridge, Edinburgh. James Thin, 54 South Bridge, Edinburgh. A. MacLaren & Sons, 360–362 Argyle Street, Glascow. E. MacKay, 54 Murray Place, Stirling.
56 p. 180 mm. EU, GU:CL, Mit.
"Prefatory Note" dated 1913.

—— [*The Lost Pibroch.*] Inverness, n.d.
Am Port Mor a bha air Chall agus Sgeulachdan eile na h-Airidh. Leis an Olla Niall Mac an Rothaich. Eadartheangaichte bho an Bheurla Sasunnaich gu Gàidhlig Albannaich leis an Urramach G. Mac Dhòmhnuill, D.D. Pris 4/–. Inbhirnis: Comunn Foillseachaidh na h-Airde-Tuath.
[4], 101 p. 250 mm. NLS.
c. 1934. English original first published 1896.

Murchadh a' Cheisteir. See MacLeod, Murdo, "Murchadh a' Cheisteir".

Murchison, Thomas M., 1907– (tr.). See Church of Scotland: Home Mission Committee. [*Tracts.*]

—— (ed.). See Lamont, Donald. [*Prose Writings.*]

—— (joint ed.). See MacLean, Malcolm. [*Alba.*]

—— (ed.). See MacLeod, Malcolm. [*An Iuchair Oir.*]

Murray, Amy. [*Father Allan's Island.*] Edinburgh, 1936.
Father Allan's Island. By Amy Murray. With a Foreword by Padraic Colum. The Moray Press. Edinburgh and London.
Published 1936.
xii, 240 p. 200 mm. Mit.
Impressions of the island of Eriskay with the words and music of a number of Gaelic songs.

Murray John 1938–. [*An Aghaidh Choimheach.*] Glasgow 1973.
An Aghaidh Choimheach. Sgeulachdan. Iain Moireach. Gairm. Glaschu. 1973.
Clò-bhualaidhean Gairm Leabhar 33.
[6] 122 p. 190 mm.
In hardback and paperback. Printed Learmonth Stirling.

—— (ed.). See Campbell, Angus, "Am Puilean". [*Suathadh ri Iomadh Rubha.*]

Murray, Murdo, 1890–1964. [*Luach na Saorsa.*] Glasgow, 1970.
Luach na Saorsa. Leabhar-latha, Bàrdachd is Rosg le Murchadh Moireach. Deasaichte
le Alasdair I. MacAsgaill. Gairm. Glaschu. 1970.
Clò-bhualaidhean Gairm, Leabhar 22.
147 p; plate. 220 mm.
Printed MacDonald Printers, Edinburgh.

Murray, Norman. [*New Method Gaelic.*] Vancouver, [*c.* 1941].
New Method Gaelic. A phonetic system of Gaelic reading. [Illus.] By Norman
Murray, M.A. Published by An Comunn Gaidhealach, Vancouver, Canada.
Copyright 1941 by An Comunn Gaidhealach, Vancouver, Canada.
[3], 17 p. 230 mm. GU:CL.

Murray, W. [*Adventure at the Castle.*] Inverness, 1974.
Leabhraichean Ladybird. Mar a thachair 'sa Chaisteal. Le W. Murray. Na dealbhan
le J. H. Wingfield. Air eadar-theangachadh le Tormod Burns. Foillsichearan: An
Comunn Gaidhealach Inbhirnis. *c.* Ladybird Books Ltd. Loughborough. Air a chlò-
bhualadh an Sasunn, 1974.
51 p; col. illus. 180 mm.

—— [*Boys and Girls.*] Loughborough, 1970.
Leabhraichean Ladybird. Balaich agus nigheanan. Le W. Murray. Dealbhan le
E. Ayton. Air eadar-theangachadh le I. NicAsgaill. Air a chlò-bhualadh an Sasunn le
Wills & Hepworth Ltd., Loughborough, 1970. A' cheud chlò-bhualadh am Beurla
1964.
Ladybird Key Words Reading Scheme, Leabhar 3b.
50, [1] p; illus. 180 mm.

Murray, W. [*Things We Like.*] Loughborough, 1970.
Leabhraichean Ladybird. Is toigh leinn. Le W. Murray. Dealbhan le John Berry. Air
eadartheangachadh le B. A. Nicillinnein. Air a chlò-bhualadh an Sasunn le Wills &
Hepworth Ltd., Loughborough, 1970. A' cheud chlò-bhualadh am Beurla 1964.
Ladybird Key Words Readings Scheme, Leabhar 3a.
50, [1]; illus. 180 mm.

Murray, W. [*We are Busy.*] Loughborough, 1970.
Leabhraichean Ladybird. Tha sinn trang. Le W. Murray. Dealbhan le John Berry.
Air eadar-theangachadh le M. C. Fhoirbeis. Air a chlò-bhualadh an Sasunn le Wills &
Hepworth Ltd., Loughborough, 1970. A' cheud chlò-bhualadh am Beurla 1964.
Ladybird Key Words Reading Scheme, Leabhar 4a.
50, [1] p; illus. 180 mm.

National Anthem, The. See [God Save the King.]

National Bible Society of Scotland. [*Comunn-Bhiobull Dutchchail na h-Alba.*] N.p., n.d.
Comunn-Bhìobull Dùthchail na h-Alba. Ciod e Comunn-Bhìobull Dùthchail na
h-Alba agus de tha e a deanamh.
[4]. 180 mm. PC.
"1928" handwritten on title page.

National Bible Society of Scotland. See Bible.

National Book League. [*The Highlands and Islands of Scotland.*] London, 1967.
The Highlands and Islands of Scotland. Prepared in association with the Highlands
and Islands Development Board. 1967. The National Book League, 7 Albemarle
Street, London, W.1.
52 p. 210 mm.
"Gaelic Language and Literature", pp 43–8.

—— [*The Highlands and Islands of Scotland.*] Edinburgh, 1971.
The Highlands and Islands of Scotland. A catalogue of books currently in print. 1971.
National Book League for Highlands and Islands Development Board.
88 p. 210 mm.
"Gaelic Language and Literature", pp 70–84. Printed Pillans & Wilson, Edinburgh.

National Mod. See An Comunn Gaidhealach.

National Spiritual Assembly of the Baha'is of the British Isles. [*Creideamh na Baha'i.*]
London, 1961.
Creideamh na Bahà'i.
Printed in Great Britain 1961. This is a publication of The National Spiritual Assembly
of the Bahá'ís of the British Isles. Bahá'í Publishing Trust, 27 Rutland Gate, London,
S.W.7.
28 p. 130 mm. PC.
Printed Heffer, Cambridge.

National Spiritual Assembly of the Baha'is of the British Isles. [*Sgriobtuirean Creidimh
nam Baha-i.*] Stornoway, n.d.
Taghadh bho Sgriobtuirean Creidimh nam Bahà-i.
Air a cho-chruinneachadh le Cuideachd Riaghlaidh Teagaisg na h-Alba, Ard-sheanaidh
Spioradail Dùthchail nam Bahà-i ann am Breatunn.
Sgrìobhadh Beurla air son eadar-theangachadh gu Gàidhlig gu litreachas nam Bahà-i 's a
chànain sin a mhaiseachadh. Air a chlò-bhualadh le Gasaet Steòrnabhaigh, 10 Sràid
Frangain, Steòrnabhagh (Eilean Leódhuis).
35 p. 190 mm.
Issued by the Scottish Regional Teaching Committee of the National Spiritual
Assembly of the Bahà-is of the British Isles.

Neill, William, 1922–. [*Despatches Home.*] Edinburgh, 1972.
Despatches Home. William Neill. Published by Reprographia, 23 Livingstone Place,
Edinburgh, EH9 1PD.
56 p. 220 mm.
Contains 7 Gaelic, 3 Scots and 28 English poems, with English translations of the
Gaelic poems. Printed MacDonald Printers, Edinburgh.

—— (joint author). See MacLean, Sorley. [*Four Points of a Saltire.*]

Newspapers. For list of newspapers which contain some Gaelic, see "Periodicals".

New Testament. See Bible. N.T.

Nic A' Phearsain, Seonaid. See MacPherson, Janet.

Nic Bheathain, Sine. See MacBean, Jean.

Nic Gilleathain, Anna. See MacLean, Ann.

Nic Gill-Eathain, Mairi M. See MacLean, Mary M.

Nic Iomhair, Mairi A. See Mac Iver, Mary A.

Nic Leoid, Babi. See MacLeod, B.

NicLeoid, Cairistiona. See MacLeod, Christine.

NicLeoid, Ciorstai. See MacLeod, Christina.

Nic Mhathain, Seonaid. See Matheson, Jessie.

Nicolson Institute, Stornoway. See School Magazines.

Nicolson, Alexander, Advocate, 1827–93. [*Gaelic Proverbs.*] Glasgow, 1951.
 Gaelic Proverbs. Collected and translated into English with equivalents from other
 European languages by Alexander Nicolson, M.A., LL.D., Advocate. Reprinted with
 Index, etc. by Malcolm Mac Innes, M.A., LL.B., Edinburgh and the Cape of Good
 Hope, Advocate. [Illus.] Published for Malcolm MacInnes, Esq. by the Caledonian
 Press, 793 Argyle Street, Glasgow. 1951.
 [10], xxxvi, 470 p. 230 mm. AU, PC.
  Section A (10 pages) consists of all the 1951 edition introductory matter. Section B
  (xxxvi, 420 p) is a reprint of Nicolson's "Gaelic Proverbs" (1st ed. 1881; 421 p).
  Section C ([423]–470 p) comprises Malcolm MacInnes' Index. The proverbs are
  arranged alphabetically. Nicolson's "Gaelic Proverbs" is based on Donald Mac-
  Intosh's "A Collection of Gaelic Proverbs" (1st ed. 1785).

Nicolson, Alexander, Lecturer in Gaelic at Jordanhill College, 1873–. [*Am Breacadh.*]
 Glasgow, 1939.
 Am Breacadh. A Basic Gaelic Reader. Compiled by Alexander Nicolson, M.A.,
 Lecturer in Gaelic in Jordanhill Training College, Glasgow. Glasgow: Archd. Sinclair,
 Celtic Press, 27a Cadogan Street. 1939.
 44 p. 190 mm. BM, Mit.

—— [*Am Breacadh.*] Glasgow, n.d.
 . . . Glasgow: Alex. MacLaren & Sons, 268 Argyle Street, C.2.
 36, [12] p. 190 mm. PC.
  The 12 unnumbered pages at the end of the book comprise 3 p of Grammar, 1 p of
  advertisements and 8 p Glossary.

—— [*Gaelic Riddles and Enigmas.*] Glasgow, 1938.
 Gaelic Riddles and Enigmas. (Tòimhseachain agus Dubh-Fhacail.) By Alexander
 Nicolson, Lecturer in Gaelic at Jordanhill College, Glasgow. Glasgow: Archd. Sinclair,
 Celtic Press, 27a Cadogan Street. 1938.
 103 p. 190 mm. BM, Mit., SS.
  English translation on facing pages.

—— [*Modern Gaelic: A Basic Grammar.*] Glasgow, [Pref. 1936].
 Modern Gaelic. A Basic Grammar. By Alexander Nicolson, M.A., Lecturer in Gaelic
 at Jordanhill College, Glasgow. Glasgow: Archibald Sinclair, Celtic Press, 27a
 Cadogan Street.
 viii, 155 p. 190 mm. AU, BM, CoS, Mit., NLS.

—— [*Modern Gaelic: A Basic Grammar.*] Glasgow, 1945.
 Modern Gaelic. A Basic Grammar. By Alexander Nicolson, M.A., Lecturer in Gaelic
 at The University and Jordanhill College, Glasgow. Three shillings and sixpence net.
 Glasgow: Alex. MacLaren & Sons, 268 Argyle Street, C.2.
 First published 1936. Re-issued 1945.
 viii, 155 p. 190 mm. PC.
  Printed Sinclair, Glasgow.

—— [*Oideas na Cloinne.*] Glasgow, n.d.
 Oideas na Cloinne. Le Alasdair Mac Neacail. Printed by Archibald Sinclair, Celtic
 Press, 2/12 Mackeith Street, Glasgow, S.E.
 103 p. 220 mm. PC.
  Reviewed in "An Gaidheal", 1948.

—— [*An Duilleag Ghaidhlig.*] See Chapbook.

—— (joint ed.). See *Alba* (newspaper).

Nicolson, Calum. See Nicolson, Malcolm.

Nicolson, Donald, 1735–1802. [*Lamh-Sgriobhainnean Mhic-Neacail.*] N.p., n.d.
Làmh-Sgriobhainnean Mhic-Neacail. An t-Urramach Dòmhnull Mac Neacail, A. M. (1735–1802).
[340]–409 p. 220 mm. FC.

Nicolson, Malcolm. [*Dain Spioradail.*] Glasgow, 1917.
Dàin Spioradail. Le Calum MacNeacail, maighstir-sgoile ann am Barabhas. Fo làimh Iain N. MacLeòid, deasaiche "Bàrdachd Leodhais". Glaschu: Alasdair Mac Labhruinn agus a Mhic, 360 Sràid Earraghaidheal. 1917.
[1], 46 p; plate. 150 mm. EPL, NLS.
Contains 1 tune.

Nicolson, Nicol, *b.* 1842. [*An t-Urramach Iain Mac-Rath.*] Inverness, 1910.
An t-Urramach Iain Mac-Rath ("Mac-Rath Mor") a bha ann an Leodhas. Beagan iomraidh m'a bheatha agus criomagan d'a theagasg. Le Neacal Mac-neacail, ministear Strath-Ghairbh. Maille ri dealbh Mhr. Mhic-Rath. An treas clò-bhualadh. Inverness: George Young, New Market. 1910.
40 p; plate. 220 mm.

—— [*An t-Urramach Iain Mac Rath.*] Glasgow, 1939.
... Maille ri dealbh Mhgr Mhic Rath. Fo làimh Eachainn Mhic Dhùghaill. Glascho: Alasdair MacLabhruinn is a Mhic, 268 Sràid Earra-Ghaidheal, C.2.
An ceathramh clò-bhualadh. 1939.
59 p. 190 mm. PC.
1st and 2nd eds. in 1894, 1915 respectively. Elegy to Macrae, pp 51–9.

Nisbet, Jessie T. D. [*La na Cloinne.*] [Ayr], [Intro. 1973].
La na Cloinne. The Children's Day. Stories in Verse, told in Gaelic and English.
[12] p. 180 mm.
Preface: "This booklet commemorates the first visit of the National Mod to the town of Ayr in October 1973. It is composed in memory of the Rev. Archibald Beaton. Proceeds from the sale of this booklet will be donated to Kilmarnock Branch of An Comunn Gaidhealach for the Rev. Archie Beaton Memorial Trophy Fund." Introduction signed, "Jessie T. D. Nisbett, 2 Hollybush Drive, Crieff. September, 1973."

Northern Assurance Company. [*Cunntas Goirid.*] London, n.d.
Cunntas Goirid. An Tuath Chomunn Urras. [Illus.] Priomh Bùthan: Lunainn, 1 Moorgate St.; Abaireann, 1 Union Terrace.
26 p, [1]. 130 mm. GU:CL.
TS-G gives date as 1902.

Obair a' Chelp. See [The Kelp Industry].

O Baoill, Colm, 1938– (ed.). See MacDonald, Silis. [*Bardach Shilis na Ceapaich.*]

—— (joint author). See Wagner, Heinrich. [*The Dialects of Ulster and the Isle of Man.*]

O Broin, Padraig (joint ed.). See Irisleabhar Ceilteach.

—— (ed.). See Teangadoir.

Oftedal, Magne, 1921–. [*The Gaelic of Leurbost.*] Oslo, 1956.
Norsk Tidsskrift for Sprogvidenskap ... Utgitt av Carl J. S. Marstrander. Suppl. Bind IV. Oslo, 1956. H. Aschehoug & Co. (W. Nygaard).
A Linguistic Survey of the Gaelic Dialects of Scotland, Vol. III. Magne Oftedal. The Gaelic of Leurbost, Isle of Lewis. Oslo, 1956. H. Aschehoug & Co. (W. Nygaard).
372 p; map. 260 mm.
Paperback.

—— [*The Gaelic of Leurbost.*] Oslo, 1956.
. . . Suppl. Bind IV. Norwegian Universities Press.
. . . The Gaelic of Leurbost, Isle of Lewis. Norwegian Universities Press.
Oslo, 1956.
372 p; map. 260 mm.
      Hardback; otherwise identical to above.

Old Highlands, The. See The Gaelic Society of Glasgow. [*Transactions.*] Volume III.

Old, Old Story, The. See Clerk, Archibald. [*The Old, Old Story.*]

Old Testament, The. See Bible.

Oldham, Joseph H., 1874–. [*The Possibilities of Prayer.*] London, 1913.
      Comasan na h-Urnuigh. Le J. H. Oldham. Translated from the English by Malcolm
      MacLeod, M.A., Minister at Broadford, Skye. T. N. Foulis, London & Edinburgh.
      1913.
      The Possibilities of Prayer. By J. H. Oldham. T. N. Foulis, London & Edinburgh.
      1913.
      81 p; plate. 190 mm. CoS, Mit.
            English and Gaelic on facing pages. Printed Turnbull & Spears, Edinburgh.
            English original first published 1912.

O Lochlainn, Colm. [*Deoch-Slainte nan Gillean.*] Dublin, [*c.* 1948].
      Deoch-slàinte nan Gillean. Dòrnan òran a Barraidh. Air na dheasachadh le Colm
      O Lochlainn, am Baile Atha Cliath, ann an Eirinn: fo Chomhardha nan Trì Coinnlean.
      Copyright Colm O Lochlainn, 1948.
      xi, 83 p. 190 mm. GU:CL.
            Contains some tunes in staff notation.

Omhain, [Iain]. [*Obair an Spioraid Naoimh.*] See Owen, John. [*The Holy Spirit.*]

O' Rahilly, Thomas F., 1883–1953. [*Irish Dialects.*] Dublin, 1932.
      Irish Dialects past and present, with chapters on Scottish and Manx. By Thomas F.
      O' Rahilly. Browne and Nolan Limited: Dublin; Belfast; Cork; Waterford; London:
      18 Red Lion Passage, Holborn, W.C.1. 1932.
      278 p, [1] "Symbols Used", [1] "Errata" (130 mm). 220 mm. AU:CL.
            Printed at the St. Catherine Press, Ltd., Bruges, Belgium.

—— [*Irish Dialects.*] Dublin, 1972.
. . . Dublin Institute for Advanced Studies. 1972.
xi, [1], 300, [2] p. 220 mm.

Orain a' Mhoid. See An Comunn Gaidhealach. [*National Mod.*] Orain a' Mhoid.

Orain-aon-Neach. See An Comunn Gaidhealach. [*National Mod.*] Orain-aon-Neach.

Orain-Caraid. Glasgow, [*c.* 1938].
      Orain-càraid. [Illus.] Price 2/6. An Comunn Gaidhealach, 131 Sràid Iar Regent,
      Glaschu, C.2. Copyright, 1938. Printed in Scotland.
      [2], 30 p. 250 mm. PC.

Orain da-Ghuthach. Glasgow, 1928.
      Orain Da-Ghuthach. Book One. Gaelic Duets. A new collection of Gaelic songs
      arranged for two voices. 1/– net. Glascho: Alasdair MacLabhruinn 's a Mhic, 360-
      362 Sraid Earra-Ghaidheal, C.2. 1928.
      16 p. 210 mm. Mit., NLS, PC.

Orain na Cloinne. See An Comunn Gaidhealach. [*National Mod.*] Orain na Cloinne.

Orain na h-Oigridh. See An Comunn Gaidhealach. [*National Mod.*] Orain na h-Oigridh.

Orain nam Beann. See Morrison, Angus. [*Orain nam Beann.*]

Oran a' Cheasar. See Morrison, Angus, of Edinburgh. [*Oran a' Cheasar.*]

Oran Mhic Illeathain. N.p., n.d.
  Oran Mhic Illeathain an "Hotel".
  1 p. 220 mm. PC.
    No music. Probably published by MacLaren, Glasgow.

Ordnance Survey. [*Glossary.*] N.p., n.d.
  Ordnance Survey of Scotland. Glossary of the most common Gaelic words (and
  corrupted forms of Gaelic), used on the Ordnance Survey Maps.
  8 p. 180 mm. PC.
    "Many years ago a small pamphlet entitled 'The Most Common Gaelic Words used
    on Ordnance Survey Maps' was issued for use with one-inch maps of Scotland.
    [About 1949] it was decided to increase the scope of the pamphlet on Gaelic names,
    this was completely recompiled by the Royal Scottish Geographical Society and was
    published in a much enlarged edition in 1951."—Preface to 1973 edition.

Ordnance Survey. [*Place Names on Maps of Scotland and Wales.*] Southampton, n.d.
  Ordnance Survey. Place names on maps of Scotland and Wales. A glossary of the most
  common Gaelic and Scandinavian elements used on maps of Scotland and of the most
  common Welsh elements used on maps of Wales.
  Printed and published by the Director, General Ordnance Survey, Southampton.
  23 p. 210 mm.
    1973. Part I: Gaelic, pp 5–12; Part II: Scandinavian, pp 13–14; Part III: Welsh,
    pp 15–23.

Ossian. [Periodical.] Glasgow, 1933, n.d., n.d., 1957, 1960, 1961, 1965, 1967, 1968,
  1972, 1973.
  Ossian. Published by Glasgow University Ossianic Society. English Section: Alex J.
  MacLean, M.A., Editor; Marion M. MacLean, Sub-Editor. Gaelic Section: John
  MacDougall (Muileach), Editor; Margaret M. MacMillan, Sub-Editor. Finance
  Managers: John M. Urquhart and Murdo MacLeod. Printed by Kirkwood & Co.,
  127 Stockwell Street, Glasgow.
  [English Section Masthead] Ossian. Vol. 1, No. 1. April, 1933.
  [Gaelic Section Masthead] Oisean. Earr. 1, Air. 1. An Giblean, 1933.
  44 p; illus. 270 mm. Mit.
  Ossian. Published by Glasgow University Ossianic Society. English Section: Mairi K.
  MacKinnon, Isobel Budge, Janette Blair, Peter W. MacLeod. Gaelic Section: Ewen
  MacDonald, Lachlan Robertson. Finance Manager: Alex. G. Matheson. "Stornoway
  Gazette", Stornoway.
  28 p; illus. 290 mm. NLS.
    c. 1950.
  Ossian. Published by Glasgow University Ossianic Society. Fifth-centenary edition.
  Magazine Committee: Betty Todd, Peggy MacFarlane, Lachlan Robertson, M.A.,
  William MacDougall, B.Sc., Tom MacDowall. Printed at the "Northern Chronicle"
  Office, Inverness.
  32 p; 4 plates; illus. 250 mm. PC.
    c. 1951; reviewed in "An Gaidheal", Feb. 1952.
  "Leansa dlùth ri cliù do shinnsre." Ossian. Celtic Chair Inauguration and Ossianic
  Club Jubilee Celebration Edition. [Illus.] March, 1957. Published by Glasgow
  University Ossianic Society.
  47 p; illus. 250 mm. NLS.
  Aireamh 3. Ossian. The Glasgow Gaelic Review. Am Foghar, 1960. Fear-Deasa-
  chaidh: Dòmhnall T. MacDhòmhnaill. Pearce Lodge, An Oilthigh, Glaschu, W.2.
  Telefon West 8541.

36 p; illus. 210 mm. Mit.
Printed Learmonth, Stirling.
Aireamh 4. Ossian. The Glasgow University Ossianic Society's Gaelic Review. Am
Foghar, 1961. Fir-Deasachaidh: Dòmhnall T. MacDhòmhnaill, D. Niall Mac-
Cormaig. Pearce Lodge, An Oilthigh, Glaschu, W.2. Telefón West 8541.
32 p; illus. 220 mm.
Printed Learmonth, Stirling.
Ossian 1965. Glasgow University Ossianic Society. Editor—Roderick M. Mac-
Kinnon. Advertisements—Duncan MacQuarrie. 8 South Park Terrace, Glasgow,
W.2.
28 p; illus. 220 mm.
Ossian 1967. Editor: Ronald I. Black. "Leansa dlùth ri cliù do shinnsre" (Fionn to
Oscar, in an Ossianic tale). Published annually in December by Glasgow University
Ossianic Society, 8 Southpark Terrace, Glasgow, W.2.
52 p; illus. 220 mm.
Ossian 1968. Editor: Ronald I. Black. Cover drawn by Donald M. Murray. "Leansa
dlùth ri cliù do shinnsre" (Fionn to Oscar, in an Ossianic tale). Published annually in
December by Glasgow University Ossianic Society, 8 Southpark Terrace, Glasgow,
W.2.
52 p; illus. 220 mm.
Ossian 1972. Editor—Donald A. MacLennan. Cover design—Donald Paterson.
"Leansa dlùth ri cliù do shinnsre" (Fionn to Oscar, in an Ossianic tale). Published by
Glasgow University Ossianic Society, 8 Southpark Terrace, Glasgow, W.2.
56 p. 220 mm.
Printed Learmonth, Stirling.
Ossian 1973. Editors—Ossianic Society Committee. Cover design—Deirdre MacLeod.
"Leansa dlùth ri cliù do shinnsre" (Fionn to Oscar, in an Ossianic tale). Published by
Glasgow University Ossianic Society, 8 Southpark Terrace, Glasgow, G12.
65 p; illus. 220 mm.
Printed Jamieson & Munro, Stirling.
Ossian 1974. Editors—Ossianic Society Committee. Cover design and cartoons—
Robert MacDonald, Deirdre MacLeod. Advertising—Roddy MacLean. [Quotation.]
Published by Glasgow University Ossianic Society, 8 Southpark Terrace, Glasgow,
G12 8LG.
60 p; illus. 220 mm.

Ossian (author?). See Dana Oisein Mhic Fhinn.

Ossianic Society of Glasgow University. See *Ossian.*

Owen, John, 1616–83. (*The Glory of Christ.*] Edinburgh, [Intro. 1916].
Cogadh mór na h-Eòrpa. Oirdheirceas Chriosd. Omhain. [Illus.] Printed by Oliver
and Boyd, Edinburgh, for The Church of Scotland, The United Free Church of
Scotland, and The Free Church of Scotland.
x, 80 p. 140 mm. NLS.
Introduction signed, "Norman MacLean, 1915". One of a series of booklets issued
to First World War soldiers. English original ("Meditations and Discourses on the
Glory of Christ", four sermons on Psalm XLV, 1–3) first published 1696.

——— [*The Holy Spirit.*] Edinburgh, [Intro. 1916].
Cogadh mór na h-Eòrpa. Obair an Spioraid Naoimh. Omhain. [Illus.] Printed by
Oliver and Boyd, Edinburgh, for The Church of Scotland, The United Free Church
of Scotland, and The Free Church of Scotland.
xi, 84 p. 140 mm. NLS.
Introduction signed, "Norman MacLean, 1916". One of a series published for
distribution to soldiers in the First World War. English original ("A Discourse
concerning the Holy Spirit") first published 1674.

F

Paipearan Deuchainn Gaidhlig. See Scottish Certificate of Education.

Parker, Winifred. [*Na Daoine Sidhe.*] Glasgow, 1907.
Na Daoine Sidhe is Uirsgeulan eile. Air an cur an eagar le Una, inghean Fear na Pairce. Na dealbhan o laimh Chatrìona Chamaroin, R.S.W., is Raoghnailt Ainslie Ghrannd Dubh. Archibald Sinclair, Celtic Press, 47 Waterloo Street, Glasgow. 1907.
[5]–48 p; 4 plates. 210 mm. BM, NLS.

—— [*Na Daoine Sidhe.*] N.p., 1907.
Na Daoine Sidhe is Uirsgeulan eile. Air an cur an eagar le Una, inghean Fear na Pairce. Na dealbhan o làimh Chatrìona Chamaroin, R.S.W., is Raoghnailt Ainslie Ghrannd Dubh. 1907.
Gaelic Fairy Tales. Edited by Winifred M. P. Parker. Illustrated by Katherine Cameron, R.S.W., and Rachel Ainslie Grant Duff. 1907.
[5]–48 p, [5]–48 p; 4 plates. 210 mm. GU:CL.
English translation on facing pages.

—— [*Na Daoine Sidhe.*] Glasgow, 1908.
Na daoine Sidhe is Uirsgeulan eile. Na dealbhan o laimh Chatrìona Chamaroin, R.S.W., is Raoghnailt Ghrannd Dubh. Glaschu: Gilleasbuig Mac-na-Ceardadh, 47 Sraid Waterloo. 1908.
Gaelic Fairy Tales. Illustrated by Katherine Cameron, R.S.W., and Rachel Ainslie Grant Duff. Glasgow: Archibald Sinclair, Celtic Press, 47 Waterloo Street. 1908.
[5]–48, [5]–48 p; 4 plates. 210 mm. PC.
Issued in aid of the funds of the Comunn Gaidhealach Feill of 1907.

—— (joint ed.). See "Sop as Gach Seid."

Pastoral Letter. See Catholic Church, Argyll and The Isles (Diocese). [*Pastoral Letter.*]

Paterson, John M. [*Gaelic Made Easy.*] Part 1. Glasgow, [1952].
"Gaelic Made Easy." A Guide to Gaelic for Beginners. Part 1. Comprising 10 lessons in Gaelic. Written and compiled by John M. Paterson. [Illus.] Dionnasg Gàidhlig na h-Alba (The Gaelic League of Scotland), 27 Elmbank Street, Glasgow.
[2], 40, [1] p. 190 mm.
Dated 1952 in 2nd ed.

—— [*Gaelic Made Easy.*] Part 1. Glasgow, 1952, 1954, 1958.
Ibid.
[2], 40, [1] p. 190 mm.
Revised 1954.

—— [*Gaelic Made Easy.*] Part 2. Glasgow, [1953].
"Gaelic Made Easy." A Guide to Gaelic for Beginners. Part 2. Comprising 10 lessons in Gaelic, including vocabulary. Written and compiled by John M. Paterson. [Illus.] Dionnasg Gàidhlig na h-Alba (The Gaelic League of Scotland). 27 Elmbank Street, Glasgow.
[2], 40, x "Vocabulary", [2] p. 190 mm.

—— [*Gaelic Made Easy.*] Part 2. Glasgow, 1956, 1959, 1969, 1973.
Ibid.
[2], 40, x, [2] p. 190 mm.
Revised 1959. Address changes to "34 Berkeley Street, Glasgow, C.3", 1959 ed.

—— [*Gaelic Made Easy.*] Part 3. Glasgow, [1958].
"Gaelic Made Easy." A Guide to Gaelic for Beginners. Part 3. Comprising 10 lessons in Gaelic, including vocabulary. Written and compiled by John M. Paterson. [Crest.] Dionnasg Gaidhlig na h-Alba (The Gaelic League of Scotland), 27 Elmbank Street, Glasgow.
[4], 51 p, v "Vocabulary", 19 p.

—— [*Gaelic Made Easy*.] Part 3. Glasgow, 1963, 1971.
. . . 34 Berkeley Street, Glasgow, C.3.
[4], 51, v p. 190 mm.

—— [*Gaelic Made Easy*.] Part 4. Glasgow, 1960.
"Gaelic Made Easy." A Guide to Gaelic for Beginners. Part 4. Comprising 13 lessons
in Gaelic, including vocabulary. Written and compiled by John M. Paterson. [Crest.]
Dionnasg Gaidhlig na h-Alba (The Gaelic League of Scotland), 27 Elmbank Street,
Glasgow.
[4], 69, ix "Vocabulary", [1] p. 190 mm.

—— [*Gaelic Made Easy*.] Part 4. Glasgow, 1967, 1973.
. . . 34 Berkeley Street, Glasgow, C.3.
[4], 69, ix, [1] p. 190 mm.
    Tapes are issued with this course.

—— [*The Gaels have a Word for it*.] Glasgow, [Fore. 1964].
The Gaels have a Word for it. A modern Gaelic vocabulary of 2,000 words. Compiled
by John M. Paterson. Price 3/6. Post free 3/10. [Illus.] Dionnasg Gàidhlig na
h-Alba. (The Gaelic League of Scotland), 34 Berkeley Street, Glasgow, C.3.
[6], 31 p. 190 mm. Mit.
    Printed Learmonth, Stirling.

Peach, L. du Garde. [*Florence Nightingale*.] Inverness, 1974.
Floireans Nightingale. Le L. Du Garde Peach, M.A., Ph.D., D.Litt. Na dealbhan le
John Kenney. Air eadar-theangachadh le Catriona M. NicDhòmhnaill. Foillsichearan:
An Comunn Gaidhealach, Inbhirnis. © Ladybird Books Ltd., Loughborough. Air a
chlò-bhualadh an Sasunn, 1974.
Sreath 561.
51 p; col. illus. 180 mm.

Peiteag Ruaidh. See Erskine, The Hon. Roderick of Mar. [*Air Eachdraidh*.]

Periodicals. [A list of serials which occasionally contain Gaelic but not in sufficient
    quantity or with sufficient frequency to warrant separate entries.]
    An Aimsir Cheilteach (C); Akros; Alba Nuadh; Aurora (C); The Barra Bulletin;
    Béaloideas; The Bee (C); Budlaven (Finland); The Canadian-American Gael (C); The
    Cape Breton Mirror (C); The Casket (C); Catalyst; The Catholic Directory; Ceann Tara
    (C); Celtica; Clan Society magazines; The Eastern Chronicle (C); Eigse; The Eilean an
    Fhraoich Annual; Eriu; Etudes Celtiques; Folk-Lore; Fraser's Scottish Annual (C);
    The Glasgow Highlander; The Glasgow Weekly Herald; The Glengarrian (C); The
    Highland News; The Ileach; The Inverness Courier; The Journal of Celtic Studies;
    The Journal of the English Folk Dance and Song Society; The Journal of the Folk Song
    Society; Lines Review; Lion Rampant; Lochlann; Maple Leaf (C); Mercat Cross; New
    Saltire; Norsk Tidsskrift for Sprogvidenskap; North Star; The Northern Chronicle;
    The Northern Evangelist; The Northern Weekly; The Oban Times; Outlook;
    The People's Journal; The Pictish Review; Planet; Poetry Scotland; Port Hood
    Greetings (C); Revue Celtique; Saga och Sed; St. Peter's Magazine; School Magazines
    (see "School Magazines" for further detail); Scots Magazine; the Scotsman; Scottish
    Art and Letters; The Scottish Australian; The Scottish Canadian (C); The Scottish
    Catholic Herald; Scottish Chapbook; Scottish Highland Weekly; The Sea Leaguer; The
    Stornoway Gazette; Studia Celtica; Studia Hibernica; The Sydney Post; Sydney
    Post-Record (C); Sydney Record (C); Thistle; Tìr; The Voice of Scotland; Weekly
    Scotsman; The West Highland Free Press; Wick Literary Magazine; Yorkshire Celtic
    Studies; Zeitschrift für celtische Philologie.
    Canadian publications are indicated by "(C)".

[*Pied Piper*.] See MacKinnon, Jonathan G. (comp.). [*The Pied Piper and other stories*.]

Piobaire Breac, Am. See MacKinnon, Jonathan G. [*The Pied Piper and other stories.*]

Place Names on Maps of Scotland and Wales. See Ordnance Survey.

Poems of Ossian. See Dana Oisein Mhic Fhinn.

Portree High School. See An Cabairneach.

Portree High School. See School Magazines.

Post, Am. Glasgow, 1969.
   Am Post. Le còmhlan a thainig cruinn aig Cruinneachadh an Luchd-teagaisg Ghàidhlig
   an Inbhirnis, 1968. Dealbhan le Cailean Spencer. Gairm. Glaschu. 1969.
   Am Post. Sreath na Sgoile (air fhoillseachadh an co-bhoinn ri Coimitidh nan
   Leabhraichean-sgoile), Leabhar 3. Clò-bhualaidhean Gairm, Leabhar 12.
   210 mm.

Prayer Books. See:
   Catholic Church. *Liturgy and Ritual.* [Iul a' Chriostaidh.]
   Catholic Church. *Liturgy and Ritual.* [Lochran an Anma.]
   Church of Scotland. *Liturgy and Ritual.* [Book of Common Order.]
   Urnuighean Airson na Cloinne.

Psalms. See Bible.

Psalmody. See:
   Church of Scotland. *Liturgy and Ritual.* [Sailm Dhaibhidh.]
   Free Church of Scotland. *Liturgy and Ritual.* [Fuinn nan Salm Ghaidhlig.]
   Hately, T. L. [*Seann Fhuinn nan Salm.*]
   MacBean, Lachlan. [*Psalmody.*]
   Whitehead, F. W. [*The Six Long Gaelic Psalm Tunes.*]

Publications of The Scottish Council for Research into Education. See Aithris is Oideas.

Puilean, Am. See Campbell, Angus.

Puirt mo Sheanmhar. Stirling, 1907.
   Puirt mo Sheanamhar. Crònain agus puirt-altruim air son a' chloinn-bhig. [Quotation.]
   Struibhle: Aonghas Mac Aoidh. 1907.
   24 p; plate; illus. 190 mm. AU, Mit.
      Foreword by T. D. MacDonald, the editor. Traditional songs, some completed by
      the editor.

Pursell, Edward (joint author). See *Learning Gaelic.*

Quiggin, E. C. (joint ed.). See MacGregor, James, Dean of Lismore. [*Poems from The
   Book of The Dean of Lismore.*]

Raspe, Rudolph E., 1737–94. [*The Adventures of Baron Munch-Hausen.*] Stornoway,
   n.d.
   Sgeulachdan Mhic-an-Teòsain. Air an tarruing o'n leabhar, "The Adventures of Baron
   Munch-Hausen". Air an rèiteachadh agus air an eadartheangachadh le Ruairidh
   Moireasdan.
   64 p of illus. 290 mm.
      In cartoon strip format. Reprinted from *The Stornoway Gazette.* First English
      ed. 1786.

Ready, Stuart, 1899–. [*Down to the Seas.*] Glasgow, 1950.
Dealbh-chluichean an Gàidhlig. Sios chun na Mara. Air eadar-theangachadh le Dòmhnall MacGhille Mhoire. Printed for An Comunn Gàidhealach by Eneas MacKay, Stirling. 1950.
24 p. 190 mm. PC.
English original first published 1947.

Rebels Ceilidh Song Book. Bo'ness, [Pref. 1965].
The Rebels Ceilidh Song Book. This Book published by Bo'ness Rebels Literary Society contains 35 Ceilidh Songs.
38, [2] p. 190 mm.
Contains 4 Gaelic songs.

Reid, Duncan. [*Course of Gaelic Grammar.*] Glasgow, 1902.
A Course of Gaelic Grammar. By Duncan Reid, F.S.L.A., teacher of Gaelic in the High School of Glasgow. [Illus.] (New and enlarged edition.) Glasgow: Archibald Sinclair, Printer, 47 Waterloo Street. Edinburgh and Glasgow: John Menzies and Co. 1902. (Entered at Stationers' Hall.)
viii, 164 p. 190 mm. AU, BM, EPL, GU:CL, Mit.

—— [*Course of Gaelic Grammar.*] Glasgow, 1908.
. . . (Third edition.) Seventh thousand. . . . 1908. (Entered at Stationers' Hall.)
viii, 164 p. 190 mm. AU, BM, GU:CL, NLS.

—— [*Course of Gaelic Grammar.*] Glasgow, 1923.
. . . Fourth edition. Glasgow: Archibald Sinclair, Printer, 47 Waterloo Street. 1923. (Entered at Stationers' Hall.)
viii, 164 p. 180 mm. CoS, Mit.
1st ed. 1895.

—— [*Elementary Course of Gaelic.*] Glasgow, 1908.
Elementary Course of Gaelic. By Duncan Reid, author of "A Course of Gaelic Grammar", etc. Issued by An Comunn Gaidhealach for use in Schools and Gaelic Classes. Glasgow: printed and published for An Comunn Gaidhealach, 68 Gordon Street, by Archibald Sinclair, Celtic Press, 47 Waterloo Street. 1908.
[4], 117, [2] p. 190 mm. Mit.

—— [*Elementary Course of Gaelic.*] Glasgow, 1913.
Elementary Course of Gaelic. By Duncan Reid. Re-arranged and enlarged by Norman MacLeod (Gaelic Master, The Glasgow High School). Published by An Comunn Gaidhealach for use in Schools and Gaelic Classes. Glasgow: Archibald Sinclair, Celtic Press, 47 Waterloo Street. 1913.
vii, 208 p. 180 mm. AU, BM, NLS.

—— [*Elementary Course of Gaelic.*] Glasgow, 1921.
. . . Second edition Published by An Comunn Gaidhealach for use in Schools and Gaelic Classes. Stirling: Jamieson & Munro, Ltd., Printers, 40 Craigs. 1921.
viii, 208 p. 200 mm. NLS, PC.

—— [*Elementary Course of Gaelic.*] Glasgow, 1928, 1935, 1952, 1968, 1971.
Ibid.
viii, 208 p. 200 mm.
1928 edition has 'Third Edition" imprint. No printer's imprint on title-page of 1935 edition. "Present Reprint" before date in 1952, 1968, 1971 editions.

Reid, George. See Beagan Gaidhlig.

Rev. Mr. Lachlan. See [MacKenzie, Lachlan]. [*Lectures, Sermons, and Writings.*]

Riaghailtean agus Clar-Obrach. See Comunn na h-Oigridh. [*Riaghailtean agus Clar-Obrach.*]

Robertson, Angus, 1872–1948. [*Cnoc an Fhradhairc.*] Glasgow, 1940.
    Cnoc an Fhradhairc. By Angus Robertson. Foreword by Alexander Nicolson, M.A., Lecturer in Gaelic in Jordanhill College, Glasgow, author of *History of Skye, Gaelic Grammar*, etc. [Quotation.] Glasgow: Alexander MacLaren & Sons, 268 Argyle Street, C.2. 1940.
    xxiii, 94 p. 190 mm. EPL, GU, Mit.
        Contains: "an attempt at eclogue in Gaelic", "Cnoc an Fhradhairc", pp 1–47; 28 shorter Gaelic poems, pp 48–83; 14 English poems, pp 81–94.

—— [*Cor, Coir agus Coirich.*] See Henderson, Angus. [*Sgoiltean agus Oilean.*]

—— [*An t-Ogha Mor.*] Glasgow, [Fore. 1913].
    An t-Ogha Mór. No, Am Fear-Sgeòil air Uilinn. Le Aonghas Mac Dhonnachaidh. Fosgrachadh le Uisdean Mac an Rothaich. Glascho: MacDhonnachaidh, Uéir & Co., 47 Sràid Waterloo.
    [8], 226 p; 4 plates. 200 mm. AU, BM, GU:CL, Mit., NLS.
        Printed John Cossar, Glasgow.

—— [*An t-Ogha Mor.*] Glasgow, 1919.
    ... Glascho: Alasdair Mac Labhruinn 's a Mhic, 360–362 Sràid Earraghaidheal. 1919.
    [8], 226 p; 4 plates. 200 mm. PC.
        A novel. 3 chapters were published in *An Sgeulaiche*, Vol. II, 1910; "Black Alpin", an early version of the novel, in English, appeared in *St Mungo*, an illustrated weekly printed in Glasgow, in 1907. An English translation, based on a version by Rev. Alexander MacKinnon, was published in 1924.

—— [*Orain na Ceilidh.*] London, n.d.
    Orain na Céilidh. Songs of the Ceilidh. By Angus Robertson. Arranged by Duncan Morrison. Foreword by D. J. MacLeod, D.Litt. Copyright. 5/– net. Paterson's Publications; London: 36–40 Wigmore Street, W.1.; Edinburgh: 27 George Street; Glasgow: 152 Buchanan Street; Aberdeen: 183 Union Street; New York: Carl Fischer, Inc., 62 Cooper Square; Canada: Anglo-Canadian Music Co., 144 Victoria Street, Toronto; New Zealand: C. Begg & Co., Ltd., Manners Street, Wellington.
    [4], 34 p. 310 mm. Mit.
        1938 (?); Mitchell Library copy acquired 1945. Contains 9 songs, with English translations.

Robertson, Angus Cameron. [*Crown and Empire.*] Edinburgh, 1911.
    Crown and Empire. Letter from Queen Alexandra and other Letters. [Illus.] Angus Cameron Robertson, Mariner and Author. Price 2/6. J. Wilkie & Co., Limited, Printers, 92 Princes Street, Dunedin. 1911.
    59 leaves. 190 mm. EU.
        Mainly English; Gaelic poem, "Chumha [sic] Righ Eideard VII" on pp 19–23; There is also an English translation of the poem.

Robertson, Atholl. See Ban-Altrumachd aig an Tigh.

—— See Ceud-Fhuasgladh do na Daoine Leointe.

Robertson, Chas. M., 1885–1949. [*The Gaelic of the West of Ross-shire.*] N.p., n.d.
    The Gaelic of the West of Ross-shire. By Rev. Chas. M. Robertson, Badcall, Lochbroom. (Reprinted from the Transactions of the Gaelic Society of Inverness, Vol. XXIV, 1899–1901.)
    49 p. 220 mm. EU.

—— [*Skye Gaelic.*] N.p., n.d.
Skye Gaelic. By Rev. Chas. M. Robertson.
36 p. 220 mm. FC.
Reprinted from "Transactions of the Gaelic Society of Inverness", Vol. XXIII,
1902.

—— (ed.). See MacGregor, Alexander. [*Songs.*]

Robinson, F. N., 1871–. [*The Gaelic Ballad of the Mantle.*] Chicago, n.d.
Reprinted from *Modern Philology*, Vol. 1, No. 1, June 1903. A Variant of the Gaelic
Ballad of the Mantle. By F. N. Robinson. Printed at the University of Chicago Press.
13 p. 250 mm. Mit.

Roman Catholic Church. See Catholic Church.

Ros, Coinneach. See Ross, Kenneth.

Ros, Uilleam. See Ross, William.

Rosarnach. Leabhar I. Glasgow, 1917.
An Ròsarnach. [Illus.] Alasdair Mac Labhrainn agus a Mhic, Glaschu. Clò-bhuailte
anns a' bhliadhna 1917.
[Cover] Leabhar I.
[8], 227p; 13 plates. 270 mm. AU, GU:CL, Mit., NLS.
Printed Milne, Tannahill ; Methven, Perth.

Rosarnach. Leabhar II. Glasgow, 1918.
An Ròsarnach. [Illus.] Alasdair Mac Labhrainn agus a Mhic, Glaschu. Clò-bhuailte
anns a' bhliadhna 1918.
[Cover] Leabhar II.
[8], 216 p; 7 plates. 270 mm. AU, GU:CL, Mit., NLS.
Printed Milne, Tannahill & Methven.

Rosarnach. Leabhar III. Glasgow, 1921.
An Ròsarnach. Leabhar III. [Illus.] Alasdair Mac Labhrainn agus a Mhic, Glaschu.
1921.
[8], 162 p; 3 plates. 270 mm. AU, GU:CL, Mit., NLS.
Printed Milne, Tannahill & Methven.

Rosarnach. Leabhar IV. Glasgow, 1930.
An Ròsarnach. An Ceathramh Leabhar. [Illus.] Alasdair Mac Labhrainn agus a Mhic,
Glaschu. 1930.
[8], 159 p; 9 plates. 270 mm. AU, GU:CL, Mit., NLS.
Printed by George Finlayson, Dundee. A series of prose anthologies.

Rosarnach. Leabhar V. [?]
An Ròsarnach. Leabhar V.
Not seen. Advertisement in "Orain a' Mhòid" (1931): "Ròsarnach V. Volume of
contemporary verse and prose. 7/6. To appear."

Rose, H. J. (joint ed.). See Campbell, John F. [*More West Highland Tales.*] Volume
One/Two.

Rosebery, Archibald Philip Primrose, 5th Earl of, 1847–1929. [*War! A Fight to the
Finish.*] Stirling, [1915].
Cogadh! "Gus an teirig treise." Gairm air na h-Albannaich gu cath. Le Tighearna
Rosebery. [Illus.] Aonghas MacAoidh, Struibhle.
16 p. 220 mm. PC.
Translation of "War! A Fight to the Finish. A martial call to the Scots." – text of
two speechs made in 1914, reprinted from *The Glasgow Herald*; English version
published 1915. Contains two Gaelic poems by Evan MacColl, pp 14–16.

Ross, James, 1924– (joint ed.). See School of Scottish Studies. [*Gaelic and Scots Folk Tales and Folk Songs.*]

Ross, Kenneth, 1914–. [*Aitealan dlu is Cian.*] Glasgow, 1972.
Aitealan Dlù is Cian. (Aistidhean.) Leis an Urr. Coinneach Ros, a bha 'na mhinistear ann an Giogha, an Lis-mór, 's a nise an Tom-an-t-Sabhail. Gairm. Glaschu. 1972. Clò-bhualaidhean Gairm, Leabhar 32.
[8], 127 p. 190 mm.
Printed Learmonth, Stirling.

Ross, Neil, 1871–1943. [*Armageddon.*] Edinburgh, 1950.
Armageddon. A Fragment. By Neil Ross, C.B.E., D.D., D.Litt., Minister of Laggan. Edinburgh. 1950.
[4], 147 p. 220 mm.
Printed by James Wilson, Edinburgh. Distributed by The Albyn Press, Edinburgh, in association with Irving Ravin, New York, U.S. Foreword by D. J. MacLeod, D.Litt. English verse translation on facing pages.

—— (ed.). See MacGregor, James, Dean of Lismore. [*Heroic Poetry from the Book of the Dean of Lismore.*]

—— (joint author). See An Solaraiche.

Ross, Thomas (tr.). See Bible. [*Psalms.*]

Ross, William, 1762–90. [*Orain Ghaelach.*] Edinburgh, 1902.
Orain Ghàelach. Le Uilleam Ros. Air an co-chruinneachadh ri chéile le Iain Mac-Choinnich ann an Inbhiriue. Gaelic Songs. By William Ross. Collected by John MacKenzie, Inverurie [sic]. Fifth edition. Edinburgh: John Grant, 31 George IV Bridge. 1902.
xvi, 107 p. 150 mm. Mit.
   1st ed. *c.* 1830; the above contains the Preface to the 2nd ed. of 1834. Pp 95–107 comprise Appendix of poems by John MacKay, "Am Pìobaire Dall", Ross's grand-father.

—— [*Orain Ghaidhealach.*] Edinburgh, 1937.
Orain Ghaidhealach. Le Uilleam Ross. Air an cruinneachadh ri chéile le Iain Mac-Choinnich. Inbhir-Iùgh.
Gaelic Songs. By William Ross. Collected by John MacKenzie, Inver-Ewe. New edition revised, with metrical translation, memoir, glossary, and notes, by George Calder, B.D., D.Litt., D.D., sometime lecturer in Celtic in the University of Glasgow. Oliver and Boyd; Edinburgh: Tweeddale Court; London: 33 Paternoster Row, E.C. 1937.
xxxii, 252 p. 210 mm. AU, BM, GU, Mit., etc.

[*Safety, Certainty and Enjoyment.*] See Tearuinteachd, Cinnte agus Aoibhneas.

Sailm Dhaibhidh. See Bible. [*Psalms.*]

Sailm Dhaibhidh. See Church of Scotland. *Liturgy and Ritual.* [Sailm Dhaibhidh.]

[*St. Columba Church Hymnary.*] Glasgow, 1906.
Leabhar Laoidhean Eaglais Chaluim Chille an Glaschu. Eadar-theangaichte o'n Bheurla. [Illus.: Church of Scotland Crest.] Glasgow: printed for St. Columba Parish Church by Archibald Sinclair, Celtic Press. 1906.
xvi, [107] p. 170 mm. FC Mit. PC.
Contains 100 hymns, all translated from English; 3 p Appendix of "Anthems".

St. Columba Collection of Gaelic Songs, The. See A' Choisir Chiuil.

School Magazines.
   Bellahouston Academy, Glasgow.
      From *c.* 1950 has occasionally contained approx. 1 p of Gaelic.
   Dingwall Academy.
      From *c.* 1930 has occasionally contained approx. 1 p of Gaelic.
   Lionel J. S. School, Lewis. [*Taintean.*]
      First printed 1959. Length varies from 20 p to 40 p; approx. half in Gaelic. Illus.
      Printed by the *Stornoway Gazette.*
   Lochaber High School, Fort William. [*Focus.*]
      From *c.* 1960 has contained approx. 2 p of Gaelic per issue. Illus. Known as *Focus*
      from 1961.
   Milburn Secondary School, Inverness.
      From 1968 has contained 1–2 p of Gaelic per issue.
   Nicolson Institute, Stornoway, Lewis. [*Sgathan.*]
      1st ed. 1901; 2nd ed. 1914; eds. in 1914–17, 1928–47, 1950, 1953–54, 1960–.
      Known as "Sgàthan" from 1972. 4–6 p of Gaelic per issue. Printed by Pillans &
      Wilson, Edinburgh (1901), Culross & Son, Coupar Angus (1914–16), The *Stornoway
      Gazette* (1917–).
   Oban High School.
      3–4 p of Gaelic per issue.
   Portree High School, Skye.
      1st ed. *c.* 1937; eds. 1937–41, 190–51, 1965–70. Approx. 6 p of Gaelic per issue.
      Replaced in 1971 by *Skyline*, a "community newspaper" (appearing on average
      every 3 weeks), which contains little Gaelic.
   Portree High School, Skye. See also An Cabairneach.
   Scalpay J. S. School, Harris. [*Boillsgeadh.*]
      First published 1973. Approx. one quarter Gaelic.
   Sir Walter Scott J. S. School, Tarbert, Harris. [*Brochan.*]
      First published 1961. Pagination increases from 16 (1961) to *c.* 50 p; approx. one
      quarter Gaelic.

School of Scottish Studies. [*Gaelic and Scots Folk Tales and Folk Songs and Scottish Music.*]
      Edinburgh, 1960.
   Gaelic and Scots Folk Tales. Gaelic and Scots Folk Songs. Scottish Instrumental
   Music. School of Scottish Studies. University of Edinburgh. 1960.
   52 p. 200 mm. PC.
      Editors: Francis Collinson (Music); Hamish Henderson (Scots Folk Tales and Songs);
      Calum I. MacLean (Gaelic Tales); James Ross (Gaelic Folk Songs). Issued with 3
      long-playing records. Translation of Gaelic material.

School of Scottish Studies. [*Music from the Western Isles.*] Edinburgh, 1971.
   Scottish Tradition. Recorded and documented by the School of Scottish Studies,
   University of Edinburgh.
   2: Music from the Western Isles.
   Produced in August 1971 by Tangent Records.
   [12] p. 290 × 290 mm.
      Issued with LP record of folk songs. Contains texts of 14 Gaelic songs, with English
      translations, and commentary by John MacInnes. Record prepared by a team of
      staff members of the School of Scottish Studies; series editor, Peter Cooke.

School of Scottish Studies. [*The Waulking Songs of Barra.*] Edinburgh, 1973.
   Scottish Tradition. Recorded and documented by the School of Scottish Studies,
   University of Edinburgh.
   3: The Waulking Songs of Barra.

Produced in 1973 by Tangent Records.

12 p.

    Issued with LP record of songs. Contains texts of Gaelic songs, with English translations. Record prepared by a team of staff members of the School of Scottish Studies; series editor, Peter Cooke.

School of Scottish Studies. See Scottish Studies.

Scott, Alexander, 1920– (joint ed.). See MacCaig, Norman. [*Contemporary Scottish Verse.*]

Scott, W. J. Edmondston (ed.). See Celtic Forum.

Scottish Catholic Society of Canada. See Mosgladh.

Scottish Certificate of Education. [*Gaelic Higher Grade.*] Edinburgh, 1967.

    [Illus.] Scottish Certificate of Education Examination Board. Gaelic: Higher Grade – Native Speakers; Higher Grade – Learners. Syllabuses and Specimen Question Papers. Edinburgh. 1967.

20 p. 250 mm. PC.

    See also Senior Leaving Certificate: Gaelic.

Scottish Certificate of Education. [*Paipearan Deuchainn Gaidhlig.*] Inverness, 1974.

    Teisteanas an Fhoghluim an Alba. Pàipearan Deuchainn Gàidhlig. Ard Ire agus Ire Chumanta. Luchd Fileanta agus Luchd Ionnsachaidh. Air fhoillseachadh an 1974 leis A' Chomunn Ghàidhealach. Clò-bhuailte le John G. Eccles, Inbhirnis.

    Scottish Certificate of Education. Examination Papers. Gaelic. Ordinary and Higher Grades. Native Speakers and Learners. Published by An Comunn Gàidhealach. 1974. Printed by John G. Eccles, Inverness.

[8], 156 p. 210 mm.

    Prepared for the press by Lachlan Dick.

Scottish Certificate of Education. See also Senior Leaving Certificate: Gaelic.

Scottish Council for Research in Education – Committee on Bilingualism. See Aithris is Oideas.

Scottish Gaelic as a Specific Subject. Glasgow, 1907.

    Scottish Gaelic as a specific subject. Stage 1. Compiled by a Committee of The Highland Association. [Quotation.] Third edition. Published for The Highland Association by Archibald Sinclair, 47 Waterloo Street, Glasgow. Norman MacLeod, Edinburgh. Hugh MacDonald, Esplanade, Oban. 1907.

128 p. 190 mm. EPL, GU:CL, Mit.

    Reprint of the 1st ed. of 1893. Printed Sinclair, Glasgow.

Scottish Gaelic Studies. Aberdeen, 1926–.

    Scottish Gaelic Studies. Issued from the Celtic Department of the University of Aberdeen. Edited by John MacDonald, M.A. [Illus.] Vol. I. Humphrey Milford, Oxford University Press: London, Edinburgh, Glasgow. 1926.

    ... Vol. V. B. H. Blackwell Ltd., Oxford. 1942.

    Scottish Gaelic Studies. Issued from the Celtic Department of the University of Aberdeen. Edited by Derick S. Thomson. [Illus.] Vol. IX. University of Aberdeen. 1961.

    Scottish Gaelic Studies. Edited by Derick S. Thomson. [Illus.] Vol. XI. University of Aberdeen. 1966.

    [Frequency] Irregular. Volumes in: 1926, 1927, 1931, 1935, 1942, 1949, 1953, 1958, 1961, 1966.

    Each vol. is issued in two parts. The interval between the appearance of the parts varies between 7 months (Vol. I, 1926) and 4 years (Vol. V, 1939 and 1942), the commonest interval being between 1 and 2 years. The Vol. title page sometimes bears the date of the 2nd part (e.g. Vol. VI), sometimes of the 1st part (e.g. Vol. XI, dated 1966, Part 2 of which appeared in 1968).

[Collation] Average: 250 p per vol. (range: 211–273 p). 220 mm.
[Locations] AU, EU, GU.
[Editors] John MacDonald (1926–58), Derick S. Thomson (1961–7).
[Printers] The University Press, Aberdeen (1926–7); R. Carruthers, The *Courier* Office, Inverness (1929–).
[Contents] A scholarly periodical.

Scottish Gaelic Texts. [Publications of the Scottish Gaelic Texts Society, an organisation set up in 1934 to encourage publication of authoritative editions of important Gaelic literary texts.] See:
Calvin, John. [*Catechismus Ecclesiae Genevensis.*]
Church of Scotland. *Liturgy and Ritual.* [Book of Common Order.]
Lamont, Donald. [*Prose Writings.*]
MacCodrom, John. [*Songs.*]
MacDonald, John, Seventeenth Century poet. [*Orain Iain Luim.*]
MacDonald, Sileas. [*Bardachd Shilis na Ceapaich.*]
MacGregor, James, Dean of Lismore. [*Heroic Poetry from the Book of the Dean of Lismore.*]
MacGregor, James, Dean of Lismore. [*Scottish verse from the Book of the Dean of Lismore.*]
MacIntyre, Donald. [*Sporan Dhomhnaill.*]
MacIntyre, Duncan. [*Songs.*]
MacKinnon, Donald. [*Prose Writings.*]
MacLeod, Mary, Seventeenth Century poetess. [*Orain agus Luinneagan Gaidhlig.*]
Morison, Roderick, "An Clàrsair Dall." [*An Clarsair Dall: Orain.*]

Scottish Studies. Edinburgh, 1957–.
Scottish Studies. Editor: J. Wrexford Watson. Advisory Board: K. H. Jackson, K. L. Little, A. McIntosh, S. Piggott, S. T. M. Newman, W. L. Renwick. Volume 1. Published for the School of Scottish Studies, University of Edinburgh, by Oliver and Boyd Ltd., Edinburgh. 1957.
Scottish Studies. The Journal of the School of Scottish Studies, University of Edinburgh. Director: B. R. S. Megaw. Editor: J. Wrexford Watson. Assistant Editors: W. F. H. Nicolaisen, S. F. Sanderson. Volume 2. 1958. Oliver and Boyd Ltd., Edinburgh.
. . . 11. 1967. Oliver & Boyd Ltd., for the School of Scottish Studies, University of Edinburgh.
. . . 12. 1968. School of Scottish Studies, University of Edinburgh.
[Continuing]
   [Frequency] Annual; vols. issued in 2 parts.
   [Collation] Average: 250 p plus plates per vol.; illus. 230 mm (vols. 1–10); 250 mm (Vols. 11–).
   [Location] AU, EU, GU.
   [Editors] J. Wrexford Watson (1957–63), B. R. S. Megaw (1964–9), John Mac-Queen (1969–). Various Assistant Editors.
   [Printers] Oliver & Boyd, Edinburgh (1957–66); The University Press, Aberdeen (1967–).
   [Contents] Chiefly products of research conducted by the members of staff of the School of Scottish Studies. *c.* 12 p of Gaelic per vol.

Scottish Television. See [*Beagan Gaidhlig.*]

Scupoli, Lorenzo, 1530–1610. [*Combattimento Spirituale.*] Perth, 1908.
   An Cath Spioradail. Le Lorentzo Scupoli. Eadar-theangaichte leis an Athair Eòghan Mac Eachainn nach maireann. Clo-bhualadh ùr fo laimh Ruairidh Arascainn is Mhairr. [Illus.] Clò-chlar Caitliceach na h-Alba. Peairt, Albainn. 1908.
   xii, 187 p. 150 mm. Mit., GU:CL.
      1st ed. 1835. Italian original first published 1660; first English edition 1742.

Sea League. [*Run agus Beachd Comunn Iasgairean na Mara.*] Stornoway, n.d.
What the Sea League stands for. Rùn agus beachd Comunn Iasgairean na Mara.
Printed at *Gazette* Office, Stornoway.
3 p. 210 mm. PC.

Sealg Bheinn-Eidir. See Fionn Ann an Tigh a' Bhlair Bhuidhe.

Seann, Seann Sgeul, An. See Clerk, Archibald. [*The Old, Old Story.*]

Seirbhis a' Chruin. Glasgow, 1943.
Seirbhis a' Chruin. [Illus.] Ar tìr 's ar teanga; lean gu dlùth ri cliù do shinnsir; guma
fada beò ar Rìgh. An Comunn Gaidhealach, 131 Sràid Iar Regent. Glaschu, C.2.
1943.
176 p. 140 mm. NLS, PC.
A selection of articles from "An Gaidheal", the official magazine of An Comunn
Gaidhealach. Foreword by Malcolm MacLeod, President of An Comunn Gaidhealach. Distributed to soldiers. Gaelic translation of "God Save the King" on
inside back cover. Printed Learmonth, Stirling. Formed part, with "Airgiod an
Rìgh" and leaflets, of "Am Feachd Gaidhealach" (1944).

Seirbhis a' Chruin. See also Am Feachd Gaidhealach.

Senior Leaving Certificate. [*Gaelic.*] Stirling, [Fore. 1946].
Senior Leaving Certificate. Examination Papers. Gaelic. Higher and Lower Grades.
A. Learmonth & Son, Printers, 9 King Street, Stirling.
47 p. 250 mm. PC.
Foreword signed, "A. J. Bedford, Edinburgh, Sept. 1946".

Senior Leaving Certificate. See also Scottish Certificate of Education.

Seolaidhean mu Shlainte. Edinburgh, [Fore. 1907].
Seòlaidhean mu Shlàinte air son feum mhàthraichean anns a' Ghaidhealtachd. An
roimh-ràdh air a sgrìobhadh leis An Urramach Iain S. MacPhàil. Edinburgh: The
Religious Tract and Book Society of Scotland, 99 George Street.
16 p. 150 mm. PC.
Foreword dated 1907. Printed Turnbull and Spears, Edinburgh.

Seonaid. Stornoway, 1929–31.
Keep this – it is valuable. 1st October, 1929. Seònaid.
Printed by Aberdeen Journals, Ltd., Broad Street, Aberdeen, for The Western Isles
Unionist Association.
Keep this – it is valuable. 1st January, 1930. Seònaid.
Printed by Aberdeen Journals, Ltd., Broad Street, Aberdeen, for The Western Isles
Unionist Association.
Keep this – it is valuable. 31st January, 1931. Seònaid.
Printed by Duncan Grant, 47 High Street, Inverness, and published by John Mac-
Donald, 3 Point Street, Stornoway.
8 p each. 230 × 210 mm. PC.
Election leaflets issued on behalf of Iain M. Moffat-Pender; contain polemical
dialogues and news items.

Seoras Gallda. See Marjoribanks, George.

Sgeulachdan Mhic-an-Teosain. See Raspe, R. E. [*The Adventures of Baron Munch-
Hausen.*]

Sgeulaiche, An. Perth, 1909–11.
A' phrìs sè sgillinn. Price sixpence net. An Sgeulaiche. Leabhar I. An naodhamh
mios, 1909. Aireamh 1. September, 1909.

[Imprint] An Sgeulaiche. Clò-bhuailte le Milne, Tannahill is Methven, Crois an Eich, Peairt, agus air a chur am mach, as leath na feadhnach d'am buin e, le Alasdair Niall Mac Neacail, 5 Victoria Terrace, Dun-fris.

... Leabhar II. An t-Earrach, 1910. Aireamh 1. Publishers: Alexander MacLaren and Son, 360 Argyle Street, Glasgow. Spring, 1910.
[Imprint] Clò-bhuailte le Milne, Tannahill is Methven, Crois an Eich, Peairt.
... Leabhar III. An Samhradh, 1911. Aireamh 2. ... [Last number seen.]
   [Frequency] Monthly up to Vol. I.5, January 1910; quarterly thereafter.
   [Pagination] 496 p in Vol. I (5 issues); 402 p in Vol. II (4 issues); 202 p in Vol. III (2 issues).
   [Size] 230 mm.
   [Locations] AU, BM, GU:CL, Mit.
   [Editor] Owned by the Hon. Roderick Erskine of Mar. Edited by Alexander Nicolson.
   [Contents] Stories and essays.

Sgeulaiche, An. See Leabhraichean nan Ceilidh. [A numbered series of offprints, chiefly from "Guth na Bliadhna" and "An Sgeulaiche".]

Sgoil Bhaltois. See Domhnull cam Macdhughaill.

[*Sguaban a Achaidhean nan Aithrichean.*] Edinburgh, 1946.
   Cogadh na Saorsa. Sguaban a Achaidhean nan Aithrichean. [Illus.] "Dhia beannaich ar Rìgh". Church of Scotland. Free Church of Scotland. 1946.
   120 p. 140 mm. PC.
      Compiled by Donald MacKinnon, of Kennoway. Printed Learmonth, Stirling. One of the series of religious booklets issued to soldiers in the Second World War.

Shakespeare, William, 1564–1616. [*Julius Caesar.*] Edinburgh, 1911.
   Julius Caesar. Dàn-cluiche Shacspeair. Eadar-theangaichte le U. M. MacGillemhoire. Sgeul mu am a dh'fhalbh. Dun-éideann: Iain Grannd, 31 George IV Bridge. 1911.
   [8], 120 p. 190 mm. AU, BM, Mit., NLS.
      Printed Oliver and Boyd, Edinburgh. English original first published 1684.

Shaw, Margaret Fay. [*Folk Songs and Folk Lore of South Uist.*] London, 1955.
   Folk-songs and Folk-lore of South Uist. By Margaret Fay Shaw. [Illus.] Routledge & Kegan Paul Limited, London.
   First published 1955.
   xiv, 290 p, 34 plates. 260 mm. AU, BM, GU, Mit.
      Music in staff. Printed W. Clowes, London.

—— [*Gaelic Folk Songs from South Uist.*] [Budapest], 1956.
   Separatim e libro memoriali cui titulus "Studia Memoriae Belae Bartók Sacra". Margaret Fay Shaw. Gaelic Folksongs from South Uist. [Illus.] 1956.
   [427]–443 p. 240 mm. AU.

—— [*Gaelic Folk Songs from South Uist.*] [Budapest], 1957.
   Separatim e libro memoriali cui titulus "Studia Memoriae Belae Bartók Sacra". Margaret Fay Shaw. Gaelic Folk Songs from South Uist. [Illus.] 1957.
   [417]–433 p. 240 mm. PC.
      Offprints from first two editions of "Studia Memoriae Belae Bartók Sacra", a festschrift edited by B. Rajeczky and L. Vargyzs, published by the Hungarian Academy of Sciences, Budapest. An English edition was published by Boosey and Hawkes, London, in 1959.

—— [*Gaelic Folk Songs from South Uist.*] See also Bartok, Bela. [*Studia Memoriae Belae Bartok Sacra.*]

Shaw, Neil (Gaelic ed.), 1881–1961. See Boulton, Harold. [*Songs of the North.*] Vol. III.

—— (joint comp.). See Cainnt agus Facail Iomchuidh air son Coinnimh.

—— (joint author). See An Solaraiche.

Shorter Catechism. Edinburgh, 1906.
Leabhar Aithghearr nan Ceist. Le Eòin Dòmhnullach, Ministear ann an Sgìre na
Tòisidheachd. Edinburgh: John Grant. 1906.
24 p. 160 mm. NBS.
V.p., 1908, 1914, 1914, 1921, 1924, 1927, 1934, 1939, 1951, n.d.
Ibid.
24 p. 150 mm.
1908 ed. by Grant, Edinburgh; eds. of 1914–51 by A. MacLaren & Son, Glasgow;
latest ed. (undated) by Knox Press, 15 North Bank Street, Edinburgh. Translated
by Dr. John MacDonald.

Sileas na Ceapaich. See MacDonald, Sileas.

Simpson, Evan John. See John, Evan.

Sinclair, A. MacLean, 1840–1924. [*Na Baird Leathanach.*] Vol. II. Charlottetown,
1900.
Na Bàird Leathanach: The MacLean Bards. By the Rev. A. MacLean Sinclair. Vol. II.
Charlottetown: Haszard & Moore. 1900.
[2], 176 p, [1] "Corrigenda". 160 mm. AU, GU, Mit.
Vol. I, 1898.

—— [*Clarsach na Coille.*] Glasgow, 1928.
The MacLean Songster. Clàrsach na Coille. A collection of Gaelic poetry by Rev. A.
MacLean Sinclair, LL.D., Hopewell, Nova Scotia. Revised and edited by Hector
MacDougall. [Quotation.] Glasgow: Alex. MacLaren & Songs, 360–362 Argyle
Street, C.2.
First edition 1881. Second edition (revised) 1928.
xxiv, 292 p; plate. 190 mm. BM, EPL, GU:CL, NLS.
Pp. 1–165 contain poems by John MacLean, "Am Bàrd MacGilleathain". Notes by
MacDougall, pp 263–92.

—— [*Comh-Chruinneachadh Ghlinn'-a-Bhaird.*] Charlottetown, 1901.
Comh-chruinneachadh Ghlinn'-a-Bhàird: The Glenbard Collection of Gaelic Poetry.
By the Rev. A. MacLean Sinclair. (Abridged.) [Illus.] Charlottetown, P. E. Island:
Haszard & Moore. 1901.
[4], 1–24, [161]–216, [265]–386 p. 150 mm. PC.
1st ed. 1890.

—— [*Filidh na Coille.*] Charlottetown, 1901.
Filidh na Coille: Dàin agus Orain leis a bhàrd Mac-Gilleain agus le feadhainn eile. Air a
dheanamh deas leis an Urr. A. Mac-Gilleain Sinclair. [Quotation.] Charlottetown,
Prince Edward Island: The Examiner Publishing Company. 1901.
197 p. 160 mm. AU, EU, Mit.
Poems of John MacLean, pp 17–130.

—— [*Filidh na Coille.*] Sydney, C.B., 1902.
Filidh na Coille.
Not seen. Reference from *Clare*; probably an error.

—— [*The Gaelic Bards*, 1825–1875.] Sydney, C.B., 1904.
The Gaelic Bards, from 1825 to 1875. By the Rev. A. MacLean Sinclair. Sydney,
C.B.: Mac-Talla Publishing Co. Ltd. 1904.
iv, 143 p. 160 mm. PC.
The fourth volume in the series. Not in *TS-G*.

—— [*MacTalla nan Tur.*] Sydney, C.B., 1901.
Mactalla nan Tùr. By the Rev. A. MacLean Sinclair. Sydney, C.B.: Mac-Talla
Publishing Co., Ltd. 1901.
vi, 126 p. 160 mm. EU, SS.
  Anthology of poetry.

—— (ed.). See Bardachd na Feinne.

—— (ed.). See MacKinnon, Alexander. [*Dain agus Orain.*]

Sinclair, Alexander (tr.). See McCheyne, R. M. [*Beatha agus Searmoinean.*]

—— (tr.). See McCheyne, R. M. [*Guth mo Ghraidh.*]

Sinclair, Donald, 1885–1932. [*Crois Tara.*] Glasgow, n.d.
  Crois Tàra. Dealbh-chluich le D.M.N.C. [Illus.] Aon tasdan. Glasgow: Alexander
MacLaren & Sons, 360–362 Argyle Street.
  [311]–362 p. 210 mm. PC.
      First advertised 1929. An offprint from "Guth na Bliadhna", X.3, 1914. In the
  same format as "Leabhraichean nan Céilidh", a numbered series of offprints from
  "Guth na Bliadhna" and "An Sgeulaiche".

—— [*Domhnull nan Trioblaid.*] [*c.* 1914?]
Dòmhnull nan Trioblaid.
  [151]–195 p. 210 mm.
      Not seen. One of a number of Gaelic plays advertised by Alex. MacLaren & Son in
  "An Deo-Gréine", X.3–6 (Dec., 1914–March 1915). First published "Guth na
  Bliadhna", IX.2, 1912, from which the above collation is taken: probably an offprint.
  See detailed note under Sinclair's "Suiridhe Raoghail Mhaoil".

—— [*Domhnull nan Trioblaid.*] Glasgow, [*c.* 1929.]
Dòmhnull nan Trioblaid.
      Not seen. Advertised by MacLaren's in 1929; advertised again in MacLaren's
  Catalogue of 1932, with quotation from a review in the *Northern Chronicle*.

—— [*Domhnull nan Trioblaid.*] Glasgow, 1936.
Dòmhnull nan Trioblaid. Dealbh-chluich le Dòmhnull Mac-na-Ceàrdadh. [Illus.]
Glascho: Alasdair Mac Labhruinn 's a Mhic, 268 Sràid Earraghaidheal, C.2.
Reprinted 1936.
  [2], 45 p. 190 mm. BM, GU:CL, Mit., PC.

—— [*Fearann a Shinnsear.*] Glasgow, n.d.
Fearann a Shinnsear. Dealbhchluich le D.M.N.C. [Illus.] Glascho: Alasdair Mac
Labhruinn 's a Mhic, 360–362 Sràid Earraghaidheal, C.2.
  [301]–340 p. 230 × 150 mm. PC.
      c. 1930. In the same format as Leabhraichean nan Ceilidh. Offprint from "Guth na
  Bliadhna", X.3, 1913.

—— [*Long nan Og.*] Edinburgh, 1927.
Long nan Og. Dealbh-chluich air son chloinne le Dòmhnull Mac-na-Ceàrdadh.
[Illus.] Comunn Litreachais na h-Alba. Dunéideann. 1927.
  290 p; plate. 220 mm. EPL, PC.

—— [*A' Mhor-Roinn agus am Fearann.*] Glasgow, n.d.
The Ceilidh Books. Leabhraichean nan Céilidh. Aireamh 18. A' Mhòr-roinn agus
am Fearann. Le Dòmhnull Mac-na-Ceàrdadh. [Illus.] A' phrìs, trì sgillinnean. 3d.
Alasdair Mac Labhruinn agus a Mhic, 360–362 Sràid Earraghaidheal, Glascho.
  [421]–438 p. 210 mm. PC.
      Reprinted from "Guth na Bliadhna", XI.4, Winter 1914.

—— [*Suiridhe Raoghail Mhaoil.*] [?]
Suiridhe Raoghail Mhaoil.
[437]–462 p. 200 mm.

> Not seen. First appeared in "Guth na Bliadhna", IX.4, 1912, from which the collation was derived: probably an offprint.
> (General Note.) In "An Deo-Greine", X.3–6 (December 1914 to March 1915), Alex. MacLaren & Sons issued the following notice: "Gaelic Plays. Why not get up a Gaelic Play to pass the long winter or in aid of Red Cross or Belgian Relief Funds? We can supply the following: 'Crois-Tara' [number of characters and price follows], 'Fearann a Shinnsir', 'Dòmhnull nan Trioblaid', 'Suiridhe Raoghail Mhaoil', 'Reiteach Móraig', 'An Gaol a bheir buaidh', 'Am Mosgladh Mór', 'Dùsgadh na Feinne', 'An Sgoil Bheag', 'An Reiteachadh Rathail'." Of these ten plays, 4 have been seen: "Reiteach Móraig" (Sinclair: 1911), "An Gaol a bheir buaidh" (Sinclair: 1912), "Dùsgadh na Féinne" (Parlane: 1908), "An Sgoil Bheag" (1910). All of these are paginated from p. 1, i.e. are not offprints. 2 of the 4 – "Reiteach Móraig" (MacLaren: 1922) and "An Sgoil Bheag" (MacLaren: 1927) – were republished later, and, significantly, reference is made in these to the earlier editions of 1911 and 1910, respectively. No pre-1914 editions of the remaining 6 plays have been seen, except that they all had appeared in periodicals before 1914. All 6 were published by MacLaren later: "Crois Tara" (*c.* 1930: offprint), "Fearann a Shinnsear" (*c.* 1930: offprint), "Dòmhnull nan Trioblaid" (*c.* 1929 and 1936), "Suiridhe Raoghail Mhaoil" (1929: offprint), "Am Mosgladh Mór" (*c.* 1926: as part of a series of Mod prize plays), "An Reiteachadh Rathail" (1929: offprint). In none of these is a pre-1914 edition of the play referred to: this gives rise to the suspicion that no earlier editions were in fact produced, presumably because of the War. *The English Catalogue of Books*, Vol. IX, Jan. 1911–Dec. 1915 and BM record none of these plays (but this is not conclusive evidence). It may be the periodicals containing these plays which are referred to in the advertisement. The price (*c.* 7d) of the plays is ambiguous evidence in this context: copies of "An Sgeulaiche" cost 6d and of "Guth na Bliadhna" 1/– but it is significant that the only play different from the rest is "An Reiteachadh Rathail", at 2/9, which also was the only one published in a book (Oiteagan o'n Iar was advertised in 1911 at 2/6 plus 6d postage).

—— [*Suiridhe Raoghail Mhaoil.*] Glasgow, 1929.
Dealbh-Chluich Ghàidhlig. Suiridhe Raoghail Mhaoil. Le Dòmhnull Mac-na-Ceàrdadh. Bald Ronald's Courtship. A Humorous Gaelic Sketch by Donald Sinclair. Glascho: Alasdair Mac Labhruinn 's a Mhic, 360–362 Sràid Earraghaidheal, C.2. 1929. 1/–.
[2], [437]–462 p. 200 m. BM, NLS, PC.

Sinton, Thomas, 1855–1923. [*The Poetry of Badenoch.*] Inverness, 1906.
The Poetry of Badenoch. Collected and edited, with translations, introductions and notes, by The Rev. Thomas Sinton, Minister of Dores. [Quotations.] Inverness: The Northern Counties Publishing Company, Ltd. 1906.
xxxvii, 1 "Errata", 576 p. 260 mm. AU, Mit., NLS.

Sinton, Thomas (ed.). See MacPherson, Mary. [*Laoidhean Bean Torra Dhamh.*]

Sir Edward Scott J.S. School, Tarbert. See School Magazines.

Siubhal air Falbh Impireachd. See Henderson, Angus. [*Ceard agus Cainnt.*]

Skye, The: One Hundred Years. See Glasgow Skye Association. [*The Skye: One Hundred Years.*]

Smeorach na Cnoc 's nan Gleann. See MacDougall, Hector.

Smith, Gregor Ian. [*Folktales of the Highlands.*] London, 1953.
Folktales of the Highlands. Gregor Ian Smith. Drawings by the author. Thomas
Nelson & Sons Ltd., London and Edinburgh.
First published 1953.
viii, 136 p. 170 mm. BM, Mit., NLS.
Contains rhymes in Gaelic. Another ed. in the same year, in "The Teaching of
English Series" (No. 255), with [137]–165 p of "notes" and "questions". Also a
Russian ed. in 1959.

Smith, Iain C., 1928–. [*Biobuill is Sanasan-Reice.*] Glasgow, 1965.
Bìobuill is Sanasan-reice. Iain Mac a' Ghobhainn. Gairm. Glaschu. 1965.
Clò-bhualaidhean Gairm, Leabhar 3.
80 p. 220 mm.
Printed A. Learmonth, Stirling.

—— [*Burn is Aran.*] Glasgow, 1960.
Clò-bhualaidhean Gairm, Leabhar 2. Bùrn is Aran. Le Iain Mac a' Ghobhainn.
Gairm: 227 Bath Street, Glaschu, C.2. 1960.
71 p. 230 mm. AU, GU, NLS.
Printed *The Stornoway Gazette*, Stornoway. Translation into Welsh ("Dŵr a Bara")
by Donald G. Howells published 1970.

—— [*A' Chuirt.*] Glasgow, [Fore. 1966].
Dealbh-chluich an Gàidhlig. A' Chùirt. Le Iain Mac a' Ghobhainn. [Illus.] Air a
dheasachadh le Dòmhnall MacThomais. An Comunn Gaidhealach.
24 p. 190 mm.
Printed Learmonth, Stirling.

—— [*An Coileach.*] Glasgow, [Fore. 1966].
Dealbh-chluich an Gàidhlig. An Coileach. Le Iain Mac a' Ghobhainn. [Illus.] Air
a dheasachadh le Dòmhnall MacThomais. An Comunn Gaidhealach.
21 p. 190 mm.
Printed Learmonth, Stirling.

—— [*An Dubh is an Gorm.*] Aberdeen, 1963.
An Dubh is an Gorm. Iain Mac a' Ghobhainn. Oilthigh Obair-Dheadhain. 1963.
Leabhraichean ùra Gàidhlig Oilthigh Obair-Dheadhain (fo stiùireadh Ruairidh Mhic-
Thómais), Aireamh 2. An Dubh is an Gorm. Le Iain Mac a' Ghobhainn.
[8], 106 p. 190 mm.
Printed Learmonth, Stirling.

—— [*An Dubh is an Gorm.*] Glasgow, 1969.
An Dubh is an Gorm. Iain Mac a' Ghobhainn. Oilthigh Ghlaschu. 1969.
Leabhraichean ùra Gàidhlig Oilthigh Ghlaschu (fo stiùireadh Ruairidh MhicThomais),
Aireamh 2. An Dubh is an Gorm. Le Iain Mac a' Ghobhainn.
[7], 106 p. 190 mm.
Printed Learmonth Stirling.

—— [*Iain am Measg nan Reultan.*] Glasgow, 1970.
Iain am measg nan Reultan. Le Iain Mac a' Ghobhainn. Dealbhan le Linda Nic-
Eoghainn agus Donnchadh MacAsgaill. Gairm. Glaschu. 1970.
Clò-bhualaidhean Gairm, Leabhar 18.
[4], 74 p; illus. 180 mm.
Printed Eccleslitho.

—— [*Maighstirean is Ministearan.*] Inverness, [*c.* 1970].
Maighstirean is Ministearan. Le Iain C. Mac a' Ghobhainn. © Club Leabhar 1970.
Air a chlò-bhualadh le Eccles Printers Inbhirnis.
[4], 92 p. 190 mm.

Smith, Dr. John, Minister of Campbeltown, 1747–1807. [*Urnuighean air son Theagh-laichean.*] Glasgow, 1942.
Urnuighean air son Theaghlaichean. Gaelic Prayers for Family Worship. By John Smith, D.D., minister of the Gospel, Campbeltown. Selected by the late Norman MacLeod, D.D., minister of St. Columba Church, Glasgow. Edited by Hector Mac-Dougall. Glasgow: Alexander MacLaren & Sons, 268 Argyle Street, C.2. 1942.
64 p. 190 mm. PC.
1st ed. 1808 (156 p).

—— See Bible. [*Psalms.*]

Smith, John, Missionary. [*Dain Spioradail.*] Stornoway, n.d.
Dàin Spioradail. Le Iain Smith, Missionaridh nach maireann.
36 p. 210 mm. PC.
Printed *Stornoway Gazette*, Stornoway.

Smith, John, of Bragar. [*Anns an Tighearna Iosa Criosd tha ar n-Earbsa.*] Glasgow, n.d.
Anns an Tighearna Iosa Criosd tha ar n-Earbsa. [Quotation.] Iain Beag Fhionnlaigh, Bràgair, Leodhas. Glascho: Alasdair MacLabhruinn agus a Mhic, 268 Sràid Earrag-haidheal, C.2.
35 p. 190 mm. PC.
Mostly hymns. Reviewed 1950. "Iain Beag Fhionnlaigh" is the patronymic of John Smith, Bragar, Lewis.

Smith, John A., 1911– (joint ed.). See Aithris is Oideas.

Smith, Kenneth J., 1918–. [*Brigh mo Sheanchais.*] Stornoway, n.d.
Brìgh mo Sheanchais. Le Coinneach Iain Mac a' Ghobhainn.
Air a chlò-bhualadh agus air a chur a mach le Paipear-Naigheachd Steòrnabhaigh, 10 Sràid Fhrangain, Steòrnabhaigh, Eilean Leodhais.
39 p. 230 mm.
1970.

Solaraiche, An. Glasgow, 1918.
An Solaraiche. Gaelic Essays. I. Aonghas Mac Eanruig; Niall Ros; Niall Mac Gille Sheathanaich; Dòmhnall I. Mac Leòid. An Comunn Gaidhealach, 108 Hope Street, Glasgow. 1918.
[4], 113 p. 190 mm. AU, GU:CL, etc.
3 essays from "An Ròsarnach", 1 from "An Deò-Gréine".

Solus Iuil. Sydney, C.B., 1925–27.
An Solus Iùil. "Is ann ad sholus dealrach glan, chì sinne solus iùil." Leabh. 1. Sidni, C.B. An Lùnasdal, 1925. Air. 1.
... Leabh. 1. Sidni, C.B. An Lùnasdal, 1925. Air. 12. [Last number.]
[Frequency] Bi-monthly.
[Collation] 96 p (total). 230 mm.
[Editor] Jonathan G. MacKinnon.
[Contents] Gaelic and English.

Solus Lathail, [An Ceud Earrann]. Edinburgh, 1943.
Cogadh na Saorsa. Solus Lathail. [Illus.] Printed by Paul & Matthew, Dundee, for The Church of Scotland, The Free Church of Scotland. 1943.
96 p. 140 mm. PC.
Daily Bible readings: Jan. 1 to March 31.

Solus Lathail, An Dara Earrann. Edinburgh, 1943.
Cogadh na Saorsa. Solus Lathail. An Dara Earrann. [Illus.] By kind permission of Messrs Samuel Bagster & Sons, Ltd.

Printed by Paul & Matthew, Dundee, for The Church of Scotland, The Free Church of Scotland. 1943.
96 p. 140 mm. PC.
April 1–June 30.

Solus Lathail, an Treas Earrann. Edinburgh, 1943.
. . . An Treas Earrann. . . .
96 p. 140 mm. PC.
July 1–Sept. 30.

Solus Lathail: An Ceathramh Earrann. Edinburgh, 1943.
. . . An Ceathramh Earrann. . . .
96 p. 140 mm. PC.
Oct. 1–Dec. 31.

Solus Lathail: A' Chuibhrionn Fheasgair, an Ceud Earrann. Edinburgh, 1943.
Cogadh na Saorsa. Solus Lathail. A' Chuibhrionn Fheasgair. An ceud earrann. [Illus.] "Dhia beannaich ar Rìgh". Church of Scotland; Free Church of Scotland. 1943.
By kind permission of Messrs Samuel Bagster & Sons Ltd. Printed by A. Learmonth & Son, 9 King Street, Stirling.
95 p. 140 mm. PC.
Daily Bible readings, as above.

Solus Lathail: A' Chuibhrionn Fheasgair, an Dara Earrann. Edinburgh, 1944.
. . . An dara earrann . . . 1944.
96 p. 140 mm. PC.

Solus Lathail: A' Chuibhrionn Fheasgair, an Treas Earrann. Edinburgh, 1944.
. . . An treas earrann. . . .
100 p. 140 mm. PC.

Solus Lathail: A' Chuibhrionn Fheasgair, an Ceathramh Earrann. Edinburgh, 1944.
. . . An ceathramh earrann. . . .
100 p. 140 mm. PC.
Bible readings. "Cogadh na Saorsa" was a series of religious publications and books published for distribution to soldiers in the Second World War.

Somerville, Arthur (joint ed.). See Boulton, Harold. [*Our National Songs.*] Volume II and Volume III.

Songs for Choral Competition. See An Comunn Gaidhealach. [*National Mod.*] Songs for Choral Competitions.

Sop as Gach Seid. Glasgow, [1907].
"Sop as gach seid". ("A straw from every sheaf.") A collection of favourite quotations in Gaelic, English and other languages, from prose and poetry. "A man's selection from books confesses his selection from life." Cover design by Finlay MacKinnon. Publisher: Archibald Sinclair, "Celtic Press", 47 Waterloo Street, Glasgow.
83 p. 260 mm. NLS.
Editorial note by Winifred Parker and Mabel C. Forbes. A fund-raiser for the An Comunn Gaidhealach Feill of 1907.

Spurgeon, C. H., 1834–92. [*Deagh Mhisneachd do na Diobarraich.*] Edinburgh, n.d.
Cogadh mór na h-Eòrpa. Deagh Mhisneachd do na Dìobarraich. C. H. Spurgeon. [Illus.] Printed by Oliver and Boyd, Edinburgh, for The Church of Scotland, The United Free Church of Scotland, and The Free Church of Scotland.
42 p. 140 p. NLS.
One of a series issued for distribution to First World War soldiers.

Sradag. Glasgow, 1960–62.
   Sradag. Aireamh 1. An t-Sultuin, 1960. A' phrìs, 1/–.
   . . . Aireamh 8. An t-Og-mhios, 1962. [Last number.]
      [Frequency] Quarterly.
      [Collation] 4p per no.; col. illus. 420 × 340 mm.
      [Publisher] An Comunn Gaidhealach; printed by Learmonth, Stirling.
      [Editor] Roderick MacKinnon.
      [Contents] Children's comic.

Sruth. Inverness/Stornoway, 1967–.
   Sruth. Scotland's Bi-lingual Newspaper. Newspaper of current events in the High-
   lands, the Islands and in Scotland. Published by An Comunn Gaidhealach – The
   Highland Association. Di-ardaoin, 6 Giblean 1967. Thursday, 6th April 1967.
   No. 1. 6d.
   . . . Incorporating the Lochaber Diary. Thursday, 10 August 1967. Di-ardaoin 10 An
   Lùnasdal 1967. No. 10.
   [Reference to the "Lochaber Diary" dropped, January 25, 1968.]
   . . . Di-ardaoin, 24amh latha de'n An Dudhlachd, 1970. Thursday, 24th December,
   1970. No. 98.
   Sruth [Continued as: fortnightly half-page in *The Stornoway Gazette*, Jan. 7th–Dec.
   1971; as 1-page supplement to *The Stornoway Gazette*, Jan. 1972–.]
      [Frequency] Fortnightly, 1967–1; monthly, 1972–.
      [Pagination] 8 p, No. 1–9 (July 27th 1967); 12 p, 10–90 (Sept. 3rd 1970); 8 p,
      91–98 (Dec. 24th 1970); half-page (300 × 480 mm), 1970–1; 1 p (600 × 480 mm),
      1972–. Illus.
      [Size] 350 mm, 1967–70.
      [Editors] Frank Thomson & Duncan MacQuarrie (Gaelic), 1967–71; John M.
      Morrison and Donald J. MacIver, May 1971–.
      [Note] Published by the Inverness Office of An Comunn Gaidhealach initially
      (printed by *The Highland Herald*, Inverness). In Gaelic and English. Replaced
      "An Gaidheal" as the official magazine of An Comunn Gaidhealach.

Sruth. See also An Gaidheal.

Steele, John (joint ed.). See Dick, Lachlan. [*Bardachd gu a Mineachadh.*]

Stevenson, R. L., 1850–94. [*Kidnapped.*] Stornoway, n.d.
   Daibhidh Balfour. Air a tharruing o'n sgeulachd *Kidnapped* le R. L. Stevenson. Air a
   réiteachadh agus air eadar-theangachadh le Ruairidh Moireasdan.
   Air a chlò-bhualadh agus air a chur am mach le: Paipear-Naigheachd Steòrnabhaigh,
   10 Sràid Fhrangain, Steòrnabhagh.
   48 p; illus. 140 mm.
      In comic strip format. Also another version (probably later edition) in different size
      (180 mm) and layout. English original first published 1886.

—— [*Treasure Island.*] Stornoway, n.d.
   Eilean an Ionmhais. Air a tharruing o'n sgeulachd *Treasure Island* le Raibeart L.
   Stevenson. Air a réiteachadh is air eadar-theangachadh le Ruairidh Moireasdan.
   Air a chlò-bhualadh agus air a chur a mach le: Paipear-Naigheachd Steòrnabhaigh, 10
   Sràid Fhrangain, Steòrnabhagh.
   64 p. 200 mm.
      In comic strip format. Also another version (probably a later edition) in different
      size (180 mm) and layout. English original first published 1883.

Stewart, Alexander, 1764–1821. [*Elements of Gaelic Grammar.*] Edinburgh, 1901.
   Elements of Gaelic Grammar in four parts. I. Of Pronunciation and Orthography.
   II. Of the Parts of Speech. III. Of Syntax. IV. Of Derivation and Composition. By
   Alexander Stewart, Minister of the Gospel at Dingwall, Honorary Member of the

Highland Society of Scotland. Royal Celtic Society Edition. Fifth edition revised.
With preface by the Rev. Dr. M'Lauchlan. Edinburgh: John Grant, 31 George IV
Bridge. 1901.
xvi, 184 p. 170 mm. EPL, Mit.
  Printed Oliver and Boyd. 1st ed. 1801; Preface by Thos. M'Lauchlan dated 1876.
  Formed the basis for H. Cameron Gillies' "The Elements of Gaelic Grammar"
  (1st ed. 1896).

—— [Elements of Gaelic Grammar.] See also Gillies, H. Cameron. [Elements of Gaelic
Grammar.]

Stewart, J. B., d. 1917. [Chì Sinn Thall Thu.] Dundee, 1918.
  Chì Sinn Thall Thu. Le J. B. Stiùbhard. Dundee: Malcolm C. MacLeod, Bookseller
  and Publisher, 183 Blackness Road. 1918.
  [Cover] MacLeod's Gaelic Booklets, No. 2.
  18 p. 180 mm. PC.
    Pref. note: "Selections from the Gaelic writings of a Highlander who fell on the
    battlefield in France, with a message from Ian MacPherson, Esq., M.P., Parlia-
    mentary Under-Secretary of State for War." Printed John Leng, Dundee.

Stewart, John, –1942. [Laoidhean agus Orain.] Stornoway, n.d.
  Laoidhean agus Orain. Le Ian Stiubhart.
  Stornoway Gazette, 67–69 Kenneth Street, Stornoway.
  [46] p. 220 mm. PC.
  c. 1967. Preface by K. MacLeod, Back.

Stewart, John Roy, c. 1700–52. [Poems.] Glasgow, 1947.
  Scottish Gaelic Poetry Series. The Poems of John Roy Stewart. Edited by Elizabeth
  E. Mackechnie. Sgoil Eòlais na h-Alba. 1947.
  39 p, [1] "Sources". 220 mm. Mit., SS.
    Printed The Caledonian Press, Glasgow.

Stewart, Kenneth. [The Five Year Plan.] Glasgow, 1950.
  Dealbh-chluichean an Gàidhlig. Dòmhnall Dearg. Dealbh-chluich an aon sealladh.
  Gaelic translation of The Five Year Plan by Kenneth Stewart. Printed for An Comunn
  Gàidhealach by Eneas MacKay, Stirling. 1950.
  15 p. 190 mm. PC.

Stornoway: Nicolson Institute. See School Magazines.

Story, Elma, –1941 (ed.). See Bolg Solair.

Suil ris an Dochas Bheannaichte. Edinburgh, 1915.
  Sùil ris an Dòchas Bheannaichte. (Eadar-theangaichte.) Edinburgh: John Grant, 31
  George IV Bridge. 1915.
  61 p. 140 mm. Mit., NLS.
    Printed Oliver and Boyd, Edinburgh.

Suim agus Feum an Eolais Shlainteil. See [Westminster Confession of Faith.]

Synge, John, 1871–1909. [Riders to the Sea.] Glasgow, 1950.
  Dealbh-chluichean an Gàidhlig. Muinntir a' Chuain. Dealbh-chluich an aon sealladh.
  Gaelic translation of the one-act play, Riders to the Sea, by J. Synge. Air eadar-
  theangachadh le Ailean Macill'eathain. An Comunn Gaidhealach, 131 West Regent
  Street, Glasgow. 1950.
  14 p. 190 mm. NLS, PC.
    Printed Learmonth, Stirling. English original first published 1905.

Synod of Argyll (sponsors). See Bible. [Psalms.]

Tailleir, Mairi. See Mairi Tailleir.

Taintean. See School Magazines. [*Lionel J.S. School.*]

Tarbert: Sir Edward Scott J.S. School. See School Magazines.

Teachdaire nan Gaidheal. Sydney, N.S., 1925–34.
   Teachdaire nan Gaidheal. "Lean gu dlùth ri cliù do shinnsreadh, 's na dìbir a bhi mar iadsan." Leabh. I. Sidni, N.S. [1925].
      The first number seen is "Leabh. I. Sidni, N.S. 15mh de'n Ghiblin, 1925. Air. 5."
      Clare and Prof. Calum I. N. MacLeod of Antigonish give 1925 as the first year of publication.
      ... Leabhar VI. Sidni, N.S., Canada. An Gearran (February), 1934. Air. 12. [Last number seen.]
         [Frequency] Irregular. The following numbers have been seen: Vol. I: 5, 11, 12 (April, Nov., Dec., 1925); II: 1–12 (Jan. 1926–Dec. 1927); III: 1 (Jan. 1928); IV: 1, 4, 5, 7, 8 (1928–29); V: 3 (Jan. 1933); VI: 11, 12 (Jan., Feb. 1934.)
         [Collation] 6–16 p per issue (average 10 p). 300 × 230 mm.
         [Locations] NLS (incomplete set).
         [Editor] James MacNeill.
         [Contents] Mainly Gaelic; contains some English from Vol. III.

Teagasg nan Aithrichean. Edinburgh, n.d.
   Cogadh mór na h-Eòrpa. Teagasg nan Aithrichean. [Illus.] Printed by Oliver and Boyd, Edinburgh, for The Church of Scotland, The United Free Church of Scotland, and the Free Church of Scotland.
   xvi, 160 p. 140 mm. NLS.
   For soldiers in the First World War.

Teagasg nan Aithrichean. Edinburgh, n.d.
   Cogadh na Saorsa. Teagasg nan Aithrichean. [Illus.] Printed by Oliver and Boyd, Edinburgh, for the Church of Scotland, The Free Church of Scotland.
   viii, 160 p. 140 mm. PC.
   Published for distribution to soldiers in the Second World War.

Teagasg nan Aithrichean. Edinburgh, n.d.
   Teagasg nan Aithrichean. (The Teaching of the Fathers.) [Illus.] Knox Press (Edinburgh), 15 North Bank Street, Edinburgh.
   [6], 160 p. 140 mm.
      Foreword by Prof. George Collins, The Free Church College, Edinburgh. The Knox Press is the Free Church's publishing agency. Printed Eccleslitho, Inverness.

Teangadóir. Toronto, 1953–60.
   Teangadóir. Focala i dtaobh litríocha ó am gu h-am. Pàdraig O Broin, Eagarthóir, 52 Derwyn Road, Toronto 6, Canada; Gl. 7461. Tàille bhliana 50 cents (3/9). Imleabhar I. Lunas 1953. Uimbir 1.
   ... Imleabhar IV, uim. 11–12.
   Lá Ochtaibhe N. Bréanainn, Abb., Bealtaine 23, 1960. Uimhir iomlán 35–36. [Last number seen.]
      [Frequency] Bi-monthly.
      [Pagination] 96 p in Vol. I (6 numbers), 120 p in II (6), 280 p in III (12), 256 p in IV (12).
      [Size] 180 mm.
      [Locations] PC.
      [Editor] Pádraig O Broin.
      [Contents] A Pan-Celtic magazine.

Tearuinteachd, Cinnte agus Aoibhneas. Stirling, n.d.
Tearuinteachd, Cinnte agus Aoibhneas. (From the English by Permission of the Author.) Ma's creidmheach thu, carson nach 'eil thu cinnteach mu thearnadh? Ma tha thu tearuinte, carson nach 'eil thu aoibhneach? Drummond's Tract Depot, Stirling. Price, one penny.
46 p. 120 mm. FC, NLS, PC.
The FC copy has 42 p, [2] Ads., [2] "Cover". In the other copies, the text ends on p 42 and pp 43–6 (i.e. including back cover) comprise Bible extracts.

[*Thangaidh, Catriona.*] See MacKay, Catherine.

Thompson, Francis, 1854–1907. [*The Hound of Heaven.*] See Laing, Hugh. [*An Sealgair Naomh agus Dain Eile.*]

Thomson, Derick S., 1921–. [*An Dealbh Briste.*] Edinburgh, 1951.
An Dealbh Briste. Gaelic Poems, with some translations in English. Ruaraidh Mac-Thómais. [Illus.] Serif Books. Edinburgh.
First published 1951.
[8], 64 p. 230 mm. AU, EU, GU, Mit., NLS.
Printed by The Stanley Press, Edinburgh.

—— [*Eadar Samhradh is Foghar.*] Glasgow, 1967.
Eadar Samhradh is Foghar. Cnuasachd de dhàintean le Ruaraidh MacThomais. Gairm. Glaschu. 1967. [Illus.]
Clò-bhualaidhean Gairm, Leabhar 4.
90 p; illus. 230 mm.
The title page illus. is the title in a stylised ogam script; this and other illus. by Henry Stuart. Printed Learmonth, Stirling.

—— [*Gaelic Learners' Handbook.*] Glasgow, 1973.
Gaelic Learners' Handbook. A new handy compendium of vocabulary, phrases, sentences, arranged under subject headings. Ruaraidh MacThómais. Gairm. Glaschu. 1973.
[4], 44 p. 190 mm.
Printed Learmonth, Stirling.

—— [*Gaelic Sources of MacPherson's "Ossian".*] Edinburgh, [Pref. 1951].
The Gaelic Sources of MacPherson's "Ossian". Derick S. Thomson. Published for the University of Aberdeen. Oliver and Boyd; Edinburgh: Tweedale Court; London: 98 Great Russell Street.
Aberdeen University Studies, Number 130.
vii, 106 p. 230 mm. AU, BM, GU, Mit., NLS.
[91]–100 p, Appendix [No. iii] of Gaelic ballads. Printed The University Press, Aberdeen.

—— [*An Rathad Cian.*] Glasgow, 1970.
An Rathad Cian. Le Ruaraidh MacThomais. Gairm. Glaschu. 1970.
Clò-bhualaidhean Gairm, Leabhar 23.
[6], 56, [2] p. 220 mm.
Winner of Scottish Arts Council Award 1971. English translation published in *Lines Review*, No. 39 (1971) and by New Rivers Press, New York, 1971.

—— (joint ed.). See Lhuyd, Edward. [*Edward Lhuyd in the Scottish Highlands.*]

—— (joint ed.). See MacDonald, Duncan. [*Fear na h-Eabaid.*]

—— (ed.). See Gairm.

—— (general editor). See Leabhraichean ura Gaidhlig Oilthigh Ghlaschu.

—— (general editor). See Leabhraichean ura Gaidhlig Oilthigh Obairdheadhain.

—— (ed.). See Scottish Gaelic Studies.

Thomson, Donald, 1907–. [*Gaelic Poems for Interpretation.*] [Glasgow], 1959.
Gaelic Poems for Interpretation. [Illus.: Crest of An Comunn Gaidhealach.] Selected
by the Central Gaelic Committee, E.I.S. 1959. Donald Thomson, M.A., F.E.I.S.
99 p. 180 mm. PC.

—— [*Gaelic Poems for Interpretation.*] [Glasgow], 1965.
. . . 1959. Reprinted 1965. Donald Thomson, M.A., F.E.I.S.
99 p. 180 mm. PC.
Published by An Comunn Gaidhealach. An anthology of poetry, with interpretation
exercises.

—— (tr.). See MacPhail, M. S. [*The Eagle's Claw.*]

Thomson, James, 1888–. [*An Dileab.*] Glasgow, n.d.
An Dileab. Gaelic Verse for Advanced Divisions and Intermediate Classes. Edited by
James Thomson, M.A., Bayble, Lewis. An Comunn Gaidhealach: 212 West George
Street, Glasgow, C.2.
[4], 48 p. 190 mm. AU, PC.
c. 1932. Printed Learmonth, Stirling.

—— [*An Dileab.*] Glasgow, 1934.
. . . Second edition. 1934. An Comunn Gaidhealach, 212 West George Street,
Glasgow, C.2.
[4], 48 p. 190 mm. GU:CL, Mit.
Printed James Cameron, Glasgow.

—— [*Fasgnadh.*] Stirling, 1953.
Fasgnadh. Gaelic Poems, with some translations in English. Seumas MacThomais.
A. Learmonth & Son, 9 King Street, Stirling. 1953.
118 p. 220 mm. AU, GU, Mit., NLS.

—— (tr.). See Gilbert, Bernard. [*The Old Bull.*]

—— (joint ed.). See Eilean Fraoich.

Thomson, Robert L., 1924 (ed.). See Calvin, John. [*Catechismus Genevensis.*]

—— (ed.). See Church of Scotland. *Liturgy and Ritual.* [Book of Common Order.]

[*Thousand and One Nights, The.*] See [*Arabian Nights.*]

Tilleadh Sheumais. N.p., n.d.
Tilleadh Sheumais agus sgeul a thuruis.
24 p. 150 mm. PC.
Canadian. Information from John L. Campbell.

Tiomnadh Nuadh. See Bible. (N.T.)

Tir nam Blath. Glasgow, n.d.
Tìr nam Blàth. Adapted from Tír nam Bláth. With grateful acknowledgements to the
McCaig Trust and to Browne and Nolan, Limited. An Comunn Gaidhealach. Printed
in the Republic of Ireland.
72 p; col. illus. 190 mm.
c. 1958.
Translated from Irish by Donald Grant.

Tir na Meala. Glasgow, n.d.
Tìr na Meala. Adapted from Tír na Meala. With grateful acknowledgement to the
McCaig Trust and to Browne and Nolan, Limited. Printed for An Comunn Gaidhealach in the Republic of Ireland.
72 p; col. illus. 190 mm.
  c. 1958.
Translated from Irish by Donald Grant.

Tir nan Og. Glasgow, n.d.
Tìr nan Og. Adapted from Tír nan Og. (With grateful acknowledgements to the
McCaig Trust and to Browne and Nolan, Limited.) Printed in the Republic of Ireland.
An Comunn Gaidhealach.
48 p; col. illus. 190 mm.
  c. 1958.
Translated from Irish by Donald Grant.

Tir nan Seud. Glasgow, n.d.
Tìr nan Seud. Adapted from Tír na Seod. With grateful acknowledgements to the
McCaig Trust and to Browne & Nolan Ltd. [Illus.] An Comunn Gaidhealach.
Printed in the Republic of Ireland.
56 p; col. illus. 190 mm.
  c. 1958.
Translated from Irish by Donald Grant. *c.* 1958. The whole series (see also "Croga
an Oir") was printed by Browne & Nolan, Dublin, with the original illustrations.

Tocher. Edinburgh, 1971–.
Tocher 1. Tales, music, song selected from the School of Scottish Studies Archives.
© School of Scottish Studies, Edinburgh University 1971.
Tocher. Tales, songs, traditions selected from the archives of the School of Scottish
Studies. © School of Scottish Studies, University of Edinburgh, 1972.
[Continuing.]
  [Frequency] Quarterly.
  [Collation] *c.* 35 p per no. 230 mm.
  [Editor] Alan Bruford.

Tolmie, Francis, 1840–1926. [*Gaelic Folk Songs.*] See *Journal of the Folk-Song Society,*
No. 16.

Tolmie, Francis, 1840–1928 (comp.). See Graves, Alfred P. (ed.). [*The Celtic Song
Book.*]

Tolstoi, Lev Nikolaevich, 1828–1910. [*Where God is, Love is.*] [Sidney, C.B.], 1924.
Far am bi Gràdh, bidh Dia. Le Count Leo Tolstoi. Air a thionndadh gu Gailig le
E.G.M.F. Air a chur a mach fo chùram Comunn Gàilig Chill-Rimhinn, Sidni, Ceap
Breatunn. Clò-bhuailte le Dòmhnull MacFhionghuin. 1924.
32 p. 210 mm. *Xavier.*
Russian original first published 1885; first English edition 1897.

Tracts. See Church of Scotland: Home Mission Committee. [*Tracts.*]

Transactions of the Gaelic Society of Glasgow. See Gaelic Society of Glasgow.
  [*Transactions.*]

Transactions of the Gaelic Society of Inverness. See Gaelic Society of Inverness.
  [*Transactions.*]

Tri Comhraidhean. Glasgow, 1930.
[Illus.] Trì Comhraidhean. Na Fasain Ura, le Morag NicDhòmhnaill, Tiriodh. Anna
Bhàn an Glascho, le Donnchadh MacDhòmhnaill, Leodhas. Na Foirfich Nodha, le
Donnchadh MacDhòmhnaill, Leodhas. A' phrìs, se sgillinn. An Comunn Gaidhealach,
212 Sràid West George, Glascho. 1930.
31 p. 190 mm. EPL, Mit.

Tuath Chomunn Urras. See Northern Assurance Company.

Turner, Neil (ed.). See MacLeod, Allan, of Bernera. [*Griasaiche Bhearnaraidh.*]

Uibhean Priseil, Na H-. Glasgow, n.d.
"Na h-Uibhean Priseil" le Feachd Thobarmhoire de Chomunn na h-Oigridh. An dara duais, 1937. [Illus.] An Comunn Gaidhealach, 131 Sràid Iar Regent, Glaschu. A' phrìs – dà sgillinn.
7 p. 220 mm. Mit.
    First advertised 1939.

Uirsgeulan Gaidhealach. Stirling, 1905.
Uirsgeulan Gaidhealach leis an do choisneadh duaisean aig Mòid A' Chomuinn Ghaidhealaich. Air an cur a mach fo ùghdarras a' chomuinn cheudna. Struibhle: Aonghas Mac Aoidh, 43 Murray Place. 1905.
62 p. 200 mm. Mit., SS.

Uirsgeulan Gaidhealach. Stirling, 1912.
Uirsgeulan Gaidhealach leis an do choisneadh duaisean aig Mòid A' Chomuinn Ghaid-healaich. An dara clò-bhualadh, fo laìmh Chaluim Mhic Phàrlain. Struibhle: Aonghas Mac Aoidh, 43 Murray Place. 1912.
64 p. 190 mm. AU, GU:CL, NLS.

Uirsgeulan na Feinne. See Fionn ann an Tigh a' Bhlair-Bhuidhe [Dwelly version].

Una, Inghean fear na Pairce. See Parker, Winifred.

United Church of Canada. [*Statement of Doctrine.*] N.p., n.d.
Aideachadh a' Chreidimh. Eaglais Aonaichte Chanada. Statement of Doctrine. United Church of Canada.
19 p. 180 mm. PC.
    Translated by Jonathan G. MacKinnon.

United Free Church of Scotland. *An Fhianuis.* See *An Fhianuis.*

United Free Church of Scotland. [*An Fhianuis Ghaidhealach.*] See *An Fhianuis Ghaid-healach.*

United Free Church of Scotland (joint sponsors). See Cogadh mor na h-Eorpa. [For cross-references to individual titles in this series.]

Urnuighean Airson na Cloinne. N.p., n.d.
Urnuighean airson na Cloinne. Prayers for the Children.
23 p. 140 mm. PC.
    English and Gaelic. Episcopalian. Attributed in *The Celtic Who's Who* (1921; ed. L. MacBean) to Rev. James MacFarlane-Barrow, Lochgilphead.

Urnuighean Sonruichte ann an am Cogaidh. See MacFarlane-Barrow, James. [*Urnuighean Sonruichte ann an am Cogaidh.*]

Urquhart, Catherine F., *d.* 1943 and David, *d.* 1950 (joint tr.). See Bottomley, Gordon. [*Deirdire.*]

Valtos Primary School. See Domhnull cam MacDhughaill.

Van Dyke, Henry, 1852–1933. [*The Other Wise Man.*] Dunfermline, 1938.
Sgeul an Draoidh Eile. Le Eanruig Van Dyke. Air a thionndadh gu Gàidhlig Albannaich le E. G. Mac Fhionghuin (a bha roimhe so 'na fhear-deasachaidh "Mac Talla"). Air a chur amach ann an Albainn le Iain Latharna Caimbeul. Chaidh an

leabhar so a chlò-bhualadh ann an Albainn le I. B. MacAoidh agus a Chuideachd, ann an Dùn Pharlain, Fiobha, gu feum an fhir-deasachaidh, anns a' bhliadhna 1938. Chaidh an leabhar so a thionndadh gu Gàidhlig Albannaich 's a chur amach ann an Albainn le cead Cuideachd Harper agus a Bhràithrean, ann an New York, a chuir amach an toiseach e.

The Story of the Other Wise Man. By Henry Van Dyke. Scottish Gaelic translation by J. G. MacKinnon (formerly editor and publisher of the Gaelic weekly "Mac Talla"). Prepared for publication in Scotland by John Lorne Campbell. Printed by J. B. Mackie and Co., Ltd., Dunfermline, Fife, in 1938. Gaelic translation published by permission of Messrs Harper & Brothers, New York. Original version in English. Copyright, 1895, by Harper & Brothers. Copyright, 1923, by Henry Van Dyke.
xvii, 45 p; plate. 190 mm. BM, PC.

—— [The Other Wise Man.] Dunfermline, 1939.
Ibid.
A' Cheud Chlò-Bhualadh – An Dàmhair, 1938 (400 lethbhric). An Darna Clò-Bhualadh – An Sultaine, 1939 (400 lethbhric).
xvii, 45 p; plate. 190 mm. GU:CL.
English original first published 1902.

Vernon, C. W. [Cape Breton, Canada.] Toronto, 1903.
Cape Breton, Canada, at the beginning of the Twentieth Century. A treatise of natural resources and development. Nation Building Series. By C. W. Vernon. Toronto: Nation Publishing Co. 1903.
260 mm. PC.
Not seen. Contains "Na Gaidheil an Ceap Breatunn" by Jonathan G. MacKinnon, pp 71–81.

Wagner, Heinrich. [The Dialects of Ulster and the Isle of Man; Specimens of Scottish Gaelic Dialects.] Dublin, 1969.
Linguistic Atlas and Survey of Irish Dialects. Vol. IV. The Dialects of Ulster and the Isle of Man. Specimens of Scottish Gaelic Dialects. Phonetic Texts of East Ulster Irish by Heinrich Wagner, Professor of Celtic and Comparative Philology, Queen's University, Belfast, M.R.I.A., Research Associate of the Dublin Institute for Advanced Studies, and Colm O Baoill, Ph.D., Lecturer in Celtic, University of Aberdeen. Dublin. 1969. Dublin Institute for Advanced Studies.
xx, 303 p; maps. 300 mm.
Appendix 1, "Scottish Gaelic Dialects", pp 189–282.

Walker, John (tr.). See Cocker, W. D. [The Miller's Wooing.]

Watson, J. Wrexford (ed.). See Scottish Studies.

Watson, James Carmichael, 1910–42 (ed.). See Carmichael, Alexander. [Carmina Gadelica.] Volume III/IV.

—— (ed.). See MacLeod, Mary. [Orain agus Luinneagan Gaidhlig.]

Watson, William J., 1865–1948. [Bardachd Ghaidhlig.] Glasgow, 1918.
Bàrdachd Ghaidhlig. Specimens of Gaelic Poetry, 1550–1900. William J. Watson, M.A., LL.D., Professor of Celtic Languages, etc., in the University of Edinburgh. An Comunn Gaidhealach, 108 Hope Street, Glasgow. Inverness: The Northern Counties Printing and Publishing Company, Limited. 1918.
lx, 350 p. 190 mm. BM, EU.

—— [Bardachd Ghaidhlig.] Glasgow, 1932.
Bàrdachd Ghaidhlig. (Second edition.) . . . An Comunn Gaidhealach, 212 West George Street, Glasgow. Stirling: A. Learmonth & Son, 9 King Street. 1932.
lxiii, 401, [1] p. 190 mm. GU, Mit.

—— [*Bardachd Ghaidhlig.*] Glasgow, 1959.
Bardachd Ghaidhlig. (Third edition.) ... 1959.
lxiv, 411, [1] p. 190 mm. GU.
Preface signed, "Angus MacLeod, Convener of the Publications Committee of An Comunn Gaidhealach."

—— [*Celtic Place-names of Scotland.*] Shannon, 1973.
... Irish Universities Press. Shannon, Ireland. 1973.

—— (general ed.). [*Leabhraichean Sgoile Gaidhlig, an Ceud Cheum.*] Glasgow, n.d.
Leabhraichean Sgoile Gàidhlig fo stiùradh Uilleam Iain Mac-Bhàtair, M.A., LL.D.
An Ceud Cheum gu Gàidhlig. Air a dheasachadh le Dòmhnall Mac a-Phí, F.E.I.S.
[Illus.] Clò-bhuailte fo Ughdarras A' Chomuinn Ghàidhealaich le Blackie agus a Mhac, Ltd., Glaschu.
64 p; illus. 180 mm. AU, BM, GU:CL.
    c. 1920.

—— (general ed.). [*Leabhraichean Sgoile Gaidhlig, Leabhar na Cloinne Bige.*] Glasgow, n.d.
... Leabhar na Cloinne Bige. Air a dheasachadh le Dòmhnall Mac a-Phí, F.E.I.S.
[Illus.] Clò-bhuailte fo Ughdarras A' Chomuinn Ghàidhealaich le Blackie agus a Mhac, Ltd., Glaschu.
80p; illus. 180 mm. AU, BM, GU:CL.

—— (general ed.). [*Leabhraichean Sgoile Gaidhlig, an Ceud Leabhar Leughaidh.*] Glasgow, n.d.
... An Ceud Leabhar Leughaidh. Air a dheasachadh le Dòmhnall Mac a-Phí, F.E.I.S.
[Illus.] Clò-bhuailte fo Ughdarras A' Chomuinn Ghàidhealaich le Blackie agus a Mhac, Ltd., Glaschu.
112 p; illus. 180 mm. AU, BM, GU:CL.

—— (general ed.). [*Leabhraichean Sgoile Gaidhlig, an Dara Leabhar Leughaidh.*] Glasgow, 1921.
... An Dara Leabhar Leughaidh. Air a dheasachadh le Dòmhnall Mac a-Phí, F.E.I.S.
[Illus.] Clò-bhuailte fo Ughdarras A' Chomuinn Ghàidhealaich le Blackie agus a Mhac, Ltd., Glaschu. 1921.
128 p; illus. 180 mm. AU, BM, GU:CL.

—— (general ed.). [*Leabhraichean Sgoile Gaidhlig, an Treas Leabhar Leughaidh.*] Glasgow, 1922.
... An Treas Leabhar Leughaidh. Air a dheasachadh le Dòmhnall Mac a-Phí, F.E.I.S.
[Illus.] Clò-bhuailte fo Ughdarras A' Chomuinn Ghàidhealaich le Blackie agus a Mhac, Ltd., Glaschu. 1922.
160 p; illus. 180 mm. AU, BM, GU:CL.

—— (general ed.). [*Leabhraichean Sgoile Gaidhlig, an Ceathramh Leabhar Leughaidh.*] Glasgow, 1923.
... An Ceathramh Leabhar Leughaidh. Air a dheasachadh le Iain Mac Dhòmhnaill, M.A. [Illus.] Clò-bhuailte fo Ughdarras A' Chomuinn Ghàidhealaich le Blackie agus a Mhac, Ltd., Glaschu. 1923.
239 p; illus. 180 mm. AU, BM, GU:CL.
The first 2 parts were first advertised in 1921. Revised by Lachlan MacKinnon and re-issued as "Leabhraichean Leughaidh" (*c.* 1949).

—— (general ed.). [*Leabhraichean Sgoile Gaidhlig.*] See also MacKinnon, Lachlan.
[*Leabhraichean Leughaidh.*]

—— [*Marbhnadh Dhonnchaidh Duibh.*] Glasgow, n.d.
Marbhnadh Dhonnchaidh Duibh. Elegy on Sir Duncan Campbell, of Glenorchy.
Edited and translated by William J. Watson. (Reprinted from An Deo-Greine.)
Glasgow: Archd. Sinclair, 47 Waterloo Street.
16 p. 190 mm. AU.

—— [*Notes on the Study of Gaelic.*] Inverness, 1908.
Notes on the Study of Gaelic. By William J. Watson, M.A. Reprinted from the
Celtic Review. Northern Chronicle Office, Inverness. 1908. 6d net.
32 p. 190 mm. GU:CL.
   Grammar. Appeared in *Celtic Review*.

—— [*Rosg Gaidhlig.*] Glasgow, 1915.
Rosg Gaidhlig. Specimens of Gaelic Prose. Edited by William J. Watson, M.A.,
LL.D., Professor of Celtic Languages, etc., in the University of Edinburgh. Published
by An Comunn Gàidhealach for use in schools and Gaelic classes. Inverness: printed
by the Northern Counties Newspaper and Printing and Publishing Company, Limited.
1915.
x, [1], 288 p. 190 mm. BM, EU, Mit.

—— [*Rosg Gaidhlig.*] Glasgow, 1929.
. . . Published for An Comunn Gaidhealach by Alex. MacLaren & Sons, 360–362
Argyle Street, C.2.
x, 295 p, [1] "Errata". 190 mm. Mit., NLS.

—— (joint ed.). See Campbell, John F. [*More West Highland Tales.*] Volume One.

—— (ed.). See MacGregor, James, Dean of Lismore. [*Scottish Verse from the Book of
the Dean of Lismore.*]

Watson, Mrs. William J. See Carmichael, Ella C.

Watt, Helen, 1908–. [*A' Bhratach Dhealrach.*] Inverness, [c. 1972].
A' Bhratach Dheàlrach. Eilidh Watt. Club Leabhar Limited. Inbhirnis.
© Eilidh Watt 1972.
127 p. 190 mm.
   Printed Eccles, Inverness.

—— [*Latha A' Choin Duibh.*] Inverness, [c. 1972].
Latha a' Choin Duibh agus Ipilidh. Sgeulachdan. Eilidh Watt. Club Leabhar,
Inbhirnis.
© Eilidh Watt 1972.
[4], 47 p; illus. 210 mm.
   Illustrated by James Dunn. Printed by Caithness Books.

Western Isles Unionist Association. See Seonaid.

[*Westminster Confession of Faith.*] Edinburgh, 1960.
   Leabhar Aideachaidh a' Chreidimh, le dà Leabhar a' Cheasnachaidh, maille ri Suim agus
Feum an Eòlais Shlàinteil: eadar-theangaichte o'n Bheurla chum Gaelic Albannaich, air
tus le Seanadh Earra-Ghaeil 's a' bhliadhna MDCCXXV; a rìs le Gileabart Mac-
Dhòmhnuill, 's a' bhliadhn' MDCCCIV; agus a nis ath-leasaichte chum na cànain
ghnàthaichte 's a' bhliadhn' MDCCCXXXVIII. Edinburgh: reprinted by The Free
Church of Scotland Publications Committee. 1960.
viii, 261 p. 170 mm. Stornoway Public Library.
   First published 1725; present ed. a reprint of the 1838 ed.

Westminster Shorter Catechism. See Shorter Catechism.

Whitehead, F. W. [*The Six Long Gaelic Psalm Tunes.*] N.p., n.d.
The Sutherlandshire version of the six long Gaelic Psalm Tunes as taken down in 1909
by Mr. F. W. Whitehead, A.R.C.O., A.R.C.M., Inverness, from the singing of Rev.
Donald Munro, Ferintosh, a native of Clyne, Sutherlandshire.
[15]–24 p. 200 mm. NLS.
> Supplement to "Seann Fhuinn na Salm . . . Taken down by T. L. Hately" (1st ed.
> 1845; 1862 ed. has 14 p). Bound with "The Scottish Psalmody . . . Published by
> authority of . . . The Free Church of Scotland. Edinburgh . . . 1910."

—— [*The Six Long Gaelic Psalm Tunes.*] See also:
Free Church of Scotland. *Liturgy and Ritual.* [Fuinn nan Salm Ghaidhlig.]
Hateley, T. L. [*Seann Fhuinn nan Salm.*]

—— (arr.). See MacFarlane, Malcolm. [*Songs of the Highlands.*]

Whyte, Henry, 1852–1914. [*The Celtic Garland.*] Glasgow, 1920.
Memorial Edition. The Celtic Garland of Gaelic Songs and Readings. Translations of
Gaelic and English Songs. By "Fionn". Third edition. Greatly enlarged. Glasgow:
Alexander MacLaren & Songs, Gaelic Publishers and Booksellers, 360–362 Argyle
Street. 1920.
xvi, 355 p; 2 plates. 200 mm. AU, BM, EPL, GU, Mit.
> 1st ed. 1881.

—— [*The Celtic Lyre.*] Glasgow, n.d.
The Celtic Lyre. A collection of Gaelic songs, with English translations. By Fionn.
[Illus.] Music in both notations. Glasgow: John Mackay, "Celtic Monthly Office",
Blythswood Drive.
[72] p. 210 mm. AU:CL.
> 68 songs. Parts I–III of the "Celtic Lyre" were published by MacLachlan &
> Stewart, Edinburgh, in 1883, 1884 and 1886 respectively and were reprinted in
> 1891; Part IV was published in 1895 by Henry Whyte (Glasgow), John Grant
> (Edinburgh) and Hugh MacDonald (Oban). The 4 parts were isued as one volume
> in 1895, this being reprinted by Grant in 1898. The date of the above edition is
> between 1895 and 1906 (the year of John MacKay's death).

—— [*The Celtic Lyre.*] N.p., 1906, 1908, 1910, 1924, 1927, 1932, 1946.
Ibid.
[72] p. 210 mm. Mit., PC.
> Reprinted as follows: Grant, Edinburgh, 1906; Sinclair, Glasgow, 1908; Grant,
> Edinburgh, 1910; MacLaren, Glasgow, 1924, 1927; Sinclair, Glasgow, 1932;
> MacLaren, Glasgow, 1946. The ed. of 1946 is described as "Jubilee Edition" and
> has a foreword by Annetta C. Scott.

—— [*The Celtic Lyre.*] Part IV. Edinburgh, 1902.
The Celtic Lyre. A collection of Gaelic songs, with English translations. By Fionn.
Part IV. Price sixpence. Music in both notations. Edinburgh: John Grant, Booksellers, 31 and 34 George IV Bridge. 1902.
[16] p. 220 mm. NLS.
> Songs no. 53–68. The above and all the 4 part volumes bear the imprint "End of
> Vol. I": no other volumes, however, were issued.

—— [*Ceol nan Gaidheal.*] Glasgow, [Pref. 1905].
Ceòl nan Gàidheal. (Songs of the Gael.) Music in both notations, with Gaelic words
and singable English translations. Edited by Henry Whyte ("Fionn"). Preface and
inscription by Angus Macintyre. Glasgow: David Bryce & Son, Bryce and Murray,
Ltd., 129 Buchanan Street.
vi, 120, [2] p. 908 mm. Mit.

—— [*Ceol nan Gaidheal*.] Glasgow, [1915, 1920, n.d.]
Ibid.
vi, 120, [2] p. 980 mm.
  There were three reprints of the 1905 ed., all without date. *MacLaren* states that the
2nd ed. was by MacLaren & Son, Glasgow in 1915, the 3rd by Collins, Glasgow in
1920 and the 4th by MacLaren (after 1931). The 4th ed. was advertised among
"Leabhraichean ura Gàidhlig" in 1938.

—— (tr.). [*Is Braithrean sinn Uile.*] N.p., n.d.
I. Braithrean Sinn Uile . . . Eadar. le Fionn.
1 p. 150 mm. NLS.
  Poem.

—— [*Mar a Dh'Eirich Cuid de na Sean-Fhacail.*] Glasgow, n.d.
The Ceilidh Books. Leabhraichean nan Céilidh. Aireamh 16. Mar a dh'éirich cuid
de na sean-fhacail. Le Fionn. [Illus.] A' phrìs, trì sgillinnean. 3d. Alasdair Mac
Labhruinn agus a Mhic, 360–362 Sràid Earraghaidheal, Glascho.
155–201 p. 210 mm. PC.
  Offprint from "An Sgeulaiche", III. 2, Summer 1911.

—— [*Naigheachdan Firinneach*.] I. Paisley, 1905.
True Stories. I. Translated into Gaelic by "Fionn". With illustrations. [Illus.]
Paisley: Alexander Gardner, Publisher by Appointment to the late Queen Victoria.
1905.
Naigheachdan Fìrinneach. I. Eadar-theangaichte gu Gàidhlig le "Fionn". Le
dealbhan. [Illus.] Pàislig: Alasdair Gardner, Clòdh-bhuailtear, le a deòin rìoghail fein,
do'n Bhàn-Rìgh Victoria nach maireann. 1905.
261 p; 5 plates. 200 mm. AU, BM, GU:CL, Mit.

—— [*Naigheachdan Firinneach*.] I. Paisley, 1906.
. . . 1906.
261 p; 5 plates. 200 mm. AU, PC.

—— [*Naigheachdan Firinneach*.] II. Paisley, 1907.
True Stories. II. Translated into Gaelic by "Fionn". With illustrations. [Illus.]
Paisley: Alexander Gardner, Publisher by Appointment to the late Queen Victoria.
1907.
Naigheachdan Firinneach. II. Eadar-theangaichte gu Gàidhlig le "Fionn". Le
dealbhan. [Illus.] Pàislig: Alasdair Gardner, Clòdh-bhuailtear, le a deòin rìoghail
féin, do'n Bhàn-Rìgh Victoria nach maireann. 1907.
263 p; 4 plates. 200 mm. AU, BM, Mit.

—— [*Naigheachdan Firinneach*.] II. Glasgow, 1929.
Naigheachdan Firinneach. II. Eadartheangaichte gu Gàidhlig le "Fionn". Le deal-
bhan. Glascho: Alasdair Mac Labhruinn 's a Mhic, 360–362 Sràid Earraghaidheal,
C.2.
First published 1907. Re-issued 1929.
[3]–263 p; 4 plates. GU.
  Vol. I contains translations of stories by Andrew Lang; Vol. II, stories by A. Mac-
Kenzie (3), Charles Lamb (1), and James Grant (1).

—— (joint ed.). See MacFarlane, Malcolm. [*An Uiseag.*]

—— (tr.). See MacKay, Thomas. [*Practical Hints on Cooking.*]

Whyte, John. [*Elementary Sounds of the Gaelic Language.*] Aberdeen, n.d.
Elementary Sounds of the Gaelic Language. Arranged by John Whyte, Inverness.
3 p. 220 mm. Mit.
  Printed by the Aberdeen University Press.

—— [*Para Piobaire agus Sgeulachdan Eile.*] Glasgow, 1925.
Para Piobaire agus Sgeulachdan Eile. Le Iain Ban Og. Peter the Piper and other Humorous Gaelic Readings. By John Whyte. 1/–. Glascho: Alasdair Mac Labhruinn 's a Mhic, 360–362 Sràid Earraghaidheal, C.2. 1925.
39 p, [1] "Clar-amais". 190 mm. BM, GU:CL, Mit., NLS.

—— [*Vocabulary for "How to Learn Gaelic".*] Inverness, 1906.
Vocabulary for "How to Learn Gaelic". By John Whyte. Inverness: "Northern Chronicle" Office. 1906.
20 p. 190 mm. EPL, PC.
From *How to Learn Gaelic* by Alexander MacBain and John Whyte, 4th ed., 1906.

—— [*Vocabulary for "How to Learn Gaelic".*] See also MacBain, Alexander (joint author). [*How to Learn Gaelic.*]

—— (joint author). See MacBain, Alexander. [*How to Learn Gaelic.*]

Willison, John, 1680–1750. [*Mother's Catechism.*] Glasgow, n.d.
Mother's Catechism (in Gaelic and English). Leabhar Cheist na Màthar (ann an Gàidhlig agus ann an Beurla). Roimh-Chuideachadh do'n Dream a ta Og agus Aineolach, chum an deanamh comasach air Leabhar Cheist Eaglais na h-Albann a thuigsinn. Leis an Urramach Eòin Willison, Ministeir an t-Soisgeil a bha an Dundeagh. A preparatory help for the young and ignorant in order to their easier understanding The Assembly's Shorter Catechism, together with Historical Questions out of the Bible and Forms of Prayer for Children and Young Communicants. Clò-bhualadh ùr, fo laimh Eachainn Mhic Dhùghail. Glascho: Alasdair Mac Labhruinn is a Mhic, 360–362 Sràid Earraghaidheal, C.2. Price threepence.
48 p. 170 mm. BM, PC.
"1926" – *MacLaren*.

—— [*Mother's Catechism.*] Glasgow, n.d.
. . . Alasdair Mac Labhruinn 's a Mhic, Reiceadairean Leabhraichean Gaidhlig, 268 Sràid Earra-Ghaidheal, Glascho, C.2.
48 p. 160 mm. PC.
MacLaren states that the ed. of 1926 was reprinted in 1940. MacLaren & Sons' address changed to 268 Argyle Street in 1932. The first Gaelic ed. of the Catechism was in 1752.

Wood, H. K. [*Is Eigin Domh an Fheill so a Choimhead.*] Stirling, n.d.
Is Eigin domh an Fhéill so a Choimhead. Na h-aobharan a ta aig a' chreideach air son frithealadh suipeir an Tighearna. Le H. K. Wood. Drummond's Tract Depot, Stirling.
16 p. 113 mm. PC.

Wright, D. Gordon. [*Love Lingers On.*] Glasgow, n.d.
An t-Suirghe Fhadalach. Dealbh-chluich àbhachdach an aon sealladh. Gaelic translation of the one-act comedy, "Love Lingers On" by Gordon Wright. Air eadar-theangachadh le Fionnlagh I. MacDhòmhnaill. Glasgow: Brown, Son & Ferguson, Ltd., 52–58 Darnley Street.
19 p. 190 mm. GU:CL, PC.
Reviewed in "An Gaidheal", Sept. 1950. English original first published 1937.

Young, Douglas, 1913–73. [*Scottish Verse, 1851–1951.*] London, 1952.
Scottish Verse, 1851–1951. Selected for the general reader by Douglas Young. With Foreword, Notes and Glossary. Thomas Nelson and Sons Ltd.: London, Edinburgh, Paris, Melbourne, Toronto and New York.
First published 1952.
xxxiv, 363 p. 190 mm. BM, NLS.
2 Gaelic poems by George Campbell Hay, 7 by Sorley MacLean, and 1 by Derick Thomson.